ANALYSIS OF THE INCEST TRAUMA

ANALYSIS OF THE INCEST TRAUMA

Retrieval, Recovery, Renewal

Arnold W. Rachman
and
Susan A. Klett

KARNAC

First published in 2015 by
Karnac Books Ltd
118 Finchley Road, London NW3 5HT

A C.I.P. for this book is available from the British Library

ISBN 978 1 78220 221 9

Edited, designed and produced by The Studio Publishing Services Ltd
www.publishingservicesuk.co.uk
e-mail: studio@publishingservicesuk.co.uk

Printed in Great Britain

www.karnacbooks.com

CONTENTS

ACKNOWLEDGMENTS

There is no meaningful way to express our gratitude to the many incest survivors with whom we have shared their life struggles. Without their willingness to open their hearts and minds to us, we would not have been able to write this book. These courageous and thoughtful people include the individuals of the case studies of "Samantha," "W.," "Winston," "Laura," and "Soma", who willingly told their stories of abuse so that both other survivors and analysts could benefit from their recovery. These individuals and many others have taught us to do the analysis of the incest trauma.

This book is the third in a planned trilogy that emerged from Arnold's research project, begun in 1976, on the life and work of Sándor Ferenczi. Susan's impressive presentation in Budapest, "The many faces of trauma", on Ferenczi's influence on her work, led to an invitation for her to join in and contribute to this significant endeavor. In some ways, it is the most natural one to write because Ferenczi's ideas and clinical work began the formal study and treatment of the incest trauma. Arnold Rachman considers Ferenczi his mentor, since his ideas, clinical work, methods, and career continue to provide him with an inexhaustible wellspring of inspiration to pursue his research and writings.

There were colleagues who provided both of us with the necessary affirmation to pursue Ferenczi studies and the study of incest. We are grateful to Beatrice Beebe, PhD, Henry Kellerman, PhD, Robert Marshall, PhD, Paul Mattick, PhD, and the late Esther Menaker, PhD. We are also grateful to Lew Aron, PhD, for originally reviewing the manuscript, and to Ernst Falzeder for reviewing Chapter Three, "The confusion of tongues drama". We have integrated their scholarly comments into the manuscript.

ABOUT THE AUTHORS

Arnold W. Rachman, PhD, FAGPA, is training and supervising analyst at Postgrad* The Institute of the Postgraduate Psychoanalytic Society; Clinical Professor of Psychology, Derner Institute, Adelphi University Postdoctoral Program in Psychoanalysis and Psychotherapy, and Associate Professor of Psychiatry, New York University Medical Center; Faculty, Trauma and Disaster Studies Program in the New York Postdoctoral Program in Psychoanalysis, Board of Directors, The Sándor Ferenczi Center. The New School for Social Research. He is an Honorary Member, Sándor Ferenczi Society, Budapest, Hungary, and the author of *Sándor Ferenczi: The Psychotherapist of Tenderness and Passion* (1997); *The Psychotherapy of Difficult Cases* (2003); *Elizabeth Severn: The Evil Genius of Psychoanalysis* (2016).

Susan A. Klett, LCSW-R, BCD, NCPsyA, is a faculty member of Postgrad* The Institute of the Postgraduate Psychoanalytic Society, where she has been a former Board Member and Past President of The Postgraduate Psychoanalytic Society. She is the Director of Professional Development of Advanced Clinical Education (ACE), a foundation of The New York State Society for Clinical Social Work. Ms

Klett is the Past Co-Director of Washington Square Institute (WSI), where she also served on faculty, as a training and supervising analyst and Director of Continuing Education. She is the Founder and Past Director of Dialectical Behavior Therapy (DBT) Training and Skills Group Program at WSI. Ms. Klett is a former contributing editor of *Issues in Psychoanalytic Psychology*. She has published articles and reviews on trauma, eating disorders, couple treatment, and the psychoanalytic process, and has presented nationally and internationally on trauma. She maintains a private practice in Manhattan.

FOREWORD

Experiences regarding the traumatic effect of genital attacks by adults on small children oblige me to modify the analytic view of infantile sexuality that has prevailed up to now. The fact that infantile sexuality exists obviously remains undisputed, yet much of what appears as passionate behavior of adults, forcibly imposed on children against their will and, so to speak, artificially implanted in them. Even over passionate manifestations of non-genital tenderness, such as passionate kissing, ardent embraces, effect the child in fact unpleasurably. Children want no more than to be treated in a friendly, tender, and gentle way. Their own movement and physical expressions are tender; if it is otherwise, then something has already gone wrong. One has to ask oneself how much of what is involved in the undying love of the child for its mother, and how much of the boy's spontaneous way, without the premature implantation of passionate adult eroticism and genitality; that is, how much of the Oedipus Complex is really inherited and how much is passed on by tradition from one generation to the other. (Ferenczi, 1988, *Clinical Diary*, p. 79, April 1932 entry)

To Nancy Ruth Wolpert-Rachman, my emotional muse and personal inspiration, who provides the necessary empathy and responsiveness for me to concentrate on my research and writing.

To my ninety-three-year-old mother, Mariane Lasky-Klett, who never ceases to amaze and inspire me, and to my loving daughter, Tiffany Laura Brodvin, who understands and respects my work, sharing her time gracefully.

CHAPTER ONE

The intellectual and emotional journey toward understanding the incest trauma

When I (Arnold W. Rachman), first started treating an incest survivor, about thirty-five years ago, I did not fully appreciate the complexities of this dark side of the human experience. Intellectually, I had not been exposed to, neither had I sought out, nor was I aware of, the professional literature regarding sexual trauma. My lack of study of incest, child abuse, and child exploitation was a combination of "emotional blindness" to these issues and almost a complete lack of academic and professional training. For example, while I was a graduate student in Human Development and Clinical Psychology during the early 1960s, I do not remember any discussion on the emotional, interpersonal, and social struggle of children with adults who exploit, abuse, torture, or murder them. Emotional and physical abuse was mentioned, but not sexual abuse. None of the academics or clinicians I studied with in the 1960s confronted the issue of the incest trauma. When studying the phenomenon of the feral child on my own (Rachman, 1978), I was emotionally moved by the monumental emotional and physical abuse that feral children suffered at the hands of their parents. Academically, the discussions about feral children focused on whether such children were autistic (Bettelheim, 1959) and the effects of deprivation on language and personality development. There was very little, or no, attention to the issue of sexual abuse, which has continued (Rachman, 2012d).

On my own, I perused research on the feral child syndrome beyond the intellectual discussions in graduate school. It was only when I went beyond these intellectual boundaries that I was able to experience the emotional darkness that was the feral child syndrome. Scientific and anecdotal reports indicated that feral children were exposed to the most extreme conditions of human degradation. Such children were raised in isolation from human contact; fed starvation level rations, were made to feel more animal than human, physically and emotionally neglected, and sexually abused. I learned more about how parents can mistreat children in every conceivable way. My own research on feral children taught me more than I was ever taught in all the many courses, seminars, lectures and discussion groups of a four-year graduate school education in child development, psychology, sociology, and social science.

Although the research on feral children was enlightening, it was only a small, dim light in the darkness of my clinical education and experience that spanned almost a ten-year period during the 1960s. This training involved very different theoretical and clinical orientations. During this period, I was a Counselor at Jewish Vocational Service in Chicago (JVS), working with intellectually limited and emotionally disturbed teenagers (Rachman, 1962). In seminars, supervision, or in discussions with colleagues, no mention was ever made of sexual abuse as a possible psychodynamic in emotional disturbance. The counseling orientation at JVS, which focused on work identity, had a vocational guidance focus. But, a more glaring omission occurred in the special agency-wide clinical seminars conducted by the late famous child psychoanalyst, Bruno Bettelheim. When I presented case material to him about a psychotic teenager I was working with in the vocational setting, he was more interested in my unconscious processes than he was in the reality of the disturbed interaction of the adolescent's family. There was no exploration of any abusive family interaction. Bettelheim was a product of a traditional psychoanalytic education. In his supervision of me, he did not view sexual trauma as a variable in childhood disturbance. In Bettelheim's work at The Orthogenic School, he focused only on the mother's emotional contribution to the development of autism (Bettelheim, 1950).

In a completely different training venue, the former Counseling and Psychotherapy Research Center at the University of Chicago, their humanistic psychology orientation, based upon Carl Rogers' person-centered psychotherapy (Rogers, 1942, 1951, 1959), also ignored the incest trauma. Although the person-centered orientation was innovative and did not adhere to psychoanalytic theory or method, it gave the incest trauma the silent treatment (Rachman, 1999a) by never addressing this phenomenon in theory or method. I do not remember one instance, in about a four-year period, when I was affiliated with the Counseling Center, ever hearing any discussion about the incest trauma discussed in a course, seminar, invited lecture series, or supervision. A unique dimension to the training program was the tape recording of all our psychotherapy sessions. Before we saw a client for our first therapy experience, we would listen to tapes of client-centered psychotherapy recorded by master clinicians. Just before the master clinician responded, there was a significant pause, edited into the tape, so the neophyte therapist could formulate a response before the master clinician spoke. We recorded the process, so we could study the differences in our response to the successful client-centered psychotherapists. In supervision, we would discuss these differences. There was no attempt made to have the student therapist conform to one acceptable standard. This method was a reflection of a student-centered, empathic, respect for individuality. It was a democratic and compassionate interaction. Yet, with all its liberal and non-traditional thinking and clinical functioning, the client-centered, humanistic approach, in retrospect, paid no attention to the issue of childhood trauma or incest.

The rounding out of my clinical education occurred during my analytic training at the Postgraduate Center for Mental Health, from 1964 to 1972. I have discussed, in other contexts, the manner in which my experiences as an analytic candidate suppressed dissidence, encouraged conformity, espoused one essential truth in psychoanalysis, and discouraged clinical creativity (Rachman, 2007b, 2009b). This is not to say that I did not receive a sound, significant, and helpful analytic education. With all my criticisms of the suppression of dissidence, I did learn to be a psychoanalyst at the Postgraduate Center, for which I will be eternally grateful. I did have some teachers, supervisors, and a personal analysis which encouraged my dissidence, most notable, Betty Feldman, LCSW, Ben

Fielding, PhD, Alice Hampshire, MD, Asya Kadis, and Claude Miller, MD.

During my tenure as an analytic candidate, I participated in a wide variety of training programs; for example, individual, group, child–adolescent, and community mental health. Once again, I repeat the observation I have already made. I do not remember one instance of recognition of the incest trauma as a variable in either diagnosis or treatment. In retrospect, I think the silent treatment regarding incest was especially evident in the child–adolescent and community mental health programs, which dealt with non-traditional patient populations. One would believe that the incest trauma would be more of a factor in the study of these populations than the traditional patients chosen for individual analytic treatment. I do remember my shock when I became a faculty member and examined candidates' case presentations where the incest trauma was studiously avoided. In one such case presentation, which occurred in the late 1980s, a candidate's case study made no mention of the incest trauma as a significant issue, although the candidate's write-up of a family history included a description of sexual seduction by the father, and possibly the brother. The candidate discussed this data and other indications of adult sexual abuse as being part of the oedipal complex. As chairman of the candidate's oral examination, I focused on the omission of the incest trauma in the psychodynamics and treatment of the case. There was another faculty member, who had a self psychology orientation, who joined me in surprise and concern about the understanding of this case. It became clear from the interaction among the three members of the faculty examination group that the candidate held a traditional Freudian orientation. She was supervised on this case by a well-respected senior Freudian analyst at the Institute. The issue of the incest trauma was never considered in the supervision, even though the analysand's adult behavior indicated many symptoms related to childhood sexual trauma. The examination group discussed the candidate's case study and clarifications were made in the discussion about the lack of focus on a sexual trauma. I was against passing the candidate but the faculty group agreed to pass with a provision that the candidate add some understanding of the theory and treatment implications of the incest trauma. The candidate reluctantly agreed to the proviso, and made minimal changes in her write-up. I reluctantly accepted the limited changes, since the administration of the Institute indicated they were satisfied, and the influential supervisor and the candidate protested against any further stipulations for passing the case study. My vigor in trying to influence a consideration of the incest trauma in the write-up of a traditionally-oriented Freudian analysis had limited effect.

* * *

Thirty years after Arnold, I, Susan Klett, embarked upon my analytic training. While I have been aware of the prevalence of incest and sexual trauma across all social economic classes through my therapeutic work with children in foster care, my involvement in attending weekly meetings with the Child Protection Team at Bellevue, as well as my work with adult patients in private practice, I also discovered that our core curriculum continued to leave out readings on theorists and treatment approaches for sexual abuse and/or incest trauma. However, I did take an elective course on trauma where treatment and work with sexually abused patients was acknowledged and discussed openly. I had later discovered Ferenczi's Confusion of Tongues trauma theory from attending a series of lectures by Arnold Rachman at the Postgraduate Center for Mental Health in 2006, 2007, and 2008, long after my graduation. I then sought out and read numerous articles and books by various authors, two that have included Ferenczi's groundbreaking work: *Treating the Adult Survivor of Childhood Sexual Abuse* (Messler-Davies & Frawley, 1994) and *The Legacy of Sandor Ferenczi* (Aron & Harris, 1993).

Sexuality, aggression, and family values

My family of origin (AWR) was defined by the ethic of gentility and the morality of *fin-de-siècle* Vienna, much like the psychosocial climate of Freud, Ferenczi, and the pioneering period of psychoanalysis. Sexuality and aggression were given the silent treatment, even though they were a part of my childhood. I grew up having the distinct feeling that my mother did not like me and was hostile towards me. Furthermore, what was especially disturbing, she encouraged others to share her feelings. She encouraged a kindergarten teacher to be controlling and critical of me. I have discussed these experiences in another context (Rachman, 2003d). During my analysis, I retrieved an aggressive and sadistic memory connected to my father. I had a distinct and disturbing image of a cat o'nine tails used by my father, hanging in a kitchen cabinet. Neither the silent hostility of my mother nor my father's instrument of child abuse was ever a topic of discussion in the family. When I tried to talk about it with my grandmother, I was given the clear message: "You are mistaken, your parents loved you, and they would never hurt you. How did you get such an absurd idea?"

Sexuality was never discussed in any way, once again the silent treatment being operative. I could not imagine bringing up the topic, although I had enormous curiosity. I learned everything I knew about sex from my peers (Rachman, 2001a).

The phenomenology of evil

I (AWR) had a naive concept of evil when I began my training and clinical experience as a psychoanalyst. The concept of evil was not a functional part of my analytic training or, for that matter, my graduate training in clinical psychology. Actually, in my graduate psychology studies as well as the postgraduate analytic training the concept of evil was considered an unscientific concept. Because I wanted to be considered a good social scientist, I rejected the concept of evil.

My analytic experience with an analysand helped me realize the value of this concept, especially in the understanding of the incest trauma. I have chronicled my clinical work with him in several articles (Rachman, 1978a,b,c, 1980, 1981, 1988a, 1991a, 1994b,c, 2003a) and Chapter Eight in this volume. What is most relevant for our present discussion is the attempt to understand the analyst's difficulties when he tried to communicate his negative feelings about his mother. Early in his analysis he talked to me about two ideas I had difficulty understanding: "my parents were trying to murder me when I was a child" and "my mother was an evil person." He told me these things about his parents, during the initial year of his analysis. At first, I wondered if they were "crazy ideas," or paranoid ideation. He never believed I really understood the evilness of his mother. At that time, I did not understand his criticism. However, he was correct. I gradually learned to better understand how a parent can be experienced as evil. The more clinical work I conducted in uncovering and analyzing the incest trauma, the more, I came to believe that evil was the only appropriate concept for the incestual behavior of parents towards their children (Rachman, 1987, 1989a, 1991b, 1992e, 1993b, 1996a, 2000, 2003b, 2010a,b).

Years later, when I had more fully metabolized my experiences with incest survivors, I was able to discuss with him the difficulty I first had with this idea of parental evil. In retrospect, I was fooled by the face-to-face contact I had with his mother. At his request, two consultation sessions were arranged with his mother because he wanted me to assess the nature and extent of his mother's psychopathology (Rachman, 1981). He wanted to know whether he or his mother, "was crazy." I experienced her in those consultation sessions as intrusive, manipulative, and dissociated. Yet, I also experienced her as warm, emotionally alive, and concerned. When he and I discussed these consultation sessions with his mother, he became angry when I did not condemn her as evil. When he became adamant about my lack of empathic attunement, I told him it would be meaningful to consult a third party about the discrepancy in our evaluations of his mother. When he agreed, I played the tapes of the consultation sessions with his mother to a colleague who was an expert in mother–child interaction (I had obtained a release from his mother to discuss the tapes with another professional). My colleague concluded that his mother was: "borderline, intrusive, narcissistic, overpowering, and manipulative." She also did not experience the mother as evil (Rachman, 1981). I now believe the expert had the same problem as myself. We were both unable to empathically attune to the concept of parental evil. It was only when I subsequently had extensive clinical experience with incest survivors, where they regularly referred to their abusive parents as evil, that I began to become more cordial to this idea (Rachman, 1990, 1991a, 1992a, 1993b, 1996a, 2003a).

Another intellectual awakening occurred when I was asked to prepare a discussion of Robert Jay Lifton's book, *The Nazi Doctors* (Lifton, 1986). I was inspired to use this case material to discuss his family experience as an emotional holocaust and his mother as an "evil human being" (Rachman, 1988c). This discussion was well received by Lifton and the audience. They felt the individual's experience of an evil mother was a meaningful concept when I used Ferenczi's confusion of tongues paradigm (Ferenczi, 1980n; Rachman, 1994a). Lifton was not familiar with Ferenczi's confusion of tongues paradigm, but felt it had meaning for understanding trauma and sexual abuse. About the same time I was grappling with the concept of maternal evil in this case study, I began my clinical work with an incest survivor who helped me finally to embrace the concept of evil.

How I learned to understand the incest trauma: the case of Samantha

About thirty-five years ago, I began an analysis with Samantha, a mental health professional who, during our first session, described a disturbing and traumatic experience with her previous therapist. She told him of her disturbed relationships with her former husband, her children, and her family of origin. Samantha also demonstrated intense vulnerability and need. She had intense feelings of subordination toward men in authority positions. Early in their contact, the psychiatrist told her he wanted to nurture her and provide her with a "soothing loving" experience. He asked her to sit on his lap, so he could hold her, and provide her with maternal affection. Samantha became frightened and resentful at this intrusive behavior, but complied. Apparently, the psychiatrist did not understand that his invitation for maternal affection was experienced as sexual seduction. Rather than provide a therapeutic experience, he created a confusion of tongues trauma (Rachman, 1994a), retraumatizing her. Samantha left this therapy soon after the trauma, detailing it to me in the first moments of our consultation session.

I remember her during this initial period as intensely anxious, obsessively verbal, emotionally and interpersonally vulnerable. She was also warm, responsive, and likeable. Although I empathized with her fright and resentment about being seduced by the psychiatrist, I was not, either intellectually or clinically, aware of the full meaning of the seduction. During this period, I was just beginning my research on Ferenczi's work and had not, as yet, applied it to my clinical understanding of the incest trauma. Later on, I understood the invitation to sit in the psychiatrist's lap was an example of an analysand experiencing a therapist as parental abuser, and herself as an incest victim. They both co-created the childhood seduction (Rachman, Kennedy, & Yard, 2005, 2009; Rachman, Yard, & Kennedy, 2009). The childhood origin of the sexual trauma did not become evident until the working through phase of Samantha's analysis.

In the unfolding of the analysis, her initial focus was on her relationships with her ex-husband and parents. It became clear her ex-husband was a domineering, controlling, and manipulative man who emotionally abused her. Not only was she victimized by him while they were married, but, during their divorce, he used his skills as a lawyer and his dominating and intimidating personality to overpower her and craft a one-sided settlement. Her vulnerability to her ex-husband's domination and her submission was also an early clue to childhood trauma.

The theme of subjugation was also evident in her relationship with her children. When her analysis began, she had three teenage girls with whom she was in constant emotional difficulty. Her middle daughter, whom she characterized as physically resembling her ex-husband, dominated and controlled Samantha in a similar emotional manner as her ex-husband. It became evident that Samantha had a negative transference to her middle daughter, experiencing her as her ex-husband. With her eldest daughter she enjoyed a less overtly negative relationship. Their relationship had elements of coldness, distance, and avoidance. In actuality, it was akin to Samantha's relationship with her mother. Samantha had the best relationship with her youngest child, as they enjoyed emotional closeness, intimate interpersonal contact, and an affectionate bond. Neither Samantha, nor I was aware, in the initial period of her analysis, of the intense emotional connection to her youngest daughter, or how it was intimately connected to her own childhood trauma.

Samantha's relationship with her mother was profoundly disturbed. Her mother was originally a patient of her father, who was a psychiatrist. The mother, according to Samantha's report, showed signs of borderline and overt psychotic behavior during her daughter's childhood, adolescence, and adult life. She described her mother as cold, detached, emotionally inconsistent, peculiar and rejecting. The mother was on psychiatric medication her entire adult life, prescribed by her psychiatrist husband. Apparently, the medication and the marriage provided a "good enough treatment regime," since the mother was never hospitalized during Samantha's lifetime. However, Samantha suffered intense rejection and emotional abandonment in her relationship with her mother. When Samantha was a child, their emotional contact was disturbing. Samantha cited several examples of the mother's disturbing and peculiar behavior: leaving her douche bag hanging in the daughter's bathroom; mentioning the father's inadequate sexual performance; buying toilet paper as a birthday gift. Samantha sought out her father as the more emotionally appropriate parent. Since his psychiatric practice was conducted in the family house, Samantha could often make visits to her father during the day when she was a child and adolescent. Apparently, one side of the father realized he had given his daughter a psychiatric patient for a mother. A darker, less nurturing side to the father was to emerge during the latter part of the analysis.

Samantha had one older and one younger brother. Both brothers were estranged from their parents and their sister during the time of the analysis. The younger brother had been hospitalized for psychiatric reasons as a late adolescent and young adult. He was distant and cold to Samantha, in the same way as the mother. The older brother was an openly hostile individual who was critical and demeaning of his sister. The older brother identified with the anger of the father.

Samantha and I easily established a therapeutic relationship, I believe, because she felt a sense of safety that she had not experienced with her previous therapist. I found her to be warm, responsive, and very willing to focus on her emotional issues. Samantha was also intensely anxious, scattered, and confused. She was very emotionally needy, and a compulsive talker who had difficulty ending our sessions. I needed to work through my countertransference reaction of being held captive by her neediness in order to empathize with the emotionally neglected wounded child that lived in her adult self.

Our focus on her analysis during the first three-year period was on several issues: the effects of the traumas of maternal deprivation and paternal domination and sadism as they were re-enacted in her marriage; distributed relationships with men; disturbed interaction with female supervisors; feeling inadequate; domination by her children; and her inadequate functioning with clients. The analysis produced change in her functioning in these areas mentioned. She became less of a victim, and became assertive in her relationship with her children and peers. She developed a career in treating trauma survivors and improved her relationships with men. Yet, I had the gnawing feeling that there was something in her early experience we had not explored. At that time I could not articulate it. My intuitive sense was there was something unexplored in her relationship with men.

The breakthrough

After feeling better and enjoying her career and children, Samantha had expressed on three separate occasions that she wanted to terminate her analysis. My orientation to termination was to provide the same empathic understanding and mutual analytic interaction as occurred during the ongoing process of the analysis, that is to say, to maintain the experience of termination as part of the therapeutic experience. The analysis includes analyzing, when appropriate, the analyst's difficulties with rejection, anger, frustration, and disappointment when someone terminates. Many analysands have complained of negative experiences with previous therapy when termination was discussed. One of the most damaging responses I have heard is the blaming of the patient for wanting to terminate. This is particularly disturbing for incest survivors, since it re-creates the confusion of tongues experience of the original trauma. As much as the idea of termination might cause emotional difficulty for the analyst, he/she must welcome an exploration of all the issues, so that there is no notion of blame, judgment, or prohibition created. After all, analysands have an inalienable right to terminate their treatment, at any time, even if it is a neurotic choice. In addition, if a termination is inevitable, the analyst should strive to let the analysand leave with a good feeling about the analyst and analysis, so that he/she would want to return to treatment when necessary.

It was with these considerations in mind that each time Samantha brought up the issue of termination, I would explore its therapeutic meaning. I felt there was some unexplored childhood experiences. She was unable to go to the zone of her basic fault (Balint, 1968; Rachman, 2003a). The third time Samantha raised the issue of termination, I shared with her my feeling that I understood her desire to terminate because she had made very significant progress. I had, however, a sixth sense that there was something significant we had not yet uncovered. Further, I said I had a strong feeling the unexplored issue was in the area of relationships with men. She had not been able, in the eight years of her analysis, to enjoy an ongoing meaningful relationship with a man, even though she was able to significantly change her role as a victim. Our interchange on the issue of this unfinished business was as follows:

AWR: "You have made significant progress in the time we have worked together and I can understand your desire to leave after all that good work you've done. What I am about to say does not take away from all that progress."

S: "I'm glad you feel I made so much progress. It's important to me to have you understand that and to tell me you appreciate how hard I've worked to make the progress. My father was critical and my mother was so rejecting and crazy."

AWR: "What I want you to consider is this: I have a feeling that something is not finished; that we haven't gotten to something—your relationships with men. As you have said to me, relationship with men still does not give you satisfaction. I don't want you to give up on this."

S: "I don't want to give up. I am just tired of always working on my stuff."

AWR: "If you can trust me on this one, I think we are approaching the last hurdle."

S: "OK, I do trust you."

We continued our clinical work, not knowing what we would uncover. A real-life incident opened up our unfinished business for exploration. Samantha's father became critically ill with a stroke. She came to her mother's aid, and moved into her family home during this crisis period. Samantha helped her father go to the bathroom, including helping him urinate. Intense undifferentiated disturbed feelings began to surface. When her father died at home, Samantha and her mother prepared his body for the undertaker. While dressing her dead husband, the mother held her husband's penis in her hand and said, "You see this little thing. He never did much with it."

Samantha was horrified to hear her mother demean her father and talk to her about her sexual difficulties with him. However, it stimulated suppressed memories of childhood seduction. During the next week, Samantha reported the following dream:

> "A child is in her bedroom. It is night. A large figure is sitting on a trunk at the foot of the bed. The figure is moving back and forth. The child is confused and frightened."

The dream was the breakthrough we both were seeking. As soon as she told the dream, we both looked at each other, as if to say, "ah-ha, this is it". We sensed the dream depicted some significant experience of childhood. We analyzed the dream over several weeks. In Samantha's associations to the dream she was first able to identify the large figure in the dream as an adult male, and then as her father. She talked about the dream from the perspective of a child. She suffered from childhood asthma. Her father, as has been mentioned, was a physician, and gave her injections for her asthma. In fact, there was a significant period during her early childhood where he probably spent nights in her room, under the guise of attending to her illness, when she had an asthmatic attack. Samantha clearly stated that it was not necessary for him to stay in her room to be treated medically, because she had the necessary training, medications, and inhalers to help herself. What is more, if she were in a medical crisis, which did not happen frequently, she was capable of alerting her father. It became clear from the analysis that the mother was emotionally and interpersonally absent in the treatment of her child's asthma. So, Samantha knew not to call her mother for help because she would not come.

Samantha came to believe that the father used the medical excuse of her asthma as a reason to spend evenings in his daughter's room, escaping from the sexual rejection of his wife, searching for passion in the guise of providing tenderness and affection to his daughter. The moving back and forth of the male figure in the dream depicted the father's masturbatory behavior. As we focused on this material, Samantha believed her father sexually abused her, not only by masturbating while in her presence, but, by fondling her genitals and encouraging her to sit in his lap while he had an erection. It was this lap sitting experience of sexuality with the father that was re-created by the psychiatrist, which led her to flee therapy with him.

When the childhood incest memories were retrieved, the analysis finally developed the depth of feeling, thought, and uncovering that had been missing in the previous years. Samantha was immersed in the analysis of her childhood sexual seduction with her father over the next several years. As the data about the incest experiences unfolded, I began to understand that something unique, significant, and disturbing was happening between us. She seemed to need a witness to the molestation, not an interpreter of it. As I empathically attuned to her suffering, confusion, betrayal, and anger, Ferenczi's concept of the confusion of tongues was transformed for me from an intellectual concept to an emotional insight. I could now co-experience the incest trauma, as Samantha journeyed backward to the level of her basic fault.

Samantha continued with her analysis for several years after the breakthrough. She did not raise the issue of termination again. Working through the incest trauma produced additional significant changes in her functioning: she became less depressed, anxious, confused, and dysfunctional; she became more emotionally present and interactive with her family and friends. Her relationships with her three daughters also changed significantly. The oldest daughter and Samantha began to enjoy a friendship based upon mutual respect in a way that she never enjoyed with her own mother. The relationship with the middle daughter, who looked and acted like her ex-husband, changed from angry interchanges based on transference reactions to a less emotionally charged, more empathically attuned experience. It was, however, in Samantha's relationship with her youngest daughter that a great deal of analytic work was accomplished. During this daughter's high school years, it became clear that she was showing signs of trauma. She became sexually active early, and there were signs of confusion, depression, and anxiety. She was in constant need of affection from boys.

When it became time to apply to college, Samantha's youngest daughter chose the furthest location in the United States. While at college, she became involved with a young man who was a Rastafarian. The daughter adopted his manner and style of dress and living. She had dreadlocks, smoked marijuana daily, and dropped out of college. The couple lived in a hut, in an isolated area of the furthest state in the USA. During the two years that this new and unusual life unfolded, Samantha did not see her daughter. It was also difficult to communicate with her, since the couple did not have a phone in the primitive conditions of hut life in the countryside. It was during this difficult period of silence from her daughter that Samantha and I tried to find meaning in her youngest daughter's behavior. We both agreed, based upon the discovery of Samantha's incest trauma, that her youngest daughter may have also been an incest victim of her father. Samantha recalled that her youngest daughter spent a great deal of time at her grandparents' home during her childhood when the grandparents were used as babysitters. Samantha became convinced that her father had committed incest on her daughter, as he had done with her. It was this realization of her daughter's incest trauma that allowed Samantha and myself to begin to understand the difficulties her daughter was having in her own life. I offered to see her daughter for a consultation, if and when she visited New York City. The daughter never came in for a session, although she viewed the offer as positive. Samantha did inquire about her daughter's experiences with her grandfather. The daughter was not offended or overtly defensive about the inquiry into whether her grandfather had molested her. Rather, the mother reported, she was in such a dissociated state that it precluded sufficient awareness of childhood traumas.

The more I thought about the incest trauma in Samantha's experience with her father, and the possibility of it in her own daughter's experience, the more meaningful became the concept of the incest trauma. Samantha felt that understanding the incest trauma helped her clear the confusion of an entire lifetime. Uncovering her incest trauma helped her, as she also said, "to recover her life". Such a change is best exemplified by the idea of empowerment. Samantha took charge of her own life. She was no longer ruled by the thoughts, feelings, or behavior of others. Samantha became aware of her own inner life and interpersonal experiences and acted upon them, while becoming emotional and interpersonally connected to significant others. I experienced her now as a mature woman, not as a childish needy person.

Toward the end of the working through of the incest trauma, she sent me a holiday greeting card with the following greeting:

1989

Dear Arnold,

All things Rare and Beautiful and best wishes for a happy holiday. You helped me through so much—I hope in 1990 the pain can be gone.

Love,

About four years after the termination of her analysis, we met at a Ferenczi Institute event to which I had sent her an invitation. She told me she was doing very well in her clinical practice, specializing in trauma survivors. Her youngest daughter had returned to the United States with her child (but without her husband). The daughter was considering continuing her education in order to become a physician.

CHAPTER TWO

Psychoanalysis's neglect of the incest trauma

Psychoanalysis has had a love–hate relationship with the seduction theory and the treatment of the incest trauma. In point of fact, the origins of psychoanalysis are based upon Freud's discovery that neurosis (hysteria) was caused by the sexual seduction of (mostly) female patients by their fathers (and secondarily by surrogate father figures). This was a remarkable discovery that established psychoanalysis on a phenomenological basis; that is to say, the data for the analysis was generated from the subjective report of the analysand.

It is one of the great ironies in modern psychotherapy and psychoanalysis that Sigmund Freud, the intellectual genius and revolutionary who helped the world realize the importance of childhood sexual trauma, would come to be identified with an orthodox position which minimizes the importance of real sexual experiences in childhood as causative in psychological disorders. What is more, Freud introduced the causal link between childhood sexual experiences and the development of adult psychopathology (Freud, 1954).

Psychoanalysis eventually became not only unreceptive, but unfriendly to the idea of real sexual experiences in childhood as a casual factor in neurosis and more severe psychological disturbances

(Rachman, 2011b). It is a matter of continuing debate as to what factors contributed to Freud abandoning the seduction theory. Much focus has concentrated on the development of the oedipal theory as Freud's intellectual *tour-de-force*. The oedipal theory was considered a significant replacement for the seduction theory. The oedipal theory of neurosis became the cornerstone of psychoanalytic theory and the idea of fantasy replaced real experiences as the etiology of neurosis.

On the basis of his work with difficult cases, Ferenczi verified Freud's original seduction theory. When Ferenczi attempted to set forth his ideas in his famous "Confusion of tongues" paper, Freud and the analytic community tried to prevent the presentation of it at the Twelfth International Psycho-Analytic Conference in Wiesbaden, Germany, and then its publication in the *International Journal of Psychoanalysis* (Masson, 1984; Rachman, 1997a,b).

There is an additional issue that has not been given sufficient attention. Freud's analysis of his daughter, Anna, needs to be considered. Both Freud's vehement reaction to Ferenczi's "Confusion of tongues" paper and his emotional blindness in analyzing his daughter suggest personal factors in the abandonment of the seduction theory (Rachman, 2003b).

Freud's monumental discovery of the seduction hypothesis was chronicled in the correspondence to Wilhelm Fliess (Freud, 1954; Masson, 1984). Masson researched both the Freud Archives, and the records at the Paris Morgue during the time Freud studied with Charcot to discern the intellectual *Zeitgeist* for the awareness of sexual seduction during Freud's training as a psychiatrist. He concluded that the French were aware of the extent and frequency of the sexual and physical abuse of women and children.

History of Freud's seduction hypothesis

In a letter from Freud to Fleiss of May 30, 1893, the sexual etiology of neurosis was noted: "I understand the anxiety neuroses of young persons who must presumed to be virgins and who have not been subjected to abuse . . . the etiology is purely emotional but nevertheless of a sexual nature. (Freud, 1954, p. 49)

In a series of two letters in October of 1895, Freud continued to chronicle growing confidence in his sexual seduction hypothesis:

Letter of October 15, 1895

> Note that among other things I suspect the following: that hysteria is conditioned by a primary sexual experience (before puberty) accomplished by revulsion and fright; and that obsessional neurosis is conditioned by the same accompanied by pleasure.
>
> Have I revealed the great clinical secret to you . . . Hysteria is the consequence of a presexual *sexual shock* . . .
>
> Presexual means before puberty, before the production of sexual substance; the relevant events become effective only as *memories* (Freud, 1954, pp. 126–127)

Letter of October 16, 1895

> I am practically sure I have solved the riddle of hysteria and obsessional neurosis with the formulation of infantile sexual shock and sexual pleasure, and I am just as sure that both neuroses are radically curable now – not just the individual symptoms *but* the neurotic disposition itself. (Freud, 1954, p. 128)

Freud described a patient who "confirms" his "theory of paternal etiology":

> Then it came out that when she was between eight and twelve her allegedly otherwise admirable and high principled father used regularly to take her to bed with him and practice external ejaculation . . . Even at the time she felt anxiety. (Freud 1954, pp. 195–196)

Freud was thrilled with his discovery and shared his enthusiasm with his confidant and friend, Fliess: "Confirmation from neurotic material keeps pouring in on me. The thing is really true and sound" (Freud, 1954, p. 130).

By the end of the year, Freud was able to add a significant discovery of sexual seduction in a male patient:

> To-day I am able to add that one of the two cases has given me what I was waiting for (sexual shock, i.e. infantile abuse in a case of male hysteria!) and at the same time further working through the doubtful material has strengthened my confidence in the correctness of my psychological assumptions . . . (Freud, 1954, p. 132)

On April 21, 1896, Freud delivered a talk before the Viennese Society for Psychiatry and Neurology. There, he eloquently presented the full formulation of the seduction theory. He claimed that the "etiological precondition" for hysteria, obsessional neurosis, chronic paranoia, and hallucinatory psychosis was to be found in sexual abuse of infants and prepubescent children by adults, or by older children who themselves had been sexually misused by adults. These molesters, he said, were parents, nursemaids, governesses, servants, teachers, and brothers and sisters.

This original formulation was not really a theory of trauma or childhood personality development. He believed that the affects and memories connected to the trauma were discovered and sequestered (repressed, dissociated) in the child's psyche. He did not formulate any affective or behavioral consequences for the child as a result of the seduction. It was at the onset of puberty that the sexual trauma became of consequence in Freud's original seduction hypothesis. The activation of sexual feelings, a normal development in adolescence, transforms the repressed experience into a trauma.

Freud and Breuer suggested that hysterics suffer from reminiscences. In other words, instead of having conscious memory of the traumatic event, they unconsciously create symbolic symptoms that connect it to the precipitating event (Freud, 1895d, pp. 4–5). Sexual seduction as trauma was to be fully explicated in Ferenczi's empirical clinical studies (Ferenczi, 1980n, 1988).

Another interesting example of the connection between hysteria and childhood sexual seduction was inadvertently discovered by Freud. During a vacation, an adolescent female, Katharina, approached Freud, since she knew he was a doctor, observing his signature at the sign-in sheet at the hotel's reception desk. She delineated a series of symptoms: "I think I shall suffocate"; "like something pressing on my eyes"; "my head gets so heavy there is a dreadful buzzing"; "I feel so giddy that I almost fell over"; "There is something crushing my chest, so I can't get my breath"; "My throat squeezed together, so I feel as though I am going to choke"; "There is a hammering enough to burst it [her head]"; "I think all the time someone's standing behind me and going to catch hold of me all at once"; "I always see an awful face" (Freud, 1895d, pp. 125–126). These symptoms seem to indicate some forceful intrusive trauma was perpetrated on her. But when Freud first inquired about the difficulties, she denied awareness of any cause of the intense symptoms. Freud asked her when the symptoms began. She said about two years prior. He offered the following interpretation: "At that time, two years ago, you must have seen or heard something that very much embarrassed you, and that you much rather not had seen" (Freud, 1895d, p. 127).

Katharina accepted the interpretation and said: "Heavens yes! That was when I caught my uncle with the girl, Franziska, my cousin" (Freud, 1895d, p. 127). Freud encouraged her to elaborate the experience, and Katharina said she found her uncle on top of her cousin having sex. She remembered her frightened reaction: "Everything went blank, my eyelids were forced together and there was a hammering and buzzing in my head" (Freud, 1895d, p. 128). Further exploration revealed this same uncle had made sexual advances to her when she was fourteen. In 1924, Freud adds a footnote to this case by saying: "Katharina was not the niece, but the daughter of the landlady. The girl fell ill, therefore, as a result of sexual attempts on part of her own father" (Freud, 1895d, p. 134).

Freud's original seduction hypothesis was a pioneering attempt to bring into scientific study anecdotal reports of sexual abuse (Levine, 1990). In addition, Freud listened and responded empathically to his female patients who were indicating that they were suffering from real events of childhood trauma. In so doing, Freud was laying the foundation for an understanding of the profound effects that overstimulation and parental narcissism can have in the etiology of psychological disorder. Freud, however, did not linger theoretically on the importance of the object relational paradigm as central to human development, but it can be said he pointed the way (Klein, 1981).

Fromm believed Freud could not extend his point of view past the patriarchal sphere of orbit and thus:

> The mother was dethroned from her paramount place as the object of love—and her place was given to the father, who was believed to be the most important figure in the child's affection. It sounds almost unbelievable today . . . Thus, Freud gives the father the place which in reality is that of the mother and degrades the mother into the object of sensual lust . . . The father is elevated to the central figure of the universe. (Fromm, 1959, p. 47)

It was Ferenczi, Freud's favorite student, who saw the profound implications of the seduction theory and elaborated a theory of childhood sexual trauma. But more of that development in an upcoming section.

The abandonment of the seduction theory

Freud's interest in the seduction theory seemed to come to an end when he wrote an important letter to Fliess on September 21, 1897. This is an important document in the history of psychoanalysis. (For the original verbatim translation of the letter, see Freud, 1954, pp. 215–218; for the revised translation, see Masson, 1984, pp. 264–267: quotations are from the Masson translation.) Freud begins this letter exclaiming his enthusiasm and dedication to his work now that he feels he has found his seduction theory of hysteria (neurosis) to be *incorrect*; "I no longer believe in my neurotica" [theory of neurosis] (Masson, p. 164). Freud discussed his reasons for changing the course of thinking about the seduction theory:

1. The failure to bring the cases of incest trauma to a successful therapeutic conclusion.
2. His difficulty in accepting that fathers were the abusers. In a very revealing sentence, Freud pointed to the possibility of a personal issue with incest: ". . . the father, *not excluding my own has to be accused of being perverse* . . ." (Freud, 1954).

In addition, Freud did not accept that the incidence of child abuse was so widespread as to match the widespread occurrence of hysteria (neurosis): ". . . the realization of the unexpected frequency of hysteria, with precisely the same conditions prevailing in each, whereas surely such widespread perversions against children are not very probable" (Masson, 1985, p. 184)

Freud may have been in a state of denial by this point, fueled by some unconscious wish to suppress the awareness of incest (Krüll, 1986). How interesting that Freud wrote this to Fleiss, whom Masson accused of molesting his son, Robert (Masson, 1984).

(3) There is no reality in the unconscious, so that the truth or fiction of an incest experience cannot be established.

(4) An incest memory is very unlikely to break through during treatment, since even in psychosis the unconscious memory is not revealed . . . even in the most confused delirium. (Freud, 1954)

Ernest Jones discussed at length Freud's change in thinking about the seduction hypothesis, agreeing with Freud's conclusions (Jones, 1955, 1957). Jones' material in the Freud biography about the abandonment of the seduction theory suggests that Freud saved himself from one of his greatest intellectual embarrassments by discarding the seduction theory. Jones accentuated that Freud's abandonment of the seduction theory was, at least in part, based on his realization that: "the stories [of parental sexual seduction during childhood] were simply fantasies . . ." (Jones, 1953, p. 295). It is this kind of argument that Jones made famous: for example, Freud always saw the error of his ways by correcting his intellectual assumptions. This kind of thinking shut down any re-examination of the abandonment of the seduction theory for almost the first hundred years of psychoanalysis's history. When the most significant re-examination of this topic occurred in 1984 by Masson, his efforts were denounced by the traditional analytic establishment.

In a discussion with an underlying note of condescension, Jones asserted that Freud was taken in by his patients in some mysterious way, as if they seduced him:

> Less astonishing and certainly more fateful for good, was the credulous acceptance of his patients' stories of paternal seduction which he narrated in his earlier publications on psychopathology. When I commented to my friend James Strachey on Freud's strain of credulity he very safely remarked: It was lucky for us that he had it. Most investigators would have simply disbelieved the patient's stories on the ground of their inherent improbability—at least on such a large scale—and have dismissed the matter as one more example of the untrustworthiness of hysterics. (Jones, 1957, p. 478)

In 1912, before Jung and Freud formally separated, Jung had a more flattering version of Freud's original belief in the seduction theory:

> You may perhaps be inclined to share the suspicion of the critics that the results of Freud's analytical research were therefore based on

> suggestion . . . But anyone who has read Freud's work of that period with attention, and has tried to penetrate into the psychology of the patients as Freud had done will know how unjust it would be to attribute to an intellect like Freud's the crude mistakes of a beginner. (Jung, 1961, p. 95)

Jung's thoughtful and affectionate comment toward Freud does put the shift from seduction to fantasy in perspective. Jones and Strachey's notion does not do justice to Freud's genius, both as the intellectual and the clinical originator of psychoanalysis. They assumed that his change in theoretical viewpoint was a mistake. As Jung correctly points out, Freud's original discovery of sexual seduction was an indication of his brilliant clinical and theoretical capacities. The change, therefore, points all the more to a series of complex issues as an explanation. In the discussion that follows, the notion of some personal issues not previously fully considered are also elaborated.

Jung, as other analysts had done during psychoanalysis's pioneering period, attempted to adjust to Freud's shifting theoretical speculations. He suggested that the seduction theory had, in essence, been "proved true in principle" (Jung, 1961, p. 95), meaning that fantasies can be just as traumatic in their effects as real traumatas" (Jung, 1961, p. 96). This view of interpreting the oedipal fantasy as having a traumatic effect became part of the traditional approach to viewing sexual trauma that greatly influenced psychoanalytic thinking and clinical practice. As we shall see later on in our discussion, a contemporary view of the analysis of the incest trauma focuses on the necessity to acknowledge, both theoretically and clinically, the actual occurrence of childhood seduction.

Freud's blindness to sexual abuse in parent–child object relations

Freud considered Ferenczi his favorite son and collaborated with him in many ways: for example, in *The New Introductory Lectures*, the role of "activity" in the psychoanalytic technique, and *Thallasa,* theory of bioanalysis. He could not follow his clinical alter ego in considering the relational implications of his original theory of neurosis. In the 1930s, Ferenczi attempted to demonstrate to Freud and the analytic community that the seduction theory continued to have meaning.

Freud was adamant about rejecting Ferenczi's "confusion of tongues" theory, which could have ushered in a modern version of the seduction theory and moved psychoanalysis toward the evolution of a relational framework (Rachman, 1997b, 2007a,b, 2011b).

In many of Freud's major case histories he actually presented evidence that destructive parental behavior was the cause of the psychopathology. However, he insisted on tracing the origins of sexual trauma to the oedipal complex (Klein & Tribich, 1982). In the Dora case, Freud ignored very disturbed family relations and sexual trauma to force an oedipal interpretation (Rachman & Mattick, 2012). Parental neurosis was overlooked for the neurotic issues of the child. It was clear that many of the parents of Freud's cases were disturbed. He overlooked this disturbed parental interaction to trace the origin of the neurosis to the child's Oedipal complex (Klein & Tribich, 1982).

It is puzzling that Freud became so emotionally blind to the mistreatment of children and its effects on the development of psychological disorder, when his original thinking was an empathic and a humane response to the sexual abuse his female patients suffered at the hands of their parents.

For those of us who believe revisionist histories of psychoanalysis need to be written, Masson's revisiting the seduction theory was most welcomed (Masson, 1984). His contribution was lost in the debate over his term as Secretary of the Freud Archives. Masson's research has explored personal issues in Freud's functioning as a variable in the change from seduction to oedipal theory. Masson presents credible evidence to suggest that Freud was aware of the data that pointed to widespread sexual abuse of children in Europe during the time he was training to be a physician, neurologist, and psychiatrist.

One of the compelling pieces of evidence that Masson cited was the result of his investigations at the archives of the Paris Morgue. According to Masson, from October 4, 1885 until February 28, 1886, while he was studying with Charcot, Freud attended autopsies at the Paris Morgue and lectures by two leading advocates of child sexual abuse theory of the day, Ambroise Auguste Tardieu and Paul Camille Hypolyte Brouardel (Masson, 1984). Both authors described the frequency of sexual assaults on children, in a Tardieu study involving 11,576 rape cases (9,125 cases of children). Some of the girls were raped by their fathers.

> What is even sadder is to see that ties of blood, far from constituting a barrier to these impardonable allurements, serve only frequently to favor them. Fathers abuse their daughters, brothers abuse their sisters. These facts have been coming to my attention in increasing numbers. I can count twelve more cases since the last but one edition of this book [A Medico-Legal Study of Assaults on Decency, 1857]. (Cited in Masson, 1984, p. 23)

Tardieu's words in citing his study of sexual assault on children by their parents almost match, word for word, Freud's original statements of about the same issue (Freud, 1954). Thirty-six years later, Ferenczi verified Freud's original clinical findings about the incidence of sexual seduction, echoing both Freud's and Tardieu's words:

> I obtained above all new corroborative evidence for my supposition that the trauma, especially the sexual trauma, as the pathogenic factor cannot be valued highly enough. Even children of very respectable, sincerely puritanical families, fall victim to real violence or rape much more often than one had dared to suppose . . . The immediate explanation—that these are only fantasies of the child, a kind of hysterical lying . . . is unfortunately made invalid by the number of such confessions, e.g. of assaults upon children, committed by patients in analysis. (Ferenczi, 1980n, p. 161)

Comparing the words of Tardieu, which Freud heard first hand, with Freud's own words and with Ferenczi's words quoted above, also known to Freud through the report of Anna Freud (Rachman, 1997a), as well as in the German publication of the paper (Ferenczi, 1933; translated into English in 1949), there is a strong indication that Freud was intellectually, clinically, and interpersonally acquainted with evidence of childhood sexual abuse within families from the time he was a trainee in Paris throughout the first thirty-seven years of the history of psychoanalysis (1896–1933).

Paul Camille Hypolyte Brouardel was Tardieu's successor to the chair of legal medicine in Paris. During the time Brouardel was Tardieu's assistant, Freud attended autopsies by Brouardel from 1885 to 1886 (Masson, 1984, p. 32). Brouardel wrote on the rape of children. Masson also states that Freud had in his library Brouardel's and Tardieu's books dealing with sexual violence against children (Masson, 1984, p. 32).

In the revisionist history of psychoanalysis, a variety of explanations for Freud's blindness to sexual abuse in parental–child interaction have been offered: Freud's promise to his father not to reveal the family secrets (Krüll, 1986); Freud's lack of courage in maintaining his seduction hypothesis in the face of opposition and ridicule from his Viennese colleagues (Masson, 1984); Freud's rigid adherence to his oedipal theory, fearing any revision would loosen the cornerstone of psychoanalysis (Roazen, 1975). Karpe (1956) associated the reversal with Freud's mourning of his late father.

Development of the oedipal theory

Freud's letters to Fliess also "hint at the theoretical revolution which was soon to come, with the abandonment of the seduction theory for a conception that saw in the myth of Oedipus a universal archetype" (McGrath, 1986, p. 197). McGrath pinpoints the central intellectual issue in the shift from seduction to oedipal theory: "The central importance of this intellectual event lies less in the issue of seduction per se than in the implied shift in theoretical focus from neurotic abnormality to the general human condition" (p. 197).

McGrath (1986), as well as Lewis (1984), clarifies that Freud did not abandon the seduction hypothesis. That is to say, he continued to believe in the actuality of sexual trauma. However, Freud did abandon the idea of sexual seduction as the frequent source of neurotic symptoms (Lewis, 1984). In addition, childhood fantasy played a more significant role in child development than he had realized:

> This realization that repressed phantasy could acquire a driving force strong enough to mold psychic reality, a realization which he experienced directly in his own case, allowed him to unify his exploration of a whole range of phenomena, both normal and abnormal. (McGrath, 1986, p. 197)

It must be noted that the cause of Freud's abandonment of the seduction hypothesis has been the subject of much debate within psychoanalysis and the intellectual community at large. In his influential book on Freud, Sulloway (1979) dates the abandonment of the seduction theory to fall 1897 [p. 191 (see Masson, 1985, pp. 264–267)] and sees it as an intellectual triumph for Freud as well as for psychoanalysis (Sulloway, 1979, p. 205). Jones also saw the event as an intellectual advance and suggested that Freud's self-analysis was the decisive factor (Jones, 1953, pp. 265–266). Other scholars have both concurred with this view and elaborated upon it (Anzieu, 1975, pp. 311–315; Schur, 1972, pp. 113–14). Masson (1984), attacked the established view, suggesting the shift from seduction to oedipal fantasy was a "loss of courage" in the face of professional opposition (pp. 105–134). Krüll (1986) also viewed the shift as a retrogressive step (p. 90) and emphasized its personal importance as "a creative solution" to Freud's ambivalent feelings for his father (p. 88). Karpe (1956) associated the reversal with Freud's mourning for his father, but saw it as an intellectual advance. Finally, McGrath (1986) also sees it as an intellectual advance, accepting there were personal motives but emphasizing the role of political forces in the process. What is more, he feels that previous scholars did not realize the importance of Freud's Hannibal fantasy while on his trip to Italy in the summer of 1897. McGrath believes that "in conjunction with his mourning, this key self-analytic success brought about the collapse of the seduction theory immediately after his return from that trip" (McGrath, 1986, p. 198).

The controversy regarding the reasons for Freud's abandonment of the seduction theory does not diminish the significance of the impact that this event had on the history of psychoanalysis. According to Freud's account, he abandoned the seduction hypothesis because, as he wrote to Fliess, he discovered "love for my mother and jealousy of my father" (Freud, 1954, p. 223). In a dream, he realized he wanted to get rid of his father and possess his mother. He generalized these personal feelings to suggest that each person was an Oedipus. Finally, Freud said to Fliess that he could not remember being actually seduced by his mother, therefore, it must have been *his wish* to have his mother:

> Almost all my women patients told me that they had been seduced by their fathers. I was driven to recognize in the end that these reports were untrue and so came to understand that the hysterical symptoms are derived from fantasies and not from real occurrences. (Freud, 1954, p. 584)

More recently, Freud's daughter, Anna, verified her father's expressed idea for abandoning the seduction theory. She said he was unable to verify that actual seductions occurred. Since he had no way to verify this, he decided it was a wish (Freud, A., 1967).

Freud generalized these personal insights in developing the oedipal conflict theory to replace the seduction hypothesis. The oedipal theory switches the issue of seduction from an actual event to a fantasized one. The conflict is thought to be between a wish for seduction in each individual (to be seduced or to seduce) and a wish to murder the rival. The oedipal fantasy is the corollary of the wish. What we think once might have happened (e.g., sexual trauma), the seduction by parent of the opposite sex, or the fear of castration, is really a projection of the individual's wish. The neurosis is an elaborate way of defending against, and retreating from, those fantasies and wishes. Freud believed that the Oedipus complex was the nucleus of the neurosis because a decisive shift or change takes place in the mind of the child during this period. This shift takes place universally, regardless of the actual experience with the parents. Whether the parent(s) are seductive or not, the child develops incestuous desires. The prototype is the male's experience. He develops incestuous desires for the mother and hate for the father. This causes tremendous conflict. The mother is also hated because she is having sex with the father, which the child experiences as rejection. It is also a natural tendency to identify with, and be like, the father.

This traditional view can result in a skepticism towards reminiscences of childhood experiences. Such skepticism can be non-verbally conveyed to the patient. It can affect the emotional atmosphere of the psychoanalytic situation. It is not farfetched to assume that an analysand would feel that his/her recall of childhood seduction was, in fact, a fantasy, since it was being treated as a fantasy. What is more, in instances of actual sexual seduction, such an attitude of skepticism encourages the dissociative process. Unwittingly, the analyst conspires to reinforce the splitting off and repression of the analysand's sexual trauma, and any other traumas suffered during childhood.

Several significant intellectual conclusions developed as a result of the switch from the seduction to the Oedipal conflict theory:

1. Real sexual seduction was diminished in importance as a causal explanation for neurosis and psychological disorder.
2. The wish or fantasy of seduction replaces the acceptance of actual sexual seduction.

3. If the conflict (wish, fantasy) of seduction is universal, there is no need to search out the actual behavior of a seducer.
4. The recognition of real seduction, and its negative consequences, is not a concern.
5. Any focus on real seduction, the actual interpersonal experience of seduction, and the need to recover from seduction would be a resistance to uncovering the unconscious oedipal wish which is the core of the neurosis.
6. The child's sexuality is at issue, not the sexuality of the parent.
7. The child who reports sexual abuse is thought to be a hysterical liar, falsifying the experience.

Sigmund Freud's analysis of his daughter Anna: implications for the seduction theory

The family secret

Freud's analysis of his daughter Anna has, until recently, been one of the most obscure and taboo topics in psychoanalysis (Roazen, 1969, 1975). It is one of the most intriguing and unusual issues in the life and clinical work of these two major figures of psychoanalysis. Is there any one of us who has not wondered about their relationship, the analysis that was conducted with Anna, and the implications for psychoanalytic theory and technique? Most distressing for those of us who struggle to understand this issue is the veil of denial, secrecy, and splitting that prevents both research and psychoanalytic discussion. What's more, there has been an implied threat of criticism and condemnation if the taboo were to be broken. Roazen (1975) has been one of the few voices in psychoanalysis who has encouraged a dialogue on the topic. His first formal mention in print of Freud's analysis of his daughter was in 1969. Roazen noted that Freud analyzed Anna Freud (Roazen, 1969). It was a "secret" confined to a small group of the inner circle (also see Young-Bruehl, 1988).

According to Kata Levy, her own analysis with Freud began at the time of the Budapest Congress (1918), and Anna was already in analysis with her father. When Oliver Freud visited home in 1921, Anna was then in analysis with their father. Mrs Edward Hitschmann, Dr Anny Katan, Dr Edith Jackson, Dr Herman Nunberg, Dr Irmarita Putman, and Dr Sándor Rado have all confirmed that Freud did indeed analyze Anna (Roazen, 1969, p. 215).

Freud's analysis of Anna is even more remarkable when you consider that he sent his son, Oliver, to Franz Alexander (Young-Bruehl, 1988, p. 115). Also, he must have sensed Anna had what he called a father fixation (Freud's idea that one of the difficult factors for a young woman about to be married is the ability to switch her libidinal desires from the father to the husband). Anna was prudish, even for the age in which she lived. She was repulsed by a male cousin who tried to kiss her goodnight (Young-Bruehl, 1988, p. 115). Freud must have seen Anna needed help to reach the genital stage.

The notion of Freud's intimate relationship with women, including his daughter, Anna, has been treated by the psychoanalytic establishment in non-analytic fashion (Bettelheim, 1990, p. 45). Freud's relationship with his sister-in-law, Minna Bernays, who lived for forty-two years as part of the Freud family in their apartment, was treated by Jones authoritatively when he stated that there was no notion of sexuality between them (Jones, 1955). Bettelheim expressed a more open view:

> One must wonder about the man, Freud, who traveled for long periods alone with this mature woman, roomed in hotels with her, but did not find her sexually attractive; one wonders even more how it was possible for this woman not to become sexually attracted to Freud. What kind of woman was she? What kind of man was Freud that he should choose as the preferred companion of his mature years a woman sexually unattractive to him? And, if he was such a man, would it not be the prime task of a psychoanalytic biographer to explain this in some detail? (Bettelheim, 1990, p. 45)

Peter Swales, the self-appointed "investigator" of Freud's first fifty years of life, has proposed a theory about Minna Bernays' relationship to Freud. He believes that Freud had an affair with his sister-in-law, but Swales's notion has been debunked by Anna Freud's biographer, Elizabeth Young-Bruehl. "This absurd theory, for which there was no documentary proof, [was] only an old rumor launched by Carl Jung and Swales's strange construal of one of the dreams Freud had analyzed in *The Interpretation of Dreams*" (Young-Breuhl, 1988, p. 449).

She felt that Freud's daughter "would have been vigilant enough to detect for herself had there been any sign of it" (Young-Bruehl,

1988, p. 449). Since the Jones biography of Freud was published, Eissler has added his voice to the aura of denial, secrecy, and splitting that pervades the attitude of the psychoanalytic establishment. Witness this recent statement on Freud's relationship to the women in his life:

> Freud is one of the few great men whose relationships with women were happy. He never entered into dramatic conflicts with them or withdrew into hostility against them—phenomena which are the exception rather than the rule in the lives of geniuses. (Eissler, 1965, p. 29)

The case of Miss Anna F

In the psychoanalytic literature, there are only veiled references to Anna Freud's analysis. The main documents for considering the course of her psychoanalysis are those she wrote herself:

> her poems and [her own paper] 'Beating Fantasies and Daydreams' . . . and Sigmund Freud's 'A Child is Being Beaten', was the 1919 essay that was Anna Freud's starting point for 'Beating Fantasies' . . . (Young-Bruehl, 1988, pp. 103–104)

> There is no documentation as to how the analysis was arranged. We do not know who proposed the arrangement, whether it was Freud or Anna. Rumors that Lou Andreas-Salomé was her analyst persisted because people were scandalized by the thought that her father had filled that role. (Young-Bruehl, 1988, p. 112)

Anna Freud started her analysis with her father in the fall of 1918 and it apparently continued into 1922 (Young-Bruehl, 1988, pp. 115, 117, 140). In 1924, after a two-year pause, they resumed their analytic work. She had written to Lou Andreas-Salomé on May 5, 1924 that:

> The reason for continuing . . .was the not entirely orderly behavior of my honorable inner life: occasional unseemly intrusions of the daydreams combined with an increasing intolerance—sometimes physical as well as mental—of the beating fantasies and of their consequences [i.e., masturbation] which I could not do without. (Young-Bruehl, 1988, p. 122)

As Anna's first analysis became part of Freud's 1919 paper, "'A child is being beaten'" (1919e), it is suggested that her second analysis became part of a 1925 paper, "Some psychical consequences of the anatomical distinction between the sexes" (1925j) (Young-Bruehl, 1988, p. 125). In this paper, many of the themes of Anna's inner life are discussed:

> her envy of her brothers and her father, her anger at her mother, who was fonder of Sophie; the early-awakened genital sensations related to masturbation; her jealousy of her mother and Tante Minna as objects of her father's love; and her identification with her father. (Young-Bruehl, 1988, p. 126)

In her second analysis with her father, 1924–1925: "she focused on being overly good and coming to terms with the inevitable harshness of people and events and not escaping into saintly hopefulness that all would turn out well in the end" (Young-Bruehl, 1988, p. 127). She later discussed this trait, under the concept of altruistic surrender, in her book, *The Ego and the Mechanisms of Defense* (A. Freud, 1936). She understood altruistic surrender as projection of forbidden or dangerous wishes on to other people. "The chief example of altruistic surrender in her book, is a governess who has lived an uneventful life entirely dedicated to other people's needs" (Young-Breuhl, 1988, p. 128). Anna Freud continued to participate psychologically in an analysis with her father through her ongoing relationship with Dorothy Burlingham.

During the pioneering period of Anna's analysis, 1918 through the 1920s and well into the 1930s, the psychoanalytic community had not yet adopted the rule of dual relationships, which discouraged an analyst from analyzing a family member, friends, or an associate (anyone with whom a relationship had already been established prior to the onset of the analysis). There were no formal recommendations for crossing boundaries of family and friendship when one wished to analyze someone in your life: "Before the First World War, both Carl Jung and Karl Abraham had worked analytically with their young daughters and written essays on their observations" (Young-Bruehl, 1988, p. 114).

In addition to Abraham and Jung analyzing their daughters, Melanie Klein analyzed her son, Erich. Apparently, she also began an analysis with her two other children, Hans and Melitta (Grosskurth, 1986).

A gender issue was perhaps the most important theoretical consideration in Freud's decision to analyze his daughter. Freud felt there were less psychological difficulties in analyzing a daughter than a son.

> Freud's assumption at the time of his daughter's analysis was that boys would be like 'Little Hans'—feel hostile and rivalrous toward a father-analyst—but girls, who were not in competition for the mother, would not. (Young-Bruehl, 1988, p. 114)

In a 1935 letter to Eduardo Weiss, who had asked Freud to comment on Weiss's desire to analyze his own son, Freud answered:

> Concerning the analysis of your hopeful son, that is certainly a ticklish business. With a younger, promising brother it might be done more easily. *With [my] own daughter I succeeded well.* There are special difficulties and doubts with a son. (Young-Bruehl, 1988, p. 114, my italics)

With this assumption that the oedipal conflict is not as intense and difficult for a daughter, Freud apparently felt that the transference would not test his capacities to negotiate hostile feelings or deal with regression, both issues with which he was known to have great difficulty (Balint, 1968; Ferenczi, 1988). The consideration of an oedipal romance in the transference relationship with a daughter did not seem to hinder Freud's willingness to analyze Anna.

Freud's emotional seduction of his daughter

In his analysis of Anna, Freud was intellectually and emotionally myopic to the emotional seduction involved. In analyzing his daughter's oedipal conflict, it is reasonable to assume that he would discuss her sexual feeling and fantasies about him, both past and present. Contemporary analysts specializing in the treatment of incest survivors would say that such discussions constitute a form of incestuously tinged seductive interaction that would be intrusive, overstimulating, and disturbing. Such interaction would violate the emotional boundaries between parent and child. It is what Ferenczi originally pointed to as retraumatization in the psychoanalytic situation (Ferenczi, 1980n). Freud's blindness to the possible psychological seduction of his daughter is particularly puzzling, since he was later to be so condemning of Ferenczi's behavior with his future daughter-in-law, Elma Palos (Rachman, 1993a), when he viewed it as sexually seductive. In a letter to Ferenczi on October 10, 1918, he was not concerned with potential seduction when he said; "Anna's analysis will be very elegant" (Young-Bruehl, 1988, p. 116). But Freud was certainly aware that his daughter's adoration of him was problematic. "He knew the extent of her idealization of him and revealed it—sometimes in jest and sometimes somberly—in his letters" (Young-Bruehl, 1988, p. 116). If Freud would not acknowledge the difficult transference situation, his daughter could. She was aware of the difficulties in her analysis:

> She acknowledged 'the absence of the third person, the one onto whom the transference advances and with whom one acts out and finishes off the conflicts ... the analyst who was supposed to be a neutral party, a blank screen,' was, in the nature of the case, missing. And, further, she understood clearly that what she called her 'extra-analytical closeness' to her father produced 'difficulties and temptations to untruthfulness' in the analysis. (Letter from Anna Freud to Lou Andreas-Salomé, May 15, 1924: Young-Bruehl, 1988, p. 472)

Freud's emotional blindness to the possible psychological seduction of his daughter seems to be consistent with other behavior. He had a vehement, moralistic, and perhaps mean-spirited reaction to Ferenczi's behavior (Rachman, 1989a, 1997a,b). Freud went to the edge of condemnation in his famous kissing letter (Jones, 1957, p. 197). The letter, written from Freud to Ferenczi on December 13, 1931, admonished Ferenczi for his physical contact with analysands. Apparently the letter was stimulated by Clara Thompson bragging that "I am allowed to kiss Papa Ferenczi, as often as I like" (Ferenczi, 1988, p. 2). The letter began with the classic phrase:

> I see that differences between us come to a head in a technical detail ... You have not made a secret of the fact that you kiss your patients and let them kiss you ... why stop at a kiss? Which after all doesn't make a baby. And then bolder ones will come along which will go further to peeping and showing ... and petting parties ... the younger of our colleagues and God the father Ferenczi gazing at the lively scene he had created, will perhaps say to himself: maybe after all I should have halted in my technique of motherly affection *before* the kiss. (Falzeder et al., 2000, p. 422)

Masson (1984), who read the original letter in German from which Jones made this original English translation, said there were significant omissions, as follows:

> . . . accordance to my memory the tendency to sexual playing about with patients was not foreign to you in the pre-analytic times, so that it is possible to bring the new technique into relation with the old misdemeanors . . . (Masson, 1984, pp. 159–160)

Ferenczi was wounded by the accusation of acting out. He replied to Freud on December 27, 1931:

> I consider your fear that I will develop into a second Stekel unfounded [Stekel was noted for a tendency to invent case histories. He resigned from the Psychoanalytic Society in 1912, to Freud's evident relief]. 'The sins of youth,' misdemeanors if they are overcome and analytically worked through, can make a man wiser and more cautious than people who never even went through such storms. . . . Now, I believe, I am capable of creating a mild, passion-free atmosphere, suitable for bringing forth even that which had been previously hidden. (Falzeder et al., 2000, p. 424)

This "kissing letter" illustrated the difficulties in the Freud–Ferenczi relationship in the last phase of Ferenczi's clinical career when he was isolated from Freud, concentrating on the analysis of the incest trauma.

There are, I believe, several significant issues involved in the Freud–Ferenczi controversy that the kissing letter illustrated.

1. The role of mothering or the tender-mother transference in the analysis of psychological disorder (Ferenczi, 1988; Rachman, 2003a).
2. Evolution of psychoanalytic methodology to treat difficult cases and the development of non-interpretative measures (Masson, 1984; Rachman, 1997a, 2003a; Rachman, Kennedy, & Yard, 2009b; Roazen, 1975).
3. The controversial analysis between Ferenczi and Elizabeth Severn (Ferenczi, 1988; Rachman, 2010a,b, 2014a,b,d).
4. The analysis of the incest trauma (Ferenczi, 1980, 1988; Rachman, 2010a);

5. Freud's unanalyzed childhood incest trauma and Ferenczi's mutual analysis (with Severn) of his childhood incest trauma (Krüll, 1984; Klein & Tribich, 1982; Rachman, 1993a, 2012d)
6. Freud's analysis of his daughter Anna (Rachman, 2003b; Roazen, 1975).

These issues will be discussed in the pages and chapters to follow. For now, a discussion of Freud's sexuality will be offered in the light of his moralistic criticisms of Ferenczi.

Marianne Krüll, a German sociologist, has written a book entitled *Freud and His Father* (Krüll, 1986). Krüll's main thesis is that Freud was led to abandon his seduction theory in deference to his father, who had died a year earlier and who had given him a covert, but urgent, dream message not to delve into the family's history. Holding on to the seduction theory might have meant breaking his father's taboo. She also referred to Freud's own admission that he had been a victim of sexual abuse with a nursemaid, one Resi Wittek (Freud, 1954; Rachman, 2012d). These experiences, she reasoned, were primary and had a fundamental influence on his personality. Did Freud's background of childhood sexual trauma become re-enacted in his seduction of his daughter? Such unconscious feelings regarding sexuality can find an outlet in moralizing and accusatory behavior toward a projective figure, which Ferenczi became for Freud.

Freud's moralizing about Ferenczi's so-called sexual behavior in the analysis of Clara Thompson (Rachman, 1993a) was a matter of executing the tender-mother transference in order to cure childhood trauma. Freud's moralizing was in keeping with his assumed role of a stern father, feeling the need to control a rebellious and free-spirited child. Such a parental and punitive role is one which Freud assumed easily, not only with Ferenczi, but with other disciples (Fromm, 1959). However, it was a role that Ferenczi contributed to by his own behavior. As Clara Thompson has pointed out, he was too concerned about his relationship with Freud to break away and form his own dissident movement (Thompson, 1964a). It is tempting to speculate, in view of these ideas about Freud's own conflicts and his own early unintegrated sexuality, that his issues led him to project this on to Ferenczi and distort the actual nature of Ferenczi's interventions. He then punished Ferenczi for something he had not resolved in himself. Ferenczi's isolation from Freud during this period contributed to his being a victim of Freud.

Freud's analysis of his daughter Anna had implications for both his oedipal theory and Ferenczi's attempt to revive the seduction hypothesis (Rachman, 2012d). No doubt, in her analysis with her father, Anna had oedipal fantasies. In Freud's theory of therapy, such fantasy material naturally unfolded as the resistances and transference are analyzed. It is logical to assume that during the period of Anna's analysis, roughly 1918–1925, Freud was practicing his analytic technique guided by the principle that the oedipal complex was at the heart of neurotic personality functioning. What is more, Freud knew that any manifestation of oedipal material was not a result of actual childhood seduction of his daughter, since there is no evidence to suggest she was the victim of sexual abuse at the hands of her father. Since the oedipal material was not a product of sexual trauma, in Freud's mind, it gave him verification of the theory that such fantasies are innate, the product of drives. This upheld his theory that sexual trauma in the etiology of neurosis is a function of fantasy, not a real-life event.

Apparently, Freud did not connect the oedipal fantasies his daughter was reporting in her analysis to any quality in the object relationship he was having with her, either in their daily life together, where she clearly idolized him, or in the psychoanalytic situation. Freud had a blind spot for conscious acknowledgment of the negative emotional effects the real relationship would have on his analysis of Anna. He did not see the associations and the material he received in her analysis as colored by their current interpersonal situation. He failed to see that the very act of analyzing his daughter seriously influenced the material of the analysis.

Freud's condemnation of Ferenczi, exemplified in his attempt to censor the reintroduction of the seduction theory, is also puzzling. He failed to see in Ferenczi's confusion of tongues theory and innovative methodology a pioneering attempt to treat patients, mostly women, suffering from the trauma of incest at the hands of their fathers (and other authority figures). Ferenczi's insistence on empathic understanding and non-interpretative clinical interaction was aimed at creating safety, honesty, caring, and trauma-free interaction. Freud was unnecessarily concerned with Ferenczi's sexuality, since there is no evidence to suggest that during his twenty-four-year career as a psychoanalyst Ferenczi ever had sexual contact with a patient (Rachman, 1993a). He might have read into Ferenczi's behavior his own unresolved and unconscious incestuous feelings for his daughter, which influenced his decision to suppress the "Confusion of tongues" paper. Ferenczi's attempt to revive the seduction theory might have triggered anxiety in Freud, regarding his unresolved notion that fathers could not perform perverted acts against children. These hypotheses are a way to understand why Freud continued to neglect, then oppose, the expansion of the seduction hypothesis into the confusion of tongues paradigm. After all, Ferenczi was Freud's favorite student and collaborator and was presenting evidence that verified Freud's original ideas. It was also clear that Ferenczi was working with the incest trauma in his difficult cases (Rachman, 1997a, 2003a). These cases would now be characterized as narcissistic, borderline, or psychotic-like disorders. He was prophetic in his observations that actual sexual seduction can be an etiological factor in these disorders and that modifications of traditional techniques need to be considered (Rachman, 2007a,b).

Confusion of tongues theory: Ferenczi's alternative view of psychoanalytic theory

Sándor Ferenczi, once considered by Freud as the heir apparent to psychoanalysis (Freud, 1919a), made an intellectual and clinically courageous attempt, during the latter part of his career, to develop a theoretical and clinical framework to explain childhood sexual seduction and trauma (Ferenczi, 1933, 1980n, 1988). Ferenczi published a series of monographs and papers that outlined his observations about sexual trauma and childhood seduction (Ferenczi, 1980l–o). These theoretical formulations and clinical observations formed a new, alternative view to psychoanalysis (Gedo, 1986; Masson, 1984; Roazen, 1975). They became the precursor for the object relation (Balint, 1968), interpersonal psychoanalysis (Wolstein, 1989), and self psychology perspectives (Rachman, 1988d). Ferenczi's theory of seduction was most fully delineated in his last clinical paper, "The confusion of tongues between adults and the child: the language of tenderness and passion" (Ferenczi, 1980n). He argued that neurosis, as well as the more severe psychological disorders, arose from actual, not fantasized, sexual experiences in childhood. Specifically, there was a greater incidence of sexual seduction of children by adults than either analysts or the society were willing to acknowledge. These seduction experiences led to a severe psychological trauma, which caused immediate and lasting problems such as dissociation, splitting, identification with the aggressor, blunted affect, depression, confusion in thinking and feeling, schizoid withdrawal, memory loss, and robotlike functioning (Rachman, 1994a). Ferenczi was the first analyst to empathically describe the psychological process of emotional trauma for children at the hands of their adult abusers. The childhood seduction experience led also to adult psychopathology. The abused child had difficulty working through the trauma because parents, society, and the analytic community unwittingly collaborated in maintaining a veil of denial about the incidence of the incest trauma.

In questioning the issue of infantile fantasy as derivative of neurosis, Ferenczi was attempting to add to Freud's cherished concept of the oedipal complex. Ferenczi wished to expand analytic boundaries to treat trauma (Rachman, 2007a, 2012a, 2014c). He believed that neutrality, silence, a blank-screen attitude, and the tendency to interpret patients' criticisms of the analyst's behavior as resistance functioned to retraumatize the child-in-the-adult. Ferenczi pleaded for an empathic emotional experience through a democratization of the analytic relationship. He encouraged the formation of a responsive, genuine, mutual encounter in the analytic situation. These and other innovative measures were developed as part of his relaxation therapy to treat trauma (Ferenczi, 1980l).

These ideas moved Freud and many of his followers to censor Ferenczi and to suppress the "Confusion of tongues" paper (Rachman, 1997a,b). In fact, the paper was not available to the English-speaking world for fifteen years after it was presented at the Wiesbaden Conference on September 4, 1932, until Balint published it (Balint, 1949). It is now clear that this deliberate unavailability prevented generations of psychoanalysts from being aware of Ferenczi's intellectual legacy (Fromm, 1959; Masson, 1984; Roazen, 1975; Sabourin, 1985; Sylwan, 1984). Psychoanalysis practiced *Totschweigen* (death by silence) to prevent Ferenczi's ideas from being part of its heritage (Rachman, 1999a).

Some thirty-five years after Freud's abandonment of the seduction theory, Ferenczi attempted to reuse it and return its significance to psychoanalysis. In his "Confusion of tongues" paper, he made a statement regarding the incidence of sexual trauma that echoed Freud's original statement of the seduction hypothesis:

> I obtained above all new corroborative evidence for my supposition that the trauma, especially the sexual trauma, as the pathogenic factor cannot be valued highly enough. Even children of very respectable, sincerely puritanical families fall victim to real violence or rape much more often than one had dared to suppose . . . (Ferenczi, 1980n, p. 166)

Freud's original words, which described this same discovery in 1897, were: ". . . it turned out that her supposedly otherwise noble and respectable father regularly took her to bed . . ." (Freud, 1954, p. 195).

Ferenczi's formulations in the confusion of tongues paradigm and in the *Clinical Diary* (Ferenczi, 1980n, 1988) provided a series of assumptions regarding the etiology of the incest trauma and its treatment that broke new ground.

1. The object relationship between parent and child was conceptualized as the focus of emotional difficulty and the development of psychopathology.
2. The nature of the emotional difficulty was the development of a sexual trauma caused by the sexual seduction of a child by a parent or parental surrogate.
3. A real event was the cause of the trauma, not the fantasy or the wish fulfillment of one.
4. The analysis of the sexual trauma was also based upon relationship issues. Trauma analysis was developed which focused on the real as well as unconscious aspects of the trauma (Ferenczi, 1988).
5. Relaxation therapy was developed to treat the sexual trauma because it introduced new ideas and methods to help the trauma survivor meet unfulfilled developmental needs. Among the non-interpretative measures used were: clinical empathy, analyst self-disclosure, mutual analytic encounter and confrontation.
6. The analytic situation is a potential source of retraumatization when the analyst behaves with clinical hypocrisy; that is, to say, he/she forces the analysand to examine only his/her side of the relationship and the analyst's contribution to the treatment process is denied, omitted, or not considered.
7. The analyst has to assume a new role in order to prevent a retraumatization of the analysand; he/she has to accept the sexual trauma as a real event in the history of the individual;

become aware of the long-ranging effects sexual trauma can have on the child's development as well as the adult personality; democratic relationship and interaction where both parties become aware of and work through their contribution to the treatment process; and highlight all interventions with a bedrock of empathy.

8. An analyst who has emotional, seductive, or sexual contact with an analysand is demonstrating the most dangerous form of retraumatization. The analysis becomes a real seduction experience that precipitates the confusion of tongues reaction. The clinical experience then becomes anti-therapeutic and cannot satisfy the survivor's need for retrieval, renewal, and recovery.
9. When impasses arise in the treatment process, the analyst is required to examine his/her contribution to the difficulty and not automatically assume that the patient is in resistance. Therefore, the analysis of countertransference becomes a significant part of the analytic process. Countertransference is seen as an essential ingredient in maintaining the therapeutic relationship. The analyst also is willing to disclose his/her countertransference in a judicious way so that the effects of retraumatization will be reduced and repaired.

Influence of tradition on the analysis of the incest trauma

The imprint of traditional psychoanalysis on our attitude toward the seduction theory, real trauma, and the deleterious effects of childhood seduction on personality development cannot be underestimated. A few examples from analysands, supervisees, and colleagues can clearly illustrate the necessity to bring these attitudes into the light of contemporary thinking and practice. A prominent senior analyst trained in Europe during Freud's time, who considered herself a "psychoanalytic liberal," told a supervisee that "some analysts make too much of sexual seduction and sexual trauma." Furthermore, she added that she had cases of individuals who had incest experiences as a child without the sexual seductions becoming detrimental to their development or adjustment. The supervisee, who was a therapist and an incest survivor, was very upset about these statements because they invalidated her personal experience.

A most interesting example of the lack of focus on sexual seduction occurred during my analytic training period. We were all excited one week during my first year of candidacy because the founder and head of the institute was going to supervise a senior member of the analytic community behind a one-way mirror. The leader was a figure we all knew but rarely got to see, since he was no longer teaching any courses, was not available for supervision, and it was the rare candidate who could afford his fee for analysis (in the early 1960s, it was $75 a session for three to five times a week). We all eagerly awaited the fish-bowl supervision to have an opportunity to see the founder of the institute at work. The supervisory problem was absolutely fascinating. A senior analyst who was a graduate of the institute had been practicing for years. Surprisingly, he was involved in an erotic transference bind. A woman he was seeing in analysis was obsessed with having his child. She spent all her time in sessions talking about his giving her a baby. Apparently, all attempts at traditional therapeutic intervention had not reduced the intensity of the erotic transference. The analyst had become increasingly more uncomfortable with this woman. He turned to the institute leader to help him resolve the problem because he was confused, depressed, totally frustrated, and felt powerless. The institute head was a leader in eclectic psychodynamic thinking and clinical practice. After hearing the story of the analyst's difficulty in the erotic transference situation, he thought that the analyst had understood the psychodynamics of the case and performed all the necessary and appropriate traditional clinical functions. The audience, as well as the troubled analyst, was eagerly awaiting any words of wisdom from the leader to help resolve this most difficult of troubling cases. During our training, we were all warned that an erotic transference was the most difficult therapeutic impasse to successfully resolve. So, in the tradition of Freud's paper "Observations on transference love" (Freud, 1915a), we were admonished never to gratify any erotic longings of a patient, never to be seductive, and what is more, not to be indulgent to, or to attempt to satisfy, any maternal or, for that matter, neurotic needs.

When the institute head made his recommendation to resolve the impasse, many of us were incredulous. I thought the recommendation was a creative response to an extremely difficult situation that could not be analyzed. He recommended that the analyst give his female patient a gift of a dog or a cat that would serve as a symbolic child, resolving the impasse. The leader reasoned if one could not analyze the resistance, one could introduce an active measure (in the tradition of Ferenczi) to create a new beginning (Balint) for the analysis. The institute head had been an analysand of Clara Thompson, who, in turn, was analyzed by Ferenczi. But what I realize now that I did not at the time, is that no one thought of another one of Ferenczi's contributions. The contribution was the one that helps psychoanalysis understand issues of an erotic transference. It is conceivable that the patient's desire to have a baby with the analyst was re-enactment in the psychoanalytic situation of a childhood sexual seduction. This woman might have been sexually abused in her childhood by a significant male, such as her father. In the therapy, the analyst became the seducer, as, invariably, the abusive parental transference emerges (Rachman, 1992d, 1993c). The working through of the erotic transference involves the identification of the issue as sexual trauma, its historical roots in childhood seduction and its contemporary manifestations in the relationship with the analyst. The identification of the childhood sexual trauma as the psychodynamic fueling the desire for sexual contact with the analyst usually resolves the erotic transference (Rachman, Kennedy, & Yard, 2005, 2009a,b).

As I look back on my own clinical practice and thinking in this area, I wonder how many individuals I saw in my early years with whom I could not detect real sexual trauma, or underestimated its importance, or was not vigorous enough in pursuing the analysis of the incest trauma. Chances are I did fail people in this way. One case involved a woman whose father had repeatedly exposed himself to her during her childhood. In fact, he had a serious history of exposing himself in public and had spent time in jail for exposing himself to children in the neighborhood. This treatment occurred during my years as an analytic candidate, when the seduction theory was only mentioned as a brief note in the history of psychoanalysis, Ferenczi was never mentioned and his confusion of tongues paradigm was totally unknown to me. I was being taught that sexual material was to be treated as an integral part of the oedipal complex. Therefore, I never focused on the issue of childhood sexual trauma in this person's analysis and was not sufficiently attuned to retraumatization in our work together. This individual prematurely termin-ated, perhaps, because I did not attune to her childhood trauma.

Contemporary psychoanalysis needs to effect several important changes in philosophy, theory, and techniques in order to correct the mistakes of the past that have seriously influenced scholarship, treatment, and the reputation of some of its pioneers.

1. The re-evaluation of its history must be continually encouraged, re-examining the behavior and assumptions of its founder and the early circle that surrounded Freud. A revisionist history of psychoanalysis is necessary, because of the practice of *Totschweigen* (death by silence) (Rachman, 1999). Significant pioneers were maligned and removed from mainstream psychoanalysis because of personal and political considerations and not on the basis of the merits of their clinical observations or technical advances. A Ferenczi renaissance has been under way now for about thirty years (Aron & Harris, 1993; Dupont, 1988a; Haynal, 1989; Masson, 1984; Rachman, 1997a; Roazen, 1975). But other forgotten pioneers such as Adler, Groddeck, and Rank need to be reintegrated into mainstream psychoanalysis. There have been some recent attempts to revive interest in Adler and Rank (Menaker, 1982; Stepansky, 1983). Yet Groddeck remains a unknown figure in contemporary analysis. Freud realized Groddeck's value as an analyst. He is considered the father of psychosomatic medicine (Grossman & Grossman, 1965). Freud, Ferenczi, and other pioneering analysts would regularly visit Groddeck's Sanatorium in Baden-Baden.
2. The incest trauma, as a real event in the lives of individuals must be acknowledged and fully appreciated. No longer can the oedipal complex dominate the dialogue about childhood sexuality. There are real events in parent–child relationships that define the structure and process of that relationship. To tell a child or analysand that what he or she feels, thinks, or experiences is not real may be the most damaging experience of all, whether it is sexual or not. It is clear now, in the twenty-first century, that Ferenczi's theoretical and clinical ideas about sexual abuse and its connection to the understanding and treatment of difficult cases were prophetic. Incest, of which Ferenczi spoke as being the most prevalent form of sexual trauma in difficult cases, was once thought to be a rare phenomenon. In the past thirty years, clinical and epidemiologic studies have demonstrated that incest is a

more common occurrence than both the professional and lay communities were willing to believe (Finkelhor, 1984; Forward & Buck, 1979; Herman, 1981, 1992; Justice & Justice, 1979; Kempe & Kempe, 1984).

3. Contemporary theory of sexual trauma can be advanced if we become acquainted with Ferenczi's confusion of tongues paradigm, which has stood the test of time as a relevant and sophisticated explanatory device (Rachman, 2011b,c).
4. In order to enhance the analysis of the incest trauma, we need to follow Ferenczi's lead when he introduced non-interpretative measures by the analyst (relaxation measures) to successfully treat incest survivors (Ferenczi, 1980k–o, 1988).
5. Freud must be given credit for his genius, whatever revisionistic views of his person and work. His empathic observations and responsiveness to his female patients in the original period of the discovery of psychoanalysis must be acknowledged as a landmark. Because he was willing to listen to their tales of sexual abuse and not label it hysterical lying, he helped retrieve memories of incest. Although Freud went on to develop the oedipal theory of trauma, he opened the door to serious consideration of incest as a problem for psychoanalytic investigation and treatment.

His devoted disciple, Ferenczi, was well aware of his mentor's early *Studies on Hysteria* (Freud, 1895d), and was inspired by Freud's early capacity to empathically attune to and respond to incest survivors (Ferenczi, 1980n). Ferenczi's intent was to extend Freud's original work on hysteria to the development of a theory for the understanding and treatment of childhood trauma. Ferenczi developed clinical empathy to respond in an unprecedented way to the emotional and interpersonal needs of sexually and emotionally traumatized analysands (Ferenczi, 1988).

Contemporary analysis still has a great deal to learn from Freud and Ferenczi's capacity to attune to trauma (Balint, Kohut, Searle, and Winnicott, among others, have been instrumental in carrying on this heritage). Extending this thinking into contemporary psychoanalysis, we need to consider the issue of analysand-informed psychoanalysis, creating an open and emotionally honest experience in the psychoanalytic situation.

CHAPTER THREE

Confusion of tongues drama: the suppression of the first theory and method for the treatment of the incest trauma

The confusion of tongues paradigm (Ferenczi, 1980n) could have ushered in a new era in psychoanalysis when Ferenczi delivered its message in 1932, but it caused such an enormous controversy that the message it conveyed was lost in the battle to deliver and publish it. In actuality, the controversy surrounding the "Confusion of tongues" paper constitutes one of the darkest moments in the history of psychoanalysis (Rachman, 1997b). At the time Ferenczi presented these ideas, he wished to have them accepted by Freud and the analytic community and integrated into mainstream psychoanalysis. He was naive about his deviations from Freud and never seemed to realize how far he had deviated and how much he represented the first dissident point of view in psychoanalysis (Gedo, 1986). There are many reasons why Ferenczi did not realize how far he had departed from what had become, by 1932, orthodox psychoanalysis. Freud had encouraged Ferenczi to experiment, expand his thinking, and develop ways to elasticize the psychoanalytic situation. But Freud and his conservative followers did not experiment. The inner circle, the "Society of Rings" (Grosskurth, 1991), functioned to maintain the status quo. Although Ferenczi was a member of this inner circle, he was still a dissident (as had been Rank). His personal and professional closeness to Freud gave him a special position within the inner circle. Freud encouraged Ferenczi to experiment with the analytic method and passed the mantle to his favorite son to develop the technical aspect of psychoanalysis (Freud, 1919a; Ferenczi, 1980c,d,f–j; Rachman, 1998b). Why should Ferenczi think the ideas in the "Confusion of tongues" paper would be so abhorrent to Freud and the analytic community when he was continuing the ideas and technical advances that Freud had previously encouraged? The basic answer is that Ferenczi was seen as regressive because he did not embrace the oedipal complex as the explanation for trauma cases. He developed the confusion of tongues paradigm, which was a more parsimonious explanation. But, it became a matter of politics not science (Rachman, 1997a,b). Was this expectation that Freud would endorse the "Confusion of tongues" paper an indication that Ferenczi was suffering from a delusion? There is no evidence, Jones notwithstanding, that Ferenczi ever suffered from a serious psychological disorder (Balint, 1968; Covello, 1984; de Forest, 1954; Dupont, 1988a; Fromm, 1959; Masson 1984; Rachman, 1997a,b; Thompson, 1964a,b,c). But Ferenczi did suffer from a confusion of tongues with Freud. He wanted tenderness (affection, acceptance, and affirmation) from his surrogate father for his new ideas. Instead he received rejection, criticism, suppression, and denunciation (Rachman, 1997a,b). In previous publications, I have chronicled the acrimonious exchanges that marked Ferenczi's desire to write this paper and Freud's vehement objections to it (Rachman, 1989a; 1992c; 1993b; 1994a,b; 1996b; 1997a,b).

There has been much discussion of what separated Ferenczi from Freud as Ferenczi became more immersed in his work with the analysis of the incest trauma (Balint, 1968; Dupont, 1988a; Grünberger, 1980; Nemes, 1988; Sabourin, 1984). The theories vary from Ferenczi's madness (Jones, 1957; Grünberger, 1980) to differences in working with regression (Balint, 1968; Sabourin, 1985) to Ferenczi's actual personal regression (Nemes, 1988). An issue that has never been fully emphasized is the differences in their clinical cases, theory, and methodology that separated Freud from Ferenczi. Freud characterized his experience as being with neurotic individuals who suffered from intrapsychic conflicts centered around the oedipal complex. Even though there is reason to question whether Freud's caseload also had incest survivors, he believed Ferenczi's deviations in theory and technique pushed psychoanalysis farther away from its mission to understand neurosis (Masson, 1984). Ferenczi had a firm grasp on the reality of his clinical work and the kinds of analysands with whom he was working. In fact, he tried to convince Freud that he was right in his seduction theory based upon his extensive clinical experience with incest survivors (Ferenczi, 1988). The more Ferenczi proclaimed his idea that psychoanalysis must become aware of the prevalence of sexual traumas as a causal factor in psychological disorder, and the need to change psychoanalytic technique in order to address the needs of incest survivors, the more he was viewed as hopelessly deranged (Rachman, 1997a,b, 1999a). It was not the first time a prophet has been maligned throughout the history of science. Freud was vilified when he introduced the sexuality of children (Masson, 1984).

Ferenczi's dissident presentation before the Vienna Psychoanalytic Society

Sterba (1982) remembered some presentations that Ferenczi had made before the Vienna Psychoanalytic Society that illustrated his dissident clinical theory and method. In 1931, on the occasion of Freud's seventh-fifth birthday, Ferenczi delivered his paper, "Child analysis in the analysis of adults" (Ferenczi, 1980m). Ferenczi's relational theory of neurosis as Sterba (1982) understood it was: ". . . a lack of adequate love in the parental care of a child is the deepest cause of any neurosis" (p. 71). In the Vienna Society meeting, Ferenczi presented the following example of his relaxation therapy, which attempted to ". . . undo the damage of infantile love privation by giving the patient as much parental love as possible":

> . . . [in] a scene from the analysis of an adult male who, in a trance like state, put his arm around Ferenczi and asked him: "Grandpa, can boys have babies?" Ferenczi answered with *most moving kindness*: "My child, why do you think so?" (Sterba, 1982, p. 71, my italics)

Sterba was clearly moved by Ferenczi's presentation, even though he might have felt the method had its exaggerations. Apparently, in the discussion of Ferenczi's presentation, a question was raised about encouraging an infantile insatiability for affection in a regressed state. The audience wondered if Ferenczi's method could have helped to create the need. In fact, one analyst had suggested that an analyst could have only one analysand if such regression was encouraged. To everybody's amazement, Ferenczi agreed. No one contradicted Ferenczi's amazing answer, attributing his deviation from Freud's classical therapeutic approach as a sign of his physical and emotional deterioration due to the disease of pernicious anemia (Rachman, 1997a). In these presentations before the Vienna Society, Ferenczi was honestly outlining his emerging relaxation therapy without defensiveness, hoping to gain approval. With these same Viennese analysts, a very interesting social episode occurred which illustrated Ferenczi's interpersonal charm:

> A very charming episode occurred in the late twenties after a society meeting in which Ferenczi had presented a paper. A group of us went with Ferenczi to a night club at which the famous American dancer Josephine Baker was performing. We all enjoyed the graceful, supple movement of her beautiful body and were enthusiastic about her performance. After her appearance on the stage, Josephine Baker joined the audience. I have no idea what made her pick out Ferenczi for an enchanting little scene. She came to our table and in a most natural fashion sat on Ferenczi's lap. She glided her hand through her own black hair, which was smoothly and tightly glued to her scalp by heavy pomade. Then she stroked the bald center of Ferenczi's head and, rubbing the pomade on his hairless scalp, said. "So, that will make your hair grow." Ferenczi and our whole group thoroughly enjoyed this episode, Josephine Baker's irresistible charm made inoffensively humorous what otherwise could have been considered an impudent transgression. (Sterba, 1982, p. 72)

The road to Wiesbaden

Sunday 30 April 1930

A two-day visit between Freud and Ferenczi produced a brief healing of their differences, as shown by this extract from a letter from Ferenczi to Freud dated April 10, 1930:

> ... I recollect the friendly and cheerful mood of those hours I spent ... I left in the conviction that my fear of my rather too independent manner of work and thought leading me into what would be for me a painful opposition to you was greatly exaggerated. So I am resuming

> work with renewed courage and firmly hoping that these small detours will never lead me away from the high road along which I have been wandering at your side for almost 25 years. (Falzeder et al., 2000, p. 392)

Wednesday 28 October 1931

After Freud and Ferenczi discussed their differences, Freud sent Eitingon a letter on November 1, 1931:

> Since he did not go into a certain point, his personal alienation from me, I am fairly well oriented about the localization of the disturbance ... Apart from the dangers of his technique I am sorry to know him to be on a track which is scientifically not very productive. The essential, however, seems to me to be its neurotically produced regression ... (Molnar, 1992, pp. 110–111)

The gathering storm: Freud and Ferenczi's personal and professional differences

There were three crucial issues between Freud and Ferenczi that set the stage for the suppression and censorship of the "Confusion of tongues" paper. These issues were:

1. Freud's criticism and condemnation of Ferenczi's relaxation therapy as exemplified in the sending of the "the kissing letter".
2. Freud's prescription for curing Ferenczi of his interpersonal withdrawal and isolation from the analytic community by pressuring him to become the President of the International Psychoanalytic Association (IPA).
3. Freud's conviction that Ferenczi was going to break away from him á la Adler, Jung and Rank (Gay, 1988).

Freud's negative reaction to Ferenczi's relaxation therapy: Winter 1931

Before the campaign to censor the "Confusion of tongues" paper, Freud instituted measures to suppress Ferenczi's work. The famous "kissing letter", which has been discussed, was one such device. The letter and the rallying of public opinion within the analytic community against Ferenczi's latest clinical innovations were intended to curtail the development of relaxation therapy. The mythology of Ferenczi's acting out with his patients has already been discussed (see Chapter Two). Dupont goes further than my assertions and repudiates the notion that he kissed an analysand:

> Contrary to rumor, Ferenczi did not kiss his patients. The story is based upon a misunderstanding between Ferenczi and Freud, created by one of Ferenczi's patients [Clara Thompson] and which his *Clinical Diary* clarifies. (Dupont, 1988b, p. 3)

Presumably, because Clara Thompson, Ferenczi's analysand, bragged to his other analysands that "I am allowed to kiss Papa Ferenczi, as often as I like" (Dupont, 1988b, pp. 2–3, n.), the so-called sexual acting out of Ferenczi's relaxation therapy reached Freud in Vienna. Freud was very upset about Ferenczi's so-called tender-mother transference method. Freud wrote him what I have termed a "hysterical and accusatory" letter, attempting to suppress his clinical work with relaxation therapy. Masson (1984), who read the original letter in German, said there were significant omissions in Jones' English translation:

> According to my memory the tendency to sexual playing about with patients . . . was not foreign to you in the preanalytic times, so that it is possible to bring the new technique into relation with the old misdemeanors . . . (Falzeder et al., 2000, p. 422)

Ferenczi's response to the "kissing letter": December 27, 1931

Ferenczi did not deny that he was entangled in a love experience with a patient earlier in his clinical career. This dual relationship with Elma Palos (his future wife's daughter) has been generally characterized by critics as being sexual. After extensive survey of this issue, I have found *no evidence of sexual contact between Ferenczi and Elma* (Haynal, 1993; Rachman, 1993a,b). What is clear is that Ferenczi fell in love with Elma and wanted to marry her. Freud disapproved of Ferenczi's desire to marry Elma and urged him to marry Gisella, her mother, ten years his senior (Covello, 1984; Dupont, 1982). Although he was happy in his eventual marriage to Gisella, Ferenczi was angry at

Freud for interfering in his love life. In the proceeding years, he felt the loss of his true love, Elma, and yearned for children, which his marriage to Gisella did not provide. What is more, Ferenczi was wounded by Freud's accusation of his acting out. He replied to Freud on December 27, 1931:

> I consider your fear that I will develop into a second Stekel unfounded. "The sins of youth," misdemeanors if they are overcome and analytically worked through, can make a man wiser and more cautious than people who never even went through such storms ... Now, I believe, I am capable of creating a mild, passion-free atmosphere, suitable for bringing forth even that which had been previously hidden. (Falzeder et al., 2000, p. 424)

Ferenczi felt it was unfair and detrimental to hold his romantic, but not sexual, relationship with Elma against him for the rest of his life. By 1931, he had been a practicing psychoanalyst for nearly twenty-five years without any actual incident of sexual acting out with a patient. In fact, sexual behavior with an analysand was completely against the theory of trauma Ferenczi proposed in the confusion of tongues paradigm. As we have seen in the previous discussion, seductive behavior, even if it is unintentional, is considered a retraumatization, and, hence, untherapeutic.

Surprisingly, Ferenczi was not devastated by Freud's reproach in the kissing letter. He thought it was a gentle reproach that was deserved. In his defense, Ferenczi shared his emotional struggles to understand and develop methods relevant to the clinical interaction with the incest trauma cases. As he wrote to Freud on May 1, 1932,

> In the last few years I have ... been ... immersed in the work of understanding my cases ... it is not altogether anything bad or reprehensible, everyone has to go through such periods. More deeply penetrating self-analysis showed me ... that since my earliest childhood I have had the tendency to get into situations which I could master only with an exceptionally large exertion of strength. (Falzeder et al., 2000, p. 432)

Ferenczi and the presidency of the IPA: August 21, 1932

Freud had been urging Ferenczi to run for the presidency of the IPA. The presidency was intended to be a curative device so that Ferenczi's isolation from the mainstream analytic community and his preoccupation with curing his difficult cases with relaxation measures would become lessened (Rachman, 1997a,b). During the 1920s, both Abraham and Eitingon had been president. "Ferenczi had been the other candidate. During the late 1920s he was hurt by refusals to elect him, but in 1930 Jones and Eitingon agreed he should become the next president" (Molnar, 1992, p. 129). But, by the 1930s, it was too late for Ferenczi and the IPA presidency. It was as if Freud and the analytic community were saying that Ferenczi was being driven mad by his work and he needed to rejoin them in more traditional clinical practice and ideas. Only then would his "clinical neurosis (psychosis)" be cured. Ferenczi did admit, in a letter to Freud dated May 1, 1932, that his clinical work was emotional, interpersonal, and intellectually demanding.

> my sense of responsibility requires me . . . to ask you whether you can accept as President one whose major interests are to some extent circumscribed in this way . . . much more is required for this position than I can offer, then I shall relinquish the role of leader without the slightest bitterness. (Falzeder et al., 2000, p. 432)

What was causing him far greater distress than his difficulties with trauma cases was Freud's criticism and lack of acceptance. Finally, Ferenczi took an enormous step toward independence and declined the IPA presidency, sacrificing politics and Freud's approval for the need to pursue his own path. The way was clear for the "Confusion of tongues" paper. On August 21, 1932 Ferenczi wrote to Freud,

> After long anguished hesitation, I have decided to renounce my candidacy for the presidency . . . which seem to necessitate in some respects not only extensions but also corrections of our practical and theoretical views . . . intellectual constitution is on no account commensurate with the dignity of a president whose main concern should be conserving and consolidating what already exists. (Falzeder et al., 2000, p. 441)

Ferenczi's withdrawal from Freud: Spring–Summer 1932

Freud's assumption was that Ferenczi's so-called detachment from him, for example, not sending letters for several months, was due to a "transparent rebellion against him, the father" (Gay, 1988, p. 582).

Freud said to Eitingon, in the Spring of 1932 (before Wiesbaden), "Isn't Ferenczi a cross to bear? Once again for months no news of him. He is insulted because we are not charmed by his playing mother and child with his female pupils" (Gay, 1988, p. 582). During the summer of 1932, Freud was certain that Ferenczi's silence was due to a personal hostility, which Freud interpreted as being a negative transference reaction. Freud was convinced that he played no part in Ferenczi's negative reaction. Ferenczi was aware in August of 1932, several weeks before the Weisbaden Conference, that his ideas and methods were dissident and Freud would never approve of them. In an act of intellectual honesty and emotional courage that demonstrated his commitment to his relaxation therapy and the confusion of tongues paradigm, he declined the candidacy for the president of IPA. Given Ferenczi's need for Freud's approval, his pursuit of his own work was his emancipation proclamation. Freud did not fully accept Ferenczi's renunciation of the presidency, and he continued to expect him to accept. The last phase in this issue would occur in a face-to-face meeting. Ferenczi and his wife would pay a visit to Freud in Vienna on the way to the Wiesbaden Conference. But, before then, Freud wrote about his feeling that Ferenczi's incest trauma work was a form of hostility towards him.

> For three years now [1929–1932] I have been observing his increasing alienation, his inaccessibility . . . his incorrect technical path, and what is probably the decisive thing, a personal hostility toward me for which I have certainly given even less cause than in earlier cases. (Gay, 1988, p. 582)

Freud clearly was viewing his favorite son now, in 1932, as a defector, about to go the way of Adler, Jung, and Rank. He was preparing himself for the break, a defection Ferenczi did not want. Freud, one can speculate, was suffering from some form of emotional trauma in this pre-Wiesbaden drama, because he began to perceive Ferenczi's negative feelings toward him as a death wish, as he had a decade before when he accused Jung of the same fantasy. Freud was condescending in his exchange of letters to Ferenczi. He used terms that were mean-spirited such as: "you will have to leave your dream island where you dwell with your fantasy children", as well as saying he was having a "crisis of puberty" (Gay, 1988, p. 583).

The suppression of the "Confusion of tongues" paper

The events surrounding Ferenczi's struggle to present and publish his "Confusion of tongues" paper are unprecedented in psychoanalytic history. I do not believe there ever has been a campaign launched by the leader of a psychoanalytic school, much less the founder of psychoanalysis, to prevent a loyal follower from giving a paper or having it published. What is more, how does the campaign to suppress this paper compare to other such dark moments in the history of science, for example, the suppression of Galileo or Semelweiss?

Freud tried to prevent the presentation of the COT paper: August 29, 1932

Before Ferenczi read the contents of the "Confusion of tongues" paper, Freud was prepared to censor it. He sent the following letter of condemnation to Eitingon on August 29, 1932:

> *He must be prevented from reading his essay* [COT]. *Either he will present another one, or none at all* ... Our behavior will depend first on his acceptance of the cancellation [of the reading of his paper] and then the impression you all have of him in Wiesbaden. (Sylwan, 1984, p. 108, my italics)

Ferenczi reads the COT paper to Freud: Thursday, September 1, 1932

On a fateful day in September of 1932, three days before the Wiesbaden Conference, Ferenczi courageously went to Freud in Vienna to read him his "Confusion of tongues" paper. It was a meeting filled with anxiety, disturbance, and interpersonal conflict for both Freud and Ferenczi. Ferenczi was devastated by Freud's very negative, and what could be called an abusive, reaction to him. The details of this experience were told by Ferenczi to his student and analysand, Izette de Forest, who, in turn, conveyed it, in detail, to Eric Fromm over twenty years after it occurred.

> I [Ferenczi] told him [Freud] of my latest technical ideas ... empirically based on my work with my patients. I have tried to discover

> from my patients' told history, from their association of ideas, from the way they behave—even in detailed respects and especially toward me—from the frustrations which arouse their anger or depression, . . . from the content—both conscious and unconscious—of their desires and longings, the manner in which they suffered rejection at the mothers or their parents or surrogates. And I have also endeavored through empathy to imagine what kind of loving care the patient really needed at that early age—a loving care and nurture which would have allowed his self-confidence, his self-enjoyment to develop wholesomely . . . It is possible to sense when I am on the right track, for the patient immediately unconsciously gives the signal by a number of slight changes in mood and behavior. Even his dreams show a response to the new and beneficial treatment. All this should be confided to the patient—the analyst's new understanding of his needs, his ensuing change of relationship to the patient and his expression of this, and the patient's own evident response. Whenever mistakes are made by the analyst, the patient again gives the signal by becoming angry or despondent. And this can be elicited from the patient and explained to him. It must be absolutely honest and genuine. (Fromm, 1959, pp. 63–64)

Ferenczi presented in this conversation a remarkably clear and compelling overview of the empirical evidence he gathered in his clinical work with incest survivors. He was, of course, talking to Freud about his "Confusion of tongues" paper, trying to convince the Professor to approve of his ideas about trauma analysis and rescind his prohibition against Ferenczi delivering the material at the Congress in Wiesbaden. Ferenczi finished his exposition of that last fateful meeting with Freud by telling de Forest the Professor's reaction to the "Confusion of tongues" material:

> The Professor listened to my exposition with increasing impatience and finally warned me that I was treading on dangerous ground and was departing fundamentally from the traditional customs and techniques of psychoanalysis. Such yielding to the patient's longings and desires—no matter how genuine—would increase his dependence on the analyst. Such dependence can only be destroyed by the emotional withdrawal of the analyst. In the hands of unskilled analysts, my method, the Professor said, might easily lead to sexual indulgence rather than an expression of parental devotion. This warning ended the interview. I held out my hand in affectionate adieu. The Professor

turned his back on me and walked out of the room. (Fromm, 1959, pp. 64–65, fn. 3)

Fromm's description of Ferenczi's last meeting with Freud as revealed in Izette de Forest's report provided American psychoanalysis with a window into the Freud–Ferenczi conflict as well as Freud's negative contribution to their difficulties that was not reported by Jones or any other members of Freud's inner circle.

Freud's reaction to the meeting with Ferenczi: Friday, September 2, 1932

> The day after that meeting [the Ferenczis met with Freud on Thursday, September 1, 1932], Freud sent Anna a report: "Without any further question or greeting he began: 'I want to read you my lecture.' This he did and I listened thunderstruck. He was totally regressed to the etiological views I believed in and gave up 35 years ago, that the gross sexual traumas of childhood are the regular cause of neurosis, says it in almost the same words I used then. No word about the technique by which he obtains this material, in the middle of it all remarks about the hostility of patients and the necessity of accepting their criticism and admitting one's errors to them. The consequences of this confused, tortuously contrived. The whole thing is actually stupid or it seems so since it is so devious and incomplete." (Molnar, 1992, p. 131)

Freud moved to censor the COT Paper: September 2, 1932

On Friday, September 2, 1932, two days before Ferenczi presented his "Confusion of tongues" paper at Wiesbaden, and one day after Ferenczi read Freud the paper, Freud sent the following telegram to Eitingon, condemning the paper: "Ferenczi read me his paper. Harmless. Stupid. Another way [for Ferenczi] to be unreachable. Disagreeable impression" (Sylwan, 1984, p. 109).

The Wiesbaden Congress: Sunday, 9 a.m., September 4, 1932

Ferenczi was the first presentation at the Wiesbaden Congress, giving his paper at 9 a.m. on September 4, 1932. Apparently, the reaction was muted in Wiesbaden. But it is clear there was a hostile reception, witness Joan Rivière's assessment in a letter to Ernest Jones:

> Its scientific contentions and its statements about analytic practice are just a *tissue of delusions* which can only discredit psychoanalysis and give credit to its opponents. It cannot be supposed that all *Journal* readers will appreciate the mental condition of the writer, and in this respect one has to think of posterity, too! (Masson, 1984, p. 152, my italics)

After Ferenczi returned from the Wiesbaden Conference and the disastrous final meeting with Freud, he was drained emotionally. Before he left for Wiesbaden, he made numerous entries in his *Clinical Diary*, for example, August 4, 7, 8, 11, 12, 13, 14, 17, 22, 24, 1932, pp. 184–211; 8/4/32, pp. 184–186. There is one entry in the *Clinical Diary* after Ferenczi returned from Wiesbaden. On October 2, 1932 he mentioned an unexpected positive response from Jones, which lifted his spirits (Ferenczi, 1988, pp. 257–258).

Jones' reaction to Wiesbaden: September 9, 1932

Jones, as could be expected, glossed over the trauma that was created for Ferenczi. He reported to Freud in a letter dated September 9, 1932, that

> He [Ferenczi] is, I am afraid, a sick man—also physically and the impression he made was very pathetic. My impression of The Congress was throughout excellent. I have rarely known one with a better stimming (mood), friendly and confident. (Paskauskas, 1993, p. 702)

Jones' enthusiasm for the Congress and his massive denial of Ferenczi's trauma was no doubt due to the fact that the Twelfth International Psycho-Analytic Congress elected him president to replace Eitingon.

March 22, 1933: Jones promised to publish the COT in the International Journal

Ferenczi was under the impression that the "Confusion of tongues" paper would be published in English. Jones had written to Ferenczi telling "him that he had translated the paper into English, and that it would appear in the *International Journal of Psycho-Analysis*" (Masson, 1984, p. 151). Ferenczi verified Jones' promise of publication in "an unpublished letter (in English) to Jones, dated March, 1932: "I thank you for wanting to publish my Congress paper in the English Journal" (Masson, 1984, pp. 151–152).

June 20, 1933: Jones reneged on his promise to publish the "Confusion of tongues" paper

In a little less than a month after Ferenczi's death on May 22, 1933, Jones wrote to Brill on June 20, 1933 instituting the final process of suppression:

> To please him [Ferenczi] I had already printed his Congress paper, which appeared in the *Zeitschrift* [German translation] for the July number of the Journal, but now, after consultation with Freud, have decided not to publish it. It would certainly not have done his reputation any good. (Masson, 1984, pp. 151–153)

Jones' accusation of Ferenczi's madness

Jones characterized the Wiesbaden trauma as difficult for Freud, rather than for Ferenczi. It was difficult for Freud because of the "progressive deterioration in Ferenczi's mental condition" (Jones, 1957, p. 166). Freud told Ferenczi not to read his paper. Brill, Eitingon, and van Ophuijsen thought the COT paper would scandalize psychoanalysis (for a fuller description of Jones' accusation, see Rachman, 1997a,b).

Spring, 1932: Symptoms of pernicious anemia

Ferenczi, by the Spring of 1932, was suffering noticeable symptoms of pernicious anemia. The idea of both Freud and Jones that Ferenczi's behavior was driven by a dissidence due to a mental deterioration was false. Witness the description of Ferenczi's stepdaughter when she first noticed the first symptoms of the disease in the spring of 1932, several months before the Wiesbaden conference:

> We found he became pale . . . Once in a while when he passed a mirror, he exclaimed: I wonder why I am so pale—old age, I guess,

and laughed. At that time he felt no discomfort and consulted no doctor. Later he got easily tired, often felt exhausted, yet, as he liked to go for a walk after dinner, with either my mother or with me, we kept up this habit for a time. *His condition became perceptibly worse during the fall, 1932. Yet he attended the International Psychoanalytic Congress at Wiesbaden in September.* From there he and my mother went to Biarritz, France, for their vacation, but he could not enjoy it because he felt very, very weak. They did not write us about this bad turn as they did not want to frighten the rest of the family and they were also hoping that it was only a passing condition . . . I do not remember what treatments he got, but he recovered his energy to a great extent and soon started to work with his patients . . . He tried not to change his way of life, and even accepted invitations, though he sometimes walked with difficulty . . . He worked with a few of his patients up to a month before his passing. He spent his last two weeks in bed and in the last days he had to be fed. The food was given to him by a maid whom he liked very much. Up to the last day he joked with her. She asked him if he would like more coffee. When she returned with it he was dead . . . (Grossman & Grossman, 1965, p.198, my italics).

Suppression of the "Confusion of tongues" paper in Hungary

I was astounded to hear that the suppression of Ferenczi's "Confusion of tongues" paper had not only occurred in English-speaking countries, but also in Ferenczi's native land. It is all the more remarkable, since Ferenczi was the founder of Hungarian psychoanalysis. The late Gyorgy Hidas, one of the former leaders of Hungarian psychoanalysis and one of the founders and former president of The Ferenczi Society, has brought the suppression to light (Hidas, 1993b). Prior to the 1990s, Ferenczi's COT paper could not be found in any Hungarian journal, even though Ferenczi has one hundred papers published in the Hungarian medical journal *Gyógyászat*. The paper was first published in Hungary in 1971 (thirty-nine years after it was presented at Wiesbaden) in a book by Béla Buda entitled *Psychoanalysis and Its Modern Tendencies*, published at a commemorative meeting on Ferenczi's work. After 1971, the paper disappeared again in Hungarian psychoanalysis. Hidas and the editors of The Ferenczi Society's official journal, *Thalassa*, Antal Bókay, and Ferencz Erős planned to keep alive material on the "Confusion of tongues" (Rachman, 1997b).

The trauma of Wiesbaden

Balint, who was a witness to the emotional difficulties between Freud and Ferenczi during this period, has noted the traumatic effect their disagreements in theory and technique had, not only for their relationship, but for the evolution of psychoanalysis:

> The tragic disagreement between Freud and Ferenczi which caused both of them so much pain, and considerably delayed the development of our analytic technique ... [and] acted as a trauma on the psychoanalytic world. Whether one assumed ... [that] the two most prominent psychoanalysts, were not able to understand and properly evaluate each others clinical findings, observations, and theoretical ideas, the shock was highly disturbing and extremely painful. (Balint, 1968, pp. 152–153)

Suppression of the "Confusion of tongues" paper and removal of Ferenczi's work from mainstream psychoanalysis

It must be noted that the suppression of the "Confusion of tongues" paper was very successful. As I have suggested in my idea of *Totschweigen*, the removal of an analyst's ideas from mainstream psychoanalysis was especially successful in silencing Ferenczi's work (Rachman, 1999a), witness these significant results:

1. The embargo on publishing the "Confusion of tongues" paper in English lasted from 1932 until 1949 (Balint, 1949).
2. The shocking fact that the paper was not published in Hungary until 1971 (Hidas, 1993b; Rachman, 1997a).
3. The loss to several generations of psychoanalysts of Ferenczi's clinical ideas and methods, his positive role as a psychoanalytic dissident who remained within the fold, and his stature as a major figure in psychoanalysis (Rachman, 1994a, 1997a,b, 2003a, 2007a).
4. The suppression of Ferenczi's ideas, methods, and significant clinical functioning was so widespread that his influence was curtailed, even in non-traditional institutes including ones where Ferenczi's former students, analysands, and colleagues had an influence in the training programs (Rachman, 1997a,b, 2003a).

5. The development of a Ferenczi renaissance has taken over fifty years to form, since Ferenczi's death in 1933.

His career and work are being re-examined, encouraging a reconsideration of his contributions as part of mainstream psychoanalysis (Aron & Harris, 1993; Dupont, 1988b; Haynal, 1989; Masson, 1984; Rachman, 1997a, 2003a, 2007a, 2010c; Roazen, 1975).

CHAPTER FOUR

Confusion of tongues theory of childhood sexual trauma

Trauma of childhood sexual seduction

There are real life traumas, such as sexual molestation, which expose a child's developing sense of self to psychologically disturbing events outside the usual range of human experience. Chodoff (1990) has discussed trauma survivor experiences in Nazi concentration camps as an experience capable of producing severe symptomatology without any other previous damaging conditions:

> . . . contrary to some psychoanalytically-derived theorizing, my experience with symptomatic survivors has convince me that childhood predispositions played little or no role in symptom formation which is a product almost entirely of the intensity of the stress itself. This point of view has recently been substantiated by a study of PTSD in Vietnam veterans that found that the diagnosis was tied primarily to the soldier's war experience experience and was not heavily influenced by preservice factors. Practically no one, whatever their previous endowment, who went through the Holocaust for a significant period of time escaped unscathed. Being a human being exposed to camp conditions was the only necessary determinant. (Chodoff, 1990, p. 3)

Childhood seduction ranks with the Holocaust, natural disasters, and world wars as horrendous reality events that profoundly alter a child's life. Psychoanalysis, especially Ferenczi's work, provides a valuable understanding of how trauma can alter human functioning. Ferenczi's ideas about trauma emerged from the study of the incest trauma over a twenty-five year period (Ferenczi, 1980b–d, f–o), reported data that suggested that childhood seduction was linked to developmental arrest, personality alteration, serious psychopathology, and certain types of psychological disorders and intense adult dysfunction.

Freud and Ferenczi's "trauma controversy"

Freud brought personal issues to the controversy about the study of treatment of the trauma disorder. One of the most significant was Freud's own childhood sexual trauma. In presenting the discovery of the seduction hypothesis with his early collaborator, Wilheim Fleiss, Freud clearly reported his early childhood dreams, memories, and recollections of sexual seduction by nursemaid, Resi Wittek (Freud, 1954). The possibility of seduction emerged from associations to a dream. Freud verified the recovered memories of seduction by discussing them with his mother. At this early point, Freud's intellect matched his personal analyses as he was discovering the importance of childhood sexual seduction in human behavior. Yet, this remarkable coordination between intellect and personal functioning was never fully realized for Freud. Quite the opposite, he went on, as has been discussed, to completely separate these data and develop the oedipal theory, which diminished the role of actual sexual seduction (Rachman, 2012g).

Freud, along with Jung (McGuire, 1974) and Rank (Goldwert, 1986), was reported to be a victim of childhood sexual abuse. Ferenczi, like Freud, had repressed his childhood seduction with a "servant girl" (Ferenczi, 1988). Ferenczi's recovery of his childhood memories of seduction occurred in the controversial analysis he conducted with his famous analysand, Elizabeth Servern (Rachman, 2014a,b,d). In this analysis, the focus was on childhood trauma, not the analysis of the oedipal conflict. What is more, the clinical interaction was based upon a two-person psychology (Aron, 1992), which encouraged Severn to ask Ferenczi to analyze his negative countertransference reactions to her. By coming in touch with his subjective experience of Severn as a woman to whom he had antipathy (Ferenczi, 1988), he recovered a childhood memory of sexual molestation by a servant girl. But, he went further than Freud had done and developed insight into negative feelings for Severn in the sexual seduction of childhood by the servant girl.

There was a difference between Freud and Ferenczi in the way they confronted their childhood sexual trauma as adults. Freud maintained the repression barrier which influenced his own theory building (Rachman & Mattick, 2012), his relationship with his daughter (Rachman, 2003b), his relationship with Ferenczi (Rachman, 1997a,b), and the development of a moralistic repressive view of sexuality (Rachman, 1993a, 1997a,b, 2012b, 2014a). Ferenczi, on the other hand was more willing to confront his repressed sexuality.

He courageously confronted these feelings to their genetic origins and uncovered his childhood sexual trauma. This personal trauma was embraced and integrated into his personal and professional life in such a meaningful way that it led to a creative change in functioning. One could conclude that Ferenczi's capacity to recover and integrate his childhood sexual trauma enabled him to develop a new theory and treatment for the incest trauma. His trauma analysis and relaxation therapy incorporated a new empathic attitude and philosophy toward children and adults who were sexually abused. Ferenczi was able to transform his own childhood trauma into a special kind of empathy for trauma survivors. Masson (1984) believed that no analyst in psychoanalytic history had the capacity to empathize with the traumatized child in the adult as did Ferenczi.

Freud clearly paid an emotional price in his valiant effort to establish psychoanalysis (Masson, 1984; Sylwan, 1984). According to his daughter, Anna, when asked why did he supress Ferenczi's "Confusion of tongues" paper, she answered that Freud was concerned that Ferenczi's alternative theory was constructed to overturn the oedipal theory of neurosis (Masson, 1984). Freud was so invested in the oedipal theory, once he formulated it, he could not let anyone, not even his closest discipline, Ferenczi, to suggest an alternative. Although it was true that the confusion of tongues was the first alternative theoretical view (Gedo, 1986), it was not intended to challenge Freudian psychology. Ferenczi wanted to help an evolution towards the treatment of trauma (Rachman, 2007a, 2010a, 2012b, 2014a). It took thirty-five years until Ferenczi's student, Balint, elaborated this integration (Balint, 1968). Ferenczi did not want to break away from Freud. He did want to provide an avenue so that psychoanalysis could have the oedipal theory stand side by side with the confusion of tongues theory (Rachman, 1997a, 2003a, 2007a, 2010a; Rachman & Mattick, 2012). It was ironic that Freud rejected Ferenczi's theory of trauma, when it was based on a mirror reflection of his original work (Freud, 1954), and the Breuer–Freud discoveries which launched psychoanalysis as a clinical science (Freud, 1895d). Freud originally believed in trauma, as he heard from his own patients (Freud, 1954).

Although Freud and Ferenczi were the closest of friends for twenty-five years or so, they were very different personalities. Their preferences in theory and technique were not only a result of contrasting views about trauma, but their views on trauma were also a function of Freud's dissatisfaction with being a clinician and Ferenczi's dedication to being a healer.

Freud was well aware of his shortcomings as a clinician, realizing his disciple Ferenczi was the clinical genius to Freud the theoretical genius (Rachman, 1997a). Freud honestly admitted to Ferenczi, in a letter dated January 20, 1930, that he was not having as much satisfaction in being a clinical psychoanalyst as his student was: ". . . I will gladly admit to you that my patience with neurotics runs out in analysis, and that in life I am inclined to intolerance toward them" (Falzeder et al., 2000, p. 386).

Freud's admission leads to the hypothesis that he was not emboldened to explore the treatment of trauma. Also, he did not want Ferenczi's work with trauma survivors to be used to develop an alternative idea to the oedipal theory. The father could stop the son from finding his own path or marching to his own drum beat. Freud could not positively resolve his oedipal struggle with Ferenczi. Ferenczi was not the rebellious son Freud had imagined. Rather, he was the son searching for his own identity, needing the approval and affirmation of the father (Rachman, 1975a). If Freud could have tolerated Ferenczi's identity struggles, psychoanalysis could have evolved toward the study of trauma as early as the 1920s (Rachman, 2007a).

Freud's opposition to the confusion of tongues paradigm

A question lingers in the history of psychoanalysis as to what motivated Freud to suppress Ferenczi's "Confusion of tongues" paper. Although Freud's voice and attitude was most influential in this regard, Abraham, Eitingon, Jones, and others carried out the actual acts which led to the suppression. Furthermore, it may be inferred that Freud encouraged an emotional atmosphere that allowed for attacks on Ferenczi's personal and professional functioning. There are many plausible hypotheses to help explain this dramatic and negative behavior by Freud. Once begun, Freud's orthodox followers continued the suppression of Ferenczi's work and launched a character assassination. It then became standard, in keeping with analytic tradition, to ignore Ferenczi's contributions and to characterize his work as a function of his deviant methods and disturbed personality.

The "Confusion of tongues" paper was a significant departure from the Freudian theory and technique of psychoanalysis that had become institutionalized by the 1930s (Rachman, 2012g). Ferenczi did attempt to minimize this departure by suggesting that he was verifying Freud's original discoveries, especially the seduction hypothesis. This attempt to minimize the departures was a genuine desire to remain within mainstream psychoanalysis. Freud had a long and difficult history of maintaining interpersonal and professional contact with analytic dissidents (Adler, Jung, and Rank, the most notable). Kohut, in modern times, was well aware of this institutionalized conservatism in psychoanalysis, and went out of his way to describe self psychology as an evolutionary step of Freudian psychology, totally ignoring the roots in Ferenczi's pioneering work (Rachman, 1989a, 1997a,b). This was an attempt to gain the favor of Anna Freud and the analytic establishment. This political move was not entirely successful, as traditionalists were very critical of self psychology, believing that Freud's work had already discovered clinical empathy.

Ferenczi did not wish to break with Freud; that is very clear. He wished to contribute to an evolution of analytic theory and technique (Rachman, 2003a, 2007a). The last meeting between Freud and Ferenczi was an attempt to gain approval for the "Confusion of tongues" paper, even though the meeting was, tragically, unsuccessful and doomed to failure (Fromm, 1959).

Freud could not give his blessings to a paper that he feared espoused an alternative view of psychoanalytic theory and method. The confusion of tongues paradigm emphasizes the real or actual occurrence of sexual seduction, not the imagined seduction of the oedipal drama. Ferenczi's trauma theory of disorder involved seduction or empathic failure in the flawed object relations of family interaction; the identification of middle- and upper-class parents as the perpetrators of sexual molestation; the psychoanalytic situation as having potential for retraumatization, both in its structure and process and in the behavior of the analyst; the development of "relaxation therapy" and the "relaxation principle", which encouraged clinical experimentation and therapeutic responsiveness. As Anna Freud pointed out to Jeffrey Masson, Freud wanted to maintain his oedipal theory of neuroses, the drive theory, and the use of interpretation as the cornerstones of psychoanalysis (Masson, 1984). Ferenczi's ideas and methods cited above threatened this view. Of course, if they did not contain kernels of truth in them, they could have been dismissed, rather than suppressed.

Freud, it could be speculated, was in denial regarding the issue of sexual seduction in his own personal life, so he could not be receptive to having the issue of sexual seduction be an integral part of psychoanalytic theory and method. Freud did not integrate his childhood sexual seduction into his adult personality. What is more, he refused to enter into an analysis with anyone else. First, Freud turned down Jung (Rachman, 1997a). When Ferenczi offered to analyze Freud, later on, Freud also turned him down (Rachman, 1997a). Ferenczi, with his focus on childhood seduction, might have been able to liberate Freud's sexual trauma material. In Freud's self-analysis, he was not able to direct the analysis to his sexual trauma. Freud also turned down a mutual peer analysis with Ferenczi, and so Ferenczi turned to Groddeck for this experience to direct the analysis to his sexual trauma (Dupont, 1982).

Freud, in addition, was in denial regarding the psychological seduction of his daughter, Anna, in analyzing her. He was emotionally blind to the fact that entering into an analytic relationship with Anna compromised her emotional development. She was not able to express and explore her sexual feelings and wishes toward her father, since he was her analyst. She entered into a clinical relationship with sexual feelings toward the parent, which are an integral part of the oedipal conflict theory of psychoanalysis. What is more, Freud was probably outraged when Ferenczi suggested in his clinical hypocrisy concept that an analyst needed to guard against seduction in the psychoanalytic situation, recreating the original trauma (Ferenczi, 1980n). Freud felt Ferenczi was in the process of breaking away from him with his confusion of tongues formulation. He exercised his power, control, and status over him to keep Ferenczi in his place and prevent him from defecting. It was imperative that the favorite son be prevented from defecting. Freud wanted to prevent his last close friendship from disintegrating as well as to save face in the psychoanalytical community that his most important relationship since Fleiss was not going to produce another defection (Rachman, 1988b). It was important to assert his authority and convince Ferenczi that his relaxation therapy and trauma analysis was a serious mistake. It is important to note that Freud and his co-conspirators, Jones, Eitingon, Abraham, and Riviere created a confusion of tongues experience for psychoanalysis. In the correspondence between them it is clear that they felt Ferenczi's "Confusion of tongues" paper was "harmless, stupid, confused, devious" (Molnar, 1992, p. 131.) But, as the epitome of a confusion of tongues experience, they made it seem as if they were preventing Ferenczi from giving his paper in order to save his reputation (Rachman, 1997a,b).

We must understand that Freud was actively opposed to the confusion of tongues formulation and made every attempt to prevent it from being introduced into the psychoanalytic dialogue and subsequently preventing its dissemination throughout the analytic community (Masson, 1984; Roazen, 1975). Freud did so with such determination and fervor that he sacrificed the positive relationship that had been built up for over twenty-five years with Ferenczi.

The irony is that if Ferenczi's ideas were regressive, harmless, and stupid, as Freud said they were (Jones, 1957), why was it necessary to launch a political assassination of Ferenczi in order to silence him (Masson, 1984; Roazen, 1975)? Freud, who apparently encouraged Jones and his orthodox followers to launch this campaign, offered his own explanation. Ferenczi's ideas were so flawed, regressive, and deviant that they were the product of an emotional deterioration in his functioning. Jones went so far as to label Ferenczi's confusion of tongues theory and his relaxation therapy as products of madness (Jones, 1957; Rachman, 1997a,b,). Ferenczi's successor to the Budapest

School, Michael Balint, who first challenged Jones' assertion of Ferenczi's madness (Balint, 1958), as well as subsequent challenges (Bonomi, 1999; Dupont, 1988a; Rachman, 1997a,b), proved Jones' assertion false. It was not until Masson (1984) interviewed Anna Freud in the 1980s, in his capacity as Secretary of the Freud Archives of the Library of Congress, that we were able to realize the real reason why Freud so severely suppressed Ferenczi. Anna Freud told Jeffrey Masson that her father was so wedded to his oedipal theory that he did not want any alteration in his theory or technique of psychoanalysis. Freud considered his oedipal theory to be the cornerstone of psychoanalysis (Malcolm, 1984; Masson, 1984). As Balint, Ferenczi's student, demonstrated, some thirty odd years later, the oedipal and confusion of tongues theories, as well as a theory of creativity, can be integrated into a coherent psychoanalytic perspective (Balint, 1968).

Ferenczi's greatest contribution to psychoanalysis may be his confusion of tongues theory and it can stand with Freud's oedipal theory as a major intellectual formulation for the understanding of human behavior. Ferenczi's formulations can be seen as a more parsimonious explanation of the phenomena of sexual trauma than the oedipal theory is of a universal explanation of neurosis. The confusion of tongues not only helped usher in a relational perspective for psychoanalysis (Rachman, 2003a, 2007a, 2009b, 2012a), but has proved to be a relevant theory for the contemporary analysis of the incest trauma (Rachman, 2000). The confusion of tongues paradigm provides a theoretical understanding of trauma and emotional disorder, such as in historical and contemporary relationships where a disparity of language, communication, and disturbed relationships produce trauma (Rachman, 1989a, 1992c, 1994a,b, 1995a,b,c, 1996b, 1997a,b, 2000, 2003a, 2010a, 2011b, Rachman & Mattick, 2012).

Confusion of tongues between Freud and Ferenczi: "The trauma controversy"

As outlined in Chapter Two, the Freud–Ferenczi relationship was instrumental for the evolution of psychoanalysis. We must remember that Freud was Ferenczi's analyst, teacher, mentor, and Ferenczi was Freud's favorite pupil, his "dear son", and potential husband to his daughter Mathilde, as well as collaborator and closest friend for over twenty-five years. In fact, their professional and personal lives were so intertwined for that twenty-five-year period that it was not possible to discern the intellectual, emotional, and interpersonal space between them.

With this creative symbiosis as a background, it is necessary to explain what occurred to drive a wedge into the Freud–Ferenczi relationship. The near fatal break in their relationship has been discussed by many authors (Balint, 1968; Dupont, 1988a; Fromm, 1959; Grosskurth, 1991; Haynal, 1989; Masson, 1984; Thompson, 1964c; Rachman, 1997a,b; Roazen, 1975). The issues put forward for the Freud–Ferenczi crisis include their differences in technique (Roazen, 1975), ability and willingness to clinically work in the zone of regression (Balint, 1968), differences in their personalities (Fromm, 1959), Ferenczi's inability to break away from Freud and find his own school of analysis (Thompson, 1964a), differences in how they conceptualize the basic analytic issues (Masson, 1984), Freud's lack of appreciation for the meaningful differences between them (Dupont, 1988a), and differences about conceptualizing and treating their incest trauma (Rachman, 1997a,b, 2000, 2012a, 2014a).

All these explanations have merit. In order to bring the present discussion into focus, it is necessary to examine Freud's "irrational" and negative reaction to Ferenczi's work on trauma. As the French psychoanalyst Barbo Sylwan has called it, the "untoward event" was the "trauma wars", the differences between Freud and Ferenczi's interest in the study and treatment of trauma (Sylwan, 1984, p. 108). The issue can be considered to be the most significant difference that separated Freud and Ferenczi. It is also the most parsimonious construct for the difficulties they had on a professional level. On a personal level, Freud had negative feelings about Ferenczi not being willing to be President of the IPA. Freud took it as a rejection (Freud, 1933c), and believed it signaled Ferenczi's desire to leave the inner circle and find his own school of psychoanalysis as Adler, Jung, and Rank had done (Gay, 1988). His authoritarian manner (Fromm, 1959) did not allow Freud to synthesize Ferenczi's desire to pursue a different path (Fromm, 1959). The resignation from standing for President of the IPA was actually Ferenczi's willingness not to cause Freud any embarrassment (Rachman, 1997a).

An important letter from Ferenczi to Freud dated December 25, 1929 described the theoretical differences that were separating these two collaborators and best friends:

1. In all cases in which I penetrated deeply enough I found the traumatic hysterical basis for the illness.
2. Where I and the patient succeeded in this, the therapeutic effect was much more significant. In many cases I had to call in already "cured" patients for follow up treatment.
3. . . . was that psychoanalysis engages too much one-sidedly in obsessional neurosis and character charter analysis, i.e. ego psychology, neglecting the organic hysterical basis for the analysis, the cause is in the over estimation of fantasy and the underestimation of traumatic reality in pathogenesis.
4. The newly acquired (although they do essentially sooner hark back to old things) experiences naturally also have an effect on details of technique. Certain all too harsh measures must be relaxed, without completely losing sight of the didactic secondary intention. (Falzeder et al., 2000, p. 376)

One could view this letter to Freud as Ferenczi's analytic emancipation proclamation from Freud. Yet, Ferenczi gently spells out the new direction in which he is headed, that is to say, the study and treatment of trauma. He is indebted to Freud for the foundation he had provided, trying to build upon his teacher's contributions rather than tearing them down. Ferenczi is aware he is walking the tightrope between rebellion and following a new path.

> . . . a certain inhibition on my part has constantly existed; . . . certainly contributed much to the fact that I was unable to give wholly free expression not only to my personal feelings, but also to certain scientific views. (Falzeder et al., 2000, p. 387).

Ferenczi spent the next four years of his life courageously pursuing the study of trauma while he struggled with Freud, the orthodox psychoanalytic community, difficulties with his own analysand, Elizabeth Severn, and the physical and emotional struggle with pernicious anemia. As Sylwan (1984) pointed out, Ferenczi was caught in an emotional turmoil, trying to be true to his own work and ideas while trying to please Freud and fend off the criticisms of the analytic community. The emotional pressure Freud exerted on Ferenczi was great, primarily through his insistence on Ferenczi accepting the presidency of IPA. Was Freud's plan to have Ferenczi become the president of the IPA so that he could have him under his control and, consequently, reign in his so-called regressive study of trauma (Sabourin, 1985; Sylwan, 1984)? This was an example of Freud's confusion of tongues (Rachman & Mattick, 2012). Freud believed he was trying to help Ferenczi come back into his inner circle by encouraging him to return to his former active role in the organization that Ferenczi first proposed to Freud. But, the hidden message was his disdain for Ferenczi's clinical experiments with incest trauma survivors (Rachman, 1997a,b,). Freud's criticism (mixed with affection) was clearly stated:

> . . . you are distancing yourself from me more and more . . . in recent times I also preferred no one else to you. It is with regret you are trying to press forward in all kinds of directions which to me seem to lead to no desirable end . . . am prepared to wait until you yourself take steps to turn around. With you it could be a new, third puberty, after the completion of which you will probably have reached maturity . . . (Falzeder et al., 2000, p. 418)

In actuality, Ferenczi was actually becoming more mature in personal and professional functioning, while maintaining an emotional and interpersonal separation from Freud. He pursued his own direction of thought and clinical functioning:

> . . . even these excursions into uncertainty also always were of significant use to me. Do you consider it out of the question that, after the maturity that is expected by you, i.e., after the turnaround, I will be able to produce something that is practically or even theoretically useful? (Falzeder et al., 2000, p. 419)

Eight months before he was to meet with Freud in Vienna to give him a preview of his latest formulations about trauma in his "Confusion of tongues" paper (Rachman, 1997b), Ferenczi communicated to Freud his developing belief in his own thinking;

> . . . I will also make an effort to exercise the strictest objectivity possible especially after objections from such a significant quarter. The time is still too short to be able to make any final statements about this work of revision. But honesty obliges me to say that, up to now, I don't feel called upon to change anything essential. On no account does that mean defiant wanting to hold fast to what is my own, I will endeavor to keep such purely personal motives (being insulted, infantile

> rebellion, etc.) in check. It is still possible that some of what I am now experiencing in the analysis also has objective validity. (Falzeder et al., 2000, p. 421)

Freud's protection of his oedipal theory

Jeffrey Mousiaeff Masson's controversial book, *The Assault on Truth: Freud's Suppression of the Seduction Theory* (Masson, 1984), stirred up an old argument about Freud's reasons for abandoning his original theory about the origin of neurosis embedded in childhood sexual seduction. Masson's assertion was that Freud abandoned the seduction theory because he had a personal failure in courage. Freud, he argued, did not pursue his seduction theory because of the vehement criticism of his colleagues at the Viennese Medical Society. The Society did not accept sexual activity in child–parent interaction. Contemporary analysts, whether Freudian or not, felt Masson insulted Freud and questioned his moral character by suggesting he had a failure of courage in abandoning his seduction hypothesis. Masson's assertion about Freud's character is questionable, since Masson admitted to anger against psychoanalysis because of his own personal Freudian analysis (Masson, 1988, 1990).

However, Freud's motives are not beyond reproach, as some traditional analysts might believe. He did have character faults, exemplified in his treatment of Ferenczi (Rachman, 1997a,b,) and the analysis of his daughter, Anna (Rachman, 2003b). Freud showed a mean-spiritedness in his treatment of Ferenczi (Rachman, 1997b). Freud's assertion that his analysis of Anna was justified and turned out well is a sign of his emotional blindness (Rachman, 2003a). Freud may have continued to believe in the actual occurrence of childhood seduction, but it is clear that his oedipal theory became the construct for neurosis. As mentioned, Ferenczi's confusion of tongues theory was perceived by Freud as a threat to the oedipal theory. First, that Freud felt the confusion of tongues concept had merit, and second, it was an actual threat to his cherished oedipal theory. Freud was not intellectually or emotionally open to entertaining an alternative view of human behavior other than his own. At the point at which Freud and the orthodox analytic community would not entertain any evolutionary ideas about psychoanalytic theory, it ceased to be a discipline informed by scientific ideas. It then became a fixed set of concepts and practices. Psychoanalysis, in this form, functioned to protect its already established standard ideas and practices. Ferenczi saw his mission as introducing the confusion of tongues paradigm to help psychoanalysis evolve towards the treatment of trauma (Rachman, 2003a, 2007a, 2009b). In 1930, two years before the presentation of the "Confusion of tongues" paper, Freud acknowledged Ferenczi was moving in his own direction, developing an alternate perspective. At that time, Freud seemed tolerant of the deviation, even supportive. Apparently, two analysands, Blumenthal and Rickman, who were in analysis with Freud, decided to continue with Ferenczi. Freud was critical of Ferenczi for not telling him he was seeing two of his former analysands. But, he also added in a letter to Ferenczi of January 11, 1930:

> Very possible that you are doing analysis better with both, or with all, your patients than I am, but I also don't have anything against that, I am saturated with analysis as therapy, fed up! [written in English] and who, then, shouldn't do it better than you? So, you see, if you can illuminate something, there is no lack of problems. (Falzeder et al., 2000, pp. 380–381)

Freud also added some other positive comments about Ferenczi's trauma analysis in a letter to Ferenczi dated September 16, 1930:

> The new views about the traumatic fragmentation of mental life that you indicated seem to me to be very ingenious and have something of the great characteristic of theory of Geniality. I only think that one can hardly speak of trauma in the extraordinary synthetic activity of the ego without treating the reactive scar formation along with it. The latter, of course, also produces what we see, we must make the trauma accessible. (Falzeder et al., 2000, p. 399)

Freud did not have the kind of optimism and flexibility in functioning to successfully deal with trauma cases. As a clinician, he was disillusioned.

Freud also saw the clinical encounter differently than Ferenczi. Freud prided himself on being the fatherly therapist who saw his patients entangled in their oedipal conflicts. Ferenczi was proposing a new foundation for the analytic relationship. This involved a tender mother transference. This form of an analytic encounter involved therapeutic regression in the object relationship between analyst and analysand. Ferenczi was free to be his anima and animus (in Jungian terms). He could express both the male and female side of his personality (Cremerius, 1983). Ferenczi and Winnicott shared the ability to be motherly in the analytic relationship and, consequently, were subjected to rumors that they had homosexual tendencies (Roazen, 1989).

Ferenczi's revision of Freud's oedipal theory of infantile sexuality: confusion of tongues theory of trauma

Ferenczi made a dramatic statement about the oedipal theory that was only known to a few close colleagues since it was written in 1932, when his *Clinical Diary* was then unknown and unpublished:

> Experience regarding the traumatic effect of genital attacks by adults on small children oblige me to modify the analytic view of infantile sexuality that has prevailed up to now. The fact that infantile sexuality exists obviously remains undisputed, yet much of what appears as passionate in infantile sexuality may be a secondary consequence of the passionate behavior of adults, forcibly imposed on children against their will and, so to speak, artificially implanted in them. Even over passionate manifestations of nongenital tenderness, such as passionate kissing, ardent embraces, affect the child in fact unpleasurably. Children want no more than to be treated in a friendly, tender, and gentle way. Their own movements and physical expressions are tender, if it is otherwise, then something has already gone wrong. One has to ask oneself how much of what is involved in the undying love of the child for its mother, and how much of the boy's murderous desire against the rival father, would develop in a purely spontaneous way, without the premature implantation of passionate adult eroticism and genitality: that is, how much of the Oedipus complex is really inherited and how much is passed on by tradition from one generation to the other. (Ferenczi, 1988, p. 79, April 5, 1932 entry)

After Ferenczi's death on May 22, 1933, a series of notes were found among his papers. These notes were published in English in 1949 (Balint, 1949; Ferenczi, 1980o). Ferenczi moved the level of discourse from solely intrapsychic to interpersonal, for example, influences in the child's environment that cause him/her trauma. In actuality, he revised Freud's concept of the death instinct by introducing the idea: "... of pressure of their environment; unfavorable change in the environment the mechanism falls to pieces and disintegrates . . . (probably along the lines of antecedent historic development)" (Ferenczi, 1949, p. 220). He conceptualized a force that allowed the individual to prevent disintegration and adapt to trauma: "[There is an] instinct of self-preservation, life instinct, [which] inhibits the disintegration and derives to a new consolidation, as soon as this has been made possible by the plasticity developed in the cause of fragmentation." The instinct of self-preservation goes beyond our capacity for conscious intelligence: ". . . it seems to have some knowledge of events distant in space and to know exactly at what point to stop the self destruction and to start the reconstruction . . ." (Ferenczi, 1980o, p. 220).

Ferenczi also described, perhaps for the first time, the process of dissociation in sexual seduction, for example, the out-of-body experience as a mechanism to prevent total self-disintegration. He called it, "to get beside oneself":

> The ego leaves the body, partly or wholly, usually through the head, and observes from outside, usually from above, the subsequent fate of the body, especially its suffering. (Image somewhat like this: bursting out through the head and observing the dead, impotently frustrated body, from the ceiling of the room . . .). (Ferenczi, 1980o, p. 222)

This description is exactly what incest survivors have reported in the analysis of their incest trauma (Rachman, 2000, 2003a, 2012b).

Judith Dupont, the editor of Ferenczi's *Clinical Diary*, noted the emerging ideas about trauma in his earlier work:

> During the year that preceded the writing of the *Diary*, Ferenczi begins noting down his ideas regarding trauma. He continues to be [preoccupied with the subject throughout the *Diary*, but at the same time he composes a set of somewhat more structured notes on 19 September 1932 (during his distressing journey after the Congress of Wiesbaden) and another, after the interruption of the *Diary*, on 26 December, a day on which he makes some other brief notations. These, it seems, are the last pages written by Ferenczi. (Dupont, 1988a, p. xviii)

Ferenczi mentioned the concept of "psycho-trauma" in a note on December 26, 1932. He noted it as a "Great unpleasure, which because of its sudden appearance cannot be dealt with" (Ferenczi, 1980o, p. 276). The concept of trauma analysis is also mentioned for the first time. Ferenczi noted the importance of a change in the emotional atmosphere in the analytic situation to what he had earlier called a relaxation attitude (Ferenczi, 1980o). In "Some thoughts on trauma," he added,

> Deep (traumatogenic) analysis is not possible if no more favorable conditions (in contrast to the situation at the original trauma) can be offered:
>
> (b) By life and by the external world
> (b) Mainly by the analyst. (Ferenczi, 1980o, p. 278)

Ferenczi began a discussion of how the trauma survivor can cope with trauma. These methods of coping were derived from his work and discussiona with Severn (1934) (Rachman, 2014a). He theorized three ways of coping, "alloplastic and autoplastic reactions; as well as substitute reactions." Alloplastic reaction was the individual's capacity to remove the "cause" of the disturbance by developing "ideas" which are "antidotes against unpleasure," or "painful influences"; "substitute reactions" are "illusory because they are a defense and removal of innocent objects and persons"; "the fantastic nature of the substitute actions remain CS [conscious] or can early be brought to consciousness" (Ferenczi, 1980o, pp. 276–277).

Another important issue in trauma analysis was the psychoanalytic view that the childhood seduction cannot be *remembered* as an adult:

> because it has *never* been CS [conscious]. It can only be *re-experienced* and *recognized* as the past. Child cannot be analyzed; analysis with a child takes place at the still UCS. [unconscious] stage no *proper experiences* mostly only *suggestions* that make up mental life. The *child* lives in the present. The unpleasurable memories remain reverberating *somewhere* in the body (and emotions). (Ferenczi, 1980o, pp. 278–279)

These emerging theoretical ideas about trauma and trauma analysis were part of Ferenczi's developing concepts that eventually became the confusion of tongues paradigm that, in part, emerged from the analysis with Elizabeth Severn (see Chapter Five). It is interesting to note that Ferenczi's analysand, Melanie Klein, who was so vigorous and intense in her clinical interaction with children, apparently did not accept Ferenczi's empathic approach. From the above extract, one could not or should not pursue deep analysis with a child. Anna Freud, following in her father's footsteps, also believed a child can be analyzed. Ferenczi's idea that the childhood trauma remains largely unconscious and the child needs to live in the present suggested that one should not disrupt this natural developmental process. The idea that the trauma is split off into somatic memory is also an important clinical precept for trauma analysis.

Ferenczi's *Clinical Diary*, written in 1932, is a very rich source of his emerging ideas about trauma, and his various notations became the confusion of tongues paradigm. The editor of Ferenczi's *Clinical Diary*, Judith Dupont, pointed out the significance of the *Diary* for Ferenczi's theoretical legacy:

> "The *Diary* contains, recorded day by day, histories of the various clinical cases of which Ferenczi based his reflections. From these cases he drew a whole series of theoretical conclusions, as they appeared to him, a number of which he elaborated in the Confusion of Tongues and in his Notes and Fragments. Some others are merely sketched out, but today they appear to us as the founding themes of certain important currents in modern psychiatry . . . Ferenczi draws parallels among the child traumatized by the hypocrisy of adults, the mentally ill person traumatized by the hypocrisy of society, and the patients, where trauma is revived and exacerbated by the professional hypocrisy and technical rigidity of the analyst. (Dupont, 1988a, p. xviii)

There are several examples in the *Clinical Diary* which hint at the fuller development of Ferenczi's confusion of tongues theory of trauma. In a July 6 1932 *Clinical Diary* entry, the heading of the entry presents two significant questions:

> Are perversions really infantilisms, and to what extent?
>
> Are sadism and anal eroticism not already hysterical reactions to traumata? (Ferenczi, 1988, p. 155)

Ferenczi was questioning the Freudian concept of the oedipal theory of neurosis. In essence, Ferenczi was implying the following ideas:

1. The issue in the concept of trauma is the *adult's passions*, not the child's oedipal desires for their parents.
2. Perversions might be the result of childhood trauma.

3. Severe psychopathology, such as sadism and anal eroticism, might be a result of childhood seduction trauma, rather than oral and anal fixations.

Ferenczi suggested an alternative to Freud's focus on the father in the oedipal theory to a focus on the mother in the "primal trauma":

> . . . the question arises whether the primal trauma is not always to be sought in the primal relationship with the mother, and whether the traumata of a somewhat later epoch, already complicated by the appearance of the father, could have had such an effect without the existence of such a pre-primal-trauma mother–child scar. (Ferenczi, 1988, p. 83, 10 April 1932 entry)

In the latter part of this same entry, Ferenczi discussed the emotional trauma in the mother–child relationship, which was the precursor for Balint's expansion of the confusion of tongues paradigm. A further discussion of a revision of the oedipal theory was noted by Ferenczi, in which he reinforced an emergency non-biological, relational explanation for the oedipal complex. Citing the case of G, where the child sought comfort with the father because of the mother's emotional unavailability and the father sexualized the relationship, Ferenczi said the following:

> This could be an example of the cases—certainly not rare—in which fixation on parents, that is, incestuous fixation, does not appear as a natural product of development but rather is implanted in the psyche from the outside, that is to say, is a product of the superego. It should be noted that not only sexual stimuli but also other kinds that neither are overpowering nor have to be overcome that (hate, fear, etc.) can have a munetic effect in the same way as imposed love. (Ferenczi, 1988, p. 175, 26 July 1932 entry)

In a series of entries in the *Clinical Diary* months before the presentation of the "Confusion of tongues" paper, Ferenczi discussed "Normal and pathological relations in the family," "What is traumatic: an attack or its consequences" (27 July, 1932, p. 178). Early August of 1932, Ferenczi presented a draft of his September 4, 1932 Wiesbaden paper where he discussed the dissociated, split-off part of the personality of an incest trauma survivor:

> ... why concern ourselves so much with the inaccessible piece of the personality, dead or encapsulated in some way ... That split off part seems to represent ... a large, indeed perhaps the most significant, part of my soul ... you could not escape the effects of the splitting ... I should never stop striving to make that portion of my personality, however painful consciously my own ... The fact of being split may make conscious recollection impossible, but it cannot prevent the affect that is attached to it forcing its way through in moods, emotional outbursts, susceptibilities, often in generalized depression or in compensatory, unmotivated high spiritedness, but even more in various physical sensations and various functional disturbances. But how are you going to make me suffer the pain that I have skillfully managed to avoid in the trauma without a renewed split, that is, without any repetition of the mental disorder, thereby restoring the unity of my personality, that is, render conscious what has never been conscious before? ... I am [convinced] of the reversibility of all psychic processes that is, all not purely hereditary ... (Ferenczi, 1988, p. 181, 30 July 1932 entry)

Again in August 1932, Ferenczi mentioned a concept that was to become a significant part of the confusion of tongues paradigm:

> The early seduced child adapts itself to its difficult task with the aid of complete identification with the aggressor, the analysis of Case F. demonstrates that such identificatory love leaves the ego proper unsatisfied. In analysis, therefore, the patient must be taken back to the blissful time before the trauma and to the corresponding period of sexual development ... One could ask whether a sense of guilt after having suffered an untimely attack (or in boys being forced to superperformances) is not bound up with guilt feelings because of having guessed and shared the aggressor's feelings of guilt. (Ferenczi, 1988, p. 190, 7 August 1932 entry)

Confusion of tongues paradigm

It is one of the great ironies in contemporary psychoanalysis that Freud, who was the intellectual genius and sexual revolutionary who helped the world realize the importance of childhood sexuality, would now be identified with an orthodox position that minimized the importance of actual childhood experiences as a causative factor in psychological disorder. The irony is especially difficult to comprehend because Freud opened our eyes and ears to the possibility of childhood sexual experiences with parents (Freud, 1954). What is more, he introduced the causal link between childhood sexual experiences and the development of adult psychopathology (Rachman, 2012g).

From 1924 to 1933, Ferenczi published a series of monographs and papers which outlined his observations about sexual seduction, trauma, and child abuse (Ferenczi, 1980d; Ferenczi & Rank, 1925). Ferenczi's ideas about trauma, childhood seduction, and etiology of psychological disorders were most fully delineated in his last clinical paper, the "Confusion of tongues" (Ferenczi, 1980n). He believed the more severe psychological disorders arose from actual, not fantasized, sexual experiences in childhood.

Ferenczi's formulation in the "Confusion of tongues" provided a series of assumptions regarding sexual trauma and its treatment by psychoanalysis that broke new ground:

1. The object relationship between parent and child was conceived as the focus of emotional difficulty and the development of psychopathology.
2. Sexual trauma, that is the seduction of child by a parent (or parental surrogate), was the etiology of certain disorders, for example, severe neurosis, narcissistic, character disorder, borderline, or psychotic conditions.
3. Childhood sexual molestation leads to developmental arrest, serious personality alterations that can occur throughout the life cycle.
4. The psychoanalytic situation can produce retraumatization by the psychoanalyst if empathy is not the central way of responding to the trauma survivor. It is also necessary to be clinically flexible and responsive.
5. Clinical hypocrisy can exist in the psychoanalytic encounter when the analyst does not acknowledge his/her emotional reactions. In the two-person experience, both analyst and analysand are responsible for analyzing any interpersonal disturbance as well as contributing to its cure.
6. Emotional honesty through countertransference analysis and self-disclosure is curative of the confusion of tongues experience. The analyst as the therapeutic parent presents a clear, direct,

empathically conceived response that provides emotional clarity, avoiding confusion and double-bind communication.

It was clear that the presentation of the ideas of the "Confusion of tongues" paper caused a trauma in the analytic community. Michael Balint, Ferenczi's intellectual and clinical heir, chronicled the negative atmosphere that existed in the analytic community (Balint, 1968). As has been discussed, examination of the correspondence relevant to the attempted suppression of the "Confusion of tongues" paper clearly shows that Freud, Jones, and others conspired to ban these ideas and methods from mainstream psychoanalysis (Covello, 1984; Dupont, 1988b; Fromm, 1959, p. 65, fn. 3; Masson, 1984, p. 152; Rachman, 1997a,b; Sylwan, 1984, pp. 108–109). An eyewitness to the trauma paper was the late Esther Menaker, one of the last psychoanalysts who trained at the Vienna Institute during Freud's time. She recounted the following story to Arnold Rachman regarding Ferenczi and the analytic community's reaction to him almost one year after the presentation at Wiesbaden:

> One day while I was in Helena Deutsch's class, we got word that Ferenczi died [Ferenczi died on May 22, 1933 of pernicious anemia]. The announcement of his passing away was made in class. A dramatic silence enveloped the class. It was clear to every student there, that we were not to talk about Ferenczi or his work. The emotional and interpersonal ban on Ferenczi was very effective. No one questioned the idea that Ferenczi was a persona non grata. (Menaker, 1986)

There were four fundamental reactions to the "Confusion of tongues" paper that developed in this post pioneering period of psychoanalysis:

1. A continuation of the idea that the ideas and methods it contained were a result of Ferenczi's psychopathology (Grünberger, 1980; Jones, 1957).
2. The ignoring of the "Confusion of tongues" paper and Ferenczi's trauma analysis period of research and practice, 1929–1933, as being unimportant (Rachman, 1997a)
3. A concern for retraumatizing the analytical community by focusing directly on the "Confusion of tongues" paper (Balint, 1949, 1968).

5. The acknowledgment of the "Confusion of tongues" paper as a significant work in the history of psychoanalysis (Fromm, 1959; Masson, 1984; Rachman, 1997a; Roazen, 1975).

Michael Balint, should be credited with the enormous task of keeping Ferenczi's ideas and methods alive so that there would be a record of his mentor's contributions for future psychoanalysts to study (Balint, 1949, 1965d, 1968). It was Eric Fromm who celebrated Ferenczi's "Confusion of tongues" paper at a time when almost everyone else ignored it. Fromm's courage in praising Ferenczi when the analytic community either ignored or condemned him is clear from the following extract:

> Freud's intolerance toward Ferenczi's new ideas was also expressed in the fact that he wanted him to promise not to publish the paper he was to give at the congress in Wiesbaden. As anybody who reads it can convince himself it is a paper of extraordinary profundity and brilliance, one of the most valuable papers in the whole psychoanalytic literature, it contains, however, certain important though subtle deviations from Freud's thought. (Fromm, 1959, p. 65, fn. 3)

The "Confusion of tongues" paper and presentation was a landmark in the relationship between Freud and Ferenczi. It can be considered Ferenczi's emancipation from his mentor and Ferenczi's growth as an independent thinker and theory builder. By April of 1932, the Freud–Ferenczi relationship was clearly strained. Ferenczi had isolated himself in Budapest, knowing Freud and the orthodox analytic community disapproved of his focus on trauma (Rachman, 1997a, 2003a). Ferenczi was not paranoid in his concerns that Freud and the analytic community would condemn his "Confusion of tongues" presentation and attempt to suppress its publication (Rachman, 1997b). They would never formally end their relationship, but for the last years of his life, Ferenczi suffered an emotional trauma from Freud's rejection. Neither Ferenczi nor Freud would recover from this trauma. Ferenczi's death on May 22, 1933 put an end to both their suffering. Unfortunately, the rejection of Ferenczi and his work would continue on through generations of analysts in such a dramatic way that for several generations his work would all but disappear from psychoanalytic institutes.

Although Ferenczi was an outgoing, warm, and responsive individual, he did not promote himself. He let his work speak for itself. It was his analysands and a select group of Hungarian and American colleagues who spread the meaningful work he was accomplishing with trauma cases. His Hungarian analysands, such as Michael Balint, Geza Roheim, Sándor Lorand, and Sándor Rado and his American analysts, such as Izette de Forest, Clara Thompson, and Elizabeth Severn, spread his ideas through Europe and the United States. Colleagues, such as Andras Anygal, Eric Fromm, Harry Stack Sullivan, and Otto Rank, who appreciated Ferenczi's clinical work with difficult cases recommended analysands to him. Harry Stack Sullivan recommended Clara Thompson, when she became dissatisfied with her first analyst. Otto Rank recommended Elizabeth Severn, who had turned to him when her analyses did not cure her misery. Andra Anygal wrote the introduction to Izette de Forest's book on Ferenczi's relaxation therapy (de Forest, 1954). Fromm poignantly wrote about Ferenczi's difficulties with Freud's attempt to dominate and control him (Fromm, 1959). Ferenczi identified himself as a healer, not as a theoretician, which was an accurate designation. But, it was also his work with trauma that pushed him into the first alternative theory to the oedipal theory of neurosis, his confusion of tongues (Gedo, 1986).

Incest trauma presentation at the Twelfth International Psychoanalytic Congress

On Sunday morning, September 4, 1932, at about 9 a.m., a stocky, balding man with a sweet face walked up to the podium in the Assembly Hall at the Hotel Rose in Wiesbaden, in southern Germany. In the gathering storm of Nazi Germany, traveling to Germany by Jews was becoming problematic. Europe was on the verge of totalitarianism. Freud could not attend the Twelfth International Psychoanalytic Congress because of illness; his mouth cancer was progressing and taking its toll on his mind and body (Rachman, 1997a). Ferenczi was also ill in body and spirit. Physically, he was suffering from the impending collapse of his body due to pernicious anemia. What is more, Ferenczi's presentation was also overshadowed by the growing personal and professional conflict between himself and Freud (Rachman, 1997b).

His presentation held the coveted place of opening the Congress and was his last appearance before an analytic congress. Ferenczi delivered what was thereafter considered his infamous Congress speech (Masson, 1984, Rachman, 1997a). Today, it should be considered his *tour de force*, originally titled, "The passions of adults and their influence on the sexual and character development of children" (Ferenczi, 1933). This original title later became the "Confusion of tongues" paper, best described as Ferenczi's theoretical and clinical contribution to the study and treatment of the incest trauma. He was focusing on *the adult's passion or sexuality, not the child's* as causing the incest trauma. This actual (not symbolic) event was also considered to have significant effect on the development of personality and psychological disorders, both in childhood and later life.

Ferenczi was the first analyst to describe and outline the psychodynamics of this kind of traumatic experience. In empathic terms, never used before, he outlined the child's inner struggle as well as interpersonal encounters with family and adult authority to maintain a sense of self-cohesion in the face of sexual seduction.

Parental sexual seduction

Children have developmental needs for nurturance, love, affection, and tenderness from parental caretakers (Balint, 1968, Kohut, 1984, Winnicott, 1965b). This is the fundamental empathic and affectionate experience to which all children are emotionally entitled. It is essential for emotional growth. Parental sexual abuse is mostly perpetrated by fathers (Herman, 1981, 1992), but Ferenczi did note maternal, siblings, relatives, family friends and strangers as perpetrators (Ferenczi, 1980n). A parent or parental surrogate misinterprets the child's natural need for affection, physical contact, and love as lust, which is the parent's own projection on to the sexually innocent child. Sexual innocence does not mean the child does not have sexual feelings. There does exist a developmentally sequenced, phase-appropriate element of sexuality. Sensuality is embedded within the relational context of the parent–child interaction. But, such sensuality must be kept at the level of fantasy. When the parent or other abusing adult, under the pressure of his/her own inappropriate needs, distorts the total motivation of the child, reducing it to a predominately sexual one, the stage is set for pathological, incestuous, acting out with the child.

The parent confuses the natural, phase-appropriate longings for tenderness, sensuality, affection, and psychosocial play by the child with sexuality, thereby reducing the complexity of normal attachment strivings to merely one of its components. In object relation terms, the parent initiates a part-object relationship, and uses the child as a discharge object rather than as a whole object in which the capacity for concern predominates.

The particular example that Ferenczi used was the remarkable discrepancy between sexuality and affection; for example, the disturbing experience when a child yearns for tenderness and receives sex. Then the child needs to cope with an unreality (Modell, 1990). The child is confused by the adult's responding to his/her need for affection with sex. In addition, molesting the child is really overpowering and aggressing against the child. It is sex and aggression that the adult is creating in the interpersonal contact with the child, not tenderness. The sexual seduction can vary from seductive verbal interaction to touching, or go as far as actual sexual intercourse. The child yearning for tenderness and love succumbs to the abuser, entering into an unholy alliance, which can be characterized as: "I will give you the sex you want because I need the affection or love you say you will give me."

If the adult seducer does not promise love, he/she then exercises power and control over the child through physical threats. As mentioned, the sexual contact between parent and child disrupts the developmental intrapsychic fantasy process. The seduction intrudes upon the child's developmental needs to have a "fantasy romance" with a parent. *The fantasy experience is not intended to be a real experience.* When it becomes a real experience, it encourages the idea of the child as a sexual object for the need fulfillment of the narcissistic parent. Fundamentally, at the deepest level of the child's subjective experience, the seduction is "a rape of the body and soul" (Shengold, 1989). "Psychological scars" persist long after the abuse has terminated. The adult seducer is also in a state of confusion, not able to distinguish his/her narcissistic and aggressive needs for passion from the tenderness for which the child really longs.

A profound sense of confusion

A series of psychological mechanisms develop that enable the child to cope with the incest trauma. One of the most fundamental mechanisms is an overwhelming sense of emotional and intellectual confusion. The seduced child is confused (traumatized) as a result of the adult's betrayal, intrusiveness, manipulation, aggression, and unempathic violation of their relationship. The perpetrator can also be confused, since he/she uses denial and dissociation to distance themselves from the abusive act. The child has developmentally become accustomed to expect tenderness and affection in the form of emotional and physical nurturance of a non-sexual nature. The child wants, and should receive, tenderness, not sexual passion. A child needs the physical affectionate embrace of a parent. There is a fundamental need to distinguish between touching as tenderness and touching as erotic. Most parents intuitively know this difference. It is the narcissistic and emotionally disturbed parent who can not distinguish between the two. Therefore, the child who has been sexually seduced confuses passion for tenderness. A child, because of his/her need for parental affection, responsiveness, and caring, is emotionally programmed to yield to an adult, to give an adult what he/she wants.

Alteration in the child's sense of reality

A child's sense of reality can be seriously altered by the confusion of tongues experience. The parent's reality overshadows the child's because the child is in the emotionally vulnerable position. A child needs the parent's response more than the parent needs the child's response. A child's sense of self is more easily threatened than the adult. And the child is in a lowered position of status, control, and power with their parent.

Parental narcissism stifles emotional availability needed to help the child understand what has happened. This is especially true when the adult denies the reality of the seductive experience or his/her unresponsiveness, and attempts to convince the child that a different experience has taken place. In the case of sexual seduction, the parent attempts to convince the child that a loving experience has occurred. In the case of emotional unresponsiveness, neglect, or physical abuse, the child also feels abandoned to his/her own feelings, without parental acknowledgment or affirmation of the reality of the abusive interaction. Under these emotionally vulnerable circumstances, the child becomes confused about the reality of his/her experience. What is more, a child can actually deny his/her own subjective experience while adapting to the parent's distorted reality.

The child is then left in a severely confused state, which, once dissociated, remains essentially the same. Because the sexual experience is traumatic, the child splits it off, including the image of her/himself as victimized, helpless, overwhelmed, frightened, angry, and confused. Once repressed, this dissociated state fails to change, becomes semiautonomous and continues unconsciously to influence the adult personality. It exerts an ego weakening disruptive effect on healthy adult functioning, especially in the area of mature object relations.

The parental seducer can influence the child's sense of reality because his/her reality testing is still in the process of developing. A child's sense of reality can easily be destabilized when trauma and reactive fantasies intrude. In the experience of sexual trauma, the child's intrapsychic functioning is flooded with intrusive fantasies as a reaction to parental sexual abuse. Such intrusive fantasies are accounted for in Ferenczi's confusion of tongues theory because they are a result of disturbance in the interpersonal relationship between the parental abuser and the child victim. Oedipal theory posits a biologically driven child–parent fantasy occurring intrapsychically. The child's subjective experience of the seduction can be stated as: "This happened to me because I am bad. I am guilty and need to be punished. There is something wrong with me."

The child is developmentally inclined to believe the parent's presentation of reality because acceptance of parental authority is associated with love, protection, and object attachment. Seduction fosters a profound sense of betrayal, not just in the parent, but in the capacity to perceive reality accurately. This, then, engenders a serious difficulty in trusting one's perceptions. Manifestation of this difficulty appears in masochistic patients who repeatedly enter into abusive relationships from which they are unable to protect or extricate themselves. The child assumes the reality of the parent, denying its own. This is an essential development of psychopathology, for example, the child denies its own subjective experience, denies it is being intruded upon, aggressed against, it is not being given love, it is being molested, wounded, etc. The child assumes the parental view of the seduction as being an act of love.

Being tongue-tied

Parental authority also prevents the child from speaking about the sense of confusion or abuse. The child is confused intellectually, interpersonally, and emotionally. At some level of awareness, the child realizes that their disturbed experience emanates from the parent. But, they cannot give voice to the difference between their definition of the seduction and the parent, since it is associated with the danger of loss of parental love, retaliation, and abandonment. In essence, the child becomes tongue-tied; he/she cannot speak about the trauma. The silence is further compounded by the fact that at this immature level of cognitive development, the child actually needs the parent to help understand and verbalize what has happened to her/him. This requires the truthful explanation given in the context of emotional support, something that the abusive parent is quite unable to do. Emotional support cannot come from a parent who is in a state of denial and dissociation.

Because the child is not helped to understand and verbalize the effects of the seduction, a pathological, split-off nucleus of traumatic affect, self-image, and relational interaction develops and becomes the basis for later psychopathology. This affects all subsequent developmental stages, including the ego functions of reality testing, self-regulation, and object relations.

Invariably, the abused child, if he/she is able to talk of the seduction, is criticized as being a hysterical liar. Often, the child victim is blamed for the seduction because the non-abusing parent does not wish to confront the reality of evil in his/her spouse, friend, cleric, teacher, neighbour, or older child. In addition, the parent does not want to be forced to take action that might compromise the tenuous emotional and interpersonal equilibrium that has been established with the abusing partner. The adult seducer also does not speak of the seduction: "The guilt that the parent or parental surrogate ought to feel but does not is then introjected by the child. The act is perceived as wrong, but there is nobody else to take responsibility for it except the child victim" (Masson, 1984, pp. 148–149). Often the adult becomes violent toward the child victim, denying his/her aggression was harmful. The "evil of the act" is projected on to the child, emotionally cleansing the adult of responsibility and negative intent.

The child is left during and after the seduction in a disrupted intellectual, interpersonal, and emotional state. The child has internalized an introject that disrupts reality oriented thinking and prohibits awareness about what actually occurred. Consequently, the child, and subsequently the adult, doubts her/his own perceptions of reality, and is often unable to perceive actual abuse in later abusive relationships to which he/she masochistically clings.

Becoming an "automata": denial, detachment, dissociation, and splitting

The child, in order to cope with the trauma, that is, to maintain self cohesion, an affectionate tie to the parent, and continue interpersonal contact necessary for survival, develops a series of defensive coping mechanisms. Ferenczi described the process of the child's psychological adaptation to the seduction trauma:

> These children feel physically and morally helpless, their personalities are not sufficiently consolidated in order to be able to protest, even if only in thought, for the overpowering force and authority of the adult makes them dumb and can rob them of their senses. *The same anxiety however, if it reaches a certain maximum, compels them to subordinate themselves like automata to the will of the aggressor, to divine each one of his desires and to gratify these completely oblivious of themselves they identity themselves with the aggressor.* (Ferenczi, 1980n, p. 162)

In this extract, Ferenczi described, for the first time, the coping mechanisms of identification with the aggressor. In addition, he described other mechanisms, such as splitting, denial, detachment, and dissociation, which enabled the child to cope with actual sexual seduction Splitting occurs because the child is unable to integrate the extremes of the parent's actual disturbed behavior; from non-seductive to suddenly seductive, as well as invasive, intrusive, and massively overstimulating. It is merely a defense against contaminating the good image of the parent with the child's innate aggression towards the bad image, but stems from the parent's actual extreme, erratic behavior. This is a non-Kleinian view of splitting. This explanation is more of a relational view than Klein's because the splitting is related to the actual quality of the parent's behavior, and not based predominately on the child's fantasies and distortions of reality. The parents real behavior is so extreme and unexpected that the child's ego is unable to integrate such a split. There is a lack of integration of self and object in the child's personality development. The capacity to integrate develops about the three-year-old period, when object constancy occurs (Jacobsen, 1964; Mahler et al., 1973). The intensity of the trauma and the painful affects are so great that it disrupts and impedes the synthetic and integrative functions of the child's ego (Rachman, 1989a). This results in the persistence of a developmental lack of integration, which is referred to as a splitting. It is manifested as the person shifting from one extreme state to another, in which the image of the self or the other are extreme opposites, which are not integrated into a whole, balanced composite. The analysand, or the self (for every object image, there is a self-image that goes with it), remains either all good or all bad. To view this phenomenon merely as a defense against aggression misses the earlier developmental interferences with normal integration caused by the parent's actual seductive behavior.

The earlier the sexual trauma, the more the capacity to integrate is arrested. If the seduction occurs before the age of three, it is likely the child will remain arrested, in a state of severe fragmentation. The self and object world and other important aspects of reality functioning will be experienced with massive discontinuities, irregularities, and bewildering confusion.

Detachment is a defense against becoming reattached to an abusive object and re-experiencing the trauma. Psychologically, it is removing oneself from the interpersonal field and from one's painful feelings.

Dissociation is a phenomenon in which the split-off parts of the individual's experience become quasi autonomous and take on a life of their own, dominating the individual's consciousness and behavior. An individual will have internal objects and split-off parts of the self that exist as pathologically motivational systems in which the original trauma is repeatedly re-enacted and replayed. This is, again, a relational view of the repetition compulsion to relive, repeat earlier internalized object relations. Freud's ego psychology did emphasize the attempt to achieve mastery over the earlier trauma by repeating it, but missed the need to remain attached to earlier abusive objects, despite conscious aversion to those objects.

Another consequence of the adaptation to the incest trauma would be blunted affect. This mechanism is the habituation of detachment and also a manifestation of feeling dead inside (Bollas, 1987). The child feels he/she has been psychologically murdered. They are the victims of a soul murder (Shengold, 1989). Incest survivors talk about being murdered by their abusers. They feel that the trusting, affectionate, loving child-self in them has been murdered. They no longer have access to a wide range of feelings that are associated with vulnerability, pain, abuse, and betrayal.

Out of body experience

Ferenczi described this phenomenon in the analysis of Elizabeth Severn (Ferenczi, 1988, Rachman, 2014a). A dramatic example of the process of detachment, dissociation, and blunted affect which had its origin in a childhood incest trauma occurred in an analysis of an adult female. The sexual abuse occurred during an early childhood period, unabated until a family member was told about it. When the father/abuser was threatened with imprisonment, the abuse stopped. Sexual abuse involved actual sexual contact with the young child. After the first such traumatic shocks to the child's body and mind, the most intense form of the confusion of tongues trauma developed to cope with the impending fragmentation of the self. During an analytic session, the incest survivor described a sexual assault where a severe dissociative reaction developed:

> He and I were in the bathtub. Usually, he would ask me to suck his cock. Actually, he would make it a playful, innocent invitation. That bastard knew how to appeal to a child. He would say: Honey, please suck on daddy's lollipop! This time, for whatever reason I didn't want to do it. So, what did that fucking bastard do? He pushed my head down under the water so I could reach his cock. I swallowed water, I thought I was going to drown. Then all of sudden I seemed to be floating in the air, moving toward the ceiling. Once I got to the ceiling, I stayed there for a while. While I was there I was looking down at the scene. I saw this child sucking on her father's cock. For a while, I thought the child would die. Then, something happened. This little girl said, I don't want to die. I began to float back down from the ceiling. All of a sudden I was back in the water choking. I spit out the water, pushed the hand away from my head, and stood up. I went out of the bathroom screaming. (Session with RT (a pseudonym), October, 2005)

The description of this individual's out of body experience was both a meaningful phenomenological description of a severe dissociative experience but, also, an emotional breakthrough in the unfolding of the analysis of the incest trauma.

Helplessly binding a child to an adult: psychodynamics of victimization

There are methods, in the confusion of tongues trauma, which form the psychodynamics of "helplessly binding a child to an adult." These three mechanisms are "passionate love; passionate punishment; and terrorism of suffering" (Ferenczi, 1988, pp. 165–166).

Passionate love

In the dynamics of passionate love, the seduction emerges from the phase-appropriate, non-erotic love of the child for a parent. In the non-pathologic form, the parent's love is also the natural psychobiological affectionate bond to a child. The child may nurse the fantasy of taking the role of the parent to the adult. There is a very important distinction between the Freudian and Ferenczian view of childhood erotic fantasies, which became one of the intellectual ideas that began to distinguish the Budapest School from the Viennesse School of psychoanalysis. This fantasy play can assume an erotic form, but remains on the level that Ferenczi termed tenderness, not passion. It is crucial to distinguish that Ferenczi's idea of tenderness is the psychic level of tenderness, not biological eroticism. The difficulty comes into play when the adult who is in contact with the child is emotionally disturbed and expresses an erotic or passionate form of love. Such adults are expressing a lack of impulse control and pathologic narcissism in their sexual desires for the child. The pathological desire of the child by the adult occurs by virtue of their own childhood sexual trauma, psychological disorder, or alcohol or drug addiction. Abusing adults use the affectionate play of a child as an excuse to express their own desires, as if the child was an adult. Fabricating the interaction as if they were involved with a peer, they rationalize that they are not responsible for the damage they are contributing to the child.

In a statement that reflects his extensive clinical work with trauma cases, which he reported in his *Clinical Diary*, Ferenczi described the spectrum of sexual abuse he reported in trauma cases: "The real rape of girls who have hardly grown out of the age of infants, similar sexual acts of mature women with boys, and also enforced homosexual acts, are more frequent occurrences than has hitherto been assumed" (Ferenczi, 1988, pp. 162–163).

Passionate punishment

The adult abuser has to deal with his/her feelings of anger, remorse, and shame for the seduction. However, the abuser behaves as if the sexual seduction has never taken place, consoling him/herself with the confabulation that a child does not know or remember the abuse. The seducer subsequently can become moralistic and religious, attempting, "to save the soul of the child by severity" (Ferenczi, 1988, pp. 162–163).

Terrorism of suffering

All children have a developmentally phase-appropriate compulsion to burden themselves with familial disorder. Rather than believe it is their parents who are causing them harm, they believe they are to blame for this disturbance. A parent who constantly complains to her/his child about her miserable life can create "a nurse for life out of their child" (Ferenczi, 1980n, p. 166). The child victim is caught in the bind of being terrorized by the parental emotional abuse and identifies with the aggressor, taking on characteristics of the abuser. By so doing, the child attempts to maintain the emotional fiction of parental love and tenderness. Ferenczi's concept of terrorism of suffering shares a similarity with Searles' "The patient as therapist to his analyst" (Searles, 1979). As the child attempts to cure the parent of his/her difficulties, the patient attempts to help the analyst with his/her emotional issues.

Identification with the aggressor

Ferenczi developed this concept to understand the perverse bond the abuser can create with the sexual seductive victim. He observed the intense emotional bond a child can develop with the very person who has abused him/her. Incorrectly, this concept had been credited to Anna Freud, which she supposedly introduced in her 1936 book, *The Ego and the Mechanisms of Defense*. But the chronology of discovery favors Ferenczi. Anna Freud attended Ferenczi's "Confusion of tongues" presentation at the Twelfth International Psychoanalytic Congress in Wiesbaden in 1932. In fact, she reported on the presentation in the official publication of the IPA (A. Freud, 1933). Therefore, she heard Ferenczi's description of this concept "identification with the aggressor" in 1932, and it appeared for the first time in print in the original German publication of the "Confusion of tongues" paper in 1933 [The passions of adults and their influence on the sexual and character development of children]; "ängstlicher Identifizierung und Introjektion . . ." (Ferenczi, 1933, p. 11). It can be translated as "fearful identification with and introjection of the threatening or attacking person" (I am grateful to Professor Paul Mattick (1984) for this translation). Sixteen years after the German publication of the "Confusion of tongues" paper (Ferenczi, 1933), Michael Balint provided the first official English translation of the concept of identification with the aggressor:

> The same anxiety, however, if it reaches a certain maximum, compels them (children who have been seduced) to subordinate themselves like automata to the will of the aggressor, to divine each one of his desires and to gratify these, completely, oblivious of themselves, they identify themselves with the aggressor. (Balint, 1949, p. 162)

The child forms a masochistic bond with the abuser. Rather than rejecting or rebelling against the abuse authority, the child attaches itself to the seducer. It is a desperate but effective way to gain, or to continue, an affectionate tie with the abuser, maintaining the fiction (delusion, if you wish) that the seduction is actually an act of love and tenderness. By introjecting the bad object, the child attempts to master the trauma by becoming like the oppressor. In instances of massive trauma where the individual is overpowered, demoralized, or senses are numbed in a pathologic environment which offers no exit (Kafka, 1948), identification with the aggressor is a child's way to cope with the overpowering trauma of incest. Incest constitutes an exercise in power, control, and aggression of an authority over a subordinate, the child.

There is an inherent communicative function in identification with the aggressor. It can be seen as the child's effort to convey his/her subjective experience. In a more dramatic fashion, it is the child's way to force an adult to feel what they feel. Contained in the concept of projective identification is this idea of putting your own subjective state into the other person, to induce in the other person what you are feeling on a visceral level. Essentially, the child is signaling his/her distress about the trauma by causing the other person to feel it (Ogden, 1979).

Ferenczi's original statement about the confusion of tongues

Ferenczi's original statement about the confusion of tongues paradigm was first noted in the *Clinical Diary* entry of April 5, 1932:

> Experiences regarding the traumatic effect of genital attacks by adults on small children oblige me to modify the analytic view of infantile sexuality that has prevailed up to now. The fact that infantile sexuality exists obviously remains undisputed, yet much of what appears as passionate in infantile sexuality may be a secondary consequence of the passionate behavior of adults, forcibly imposed on children against their will and, so to speak, artificially implanted in them. Even over passionate manifestations of non-genital tenderness, such as passionate kissing, ardent embraces, effect the child in fact unpleasurably. Children want no more than to be treated in a friendly, tender, and gentle way. Their own movements and physical expressions are tender, if it is otherwise, then something has already gone wrong. One has to ask oneself how much of what is involved in the undying love of the child for its mother, and how much of the boy's murderous desire against the rival father, would develop in a purely spontaneous way, without the premature implantation of passionate adult eroticism and genitality; that is how much of the Oedipus complex is really inherited and how much is passed on by tradition from one generation to the other. (Ferenczi, 1988, p. 79)

Freud had known about the more developed idea of the "Confusion of tongues" when Ferenczi read him the presentation for the Wiesbaden Congress. Although Ferenczi was desirous of Freud's approval, the lack of it did not deter him from pursuing his presentation or publication of his ideas. It took a great deal of emotional courage to do so, since Freud tried to prevent him from presenting or publishing the paper (Rachman, 1997b).

Eric Fromm pointedly wrote about Ferenczi's difficulties with Freud's attempt to dominate and control him (Fromm, 1959). Ferenczi identified himself as a healer, not as a theoretician, which was an accurate designation for his motivation and clinical work with difficult trauma cases. But, he was also intellectually curious and adventuresome. His work with trauma pushed him into the first alternative theory to the oedipal theory of neurosis, the confusion of tongues (Ferenczi, 1980n). He did not formulate this paradigm because he wanted to rebel against Freud and challenge his authority or belief. The formulation was what Ferenczi thought was a necessary evolutionary step for psychoanalysis in order to expand its clinical therapeutics toward treating and studying trauma. As we know, initially there was almost universal condemnation of Ferenczi's ideas and methods of treating trauma (Balint, 1968; Rachman, 1997b). His *Clinical Diary,* which contained the clinical data and the theoretical origins of the confusion of tongues paradigm, was not published until 1985 in French (Ferenczi, 1985) and in English until 1988 (Ferenczi, 1988). These delays were a deliberate attempt by Freud and his orthodox followers to suppress Ferenczi's ideas. Balint attempted to protect his mentor by delaying the publications until there was a more favorable environment for the acceptance of Ferenczi in the analytic community (Balint, 1968). Of course, that longed for favorable environment took over fifty years to occur, a sign of the difficulties that Ferenczi's work was subjected to through the twentieth century. In spite of these difficulties, the confusion of tongues paradigm and the *Diary*'s clinical data on the incest trauma were prophetic statements about the need to focus psychoanalysis on the theory and treatment of trauma.

Balint's extensions of Ferenczi's confusion of tongues theory of trauma

Balint's extensions of Ferenczi's confusion of tongues theory of trauma made a significant and unique contribution to psychoanalysis (Balint, 1965d, 1968).

1. He used Ferenczi's ideas and methods as a conduit to help contribute to the British object relations perspective.
2. The confusion of tongues paradigm was extended to emotional experiences between mother and child. A confusion of tongues also arises from non-sexual interaction in the object relationship with a caretaker. The concept of primary object love recognized deficits in empathic unresponsiveness to a child's developmental needs. Understanding emotional trauma involves parental unresponsiveness, or a need for love, affection, and empathy (Balint, 1965a).
3. The child does not understand either cognitively or emotionally why the parent is not responding to their needs. The child is confused and blames him/herself. The child wants and needs passion-free love and erotic-free affection.
4. The concept of a new beginning emphasized the expansion of psychoanalysis to the perspective of the analyst and the ambience in the psychoanalytic situation.
5. The concept of the basic fault provided a non-drive theory for understanding narcissistic, personality, borderline, psychotic disorders (Balint, 1968).
6. Reformulation of a contemporary view of regression. A distinction was made between "benign and malignant regression."

Balint and his first wife, Alice, were early contributors to the emerging British object relations orientation (Rachman, 2003a). The Balints, in the 1930s, expanded on Ferenczi's early relational ideas. The new beginning is the ultimate force that compels an analysand to keep at their analytic work: ". . . their wish, often unconscious, is to be able to love free from anxiety, to lose their fear of complete surrender" (Balint, 1965b, p. 159).

The analyst may decide to respond to a particularly worthy analysand and help create a course of treatment to deal with the psychological difficulties of the individual that emphasizes the emotional trauma and a new way of therapeutic interaction. The new beginning focused on the analyst becoming aware of his/her functioning. The Balints focused on the analyst being capable of perceiving what he/she does, what he creates, what he causes as the subjective observation of the analyst (Balint & Balint, 1939). This orientation expands Ferenczi's phenomenological view of both analysand and analyst as subject, both members of the therapeutic dyad contributing to the analyst encounter. The Balints opened up study of the person and functioning of the analyst and how this effects the analytic encounter.

Michael Balint offered fundamental concepts for understanding the concept of emotional trauma as an important issue in the understanding of personality development and psychological disorder. Emotional trauma is derived from the individual's need for primary object love:

> I consider primitive or archaic, object love to be the *fons et origo* [source and origin] of human libido development. The original and everlasting aim of all object relations is the primitive wish: I must be loved without any obligation on me and without any expectation of return from me. (Balint, 1965b, p. 50)

The implication of this theoretical view is that the transference reaction in the psychoanalytic situation contains the basic element of primary object love: "The desire to be loved, always, everywhere, in every way, my whole body is the primary tendency in transference" (Balint, 1965b, p. 50).

Unlike the Freudian theory, which maintains that the infant is born with a primary narcissism where the infant is turned inward on itself, Balint maintained that the infant is born with a need to relate to its environment and an object (another human being). Development proceeds along the line of object relations, moving from archaic to mature object love.

Balint outlined three levels of personality organization and functioning. This theory of emotional trauma was an attempt to expand Ferenczi's ideas into a comprehensive analytic view of trauma. These zones of maturation were viewed as differences that were brought about in the object relationship with the primary love, usually the mother. Zone I is the zone of the basic fault. Balint used a geological metaphor to refer to the most primitive level of personality. Basic fault referred to a flaw, having a fundamental crack or fault (as in a geological fault, which can cause fundamental damage to the earth). This would be a level of adaptation due to serious emotional trauma with the caretaker usually causing a borderline or psychotic disorder. This is the pre-oedipal zone of functioning most relevant to the analysis of difficult or regressed cases (Balint, 1965d, 1968). In Balint's conceptualization of the basic fault, he articulated Ferenczi's original idea of a two-person relationship. The fault was due to lack of empathy, compassion, neglect, or abuse in the primary object love with the mother (and, when applicable, with the father). Deficits in the personality remain as a result of emotional trauma. These are severe dependent, and, in certain instances, symbiotic relationships. Another significant characteristic of the relationship at the basic fault is:

> . . . the immense difference of intensity between the phenomena of satisfaction and frustration. Whereas satisfaction the "fitting in" of the object with the subject brings about a feeling of a quiet tranquil well-being . . . frustration the lack of fitting in of the object, evokes highly vehement and loud symptoms. (Balint, 1968, p. 17)

Balint acknowledged that Ferenczi's difficulties in treating Elizabeth Severn were influential in his conceptualizations (Balint, 1968). He characterized object relationships with analysands at the level of the basic fault by moments of crises, where there are intense changes in the emotional atmosphere. At such moments, the analyst's behavior, especially if traditionally interpretations are employed, can be experienced as an attack, an insult, or as seductive or abusive. Or, on the other hand, these same interpretations can be experienced as soothing or exciting later on in the relationship when the crises have subsided. Such intense changes in affective functioning illustrates how easily traumatized an individual can become at the level of the basic fault. These individuals induce an intense countertransference reaction, which derives ". . . from an uncanny talent that enables the patient to understand the analyst's motives and to 'interpret' his behavior" (Balint, 1968, p. 19).

Zone II, in Balint's theory, is the zone of the oedipal level. The oedipal level is developmentally a more mature level of functioning in terms of psychic and affective functioning, as well as ego integration, object relationships, and reality testing. An analysand functioning at this level has had a good enough early primary object love experience and developed meaningful ego structure. Furthermore, the individual has internalized most of his/her significant early experiences (Balint, 1968).

Balint, although questioning the idea of need satisfaction, did believe in the treatment of the oedipal issues from a Ferenczian viewpoint. He emphasized the analysand's need for empathy from the analyst, and the concern that intrusive interpretations can create retraumatization.

Zone III, is the zone of creativity. This is the highest level of affective, psychological, emotional, and intellectual functioning. These are the individuals who are at the level of Maslow's concept of self-actualization (Maslow, 1954). For Balint, the level of creativity is an object related issue. This capacity develops from the meaningful, non-traumatized relationship with the mother. At this level, the individual can function on his/her own, without a dependency on a primary object. But, of course, in order to reach the zone of creativity the individual needs to have a primary positive experience with a primary object love. As can be seen from the case of Winston (see Chapter Eight), a disturbed relationship with a primary love object, his mother, produced a dysfunction in his capacity to be creative. It was only when he was able to work through this trauma in his analysis that his creative impulse could be developed.

The concept of therapeutic regression is a major contribution Balint made to the theory and technique of trauma analysis. He provided an alternative theory to the classical view of regression. For Balint, regression in the psychoanalytic situation is always in response to the prompting of an object. Hence, regression is not solely an intrapsychic phenomenon, but a two-person, object related, relational experience. Regression is also related to pre-genital development.

This view of regression takes into account an interpersonal need of human beings. In an ongoing, intensive, therapeutic relationship, dependencies can develop which recreate the childhood experience of the mother–child dependency. Balint believed that it is necessary for therapeutic regression to take place in the safety of an analytic relationship. The early mother–child relation is recreated within the transference, in the hope of repairing the basic fault trauma of childhood. Both Balint and Winnicott believe that the analytic situation, when treated as a holding environment, can recreate the archaic mother–child relationship.

Balint made a valiant and significant attempt to translate and extend Ferenczi's clinical experimentation with regression (Rachman, 2010a,c) into mainstream psychoanalysis. He distinguished between benign and malignant regression (Balint, 1968). Benign regression is a necessary emotional experience in the psychoanalytic situation in which the analyst relates to the analysand to sustain him/her. As a primary object, the analyst has a therapeutic function to recognize the individual's internal life and unique individuality. The relationship with the analyst is necessary for survival. The analyst must allow the individual to proceed through the regression, and to be there in a nurturing, empathic way, allowing for permeability in boundaries. It is a therapeutic presence characterized "... by consent, participation and involvement ... tolerance and understanding ..." (Balint, 1968, p. 145).

This description is of a creation of a therapeutic ambience, which can be integrated with Ferenczi's clinical experimentation and activity oriented approach to dealing with trauma. Balint's description of the necessary therapeutic ambience parallels notions of an emphatic atmosphere, and runs parallel to Winnicott's concept of a holding environment.

Malignant regression is dependent upon the object relationship between analyst and analysand, a two-person experience. The analyst's contribution comes from his/her psychopathology and the nature of the interpersonal relationship established. Severe regression occurs because the experience repeats the original traumatic injury. The analysand loses trust and hope of a new beginning with the analyst. The analysand feels that the promise of a new, reparative parental response will not be realized. Or, more dramatically, the analyst acts, or is perceived as acting, in the same way as the original traumatogenetic object, creating a retraumatization experience. This is not a time to use interpretation, but a time to recognize the analysand's need for primary object love. The analyst must respond to the growing disharmony, aggression, destructiveness with "... need recognizing, need satisfying and need understanding ..." (Balint, 1968, p. 181).

If the analyst communicates his understanding of the need for primary object love, the harmony can be restored. Malignant regression is returned to a state of benign regression.

Balint set the stage for a change in analytic thinking about the positive functioning of regression, later reflected in Winnicott's (1965b) and Kohut's (1977) works. These formulations were shaped by Ferenczi's work with Severn (Ferenczi, 1988; Rachman, 2014a). He saw the need to regulate the regression (Rachman, 2012g). The idea of regression as a significant contribution to the analytic encounter was stated by Balint:

> I cannot see why the analyst should be afraid of fostering a dependent, infantile, regressive transference relationship. I must say that in my analysis this stage is almost always reached . . . my idea of a new beginning, which is of paramount importance . . . for a proper termination of analysis, presupposes such a situation as a transitory period. (Haynal, 1989, p. 82)

Balint's ideas on trauma also present a new role for the analyst and clinical interaction in several important ways.

1. Clinical responsiveness is not ruled by the classical role of interpretation. The analysand's developmental needs have to be understood and responded to. Responsiveness then becomes a matter of non-interpretative clinical interaction, such as, need recognition, empathy, and therapeutic responsiveness aimed at need fulfilment (Rachman, 1998b).
2. Therapeutic optimism is embedded in the concept of a new beginning. Ferenczi clearly believed that as long as an analysand was willing to come to see him, he was willing to continue the analysis (Rachman, 1997a). Therapeutic optimism refers to maintaining hope that the analysand is capable of change and the analyst does not emotionally distance him/herself, or give up on the analysand. This attitude points to the importance of Ferenczi's two-person psychology and mutual analytic encounter (Rachman, 2003a, 2007a, 2014a). The intersection of the analysand–analyst subjective experience informs and maintains the analysis (Rachman, 2010c).
3. Balint reformulated the traditional idea of optimal anxiety for learning to the optimal level of satisfaction:

> And it is in this context that the analyst's behavior and contribution toward the creating and maintaining of the clinical situation becomes of paramount importance . . . how much and what kind of satisfaction is needed by the patient on the one hand, and the analyst on the other, to keep the tension in the psychoanalytical situation at or near the optimal level. (Balint, 1968, p. 218)

Bacal's concept of optimal responsiveness is related to this idea, which helped continue the Ferenzi–Balint dialogue in contemporary psychoanalysis (Bacal, 1988). Balint's attempt to reformulate and extend Ferenczi's work on trauma was not only ignored by the so-called mainstream (traditional) psychoanalysis, but also by the same object relations perspective to which Ferenzi and Balint made such a significant contribution (Balint, 1968). I have discussed Kohut's lack of recognition in his work of Ferenczi and Balint's contributions (Rachman, 1989a), even though he was well aware of the work (Gedo, 1987). The most personal blow that Balint experienced in this regard was the lack of recognition by Winnicott, his fellow member of the Independent Group of the British Psychoanalytic Society and Institute. The tale of Winnicott and Balint's disagreement is worth telling.

Winnicott's lack of recognition of Ferenczi and Balint's work on trauma

In a series of personal and written exchanges in the 1960s, Balint openly criticized Winnicott for failing to recognize and credit Ferenczi for some of his ideas that Winnicott integrated into his thinking but never credited to Ferenczi. Balint was particularly concerned because he had been "Winnicott's most distinguished ally in The Middle Group of the British Psycho-Analytical) Society . . ." (Rudnytsky, 1991, p. 87). Winnicott finally admitted his error, however reluctantly. First, he said Ferenczi and Balint have said what he has said were his own ideas.

Later, in 1967, Winnicott self-disclosed a personality fault as the issue: "I've realized more and more . . . what I've lost from not correlating my work with the work of others. It happens to be my temperament, and it's a big fault" (Winnicott, 1967, p. 573).

It is particularly distressing to read of Winnicott's neglect of Ferenczi's and Balint's ideas, since they made a significant contribution to the origin and development of the object relations perspective, of which Winnicott became the most renowned spokesperson. Winnicott's neglect of the Budapest School contributed to the neglect and suppression of Ferenczi's work. The narcissism of Freud, Kohut, and Winnicott interfered with crediting Ferenczi as a forerunner.

CHAPTER FIVE

A pioneering analysis of the incest trauma: Sándor Ferenczi's analysis of Elizabeth Severn

Elizabeth Severn, Ferenczi's most famous case, extensively discussed in his *Clinical Diary* as "RN" (Ferenczi, 1988), was called an "evil genius" by Freud (Jones, 1957, p. 407). Freud's very negative view of Severn as a person and an analysand seemed based upon what was reported to him by other analysts, such as Ernest Jones and Clara Thompson. I believe Freud's first-hand knowledge of the Severn analysis was very limited, since he was not privy to Ferenczi's *Clinical Diary* (Ferenczi 1988), which was known only to Michael Balint, Ferenczi's heir apparent to the Budapest School, and other Hungarian colleagues. The *Clinical Diary* was an uncirculated private document by Ferenczi which illustrated his work on trauma, his analysis with Elizabeth Severn, his clinical experiments with non-interpretative measures, the development of mutual analysis, and his dissatisfactions in his analysis with Freud (Dupont, 1988a). Its publication was a landmark that documented pioneering analyses of trauma, highlighting the analysis of the incest trauma with Elizabeth Severn.

Ferenczi considered Severn his most difficult case: a case that he said he saw as complex and very difficult (Ferenczi, 1988). He had a variety of designations for her, such as calling her the Queen and La

Contessa, which seemed negative, as well as ones which seemed positive, such as viewing her as "my colleague" and "Dr. Severn" (Rachman, 2009a). Severn was a profoundly disturbed individual who had been in several unsuccessful analyses in the United States. She had several consultations with Otto Rank, a collaborator of Ferenczi (Ferenczi & Rank, 1925). Rank suggested to Severn that she consider an analysis with Ferenczi, who, by the time Severn consulted him, had become known as the analyst of difficult cases. Their analysis occurred between 1925 and 1933, while Severn lived and worked in Budapest. Their relationship lasted until February 1933, when Ferenczi, because of ill health, terminated the analysis. At that time he was beginning a serious physical decline due to pernicious anemia. He died on May 22, 1933, four months after the termination. Shortly before his death he was confined to bed, having to be hand-fed. He was, however, lucid in his thinking and joked with his caretaker (Rachman, 1997a). Severn was upset at what seemed a premature termination and complained in letters to her daughter, Margaret Severn (Rachman, 2011a, 2014c).

The analytic community had a very negative reaction to Severn. Thompson was in analysis with Ferenczi at the same time as Severn. Thompson felt Severn was emotionally dangerous for Ferenczi, sapping his energy with her endless demands. It is also thought that Thompson was jealous because Severn received Ferenczi's greatest time and attention. Ferenczi was willing to take Severn on as an analysand, knowing the difficulties. This analysis laid the foundation for the evolution of the analysis of the incest trauma and other traumas, for example, severe neurotic, narcissistic, character disordered, borderline, and psychotic disorders (Rachman, 2012b,c). The analysis was a courageous attempt to analyze a very difficult trauma case in order to elasticize the boundaries of psychoanalytic theory and technique (Rachman, 2007a, 2014a). Ferenczi never encouraged his students, whether they were Michael Balint, Izette de Forest, or Clara Thompson to leave psychoanalysis. His students did, however, have an effect on the evolution of psychoanalysis by contributing to new approaches, for example, object relations (Balint), interpersonal analysis (Thompson), self-psychology (Balint via Paul Orstein), and humanistic psychotherapy (de Forest).

The innovations which emerged from Ferenczi's treatment of Severn, as well as other difficult cases in the period from 1925–1933, were considered "wild analysis" because Freud and his orthodox followers considered Ferenczi's deviations as encouraging neurosis rather than curing it. This issue was addressed by redefining the concept of indulgence which was originally attributed to Ferenczi's new method: In this discussion, the suggestion is made that the original concept *Nachgiebigkeit* (to bend towards) should have been translated as flexibility or elasticity, which reflected Ferenczi's idea of responding to an analysand's development needs rather than indulging his/her neurotic tendencies (Rachman, 1997a, 2003a).

As we have seen, Ferenczi's confusion of tongues paradigm (Ferenczi, 1980n) was a meaningful extension of the seduction hypothesis (Freud, 1954). Freud, actually, led the evolution of psychoanalysis toward change (Freud, 1919a) and passed the mantle to Ferenczi (Rachman, 1997a). The introduction of activity into psychoanalysis and Ferenczi's use of it in treating difficult cases (Ferenczi, 1980c,d, f–n) was the precursor of the evolution of the analytic method towards the treatment of the incest trauma. There are many ironies in the issues that began the Freud–Ferenczi controversy and maintained professional and personal conflict between them. One of these ironies was working with difficult cases. Many of Freud's cases could also be classified as difficult cases, such as the Rat Man and the Wolf Man. In fact, there is an important introduction to the case of the Wolf Man, written by Freud in 1918, which seems to be overlooked in discussion of working with difficult cases. This quotation is a rallying point for analysts to work with difficult cases because they provide the opportunity to expand the clinical boundaries of psychoanalysis:

> Something new can only be gained from analysis that presents special difficulties, and to the overcoming of these a great deal of time has to be devoted. Only in such cases do we succeed in descending into the deepest and most primitive strata of mental development and in giving from these solutions for the problems of the later formulations and we feel afterwards that, strictly speaking only an analysis which has penetrated so far deserves the name. (Freud, 1918b, p. 476)

The Wolf Man's analysis was very difficult for Freud. Interestingly, this analysis continued way beyond Freud's efforts. For a period of twenty years or so, psychoanalysts, beginning with Ruth Mack Brunswick, traveled to Europe each summer to continue the treatment of the Wolf Man (Roazen, 1975). As one considers the meaningful words in Freud's introduction to the Wolf Man, it seems to echo Ferenczi's struggles with Severn. What is so puzzling is that Freud did not support his student when he followed in his footsteps and courageously accepted the task of the analysis of one of the most difficult cases in the history of psychoanalysis, Elizabeth Severn.

It is my belief that Severn was an unsung hero of psychoanalysis because she used her illness to push herself to recovery, helping pioneer an evolutionary treatment for the incest trauma and contribute to the confusion of tongues theory of trauma (Rachman, 2010b).

She used her intellect, assertiveness, knowledge of therapy, and her illness to relentlessly explore the darkest recesses of her own mind, while pushing her analyst to do the same. Her analyst, for the first time in analytic history, developed an "in vitro" experiment in the use of subjectivity to analyze an individual suffering from trauma (Rachman, 2010a).

Pioneering treatment of the incest trauma

This material to be described in the clinical interaction between Ferenczi and Severn was derived from a page-by-page analysis of his *Clinical Diary* (Ferenczi, 1988). By inspecting every entry in the *Clinical Diary*, an attempt was made to reconstruct the treatment process. This reconstruction of the analysis is divided into seven stages.

Stage 1: Feelings of antipathy.
Stage 2: Unfolding of symptomatology.
Stage 3: Dream interpretation and traditional analytic measures.
Stage 4: Trauma analysis.
Stage 5: Analysis of countertransference/analyst self-disclosure.
Stage 6: Erotic transference reaction.
Stage 7: Emotional and behavioral changes in analysand and analyst.

These stages will illustrate the Ferenczi–Severn analysis:

Stage 1: Early feelings of antipathy

Ferenczi made a revealing and emotionally open statement about how the analysis with Severn began with feelings of what he called antipathy:

(a) [Severn had] excessive independence and self-assurance:

(b) Immensely strong wlll powered as reflected by a marble-like rigidity of her facial features:

(c) Altogether a somewhat "sovereign, majestic superiority of a great or even the royal imperiousness of a king—all these characteristics that one cannot call feminine". (Ferenczi, 1988, pp. 96–97, 5 May 1932 entry)

In a remarkable statement that examined his antipathy to Severn, Ferenczi said:

> Instead of making myself aware of these impressions I appear to proceed on the principle that as the doctor I must be in a positive of superiority in every case. Overcoming my obvious apprehensions when faced with such a woman. I appear to have assumed, perhaps unconsciously, the attitude of superiority of my intrepid masculinity, which the patient took to be genuine, whereas this was a conscious professional pose, partly adapted as a defensive measure against anxiety. (Ferenczi, 1988, p. 97, 5 May 1932 entry)

It should come as no surprise, as we examine Severn's analytic experience with Ferenczi, that the analysis was filled with intense emotionality, emphatic failures, interpersonal difficulties, and crises in the transference and countertransference relationship.

Stage 2: Unfolding of the symptomatology

Ferenczi described how Severn suffered for weeks from lack of sleep and breathing difficulties. She was enraged with Ferenczi and the analysis. She was angry and dissatisfied because the analysis caused her pain; it opened old wounds: "Swearing and screaming during the entire session, accusation, insults, etc. She insists I should admit my helplessness, finally she even has the idea that I should repeat the trauma if it will only help" (Ferenczi, 1988, p. 156, 6 July 1932 entry).

Severn's behavior and Ferenczi's capacity to deal with it is the beginning of the concept of therapeutic regression that Balint developed over thirty years later (Balint, 1968; Rachman, 2013). As Ferenczi struggled to understand and analyze Severn, she did not let up in her complaints about his functioning: "complaints about the absence of the degree of interest and sympathy, even love, that alone give her confidence in my ability to glue her lacerated soul into a whole" (Ferenczi, 1988, p. 155. 6 July 1932 entry).

Ferenczi felt assaulted by these outbursts and criticisms. He had great difficulty with the countertransference reactions that Severn's personality and difficult functioning triggered in him. He became defensive, unempathic, and angry toward his analysand. A particularly difficult moment occurred when Severn would point out his countertransference. To his credit, Ferenczi tried to be open and honest when this happened to him: "my reaction to this was formerly a marked increase in antipathy and the feeling of being forced into feelings" [Followed by corresponding inner defenses] (Ferenczi, 1988, p. 155, 6 July 1932 entry).

Rather than blame Severn for the difficulties between them, Ferenczi vigorously employed countertransference analysis to become aware of his own contribution to the therapeutic difficulties: "Since the more profound investigation of the causes of my sympathies and antipathies, a large share of the latter have been traced back to infantile father and grandfather fixation with corresponding misogyny" (Ferenczi, 1988, p. 15, 6 July 1932 entry).

Ferenczi's countertransference analysis demonstrated his vigorous self-analysis which allowed him to go from antipathy to empathy: "appreciable increase in compassion for the person who has been tortured the point of death and falsely accused in addition" (Ferenczi, 1988, p. 155, 6 July 1932 entry).

Stage 3: Dream interpretation and other traditional analytical interactions

Although Ferenczi's analysis of Severn was a pioneering demonstration of the use of non-interpretative measures in the analysis of the incest trauma, it was also a demonstration of integrating standard analytic methods, such as the use of dream interpretation, analysis of transference and countertransference, and recall of childhood experience, in the analysis of the incest trauma. The following material will illustrate the use of dream interpretation in the analysis of trauma. Severn told Ferenczi about a dream about a former patient that she had seen. The dramatic part of the dream on which they focused was: "Former patient Dr. Gx forces her withered breast into R.N.'s

[Severn's] mouth. 'It isn't what I need; big, empty—no milk'" (Ferenczi, 1988, p. 13, 19 January 1932 entry).

Severn's associations were that the dream reflected the transference (and/or real relationship) as well as "unconscious contents of the analysand and the analyst" (Ferenczi, 1988, p. 13). The dream reported was a part of the unique mutual analysis that Ferenczi and Severn cocreated. Severn translated her interpretation into a demand that Ferenczi let himself go emotionally and interpersonally, so that he could analyze his own emotional issues in their transference relationship. Ferenczi also associated to Severn's dream in a particularly dramatic way. The fragment of the dream which was reported as "Dr. Gx. forces her withered breast into R.N.'s mouth" (Ferenczi, 1988, p. 13) apparently triggered a recall for Ferenczi of a childhood trauma: "szaraz dajka affair ... infantile, traumatic: affair of the nurse, plus housemaid" (Ferenczi, 1988, p. 14, 19 January 1932 entry).

Ferenczi linked the trauma association to his lack of empathy for Severn, that is, his wish to be rid of her as an analysand and to a lack of willingness to respond to several of Severn's stated needs. Severn believed Ferenczi's trauma association might be connected to the issues in their relationship.

A second dream analyzed was as follows:

> ... she dreamed of a bull, which attacked her; she actually feels the horn against her skin, and she gives up. This saves her life, since the animal loses all interest in the creature that is no longer struggling and appears to be dead, and leaves her lying there. (Ferenczi, 1988, p. 156, 6 July 1932 entry)

Ferenczi's interpretation of the dream was:

> The patient finds me quite repentant enough, on the other hand as this shows, she is now perhaps inclined to appreciate my admission and my friendliness and to do without some of the other things. This up to now has been worth it to keep the occasional fits of impatience firmly under control, and even to accept. (Ferenczi, 1988, p. 156, 6 July 1932 entry)

Ferenczi believed the dream showed Severn's struggle in the transference with him, where she felt attached. Severn is able to end the struggle because she began to experience his genuine concern and empathy. What is more, she also experienced him as more in control of his functioning and self-disclosing. Ferenczi's functioning foreshadowed the theoretical expansions about the crucial dimension of empathy in psychoanalytic theory and clinical functioning (Rachman, 1989b).

There were references in the dream to the circus: "The historical analysis of this male (who acts like a clown in the dream and instead of showing his own pain amuses others and performs comical acrobatic tricks)" (Ferenczi, 1988, p. 157–158, 7 July 1932 entry).

Ferenczi interpreted the tent idea in the dream as akin to childhood references to the circus; for example, clowns, acrobats, circus performers as Severn's own infantile life story to the transference relationship with him. The reference in the dream to the mirror-writing and hearing the caller as though from a great distance refer to both her dissociative experience with her father and the feeling of distance with others generated from this experience. In summing up the meaning of the dream, Ferenczi eloquently stated the courageous attempt to maintain self-cohesion in the face of staggering childhood trauma:

> The most comprehensive interpretation of this nightmare, however, is that this personality, shattered and made defenseless by suffering and poison, is attempting, over and over again but always unsuccessfully, to reassemble its various parts into a unit, that is, to understanding herself (realizing her own misery) she can only display in an indirect and symbolic way the contents that relate to her and of which she is herself unconscious; she must concern herself with analogous mental states in others (the reason for her choice of career), perhaps in the secret hope that one day she will be understood by one of these sufferers. (Ferenczi, 1988, p. 158, 7 July 1932)

Stage 4: Trauma analysis (traumatize analyze)

The more empathically attuned Ferenczi became to Severn's childhood traumas, the more she could recover from them and believe in their reality:

> At the same moment the patient opens up, is permeated by a feeling that I have at last understood (that is, felt) her suffering, consequently with an increased sense of certainty (a) the reality of her own experiences, (b) . . . of being listened to sympathetically. (Ferenczi, 1988, pp. 26–27, 19 January 1932 entry)

The capacity by the analyst to listen and respond to the childhood trauma as the analysand's reality (not a constructed developmental fantasy) helped to pave the way for an altered stage of consciousness. Her referred to it as a "semi-trance" (Ferenczi, 1988, p. 30, 4 February 1932 entry; Rachman, 2013), which Severn would enter when feeling safe, trusting, and affirmed. At first, Ferenczi was alarmed with her behavior: "shortness of breath, interruption of pulse and breathing, pallor, coldness and cold sweat, etc." (Ferenczi, 1988, p. 30, 4 February 1932 entry).

Ferenczi believed that Severn was suffering greatly when she demonstrated these symptoms. His active interpretations were an attempt to end her suffering (and, perhaps, his own).

Severn would get angry with his active and intellectually oriented interventions. She would tell him to "shut up" (Ferenczi, 1988, p. 30). Apparently, Severn understood what was taking place more than did Ferenczi. She had to teach him that her semi-trances were an attempt to recall and re-experience her childhood trauma. Ferenczi did eventually become a good student of Severn. The two of them developed this therapeutic regressive method into a fundamental dimension of treatment for analyzing the incest trauma, which has become standard methodology in contemporary psychotherapy and psychoanalysis (Rachman, 2000, 2003a). Six years into the analysis, he allowed Severn to remain in the semi-trance for about ten minutes before he intervened. It was then they could analyze her anger towards Ferenczi for disturbing her peace while she was in her semi-trance. Ferenczi was then able to provide an empathically based intervention:

> Since you cannot say anything about the cause of this anger and rage, we can only assume that impressions of the external world are being retained and reproduced in the unconsciousness, impressions that correspond in quality to those emotional reactions. Indeed, one must assume that whatever you do not want to feel, know of, or remember is far worse than the symptoms you escape into. (Ferenczi, 1988, p. 30, 4 February, 1932 entry)

It was through this type of clinical interaction that allowed Severn to influence Ferenczi's functioning towards greater clinical patience, empathetic understanding, and non-interpretative measures. Ferenczi, with Severn's help, co-created the clinical concept and methodology that allowed the semi-trance experience to evolve into the concept and clinical practice of therapeutic regression (Balint, 1968). Therapeutic regression sessions are demanding for both analyst and analysand. Ferenczi described the emotional drain on being Severn's analyst during these sessions:

> The most trying of the demands on me arose from the fact that toward the end of the sessions, the patient would have an attack, which would oblige me to sit by her for another hour or so, until the attack subsided. My conscience as a doctor and a human being prevented me from leaving her alone and in this helpless condition. But the overexertion appears to have provoked immense tension in me, which at times had rendered the patient hateful to me. (Ferenczi, 1988, p. 30, 4 February 1932 entry)

Ferenczi's experience of seeing the analysand as provoking a hateful attitude can be seen as a forerunner of Winnicot's concept of "Hate in the countertransference" (Winnicott, 1949). Ferenczi was amazed how powerful it was to show empathy and allowed Severn to contribute to his understanding of how to treat her. In fact, he found that until he could respond to Severn's pleas for empathy and understanding, she could (would) not come out of her therapeutic regression: "Sometimes, a bit of intelligence in the patient remains in contact with me even during the repetition of the trauma, giving me wise guidance as to how to handle the situation" (Ferenczi, 1988, p. 155, 6 July 1932 entry).

Stage 5: Analysis of countertransference and the analyst's self-disclosure

Ferenczi became defensive, unempathic, and angry when Severn first pointed out his countertransference reaction: "My reaction to this was formerly a marked increase in antipathy and the feeling of being forced into feelings (followed by corresponding inner defense)" (Ferenczi, 1988, p. 155, 6 July 1932 entry).

With continued self-scrutiny, Ferenczi reached the following conclusion, which added insight about his father role in his negative feelings towards women: "Since the more profound investigation of the causes of my sympathies and antipathies, a large share of the latter have been traced back to the infantile father and grandfather fixation with the corresponding misogyny" (Ferenczi, 1988, p. 155, 6 July 1923 entry).

When Ferenczi could reach the emotional depths of his countertransference reaction, he was now able to change his negative feelings about Severn and respond with empathy: "appreciable increase in compassion for this person [Severn] who has been tortured almost to the point of death and falsely accused in addition" (Ferenczi, 1988, p. 155, 6 July 1932 entry).

Ferenczi also analyzed his negative maternal countertransference reaction toward Severn in order to develop insight into his antipathies. He stated the countertransference issue clearly:

> The patient's demands to be loved corresponded to analogous demands on me by my mother. In actual fact and inwardly therefore, I did hate the patient, in spite of all the friendliness I displayed, this was what she was aware of, to which she reacted with the same inaccessibility that had finally forced her criminal her to renounce her. (Ferenczi, 1988, p. 99, 5 May 1932 entry)

> Reciting word for word, some-what ashamed, whatever the patient insisted upon. When I uttered these very words, exactly and word for word as requested, they often work wonders. (Ferenczi, 1988, p. 106, 12 May entry)

Stage 6: Erotic transference reaction

Ferenczi admitted he had a negative maternal transference to Severn: "in R.N. [Severn] I find my mother again, namely the real one, who was hard and energetic and of whom I am afraid. R.N. knows this, and treats me with particular gentleness" (Ferenczi, 1988, p. 45, 24 February 1932 entry).

This negative maternal transference not only triggered off antipathy towards Severn, but helped to create an emotional vulnerability that would endure throughout their relationship. Ferenczi described a very significant session of mutual analysis where he moved from his analysis of maternal transference to recovering his childhood sexual abuse. During this session, Ferenczi got a severe headache during a three-hour long period. He took Severn's advice and: "I submerged myself deeply in the reproduction of infantile experience; the most evocative image was the vague appearance of female figures, probably servant girls from earliest childhood" (Ferenczi, 1988, pp. 60–61, 17 March 1932 entry).

Ferenczi had an additional association: "[a] mad fantasy of being pressed into this wound in the corpse" (Ferenczi, 1988, p. 61, 17 March 1932 entry).

The interpretation made of these recovered memories, which Ferenczi seemed assured took place. involved childhood sexual abuse, a trauma he now realized he shared with his analysand, Severn. As his childhood sexual seduction was re-emerging, he needed to use the same empathy, understanding, and analysis he practiced with Severn and apply his trauma analysis to his own childhood trauma. The "mad fantasy" was a result of the sexual abuse by a servant girl, which he believed was not a fantasy but an actual event. He was able to analyze his childhood experience and self-disclose in the following: "a house maid probably allowed me to play with her breasts but then pressed my head between her legs. I became frightened and felt I was suffocating" (Ferenczi 1988, p. 61, 17 March 1932 entry).

These recalled memories about his childhood seduction and its negative emotional consequences set the stage for Ferenczi's next interpretation: "That is the source of my hatred of females. I want to dissect them for it, that is to kill them" (Ferenczi, 1988, p. 61, 17 March 1932 entry).

A final sequence in his countertransference was analyzing the role that his relationship with his mother played in his negative feelings toward women. The insights Ferenczi developed about his relationship to women were:

> (1) A compulsive desire to help anyone who is suffering, especially women.
>
> (2) A flight from situations in which I would have to be aggressive. This is the feeling that in fact I am a good chap, who exaggerated reactions of rage, even at trivial affronts, and finally exaggerated the reactions of guilt at the slightest lapse. (Ferenczi, 1988, p. 61, 17 March 1932 entry).

Very early in their relationship, Ferenczi reported that Severn had developed an erotic transference, which he took as a serious breach: "The misunderstanding [occurred] during the third or fourth session, when the patient made the observation, in her association, that I had said I was growing fond of her" (Ferenczi, 1988, p. 97, 5 May 1932 entry).

He became fearful and defensive. He felt falsely accused, as other analysts had been, of having made a declaration of love to their patients (Ferenczi, 1988, p. 97, 5 May 1932 entry). He was alarmed at the accusations: "I denied categorically and immediately ever having said anything of the kind, but I did not seem to be able to convince the patient" (Ferenczi, 1988, p. 97, 5 May 1932 entry).

Ferenczi found the analysis of Severn's erotic transference very difficult. Severn had apparently, begun to view Ferenczi as a perfect male (or father). By intervening with interpretations into Severn's erotic fantasies, in an attempt to reduce the intensity of the erotic feelings, Severn was shocked that Ferenczi's interpretations were intellectual. Severn insisted that there was a sexual side to her reaction that Ferenczi did not understand.

The attempt to deal vigorously with the intractability of the erotic transference began with Ferenczi's cessation of the relaxation measures he had previously introduced to help Severn repair her childhood trauma. He no longer allowed her to accompany him on vacations and the number of sessions was reduced. In essence, he reduced the intensity of the emotional and interpersonal contact between them. As the tension mounted in their relationship, Ferenczi offered Severn an interpretation that was intended to resolve the issue. *She hated him because he had not returned her erotic advance and had emotionally withdrawn from her.*

What was to occur next made analytic history. Severn corrected Ferenczi, saying *she felt he hated her*. What is more, she asserted that her analysis would never be successful *until Ferenczi analyzed his hate.* It was a struggle for Ferenczi to give into Severn's wishes: "[Severn said] her analysis would never make any progress until I allowed her to analyze those hidden feelings in me. I resisted this for approximately a year, but then I decided to make this sacrifice" (Ferenczi, 1988, p. 99, 5 May 1932 entry).

Stage 7: Emotional and behavioral changes in analysand and analyst

Ferenczi believed that intense and severe childhood trauma so damages the individual that the analysis can offer these individuals help, but perhaps not cure: "with regret [the] analysis does not offer them anymore for their lives than understanding and sympathy and only fragments of happiness" (Ferenczi, 1988, p. 156, 6 July 1932 entry).

These emotionally explosive sessions caused stress for both Severn and Ferenczi. He had the emotional courage to change to do the clinical work.

> The obstacles and amnesia in the analyst himself have delayed the emergence of an understanding (in the analyst; see her complaints about my enormous judgments), and only now, as I begin to realize my mistakes and recognize and exonerate her as an innocent and well intentioned person (I did in fact describe her in the most favorable terms). (Ferenczi, 1988, p. 158, 7 July 1932 entry)

Ferenczi believed that the changes in his own functioning would add a curative function to the analysis:

> we are approaching the possibility of fitting the fragments of her personality together and of enabling her, not only indirectly but also directly, to recognize and remember the actual fact and causes of this disintegration. Now, however, she has found someone who can show her in a convincing manner, that what she has uncovered about the analyst she must acknowledge as a distant reflection of her own suffering. (Ferenczi, 1988, pp. 158–159, 7 July 1932 entry)

After much analytic work, he reported a change in Severn's attitude toward him: "with particular gentleness: the analysis even enables her to transform her own hardness into friendly softness" (Ferenczi 1988, pp. 43–44, 24 February 1932 entry).

Severn's positive reaction to Ferenczi was not transitory. Ferenczi reported a new way of relating by Severn: "I was received with a radiant face and a conciliatory gesture: numerous apologies for having provoked and infuriated me through lack of self-control" (Ferenczi, 1988, p. 48, 6 March 1932 entry).

Ferenczi was able to use the empathic atmosphere to explore deeper levels of the Severn trauma to move the analysis toward individuation, separation and termination.

> As the final act, following "deep catharsis," I imagine a period of reconciliation and finally separation with the feeling of being

> delivered from traumatic fixation from emotions of a compulsive nature with regard to love and hate. The traumatically oriented character ceases to exist, and the other, natural aspects of the personality are able to unfold. (Ferenczi, 1988, pp. 49–50, 6 March 1932 entry).

Ferenczi reported an essential change in Severn as a result of his self-disclosure: "once I had openly admitted the limitation of my capacity, she even began to reduce her demands on me" (Ferenczi, 1988, p. 99, 5 May 1932 entry).

Ferenczi believed the changes in Severn's functioning would continue: "Then the former disintegration and consequently the tendency to project (insanity) will in fact be mutually reversed" (Ferenczi, 1988, p. 159, 19 July 1932 entry).

CHAPTER SIX

Listening to the voices of the abused

Freud's veil of denial

If one studies the history of psychoanalysis during its pioneering days, roughly from its inception in 1895 to Ferenczi's death in 1933, what becomes clear is Freud's dominance, control, and manipulation of political, personal, and professional issues. His vision of psychoanalysis was that of a movement, a political force, speaking with one voice to influence professional and public thought. Psychoanalysis was shaped into a movement by Freud's personality and the colleagues he chose to be in his inner circle. He chose "company men" and women, that is to say, individuals who would *conform* to the policies of his orthodox position (Fromm, 1959). The most dramatic example of such conformity was Ernest Jones. He contributed to the movement in several significant ways: he initiated the idea of a secret group (Society of Rings) to protect Freud from attack from the profession and the public and to pass judgment on analytic contributions from within. Jones used his position as editor of the *International Journal of Psychoanalysis* to suppress dissident viewpoints; most notably, he organized a political assassination of the life and work of Ferenczi (Rachman, 1997a, 1999a). One cannot overestimate the potency of Jones's political activity in suppressing dissident ideas or solidifying psychoanalysis as a movement. Jones was successful in his political assassination of Ferenczi, having the support of Freud and the orthodox analytic community. His false assertions that Ferenczi's innovations were a result of his madness went unchallenged by Freud's inner circle then, and now. Traditional analytic institutes did not teach Ferenczi's work during that fifty-year period (Rachman, 1997a). Freud's participation in suppressing Ferenczi's work, using his company man, Jones, as his political assassin, was not the only attempt at denial of interest in the incest trauma (Rachman, 2012d). Revisionist histories of psychoanalysis (Aron & Harris, 1993; Balint, 1968; Fromm, 1959; Grosskurth, 1991; Haynal, 1989; Masson, 1984; Rachman, 1997a,b; Roazen, 1975; Sabourin, 1985) have made a very significant contribution. They have broken the unstated taboo, and put Freud under analysis. Since Roazen's pioneering critique of Freud (Roazen, 1969), an intellectual climate has been created of alternative explanations for the orthodox analytic position. With this new viewpoint in mind, Freud's personal functioning is relevant to his intellectual and clinical rejection of Ferenczi's attempt to reinstate the theoretical and clinical link between actual childhood sexual seduction and the development of psychological disorder.

Freud's inability to accept Ferenczi's significant and visionary findings and his denunciation of his favorite son on the issue of the incest trauma can be linked to several personal considerations.

1. Freud's personal reason for the abandonment of his original seduction hypothesis can be linked to the back of integration of his own childhood sexual seduction, which he reported in his letters to Wilhelm Fliess (Freud, 1954). He openly described his incest trauma in these letters, but never used the experience to better understand the incest trauma (Rachman, 2012d).
2. Freud was acquainted with child sexual abuse in the professional reports of child abuse and murder in the newspapers. Masson (1984) reported that, while studying with Charcot, Freud performed autopsies on children who were so severely abused that they died from their wounds. What is more, reports of children missing, abused, and found dead were dramatically reported daily in Viennese newspapers during the period when Freud was training. Shortly after Freud's abandonment of the seduction

theory, he reported his first case of analysis, the case of Dora (Rachman & Mattick, 2009).

3. In a re-analysis of Freud's case, Rachman and Mattick focused on Dora's clinical symptoms, family interaction, and subjective experience (Rachman & Mattick 2012). They reached several conclusions that bear on Freud's personal and professional attitude towards sexual matters: Freud was obsessively focused on proving his newly developed oedipal theory at the expense of being attuned to the data which provided an alternative, more parsimonious, explanation for Dora's emotional problems; Dora's history clearly indicated she had a longing for maternal affection, of which Freud was aware, but chose to ignore in formulating his diagnosis and treatment plan; Herr K., the family friend, who was forty years old, married, and who attempted a sexual advance towards the fourteen-year-old Dora, was never considered as sexually harassing, or trying to molest the teenage girl. Rather, Dora was asked to analyze the proposition that her rejection of Herr K.'s grabbing and attempting to kiss her was an indication of her oedipal problem with her father. Freud seemed unaware that he might have been involved in a sexually seductive countertransference reaction. Although Freud did not mention the idea of a countertransference reaction until 1912 (Freud, 1912b,e) the experience was present in the Dora case for him to identify. Freud was forty years old (as was Herr K.) when he analyzed the teenage Dora. He bombarded her with oedipal interpretations. In a dramatic example of this interaction, he told her that her behavior of opening and closing the purse she brought to a session was an indication of symbolic masturbation. A parsimonious response might have centered on her being anxious in the presence of an older man in an analytic session, particularly where an older man was aggressively bringing her attention to confront sexual matters. Freud mentioned that he could have responded to Dora's need for tenderness (mothering), but this kind of response would not have been analytically appropriate. Freud suffered from his own confusion of tongues, being unaware his analytic zeal was emotionally seductive and traumatizing (Rachman & Mattick, 2012).

4. Freud's analysis of his daughter, Anna, was an indication of emotional blindness to the serious pitfalls of such an endeavor,

and massive denial of the emotional seduction of one's child (Rachman, 2003b). It might have been an indication of affection that Freud wished to analyze his daughter, giving her the precious gift of his intellectual mind. But, the wish to analyze should not have become a reality. Freud was blind to the emotional seduction of analyzing his own daughter's oedipal (sexual) feelings and thoughts about one's father, when the father is one's analyst.

5. Freud's moralistic and mean-spirited behavior towards Ferenczi over their disagreements about Ferenczi's confusion of tongues theory and relaxation therapy was not justified on intellectual or professional grounds. Freud dismissed the confusion of tongues theory as showing regressive tendencies, returning psychoanalysis to the seduction theory, long abandoned. What Freud was unable to see was that Ferenczi extended his original findings to elaborate a theoretical structure that detailed the way incest produces arrested development. Rather than a regression, Ferenczi's theory was visionary (Rachman, 1993a, 2000, 2003a, 2007a).
6. Freud's criticisms of Ferenczi's relaxation therapy, as evidenced by the already discussed "kissing letter" (Jones, 1957), contained moralistic and false accusations of sexual conduct by Ferenczi. Freud confused Ferenczi's reparative therapeutic experiences through empathy for sexuality (Rachman, 1998b).
7. Finally, Freud's refusal to shake his best friend's hand and bid him adieu at their last meeting was a mean-spirited retaliation for Ferenczi's desire to present his "Confusion of tongues" paper (Fromm, 1959).

Lifting the veil of denial

In the twenty-first century, as we can now look back at the changes in the social/psychological climate for incest, it is clear that a significant shift has occurred in the professionals' and in the public's capacity to be aware of, and confront, the incest trauma. In fact, the incest survivor's peer movement can be said to have led the way in lifting the veil of denial regarding the occurrence of incest in family interaction. In particular, the women's movement rape victims and (survivors) of childhood incest have found their voices. Women are abused in a much higher proportion than men (Herman, 1981), and have been significantly helped to give voice and publicly disclose their real experiences of childhood seduction and adult sexual trauma. Judith Herman (1992), one of the most respected voices in the study of women's sexual trauma, welcomed the new emphasis on identifying the reality of actual sexual abuse in women's lives.

Herman makes several significant points regarding the new climate for disclosure. The change in the emotional climate when women are self-disclosing their childhood incest now prevents the abuser from maintaining silence and committing the crime without detection. Such confessions by the abused force church, school, and state to confront the issue of child abuse in their institutions.

As we have discussed in Chapter Four, Ferenczi was the first psychoanalyst to discuss the negative dynamic of blaming the child for the incestuous experience in his confusion of tongues paradigm of trauma. Influenced by the oedipal complex, analysts, parents, authorities, and social institutions suggested that *the child's sexuality seduced the adult. In actuality, it is the adult's sexuality that is at issue.* Adults, mostly family members, project their unresolved sexual needs on to the innocent longings of their children for tenderness and affection. An interesting point can be made about incestuous behavior by the adult seducer. Because the child partner is extremely vulnerable, in a position of unequal power, status, and control, the adult seducer does not have to cope with the difficulties of an adult relationship. He/she literally seduces an innocent. The male molester does not have to work through the emotional difficulties in initiating and sustaining a relationship with another adult who is his peer. These issues of power, control, and status are at the heart of what Ferenczi described in his "identification with the aggressor" (IWA) concept (Ferenczi, 1933) (also see Chapter Four). It is the psychological dynamic that allows for the seduction, as well as the explanation for the child continuing in the abusive experience. Seducing a child, as has been pointed out, is a step beyond pathologic narcissism. Miller (1986) described this situation clearly as the incestuous experience between child and adult. Incest is a grotesque act by an adult on the physical and psychological body of a child. It is an act so perverted that it robs the child of the capacity to think, feel, and behave. But the incest trauma also produces an unholy alliance between the abuser and the child.

Ferenczi's description of the psychopathologic adaptive mechanisms of IWA suggested that adult–child sexuality is psychologically damaging. Ferenczi's extensive clinical experience indicated that psychological damage can occur without actual sexual contact. Ferenczi described nakedness as a means of inspiring terror, as in an example of severe disturbance in a mother–son seduction (Ferenczi, 1980n). This mother produced panic in her son by undressing in front of him. He was flooded with feelings, overwhelming his vulnerable sense of self. As in the description of actual sexual contact, Ferenczi pointed out, this kind of behavior toward a child contains hostility. Balint (1968) also discussed the rage a parent can express in his/her unempathetic behavior to a child.

The voice of the abused

No form of intellectual debate can convince skeptics in the academic or psychotherapeutic communities of the efficacy of retrieving memories of childhood molestation and abuse because their definition of science, which relied on empiricism via experimentation, will devalue phenomenology. In fact, intellectual arguments have validity. Any thoughtful clinician must acknowledge the efficacy of two fundamental arguments. The first set of data that is convincing is that studies of memory do leave open to some question the veracity of recall of childhood abuse (Loftus, 1979, 1991; Loftus & Ketcham, 1991, 1994; Loftus & Loftus, 1976).

Secondarily, we must also acknowledge that inexperienced, inadequately trained, overzealous, or sociopathic therapists have inappropriately encouraged recall of early childhood memories, when it certainly would have been empathic and better technique if they would have allowed the individual to set the style, pace, and content of the therapeutic process. We have been concerned with the issue of what constitutes empathic therapeutic activity for some time now, attempting to integrate the most innovative contributions in our field, while being ever cognizant of the necessity to have any intervention based on empathy, democratic principles, and a concern for intrusion, control, manipulation, or coercion (Rachman, 1975a, 1981, 1988a, 1991a, 1997a, 2003a, 2012a, 2014d).

We believe the only way to charter a meaningful therapeutic course in the treatment of trauma, including sexual, molestation, is to pay serious attention not only to academics and dissenting clinicians, but *to hear the voice of the abused*. In the history of the field of psychotherapy, the controversy between Freud's and Ferenczi's ideas about the existence of trauma disorder was the first such debate (Rachman, 1997a,b). Freud began a series of mean-spirited attacks on Ferenczi's technical innovation of relaxation therapy when he felt his once-favorite student was experimenting with a change in the standard procedure to cure neurosis. First, the criticisms were in the form of intellectual arguments that intended to point out Ferenczi's lack of understanding of the classical technique for analytic practice (Jones, 1957; Grünberger, 1984), but then it became a personal issue when Freud criticized Ferenczi's personal and professional functioning (Fromm, 1959; Masson, 1984; Rachman, 1997a,b, Roazen, 1975). One of the fundamental issues that fueled this debate was the difference in their patient populations and, subsequently, their ideas on treatment (Rachman, 2003a, 2012g). By the time Ferenczi had developed his new methodology to deal with treating incest survivors, Freud's practice was almost exclusively psychiatrists, psychologists, and other mental health professionals looking for training from the Master. Freud had long abandoned his experiences with incest survivors and his earlier ideas about the traumatic origins of neurosis (Masson, 1984).

When a truly poignant and thoughtful account comes into print by a survivor of trauma, we believe the efficacy of listening attentively to the analysand helps to focus the debate in a meaningful way. One such recent account is the touching story of a woman who had suffered from multiple personality disorder (Mason, 1997). Laura Emily Mason (a pseudonym) recounts her lifetime struggle to survive the lasting effects of emotional and physical abuse primarily by her father (and her mother as well). Her experiences of cruelty by her father in his attempt to shape her behavior as if she were a bonsai tree include: "He was intent on molding me to his vision of complete self-reliance with the patience of a horticulturist shaping a bonsai tree, knowing it would take years to painstakingly twist it into crippled perfection" (Mason, 1997, p. 45).

In what can be a typical scenario for a trauma survivor, Laura escaped the physical abuse (which she could not control): "by becoming divided internally . . ."; living a life as if she were free of "the fear, anger, humiliation and helplessness . . ." (p. 45). Different selves emerged as Laura grew older, emerging into awareness, speaking and acting differently. She could make no sense of her internal chaos until:

> One summer evening in 1988 I was wandering the aisles of a video store, picking up one empty box after another. Nothing grabbed me. Then I saw *Sybil*. I don't know what made me decide to rent it, but as soon as I watched it, I knew. I was 46 years old, and things made sense for the first time. (Mason, 1997, p. 47)

After viewing *Sybil*, Laura began searching for information about multiple personality disorder (MPD). She found two publications that helped her understand her disorder; a book by a professional, Frank Putnam's *Diagnosis and Treatment of Multiple Personality Disorder* (1989) and a self-help publication, *Many Voices*. These publications and a support group for people with MPD helped Laura begin a process that helped solve the mystery of all the split-off inner selves. She realized that the fragmentation of the self that was necessary to psychological survival as an abused child was not viable as an adult:

> . . . problems arise because some of us continue to react with patterns of behavior that remain frozen in the past. Harmless situations trigger flashbacks and sudden switches . . . If a man inadvertently blocks my way in a D'Agostino aisle, a child pops out and freezes with fear . . . and we fly home, muttering, "Goddammed fucking son of a bitch!" . . . Anyone hearing us scream, curse, rant and rave would be surprised to look in and see only one person—one body in our apartment. (Mason, 1997, p. 48)

On the basis of the principle of mutuality that we have extracted from Ferenczi's work (1988), we are interested in being informed by the analysand as to what ideas and methods are meaningful for their therapy (Rachman, 2000, 2004, 2012a). Laura, after years of searching for understanding and healing of MPD said the following:

> Becoming free of my no-longer-needed divisions is difficult. MPD is not an organic disease; it can't be cured with drugs. Long and intensive psychotherapy is the only known cure. Each part must re-experience its own individual trauma, sometimes with the intensity of the original events, then must come to know and feel what other parts know and feel. This work takes a great deal of strength and commitment on the part of the patient as well as much skill, compassion, and patience on the part of the therapist. (Mason, 1997, p. 48)

Laura's statements about the curative process should also add a meaningful perspective to the false memory debate:

> The literature defines a cure as integration—the repeated merging of one personality with another until only one remains. There are many steps along the way. The first is building trust. Multiples have been betrayed by people they should have been able to count on, and they constantly trust their therapists.
>
> Next comes the recovery of memories. In theory, once a memory is recovered, the personality that held it will no longer be tortured by it. The false-memory-syndrome movement claims that some therapists implant memories in their patients, causing them to unjustly accuse their parents of abuse. That may happen occasionally, but I believe most therapists follow their patient's lead and don't make suggestions. There are also people who question the accuracy of memories. It's not always easy to know whether something I remember happened exactly the way I remember it. But therapy isn't a court of law, where the goal is to establish facts. Therapy aims for emotional healing, and for that, emotional truth is what matters. (Mason, 1997, p. 49)

The present more open and self-revelatory emotional climate can produce significant positive results in encouraging recovery from sexual trauma, which is illustrated in another publicized case. An educator was apprehended for making obscene phone calls. First, an explosion in the media chronicled his public disgrace, then, in his own book, the ex-president of an American university, Richard Berendzen, revealed the psychodynamic behind his compulsion to make obscene phone calls to women with whom he could talk about having sex with children (Berendzen & Palmer, 1993). Berendzen revealed that he was forced to have sex with his mother, from 6–12 years old, with his father's awareness. His mother was obsessed with her son and was institutionalized for emotional illness. He felt he was his mother's passion and her prey.

The climate of exposure of the incest trauma has also been the subject of fiction. The main subject is someone who has been sexually abused by both her parents. The mother fondled and humiliated her. The father repeatedly raped her. The individual spent her childhood serving as the model for her famous photographer father (Harrison, 1993). In his photographs, she appeared nude, sometimes mutilated, sometimes pretending to be dead. The father's work received critical acclaim, but she leaves childhood feeling as if her father has stolen her soul. In treatment, she tries to come to terms with years of childhood abuse. The description of the abusive sexual experience is akin to the experience of an emotional holocaust in the family interaction where she felt her soul had been taken away from her (Shengold, 1989).

There is a motion picture, entitled *Henry Fool* (Hartley, 1997; Maslin, 1998), which is a low-budget art film made in New York City. It is a film that has received critical acclaim for the writing, cinema-photography, acting, and story. The central character, Henry Fool, appears to represent a failed hero, someone who has the capacity to inspire others to change their lives, but cannot make the necessary changes to conquer his own demons of alcohol addiction, pedophilia, laziness, slovenliness, and career failure. He had exceptional intelligence. One of the (minor) subplots of the movie is the theme of incest, which appears in two different currents intersecting in the life of Henry Fool. Our hero had served a seven-year jail term for molesting a thirteen-year-old girl. His parole officer becomes a shadowy figure in the movie, reminding him, in a gentle but persistent way, to pursue getting a job, stop drinking, and conquer his desire to have sex with minors. (The kindly parole officer is like a gentle superego, urging the traumatized self to grow through the trauma towards self-actualization.) Although there are moments when Henry Fool (an apt designation for a flawed hero) seems transfixed on the form of innocent beauty, he never seems ready to break the incest taboo again. He reserves his active libido for a legally aged girlfriend and her mother. He does have sex with the girl and her mother. Although the incest theme is veiled rather than overt, it is clearly evident (Maslin, 1998).

The most influential book of the incest survivor's movement has been *The Courage to Heal*, by Bass and Davis (1988). We can readily agree with some of the criticisms of the book, which has clearly become the bible of the incest survivors' movement. Wakefield and Underwager (1992) wrote of lawsuits arising from recovered memories of alleged sexual abuse. *The Courage to Heal* has questionable ideas, such as encouraging survivors to file lawsuits against the alleged perpetrators in order to work through the recovery process. There is also a lack of skepticism regarding certain allegations of abuse, blanket acceptance of all reported retrieval incest memories, lack of criticism for invasive, intrusive, and manipulative therapeutic interventions which might seriously contaminate the process of retrieval and recall, and no questioning of the veracity of ritualistic abuse, murder, sacrifice, and reported cult behavior. An analysand incest survivor also verified a suspicion we had gathered from reading the book. She strongly felt there was a decided lesbian/feminist theme, which hints at women turning to women for all their emotional, interpersonal and sexual needs. But, despite these shortcomings, *The Courage to Heal* has made a positive contribution to the treatment of incest survivors. In our clinical experience, many incest survivors suffer from intense ambivalence about whether they have had childhood sexual trauma. On the one hand, they have a sixth sense that something bad, dark, disturbing, or disgusting might have happened to them during their childhood. Some describe these feelings as if a dark cloud is hanging over his/her head. Others experience depression anxiety and confusion of unknown origin. In almost every instance, however, when an incest memory, somatic experience, flashback, obsessive thought, disturbing sexual fantasy, or dream appears during the uncovering process, there is a questioning by the individual of its veracity. Often, an individual has said the following: "How do I know I didn't make this up? Maybe, I thought this to please you"; "I don't want to accuse anyone of anything, if I'm not sure"; "I must be crazy to have these thoughts, no one would have done this to me."

Without trying to convince the individual, especially at a time of intense ambivalence, we have recommended bibliotherapy. There is a need, at a time like this, to recommend material, written in a non-technical, informed manner from the subjective experience of the survivor. We originally became interested in *The Courage To Heal* when it was repeatedly recommended by several incest survivors. In every instance, where we have recommended it to an analysand, there has been a positive response, ranging from reducing anxiety and ambivalence to verification of incest experiences. Such positive response has been forthcoming from survivors who themselves were counselors, therapists, and analysts, as well as those who did not have a mental health background. We believe these endorsements by incest survivors, some of whom are mental health professionals, can be viewed as positive subjective data.

On the other hand, those of us who work extensively with trauma survivors feel the debate over recovered memories in scientific journals and the mass media has been destructive. Academics, overzealous critics of psychotherapy and psychoanalysis, self-appointed social critics, as well as uninformed clinicians, have created a social atmosphere of retraumatization for incest survivors. Re-evoking the veil of denial recreates for incest survivors the blame-the-child experiences of their original trauma. In analytic sessions, survivors have expressed their despair that the social system, once again, will not believe the abuse they suffered. It is clear to those of us who work with trauma survivors that they need an empathic emotional and interpersonal social climate, so that they can uncover the experiences and feelings connected to their incest.

If incest survivors cannot gain this support in the social system, they should be able to have this necessary empathic experience with their psychoanalyst or psychotherapist. A thoughtful assessment of this has been offered by Grossman (1997):

> Some therapists are not sufficiently knowledgeable or are too driven by their own agendas to respect a client's own recovery process. These therapists can influence clients to believe that fictitious events actually happened, or that real events did not happen.
>
> On the other hand, many psychotherapists are well trained and informed, and do assist clients to recover memories safely and accurately, which can dramatically help their healing. Such treatment is extremely beneficial to many trauma survivors, although others may not be pleased with the results. (p. 75)

CHAPTER SEVEN

Incest trauma, psychoanalysis, and the brain

When a young child wakes up screaming from a nightmare, it usually is the parent who comforts her, but what happens to the child whose nightmare is a recurrent distressing dream of the replay of sexual abuse by one's own father? Delayed and chronic post traumatic symptoms have been described in adult incest victims (Albach & Everaerd, 1992).

Sándor Ferenczi's confusion of tongues paradigm is instrumental for helping make sense of how a child survives such a disorganizing experience. He states:

> These children feel physically and morally helpless, their personalities are not sufficiently consolidated in order to be able to protest, even if only in thought, for the overpowering force and authority of the adult makes them dumb and can rob them of their senses. The same anxiety, however, if it reaches a certain maximum, compels them to subordinate themselves like automata to the will of the aggressor, to divine each one of his desires and to gratify these; completely oblivious of themselves they identify themselves with the aggressor. Through the identification, or let us say, introjection of the aggressor, he disappears as part of the external reality, and becomes intra- instead of extra-psychic; the intra-psychic is then subjected, in a dream-like state as is

> the traumatic trance, to the primary process, i.e. according to the pleasure principle it can be modified or changed by use of positive or negative hallucinations. In any case the attack as a rigid external reality ceases to exist and in the traumatic trance the child succeeds in maintaining the previous situation of tenderness.
>
> The most important change, produced in the mind of the child by the anxiety-fear-ridden identification with the adult partner, is the introjection of the guilt feelings of the adult which makes hitherto harmless play appear as a punishable offence. When the child recovers from such an attack, he feels enormously confused, in fact, split—innocent and culpable at the same time—and his confidence in the testimony of his own senses is broken. (Ferenczi, 1980n, p. 162)

A century ago, Ferenczi reported that incest trauma contributes to personality disorders, emotional disturbances, and the development of psychopathology, which we have demonstrated in case illustrations throughout this book. In the twenty-first century, technical advances aid neuroscience researchers, and have provided further proof of the pervasive neurobiological effects of cumulative trauma on the brain, the central nervous system, and the physiological systems of the body. It is vital for psychoanalysts to have a full understanding of the shattering aftermath of trauma. For example, Cozolino (2002c) discovered that "chronic high levels of stress release surges of cortizol and compromise hippocampus functioning which decreases the brain's ability to control amygdala functioning and increases emotional dysregulation" (p. 282). Further studies indicated that "self harm during dysregulated states results in endorphin release and a sense of calm which puts these individuals at risk for repeated self-abusive behaviour" (p. 282).

Bryer and colleagues (1987), Herman (1986), and Landecker (1992) discovered that most patients with borderline personality disorders (BPD) have been physically and sexually abused. According to Bryer, "the incidence of child abuse among persons with BPD is significantly greater than other diagnoses" (p. 1429). A connection between self-injurious behaviors and histories of sexual abuse was discovered by Bryer and colleagues (1987); Herman (1986), Anderson (1981), Carroll and colleagues (1980), and Greenspan and Samuel (1989). The amygdalae of patients found to have early exposure to trauma were smaller in size compared to the normal brain (Weniger et al., 2009).

Schore (2001, 2003) explored the traumatic impact of disrupted attachment by reviewing studies of infants separated from their mothers in hospitals and residential treatment centers; he linked the construction of defenses such as dissociation, numbing, and an impoverished affect to Bowlby's (1969) attachment theory. These infants were observed to cry in a state of extreme hyperarousal; when neglected and not responded to, they gave up by withdrawing inward and progressing into a dissociated state. Perry and colleagues (1995) find that dissociation and hyperarousal states are on a continuum. Cutting and eating disorders are means often used to regulate these intolerable affective states.

Cozolino (2002a) also speaks about the brain's plasticity and the benefits of relational psychotherapy; he writes that

> language, in combination with emotional attunement is a central tool in the therapeutic process; it creates the opportunity to blend words with feelings, providing a means of neural growth and neural network integration. (p. 210).

He reports that

> The therapist must provide an external scaffolding within which the patient can rebuild these brain networks of memory, self-organization, and affect regulation; on another level, the therapist serves as an external neural circuit to aid in the integration of networks left unintegrated during development. (2002c, p. 283)

Based on this current neuroscience research, its link to the attachment theory and the aftermath of trauma, we believe a contemporary relational approach informed by the Budapest School of Psychoanalysis is effective in treating patients suffering from a wide range of dissociative patterns. The application of this theory can be seen through the case of Laura.

The case of Laura

This case illuminates the impact of cumulative trauma on one's sense of self and self in relationships. Traumatic episodes have contributed to the development of Laura's personality disorder consisting of obsessive, compulsive, narcissistic, borderline, and paranoid features. Laura suffers from chronic PTSD and dysthymia with masochistic features. In order to survive multiple onslaughts from both parents, Laura constructed a wide range of dissociative patterns consisting of denial, splitting, neuro-genic amnesia, numbing, dissociation, hyper-arousal and panic attacks.

Laura walked slowly and gracefully into my office for the first time with an air of confidence. She was dressed in a tailored black pantsuit with a white silk V-neck sweater. Her perfect posture gave her the appearance of being taller than her 5′4″. At twenty-six, with high cheekbones, fair porcelain-like skin, and shiny chin-length reddish-brown hair, she resembled a famous model. Her tense, fixed smile betrayed her palpable anxiety as she looked around the room and asked where to sit. Once seated, she looked directly at me with huge green eyes, filled with deep sadness. I was struck by the juxtaposition between the aloof air of confidence she portrayed as she entered my office and her sad anxious affect. She sat in a stiff position on the edge of her chair and began cautiously explaining, in a self-protective manner, that it was important for her to understand what she was getting into before she began. I felt compassionate toward her and attempted to put her at ease, realizing how difficult this encounter was and the courage required of her to pursue treatment, and responded by commenting that therapy was a mutual agreement between us, whereby we work together at a comfortable pace to explore her thoughts and feelings, past and present, in order to increase her self-awareness and gain understanding of how her past may contribute to her present problems. I then asked, "What brings you into therapy at this time?" She spoke about her most recent attempts at a relationship with a good friend, which suddenly failed once it shifted to a more intimate stage. She became choked up as she explained that she became uncomfortable around him and that she could no longer be herself.

L. "I don't know what happens; I either talk too much or clam up. I become so anxious that I cannot think, I freeze/feel paralyzed. I edit my thought to the degree where it interferes with my ability to speak."

A. (listens attentively and looks questioningly) "I wonder if you have any thoughts on what creates the shift?"

L. (silent for a few seconds) "I become self-conscious, worrying if I talk too much, speak too quickly or if I laugh too loudly; it seems that I am always double checking myself, then I feel inadequate and humiliated."

A. Nods.

L. "I am almost twenty-six years old and I just cannot go on like this; I want to get married and have children someday. I long so much for an intimate relationship but I am also terrified of it" (she shrugs her shoulders, tears streaming down her face) (Klett, 2014).

Her relationship to both parents and her brother

Laura describes her mother as a young parent, unpredictable, impatient, without boundaries and easy to anger. She reported that her mother often complained that she was difficult to soothe, a sensitive child allergic to milk. Laura recollected stories that she vomited often due to this undiagnosed allergy to milk and at one time, as an infant, she lost quite a bit of weight.

She spoke of her brother as being similar to her mother, somewhat sadistic, tickling her until she laughed hysterically and then unexpectedly smacking her across the face until she cried. She described him as enjoying having control over her emotional state. Laura's tone changed when she spoke about her father. Her face lit up as she referred to him as a "happy drunk," affectionate and playful. The juxtaposition between bad mother and good father was extreme (Fairbairn, 1954). Laura teared up as she spoke of her mother divorcing her father when she was twelve years old, stating that she felt as if he abandoned and divorced her.

I created a safe and secure environment by being a reliable, consistent, attentive, responsive, and durable object. I developed a maternal countertransference toward Laura which I carefully monitored in order to prevent an enactment: Vigilant not to impinge upon her, cautious not to repeat an early environmental failure or to become overprotective and also mindful of Ferenczi's (1980n) concept of "wise baby" (p. 165), understanding the patient's hypervigilance to the therapist's needs, which guided careful listening to her nuance-implicit communications (Klett, 2014). Throughout the first year of treatment, Laura used intellectualization and isolation of affect as a defense. Her needs for a good maternal object and mirroring manifested themselves as her exhibitionist desires emerged. She would constantly bring in examples of her work, letters, and pictures, displaying a need to be seen as special and to engage me while also keeping me at a distance. I was flexible, engaged in this activity, and meeting Laura where she was, without colluding with her, realizing that this was not just resistance, but something more. Our working alliance developed into a strong and positive one. She needed to see the analyst as the ideal object and also for her analyst to only see the good parts of her. The importance of understanding her internal and external splits, resulting from severe trauma, was evident throughout our work and my need to respect and understand them in order to provide some sense of safety and predictability was necessary in order to form an attachment (Klein, M., 1935). In staying closely attuned to Laura throughout the first year of treatment and in recognizing and providing her self-object needs for mirroring, idealizing, and twinship, which, according to Kohut (1971), reactivates thwarted developmental needs of the self, Laura's ego strengthened and trust between us deepened. Her anxious and hypervigilant states no longer blocked our work, defenses softened, and she was beginning to listen to, and to trust, herself.

In the second year of treatment, I noticed a shift from earlier sessions in that Laura was now beginning to discuss her observations of her emotional life. She became less reliant on isolation of affect and intellectualizations.

I shall bring you into the first session in which Laura gained access to memories and her connection to her feelings regarding a life-threatening experience when being physically abused by her mother. Within this session, she precisely explains the dissociative process of depersonalization, the function of this defense, and how it helped her to survive at the age of twelve. In speaking of this episode, Laura was able to connect to her dissociated feelings of terror and to process them for the first time.

Within this session, I (analyst) demonstrate the use of empathic attunement to the patient's implicit communications which was vital in facilitating safety, in reaching the split off parts of the self, and loosening the defenses to mobilize frozen experiences so that they could be metabolized and integrated into a cohesive sense of self. It would not have been possible for me to enter into areas of severe trauma without first forming a secure attachment with Laura, otherwise, I would have placed her at risk for retraumatization.

> Laura begins the session. "When my mother left my father, I was angry and became defiant."

L: "My mother told me to clean the dishes. I said no and challenged her, standing up to her, not giving in, not responding to her screaming. I believed that if I acted unafraid, she would back down. She looked at me with rage and hatred in her eyes. I just left my body as she put a knife to my throat and pushed me against the window pane. My brother entered the room and screamed causing her to regain self-control. She ran out of the house. I did not feel any pain until the next morning when my throat was scratched, and my head hurt. I then discovered a large lump on the back of my head. I was the victor, for my mother could not beat me into submission or take my spirit or soul away, as long as I did not exist."

A: "As long as you did not exist . . ."

L: "You should have seen the rage and hatred in her eyes." She sobbed, "My mother would have killed me." (Her tone increases.) "She would have killed me." (Her face is pale. She takes a deep breath. She realized how close she came to death.) "If my brother did not walk into the room . . ." (Her face turns white, an expression of a shocking realization spoken for the first time.) (Klett, 2014).

Within this session, Laura connects to her lost self as a result of my comfort with, and acceptance of, her silence and of her not knowing. With encouragement to trust and to stay with the feelings, both Laura and I listened to the silence, which enabled her to find her voice and to release feelings of intolerable pain. I believe that her secure attachment with me has provided a container for previously unmanageable affects.

Laura allowed me to enter her experience and to gain understanding of the function of self-mutilation, through projective identification, whereby I came to grasp the physiological effect of trauma. In the following session, Laura showed me scars on her arms and spoke about a desire to cut. She stated that she did not know how to describe what she was feeling. I encouraged her to just stay with the feelings and said that words are not always necessary. I continued to encourage Laura to stay with her feelings and to notice any feelings in her body. After a few minutes passed, she began crying uncontrollably. The intensity of her pain was immense. I felt that she would be all right. I was in this with her, not interfering with words or interpretations or making efforts to rescue her, but staying very closely attuned and connected. Laura's facial expression was one of great despair, which shifted to horror, then fear. She stayed with overwhelming emotions, her whole body shook and she continued to sob. She then said, "There is such an emptiness, a core sense of emptiness, a dark abyss." (Her facial expression indicated she was horrified and lost.) I sat with her through these intense feelings. An atypical feeling came over the me, as I suddenly had a strong desire for relief. I believed that Laura split off her impulse to cut herself and projected it into me through a typical primitive defense of projective identification. Laura continued: "I do not have any sense of who I am, other than one who takes care of others' needs or for my career and academic achievements." This was a part of who she was and the only part she knew. She reached for, and became aware of, her true self in this session, as I reminded her that the self does exist, as I just heard her voice, and explained that it will need nourishment and safety to continue to grow (Klett, 2014). (See Winnicott, 1960 for the false self; Ferenczi, 1980n for the wise baby; Miller, 1979 for the gifted child; Brandchaft et al., 2010 for pathological accommodation.)

We now move on to another vignette which provides me with the opportunity to highlight the use of a dream as a transitional space, allowing safety for Laura to recall and to re-experience sexual abuse. However, this time, she showed renewed strength and resilience as demonstrated through her associations to her dream through which she expressed and connected to her murderous rage for the first time and gave voice to her childhood longings through co-constructed dream interpretation.

L: "I had a dream, I was back at a party when I was thirteen and a half years old. It felt more as if I was reliving this experience, rather than a dream. I was with the seventeen-year-old male, Eric. I could feel his breath, the heaviness of his body weight, the smell of Old Spice cologne and the whiskey on his breath. But, this time things were different, I was not as frightened. I was more angry. I forced him off of me. I picked up a high-heel shoe and kept hitting him over the head. His head was bleeding and he fell to the floor. I was afraid that he may get up, so I hit him some more until he lay motionless. Hours later, I discovered that he was dead. The police came and this incident was in the newspapers." As Laura had her hand on the doorknob, she added, "Oh yes, one more thing, it happened in Susan's room."

A: (replies questioningly) "In Susan's room?" As Laura was leaving the office, she replied, "Susan was a writer and she was accused of his death."

The following week, we continued to associate to her dream. Within this dream, murderous rage surfaced and Laura was able to talk about her anger for the first time. She also began to express her longings for me to protect her, as well as her anger at me for releasing her murderous rage. What is more, she realized that her worst fear was being like her mother, becoming her mother.

A: I asked, "Is there anything else?" Laura reported that she felt different this time because she was able to hold on to herself and not to submit to another's will. Submission forced her into something for which she was not ready. She had a mixture of feelings, those of shame, guilt, curiosity and power. She discovered she could easily control and please men through sex, and this power over them soon turned into contempt.

A: (nodded) . . . I followed up by asking what she thought of this crime taking place in Susan's room. She could not think of anything, but she knows someone by the name of Susan. I mentioned that in dreams, one person may represent many and spoke of note-taking when Laura and I are together in my room, as I always note dreams verbatim (Klett, 2014).

(I tolerated her unconscious anger and did not interpret it further, in the transference within the dream). Laura then raised her voice.

L: "I am angry, I am angry that this has happened to me. It changed my life, in one moment I lost my innocence." (She also talked about her relationship with men and how when the relationship became intimate, during sex she would have panic attacks. She then recalled that this acute anxiety was the feeling that she would have when she woke up from the nightmares as a child.)

I reflected on Cozolino's definition of a panic attack as an intense physiological and emotional experience which occurs in the absence of real danger. He finds that panic attacks are often triggered by stress or other conflicts in the sufferer's life, but he or she seldom makes the connection between these events and panic attack. The associations are contained within hidden neural layers. They are experienced as "coming out of the blue" leaving the victim to struggle to comprehend what is happening and why (2002b, p. 243)

A: "Can you tell me about your nightmares?"

L: "I was always being chased by a monster who would transform into my father. I would wake up screaming with my heart racing and drenched in sweat, my father would come in to comfort me. In the dream I was running from him, it was fuzzy . . . I was horrified, I could not get away, now he was here, but he was here to comfort me, I was confused, possibly I wanted him."

Laura needed to see her father as the good object; he was the caretaker in the family. Now, she realized that he exploited her. His impulsive narcissistic passions were difficult to accept. She now recalled that Old Spice was the cologne he wore, surely, not the seventeen-year-old boy, his breath smelled of whiskey, while Eric, the boy, her brother's friend, drank beer. She was revictimized and her brother told her it was her fault as she was at a party (aged thirteen) with his friends, seventeen-year-old boys, whom she was kissing. While Laura thought she was first sexually abused at this party, uncovering and processing this abuse led to the uncovering of childhood incest.

Laura was silent, in a daydream-like state, and then she began to speak.

L: "I just had this vision, of my father now with his head split open and with a glass of Wild Turkey in his open hand, half full, I, as my adult self, walked up to him and drank it, not feeling a thing, needing to remain numb." She cried and recalled her adolescent years when he left and she need to numb herself.

L: "I lost all the years when my father left. I began drinking, hanging out with an older crowd. I became promiscuous, began cutting and developed an eating disorder."

We processed and worked through Laura's acting out. She came to understand how, in longing for her father, she numbed herself through drinking, promiscuity, cutting to feel alive, and at times to ease overwhelming emotions. She described her eating disorder as a form of control over her body, the only thing that she felt she had control over in her life at this time. She came to understand her injurious behaviors as a need to remain attached to and identified with the aggressors, both parents. Her memories were too traumatic to be processed and became somatic memories; many authors report that "the body keeps the score and becomes the storehouse for abusive experiences."

Farber's research (2002) resonates with Laura's experience when she notes that: "eating disorders and acts of self harm are the result of traumatic disruption of attachment, as well as impairment in attachment to internalized objects," she also reports

> that lack of secure attachments may lead to eating disorders characterized by insatiable hunger or yearning. Self harm is also characterized by painful attempts to enliven a deadened or depressed self. Attachment to suffering is both the cause and the result of self harm, and represents an attachment to early experiences of neglect, abuse and trauma. (p. 42)

In a similar vein, Shapiro and Dominiak (1992, p. 39) and Ferenczi (1980n) describe this defense as a means by which the victim gains mastery over previous experiences of learned helplessness by "identification with the aggressor" (p. 162). Laura demonstrates a harsh and often sadistic superego, which indicates an early identification with her mother. Her negative introject inflicted punishment and pain. Nusbaum (2000) finds that the patient protects the loved parent through defenses of idealization and denial and turns her anger inward toward the self (p. 300); this precisely captures Laura's relationship to her father. Howell (1997) concurs; she states, "this form of masochism adaptively preserves attachments" (p. 241). Laura's acting out behavior throughout ages 13–17 in relation to her internalized objects would be indicative of her separation–individuation difficulties, which, according to Mahler (1963), are revisited during adolescence.

Only after reaching Laura and facilitating her expression of unarticulated experience was she able to give voice to the complexity of her relational experience of cumulative traumas. She now was able to separate without a fear of disappearing and she relinquished her need to identify with the aggressor. Laura's relationships outside of treatment changed. She began a relationship with a stable, healthy male. There was a reduction in her repetition compulsion to draw men to her who were projects, whereby she maintained her familial stance as the caretaker, leaving her to feel needed and in control, only later to be filled with resentment and to feel neglected and drained. This type of male relationship no longer interested or appealed to her. She relinquished masochistic suffering as she achieved a healthy separation–individuation.

Discussion

The concepts in this chapter are informed by neuroscience research, attachment theory, and a contemporary relational psychoanalytic approach strongly influenced by Sándor Ferenczi, specifically regarding the incest trauma, identification with the aggressor, the significance of empathy, the confusion of tongues trauma theory, countertransference, and a two-person psychology.

The profound impact of trauma on the body, brain, self, and self in relationships has been evident in the analysis with Laura. The splits in her ego, the fragmentation and shattering of the self, and the disruption to her development were astonishing. Cozolino (2002c) finds that

> the impact of trauma depends on a complex interaction of the physical and psychological stages of development during which it occurs, the length and degree of the trauma and presence of vulnerabilities or past traumas. (p. 263)

Cozolino discovered the negative impact of long term stress on the brain results from the impact of early bonding failures (p. 282). His research regarding neural plasticity and the effectiveness of working from a relational approach to rebuild brain structure confirmed my experience of the necessity of using this approach for effective treatment of complex relational trauma and, most importantly, for working through the transference.

Throughout the course of the first year of Laura's therapy, a transference surfaced which became a central and ongoing theme related to Laura's fear of dependency on me, together with her concerns regarding my ability to tolerate her neediness and handle her intense affective states. She feared that she might have a breakdown. She also had concerns over my seeing her as imperfect, the bad object. She worried that I could arouse her anger at her mother and cause a break in their relationship. Through exploration of this transference, Laura became aware of her profound difficulty with trusting and an acute fear of losing control. She also realized that she was projecting her defense of splitting on to me. I often reminded her that examining the less than perfect aspects of a person does not contaminate their good qualities. Laura was able to make a connection to her early relationships and understood the transference which she articulated as follows: "I am afraid of overwhelming you, of being a burden, my mother always complained that I expected too much and I was too needy."

The transference shifted over time. Later on in the treatment, when I returned from a two-week vacation, Laura came into the session and an intense, negative, primitive transference surfaced. She was very angry and wanted to end treatment. She perceived me as strict and controlling. She insisted that her suffering was caused by being in the analytic relationship with me; she now perceived our relationship as sadomasochistic. She wanted to vomit out her rage. She expressed a desire to throw up on my couch. I embraced this spontaneous gesture. I believed allowing this to unravel, without an immediate interpretation, was effective. As a result, Laura experienced a benign regression in the service of the ego (Balint, 1968). She discovered the basic fault, the area where she was hurt because she felt unwanted; her mother was repulsed by her vomit. She now realized that she was not damaged. She understood that her mother could not take her vomit; she only wanted the clean, good baby. She experienced my acceptance of her when she loved me as well as when she hated me. I was interested in the good and the bad, the whole object. Laura was able to experience herself in relation to a new object, a new relational experience.

Our treatment has moved from object relating to object usage (Winnicott, 1969). Winnicott's concept of object usage illuminates the importance of the infant's ability to use the mother ruthlessly as an object without fear of her destruction. Laura's mother's narcissism, anxiety, and anger caused her to fail Laura through this important developmental phase. She was not capable of temporarily giving up her own control, subjectivity and omnipotence to facilitate and support Laura's subjective omnipotence. Her mother could not survive her usage of her, which resulted in Laura's premature focus on the other people's needs and on the external world. The impact of this early failure has resulted in Laura's formation of a false self construction. This impingement in the mother–child experience impaired Laura's ego structure, causing a lack of ego continuity. It has contributed to her core belief that if she takes something for herself, it will be damaging to another. She is beginning to assert her needs in relationships, to set boundaries, and to master her fear of losing herself in caring for others.

Laura became able to use symbols, to connect to her inner child, and to express her needs. She hugged herself and patted herself on the arm as she stated, "When I was a baby and I would cry, my mother would not hold me close and say poor Laura there, there." She held her arms out straight before her as if she is holding a child upright in front of her, then she said: "My mother would hold me out as if she were disgusted with me as if she wanted to throw me." She sobs, "It is weird, I just want to throw up, it is so satisfying, it is a release, like a scream." Laura's attempt at providing self-soothing to her internal infant encouraged me to address her relationship to herself and her guilt and shame over past self-abusive behaviors. I reflected on the importance for Laura to have compassion and forgiveness toward herself. She was able to synthesize the good and bad aspects of self and others, to see the whole object that reflected increased ego strength and a cohesive sense of herself. She now could take in the whole object, which provided her with the courage and a desire, expressed by her without any prompting or suggestions from me, to speak to her parents about the abuse. As she now achieved separation and individuation through the treatment by being able to fully mourn early losses, and to process and voice previously unarticulated experiences, she needed validation of her experience by those who caused it, and possibly an apology. Although, Laura did not feel that she could forgive her parents, she had a need to speak with them about the abuse.

When she confronted her mother, she found her defensive; however, her father apologized. Laura accepted their reactions, mourned the loss of what she did not have, and, more importantly, of what she will never have. She realized her parents' limitations and accepted them as they were, no longer as she hoped they would be. Laura claimed, "I am no longer invested in convincing my mother to go into treatment for me in hopes of having the mother that I never had. I want my mother to embark upon therapy for herself, for her own happiness and I will support that." She then stated that when she comes to a place of forgiveness, which she hoped to do if she could some day, she will never forget and will maintain realistic expectations of both parents. As she processed this reality, she was in excruciating pain, severely disappointed. Her father, the good parent, betrayed her. Ferenczi's concept of "Confusion of tongues" (1980n) helped make sense of something incomprehensible for both of us and has helped me to gain some understanding of the mind of the perpetrator who was her father, the father she loved and now both loved and hated. This concept captured Laura's experience of betrayal of the adult who spoke the language of passion, the father who was impulsive and gave in to his own narcissistic needs rather than attending to his child's need for tenderness; he offered her sex in the guise of love (Rachman, 1997a). It also clarified Laura's self-injurious behavior as an identification with the aggressor and her personality organization as the wise baby.

The confusion of tongues theory further contributed to my understanding of Laura's low self-esteem and the shame and guilt that she carried resulting from the confusing messages she received from both parents; she did come to realize that the badness did not reside in her. She cried because of the pain her parents hadcaused her. She was uncertain whether she could forgive them, but she came to be able to accept the situation because she had realized that she had no control over it. She did not have to numb herself to this reality, she felt empowered, not numb or anxious, just very sad. She did have parents; she realized and accepted that they were the only mother and father she would ever have; she did not want to abandon them. Laura no longer had a need for the attachment. She was able to separate and individuate. The sadomasochistic relationship to herself discontinued, partly because she was able to forgive herself for taking on the blame and for years of self-injury. I shared with her the following quote by Mark Twain, which we agreed captured her experience of forgiving herself. "Forgiveness is the fragrance that the violet sheds on the heel that has crushed it."

CHAPTER EIGHT

Analysis of an incest trauma in a difficult case

It is our opinion that most analysts do not publicly admit to the length of treatment for their most difficult cases. Ferenczi's treatment of Elizabeth Severn covered a span of eight years (Ferenczi, 1988). It is likely that the analysis of Severn would have continued, if not for Ferenczi's premature death. Freud pioneered the long-term analysis of a difficult case, for example, his analysis of the Wolf Man (Freud, 1918b), extended for a significant period, but what is even more important is that the analytic community continued the treatment for many years after Freud's death. First Ruth Mack Brunswick, then a series of analysts from America would come to Europe during the summer months to treat the Wolf Man. The analytic community realized, as did Freud, that the Wolf Man was a difficult case who needed prolonged and intensive treatment without a preset termination date. Roazen (1975) made a significant assessment of this unconventional treatment of a trauma case:

> He did progress better under Freud's care than with other therapists of the day, but can one say that in the end it was analytic insight which helped, or rather the continuing emotional support of Freud and the psychoanalytic movement? (p. 157)

Winston was seen in psychoanalysis from September of 1964 until the Spring of 2013. When he began the analysis at the age of twenty-four years, he was in a state of profound confusion, dissociation, and severe dysfunction. He was suffering from a profound confusion of tongues trauma. He had dropped out of graduate school, after receiving his baccalaureate degree with the highest honors from a very prestigious college. Upon graduation, he had been employed as a welfare investigator, a job well below his intellectual accomplishments. His intellectual, emotional, and interpersonal functioning was at its lowest level in his life at that time. What is more, he had no idea what was happening to him, and certainly he had no idea why. Previously, he had a one-year therapeutic experience with a psychiatrist. In discussing his previous therapy, there were no indications that trauma, and the incest trauma in particular, was a focus. The focus on the incest trauma resulted from an emphatic inquiry into Winston's family life and interaction, which made it clear that trauma was a central issue. Winston was very receptive to this trauma focus. Because the analyst employed empathy rather than interpretation, the analysand experienced him as understanding, responsive, engaged, and compassionate. He voiced the importance of empathy for the relationship. Second, the empathic inquiry did not challenge the authenticity of the subjective report of abuse. The trauma was not seen as an indication of an internal process of distortion, but as a *real event* in the interpersonal history of the individual. Empathetic understanding was essential through the entire course of Winston's analysis.

Unfolding the family psychopathology helped Winston become aware of how trauma shaped his personality development. He had the special gifts of eidetic imagery (photographic memory), superior IQ, understanding of the meaning of symbols, and the capacity to free associate using a vast knowledge of mythology, history, and language. He was able to integrate that his traumas with his mother and father was causative to his severe emotional and interpersonal dysfunction. Winston's case is similar to Ferenczi's Elizabeth Severn (Rachman, 2009a, 2010a,c, 2011a, 2012b,c, 2014a,c, 2015). Ferenczi's analysis of Severn is a model to pursue a co-created democratic and mutual relationship (Ferenczi, 1988).

When the analysis began, the diagnostic impression was a severe borderline with psychotic features. At the onset of contact, Winston was in a state of regression, unable to function in school, work, and socially. The only activities he could maintain were smoking cigarettes, listening to music on the radio, and masturbating. His emotional life was filled with fantasies of murderous rage toward his mother, being preoccupied with her dismemberment. A parallel fantasy involved intense prejudicial feelings toward negroes. He harbored fantasies about rounding up negro children in garbage trucks, which would be used to eliminate them. Occasionally, he would have breaks with reality. During these periods of intense anxiety when he felt unnurtured he would fantasize being an animal grazing in a meadow. At these moments of intense need, he felt intensely frustrated. There are no adequate words to express the anguish, frustration, and resentment Winston expressed over his unfulfilled needs, which he shared in an endearing way. On the other hand, experiencing his hatred, prejudice, murderous rage for his mother and African-Americans was very difficult.

He described his childhood traumas as serious, severe, disturbed relations with his mother and father. The mother was described as a giant mole who burrowed her way into every cell of his body. He experienced her as controlling, manipulative, domineering, intrusive, and sexually seductive. His childhood was spent emotionally and physically hiding from her, by developing a false self into which she could not intrude. She was more emotionally connected to her son than her schizoid husband. She literally used him, when an infant, as an instrument of masturbation.

Winston characterized his father as a severely schizoid individual, whom he described as a cloud, someone whom he could not reach interpersonally or emotionally. The father's sister had been hospitalized for psychosis for much of her adult life. The father was an unsuccessful lawyer, intelligent, but incapable of earning a meaningful living.

A younger brother, who was symbiotically tied to the mother, functioned to help separate Winston from the mother's narcissistic hold. This was a life-saving device, as he was able to push the mother away when his younger sibling became the mother's new emotional focus.

A central psychodynamic of the analysis was a negative maternal transference that focused on control, manipulation, domination, and intrusion. Winston was hypersensitive to any indication that the analyst was trying to control him. Very early in our relationship, he was told that he was showing signs that his dysfunctional behavior was changing. No sooner had the word "changing" been said than Winston became very confrontational and angry. I (AR) was surprised by his reaction because it was intended to give him hope by saying he was no longer stuck in a depression and negative cycle of behavior. In actuality, he walked out of that session. He did return for the following session, where the focus was on the interpersonal encounter.

He was asked to tell openly and honestly what had been said or done that had so angered him. His response was very instructive. It helped co-create his analysis, and, provided a blue-print for pursuing a psychoanalysis of a trauma survivor. Winston said the problem was that when I said he was *changing*, he heard, "You were changing me." What is more, he experienced me as "being proud" that I was *changing him*. These words and his experience of them, meant, to him, that I was interested in being domineering, intrusive, and controlling.

Such an experience was a re-creation of his entire childhood with his mother, which he found unacceptable. When I first heard the negative evaluation in that crisis session, I was not aware of being domineering, intrusive, or controlling. In fact, I thought the response reflected empathy. I was trained to be empathic in my training experiences at the Counseling and Psychotherapy Center at the University of Chicago (Rachman, 1997a, 2003a). Being empathic also suited me personally. After my training at the University of Chicago, Ferenczi's (1988), Rogers' (1950), Kohut's (1984), and Winnicott's (1965) ideas about empathy became an integral part of my clinical thinking and behavior (Ferenczi, 1980f; Kohut, 1984; Rogers, 1942, 1951, 1959; Winnicott, 1965b). When I began the analysis with Winston, it was characterized by "accurate empathic understanding". Clinical empathy clearly helped me establish a meaningful working relationship with Winston. He verified this functioning by filling out a form the institute used to assess the analyst's functioning. He said he was happy with his analyst because: "he understands me and what I tell him about my background" (Session #10). Although I was proud of my capacity for empathy, it was not sufficient for this difficult case.

When I asked Winston to assess my functioning, I learned what Ferenczi had learned from Severn. When you *listen* to the analysand *rather than defend yourself*, and *not rush to interpret*, you learn a great deal about the individual and the subjective experience of the analysand. I learned in that session that a well-meaning analyst, who prided himself on being empathic, could act defensively and be experienced as controlling. Although it was difficult to accept, I did have to admit, I could be controlling. Someone else, close to me at that time, also said I was controlling. Apparently, having experienced a controlling mother myself as a child, it had its effect on my personality development (Rachman, 2003a). It was time to accept the capacity to be controlling both in my personal and professional life. In this analysis of Winston, as well as with others, I became more attuned to the capacity to retraumatize by my non-therapeutic behavior.

The "changing" response was intended to reflect empathy. But, as is often the case in the analysis of trauma cases, where clinical empathy is such a fundamental relational issue, empathic failures provide important opportunities for the analyst to increase his/her understanding. In this instance, I was, at first, incredulous that Winston was suggesting there was a lack of empathic understanding in my response of pointing out that he was changing. I was trained in the empathic approach, valued it, and had published about it. Yet, when an analysand becomes angry and dramatically walks out of a session, it is a moment to reflect not only on the analysand, but the analyst's functioning. This is the model of a two-person psychology Ferenczi introduced in his analysis of Elizabeth Severn (see Chapter Five).

What Ferenczi learned from Severn in the famous mutual analysis sessions was that if the analyst can examine his own functioning, rather than blame the analysand for the clinical difficulty or impasse, the analysis can proceed (Rachman, 2014a). In this instance, Winston was informing me that the issue of controlling and manipulative behavior needed to be examined and acknowledged in order for him to feel safe and empathically understood. When I was willing to examine these issues, from the analysand's subjective experience, the clinical crisis was diminished. I was willing to disclose that control and manipulation was a possible factor in Winston's being angry. Winston was grateful for the disclosure. He never again walked out of a session.

From then onward, the analysis with Winston was co-created. An empathic atmosphere was improved, so that when an impasse was reached in transference–countertransference crises, or an interpersonal crisis, Winston would feel free to openly express his feelings about the analyst. Then, both would struggle to examine their functioning. A good example of this mutual analytic process occurred later on in the analysis. As I have mentioned, Winston had severe prejudicial feelings toward African-Americans. He also identified himself with killers such as Richard Speck and the Son of Sam. Furthermore, he admired Adolf Hitler and had, on several occasions, said: "Hitler had the right idea to exterminate the Jews." This was difficult to hear. I refrained from criticizing him, but it always caused emotional difficulty. His anti-Semitism, his hatred, and murderous rage were a function of his feelings toward his seductive and controlling mother and his distant and unavailable father. In one session, after many years of my enduring these horrendous remarks, Winston said: "I just saw a documentary about Hitler on TV. He was a great man. Exterminating the Jews was the right thing to do."

Perhaps he said this about Hitler one time too many. Perhaps I was struggling with my own feelings of anger that day. Or, perhaps, there was a countertransference reaction of anger and disgust toward Winston. Whatever it was that day, I responded: "I don't appreciate your continuing to talk about Hitler as a hero for attempting to exterminate the Jews."

He responded with: "I can say anything I want about Hitler and killing the Jews."

What was said in response was a countertransference disclosure: "You can say what you wish. But I can only say, if you continue to talk about Hitler's positive functioning in killing the Jews, I will not be able to maintain empathy toward you during this session."

Winston became very angry, saying: "You are my therapist. I can say whatever I want to my therapist. You should not control me and what I say. You should not be like my mother. You should be different from her."

No sooner had Winston uttered these words than I knew he was right in what he had said. I did not hesitate to say the following to him:

> "You are right, you *can and should* say whatever you want to me. And, I want you to continue to do so. You are also right, *I should not try to control what you say or do*. I don't want to be like your mother. However, please consider why you continue to tell me about Hitler's extermination of the Jews. Perhaps you are trying to taunt me."

The emotional atmosphere changed dramatically with the countertransference self-disclosure. Winston accepted my emotional honesty and responded positively. He was appreciative that I admitted to being controlling and that he had a right to be angry. It was his emotional right to say what he wanted. It was my job to create an atmosphere where Winston could express his deepest thoughts. On the other hand, I needed to deal with the negative feelings about Hitler and exterminating the Jews. Winston admitted that there were times when he was seeing how far he could go in expressing his anger and sadism toward me. It was a transferential expression of feelings toward his mother.

My judicious self-disclosure, as just described, was a significant part of an overall employment of non-interpretative measures (see Chapters Twelve and Thirteen, and Rachman et al., 2005, 2009a,b). The analysis of severe trauma can be seen as predicated on the capacity of the psychoanalyst to be theoretically and clinically receptive to the employment of non-interpretative measures.

Winston's analysis, as was Severn's (Ferenczi, 1988), can be characterized as an analysis that illustrates the way non-interpretative measures can be meaningfully integrated into the psychoanalysis of trauma. The analysis began and was maintained with the reliance on accurate empathic understanding as the mode of observation and response. This can be characterized as Phase One of the analysis: The emphatic phase. The phases are not discrete demarcations, but periods when a particular dimension of clinical activity may predominate (Rachman, 1988a, 2003a). Phase Two, which began toward the end of the first year, was characterized as the analytic phase. During this phase, Winston brought in hundreds of dreams during his thrice-weekly sessions with which he was able to readily associate. As has been mentioned, he had superior capacities to employ a knowledge of history, mythology, language usage, metaphors, and symbols in their interpretation. Also of great importance was his motivation to understand himself, which never wavered. If only he had had therapeutic help as a child, his severe emotional disturbance and dysfunction would not have haunted him as an adult. The extent of the analytic phase lasted for years as he eagerly analyzed dreams, fantasies, and uncovered early recollections as well as the transference–countertransference issues. During this period the traumas were retrieved. Winston became a psychologically sophisticated individual. Instead of being a repressed, confused, enraged individual, he became aware of, and confronted, the dark issues of his family interaction and the profound influence the traumas with his mother and father had on his personality development. In essence, the details of Winston's traumas were delineated, but there was something missing. The analytic phase was predominately a cognitive experience for Winston. He showed enthusiasm, delight in self-reflection, analyzing conscious and unconscious data, and developing insight. Emotional expression and connection to the material and experiences were limited. On reflection, Winston was not yet ready for emotional insight. It was Winston who suggested a turn in our analysis. In essence, he said that he: "had analyzed hundreds of dreams, fantasies, went over my childhood experiences talked about our relationship, but, I still don't feel things; I feel blocked, frustrated and unfulfilled."

Although Winston had painted a clear picture of his mother's emotional seduction, I also felt there was something missing. He had mentioned, but never analysed, his mother's sexual seduction. One of the significant aspects of the third phase, the active phase, was the recovery of his childhood incest trauma. The process occurred by integrating analytic group psychotherapy and active individual analysis with non-interpretative measures. Winston's request for greater activity in the analysis was seen as a developmental need to become more assertive, feel empowered, and become emotionally expressive. His childhood traumas had left him feeling powerless, fearful, and suppressed. Winston had made it clear he was very satisfied with the empathic and analytic phases of the analysis, but he was asking for help to be more emotionally open, expressive. He wanted to be able to act upon his own desires.

Group analysis became the initial vehicle for introducing greater activity into the analysis. Both Winston and I had some concern about his joining a therapy group because he had such negative feelings about people, including intense prejudicial feelings about African-Americans. He also voiced his lack of empathy for people. Winston was willing to join the group when he was told there were no Blacks in the group and that the members were intelligent, educated, and high functioning in their careers. Winston readily became a leader of the group because of his likeability and his false self, which showed him as positive in public interaction. In his interaction with group members, he was concerned, even kind, intelligent, insightful, and emotionally responsive. There was one female member to whom he had a negative transference reaction because she reminded him, very much, of his mother. In spite of this negative transference reaction, he genuinely tried to help her. The group member voiced her appreciation.

Clinical interaction in group analysis was a natural avenue for Winston to feel more active. This analytic group was conducted for an eight-year period during the late 1980s to the 1990s and integrated encounter and non-interpretative measures (Rachman, 1988a), which was seen as a contemporary extension of Ferenczi's non-interpretative measures (Rachman et al., 2005, 2009a,b). There was a significant use of non-interpretative measures during Winston's participation in group. Six non-interpretative measures were integrated in Winston's working through of his childhood incest trauma: for example (1) the dart game; (2) flotation tank/immersion experience; (3) the Greek Chorus; (4) exorcism of the symbolic mother encounter; (5) light illumination session; (6) the building block encounter: Suppression of creativities.

During the first year of the group's interaction, one of the major emotional themes was the members' anger towards their mothers. After a significant period of verbal expression of their anger, a group member, Harold, said he would like to have a more active way to express his feelings. This request for active, non-interpretative measures was not seen as a resistance, or an acting out, but, rather, as an expression of a developmental need to contact early non-verbal traumatic feelings and experiences (Rachman et al., 2005, 2009a,b). With this developmental view of non-interpretative measures, I responded to the expressed needs of group members by helping them co-create non-interpretative measures that would address their specific, unfilled developmental needs.

The dart game

Harold took the initiative in helping create this non-interpretative measure. He used his design and technical skills to create enlarged pictures of the group members' parents. Each group member who wished to participate in the experience was asked to bring in a family portrait of their choice. Each group member brought in some photographs. Each photograph was significantly enlarged and attached to a foam board. Harold also brought in darts. The therapeutic task was to throw the darts at your own family photograph or any other member's, expressing any sounds, feelings, or thoughts when releasing the darts.

Harold volunteered to start. At first, he threw several darts at the photograph of his mother and father, expressing statements of hatred and disappointment. Harold's open statements of parental anger galvanized the emotionality of the members as three other members threw darts at their parental photos while releasing angry feelings. Two members, Bobby and Winston, did not want to participate. They remained at the edge of the interaction as observers. There was an agreement with all members that they could choose not to participate in the experience. Winston chose to remain on the sidelines during the dart game because he was not emotionally ready to release his feelings. He was encouraged to titrate his own anxiety and when he was able to participate he was free to do so.

All members who participated, as well as those who remained as observers, reported they had a meaningful therapeutic experience. When Winston's reaction was explored, he said he was ready to be more active in this next non-interpretative measure.

Flotation tank/sensory deprivation experience

Winston, once we began to integrate non-interpretative measures into our analysis, began his usual curiosity and research into alternative ways of treatment. In the 1980s, as part of the non-traditional therapy movement, an immersion tank experience had been developed. Intuitively, he felt the experience of being suspended in an isolation tank with all outside stimuli removed would produce a therapeutic effect. Winston was convinced the immersion experience would help uncover dissociated feelings and recover data about childhood trauma. I investigated both the commercial use of the immersion tank and the scientific research on sensory deprivation experiments (Goldberger, 1966, Solomon et al., 1966; Zubek, 1969). There was trepidation about Winston's participating in the immersion experience because of the possibility of emotional flooding, which could produce a dramatic lifting of the repression barrier. I expressed my concern about emotional flooding; Winston was determined to pursue this measure. I told him to tell the technician about the issue and call me if any concern was evident, or difficulties arose. Winston trusted his own capacity to titrate emotional experiences, which was clearly evident in the countertransference crisis previously described. Since he was determined to pursue this activity, over any concerns I had, his psychic wisdom needed to be trusted. Winston contacted me by telephone before and after the procedure. A time-extended session was conducted the next day after the immersion tank experience. He described the immersion experience in very positive terms, in a way that verified the sensory deprivation research. He said he found the experience of being immersed for one hour "very soothing, calming." He said: "I could have continued in the tank indefinitely." As the research had indicated, the more disturbed the individual, the greater the soothing effect sensory deprivation can have. Internal emotional bombardment, from delusions, hallucinations, or obsessive compulsive thoughts caused by childhood trauma are reduced or silenced. Apparently, this was the effect the immersion tank experience had on Winston. When asked about any disquieting feeling, thoughts, or emerging fantasies or early experiences, there was some sense during the end of the experience, which Winston described as: "that something, was loosening up inside of me." We both wondered if the something was related to the present focus of the analysis, which was the intensely angry feelings towards his mother. The next emerging non-interpretative measure would satisfy our curiosity.

The Greek Chorus in the intensive group experience

The employment of non-interpretative measures in group analysis occurred as an intensive group experience (IGE), a time-extended group session which integrated non-interpretative measures for the therapeutic purpose of uncovering childhood trauma in a relational analysis framework (Rachman, 2003a, 2007a, 2009b). By the time this third non-interpretative measure was planned, all members were participating, including Winston. In particular, Winston became the leader in conceptualizing and planning these non-interpretative measures. In the Greek Chorus, a group member, Rebecca, wanted to deal with her controlling, manipulative, and domineering mother, to whom she wished to express her rage. She wanted help to release her rage so she could liberate her functioning. Winston conceived of a Greek Chorus encounter. The group members surrounded Rebecca as she was seated on a chair in the middle of the group circle. The lights in the consultation session were dimmed. A mask was placed over Rebecca's face, so she could concentrate intensively on only the voices of the group members. The group analyst stood directly behind

Rebecca holding her shoulders, intended to give her emotional support while she was going through a potential emotional upheaval. The analyst agreed to Rebecca's request that she could talk if she needed help during the Greek Chorus encounter.

The Greek Chorus began with group members shouting out loud, negative, hurtful, critical, demeaning things Rebecca had reported that her mother had said. Immediately, Rebecca began crying and appeared to act like a victim. She turned to the analyst to help her. She was encouraged to release her suppressed anger. When she was able to do so, after about five minutes or so, she released what sounded like a primal scream. She raged, telling her mother to stop criticizing her and stop making her feel like a child who could not please her. When Rebecca expressed her anger, the Greek Chorus encounter was terminated.

All group members were encouraged to take a turn interacting with the Greek Chorus. Three members, Harold, Shirley, and Winston did take turns. As Winston took the seat in the middle of the group, the members of the Greek Chorus expressed to him the seductive, manipulative, and intrusive things he had reported his mother had said to him as a child:

> "Winston you will be the youngest Supreme Court Justice in the history of the United States; I know what is best for you; only a mother can look at you with a mother's eyes and know what you need; come be by your mother so I can take care of you; you're such an intelligent, handsome, good boy."

After a while, Winston raised his hands so as to tell the group to stop the Greek Chorus, which they did. He took off his face mask and said the following:

> "I can now feel the anger that has been building up inside of me all my life for my mother. She is stupid, an emotional pygmy, and like an animal who is trying to bore her way into every cell of my body. I really felt the group was like my mother. It did not seem like make-believe or a game. No wonder I wanted to kill and dismember my mother."

He went on to discuss co-creating a new non-interpretative measure to deal with the emerging rage toward his mother and his sense of powerlessness. Winston emphasized that he now needed an active measure to more fully release both his anger and to develop a sense of power.

Exorcism of the symbolic mother measure

The exorcism of the symbolic mother was co-created by the group, Winston, and the analyst. Winston wanted to express his anger in a direct way, to feel powerful in doing so, giving expression to a fantasy of wanting to kill his mother for attempting to destroy his life by her intrusive, controlling, and seductive behavior. His desire to express his rage towards his mother was enthusiastically supported by the group. The analyst had trepidations about co-creating a therapeutic encounter where a group of individuals would be free to release murderous feelings. In order to find a therapeutic zone to co-create a safe and meaningful non-interpretative measure to provide an avenue to express rage, the analyst needed to deal with his countertransference about expressing rage; unresolved issues about his/her mother, encouraging release of murderous feelings. The analyst had worked on relevant material connected with anger, so that countertransference was at a minimum (Rachman, 2003a). In this way, there was a separation between the analyst's maternal transference and Winston's. According to the theoretical and clinical ideas developed for treating the effects of intense childhood trauma (Rachman et al., 2005, 2009a,b), Winston needed a symbolic opportunity to express his rage which may have predated language. Preverbal trauma is often encapsulated in somatic memory, where the traumatic feelings and experience are embedded in the parts of the body most relevant to the original trauma. At first, Winston's idea was: "to burn my mother in effigy in a giant bonfire."

He had the idea of a bonfire on a beach, which he presented in an individual session. I empathized with his need to have a powerful, dramatic way to express a lifetime of rage towards his mother, but suggested that any non-interpretative measure needed to be within the confines of a therapeutic session. As so defined, for safety and confidentiality, a beach bonfire would be ruled out. Winston accepted the limit setting without any argument.

Winston, Harold, Shirley, and Winston's wife were instrumental in co-creating the exorcism of the symbolic mother encounter. Winston wanted to be in a position of power during the encounter. Harold created a king's crown. He also created an Egyptian Pharaoh's outfit for himself. Winston's wife created a monarch's robe to go with the crown. Winston brought in a carving knife and fork as his symbolic indications of power and status. Shirley created a large stuffed female doll with very large piercing eyes, a seductive face, and a triangular-shaped, brown vagina. All items highlighted Winston's emotional issues; in addition, she created a large wall-hanging with the same features. The experience unfolded as follows:

> Winston sat on a chair with a large pillow so he was elevated. He had on his crown, cape, and knife and fork in hand. Harold wore his Egyptian outfit. The symbolic mother doll was placed on a separate smaller chair in front of Winston so he could look down on it. The remaining group members surrounded Winston, providing support and encouragement to express his anger.
>
> The lights were dimmed and members began to repeat the statements that Winston's mother made to him which were used in the Greek Chorus. The Greek Chorus was also integrated into this experience. After one chorus, Winston became agitated, angry, and shoved the knife and fork into the symbolic mother doll. He had a smile on his face from ear to ear. After lingering with the knife and fork while it was in the symbolic mother doll, he returned to his symbolic throne. Every member took turns stabbing the mother doll, expressing their own statements of maternal anger.

After the experience ended, there was a full discussion of what had transpired. Winston continued to wear a big smile on his face, voicing his delight in releasing his anger towards his mother. In the past, he was only able to speak in a distinct, detached way when describing his hatred, anger, and fantasies of dismembering his mother. Now, he addition, he said he felt a sense of power. This was a very important breakthrough for him. He developed a fantasy that he would be able to reclaim a lost part of himself. And, just as important, he felt he was getting closer to retrieving his childhood traumas.

The other members of the group were also excited about their release of therapeutic anger and were looking forward to exploring these feelings in their individual sessions. They all felt that Winston was on the verge of being able to make a breakthrough. It is also important to note that the group members and the analyst experienced a sense of anxiety, fear, and, yet, emotional release during the encounter.

The aforementioned five non-interpretative measures were all developmental stages in Winston's emotional recovery from his childhood sexual and emotional traumas. The dart game allowed Winston to be emotionally expressive in the safety and trust of his peers. Feelings of anger toward his mother were expressed in a symbolic, projective way, which was the appropriate phase of his emotional development. The immersion experience encouraged a quieting of intrapsychic conflict, stress, and negative affect. Being able to perform this kind of intense emotional attunement in the privacy of his own inner space was essential for Winston as a second phase in his emotional recovery. He began to emotionally attune to his parental involvement in his traumas. Group analysis provided, for the first time in his life, a peer group for emotional and interpersonal holding. This was not accomplished in his family, and neither was he able to become emotionally open enough to share his true self. As has been mentioned, the group did coalesce around an emotional contagion of angry feelings towards parents, especially their mothers. In the third and fourth phases of his emotional recovery, Winston was able to co-create with the group and the analyst a narrative for emotionally and symbolically confronting his mother regarding her sexual and emotional seduction of him. Exorcism of the symbolic mother helped Winston and most of the group members to begin emotionally to confront their intense and repressed negative feelings toward their mothers.

They could translate their feelings into an activity that bypassed an intellectual or cognitive avenue of expression. The use of a symbolic depiction of a mother against whom one could aggress without any emotional or physical retaliation was therapeutic. Finally, the light illumination session, to which we will now turn, took place individually and allowed Winston to therapeutically regress to the earliest part of his "basic fault" (Balint, 1968), where his mother not only involved him in sexual acts, but actually used him as a sexual object.

Light illumination session: self-hypnotic therapeutic regression

Winston had suggested we create a session where he could attempt to therapeutically regress, because he felt all the therapeutic work he had done in the intensive group experiences was helpful in stimulating an emotional awakening: Feelings, images, and fragments of experiences he believed had something to do with childhood sexual seduction. Winston, in his usual way, was determined to establish a breakthrough in his earliest and most intense trauma. We had an agreement that he could take the lead in creating non-interpretative measures to reach his trauma. Winston had found a plastic tube containing a florescent glow that is activated when the plastic tube is shaken vigorously. When Winston told me about the illumination stick, we co-created a non-interpretative measure to reach the trauma of childhood seduction.

The following session helped define this next non-interpretative measure. As soon as Winston sat down in his chair, I saw him attentively staring at a large African poster which hung on the wall. His chair faced this poster, on which was drawn in sepia, dark brown, and tan colored ink a series of abstract designs of triangles, flowers, and leaves demarcated in squares of various lengths and widths. After observing him for several minutes, believing he was in an internal space which should not be intruded upon, he turned to the analyst and said: "I don't know why but I am drawn to this poster, even though it looks like an African type drawing. You know what I think about blacks. It's something about the color and designs."

I responded by asking whether he wanted to develop an active measure to see if we could focus on his feelings. He readily agreed. Spontaneously, we created a non-interpretative measure. Outside stimuli were reduced: the blinds were shut; the phone was shut off; the lights were dimmed. Then Winston was asked to turn his chair so that he was directly in front of the African poster and to focus his attention on any part of the poster to which he was drawn.

He was told to indicate when he found a part of the poster on which to focus by raising his right hand. Silence was respected so he could concentrate. Winston then had the opportunity to focus on a particular section for fifteen minutes, when he felt he had reached a breakthrough or reached his limit. Winston focused on the design for about ten minutes and then said he was ready to talk about the experience.

There were two basic reactions to which he responded: the earthy colors, particularly dark brown, and the triangular shapes. Taken together, we concluded a dark brown triangular-shaped object was the main issue. Winston had an idea that an intensive individual session, where a special device was used, the aforementioned illumination stick, would be used to help solve the mystery. We arranged for an intensive individual session that lasted for one and half hours. Before the session formally began, the consultation room was prepared. The window blinds were closed. The phone was turned off, classical music chosen by Winston was played. The lights were turned off, with the exception of a small desk lamp so that I could see the proceedings. Winston was situated on the analytic couch facing away from me. He orchestrated the session. After he was convinced all external stimuli were significantly reduced, he said: "Let us begin." The agreement was for him to speak, but I was to remain silent. He did agree that the session could be recorded. The silence would insure he would not feel, in what we anticipated would be a developmentally regressive state, that I was an intrusive presence, like his mother had been. After lying on the couch, he vigorously shook the illumination stick. Then, it began to glow, and he held it up to his face at eye level. He starred silently at the illumination rod for several minutes, while I continued to remain silent. Winston began to speak by describing what seemed to be an early childhood experience.

I checked the notes I made during the experience with the tape recording of the session. In terms of Winston's voice quality, manner of speaking, emotional expressiveness, and interaction described during this session, he seemed to be in some form of altered state. His voice appeared to have the quality of a younger person, and emotionally he appeared to indicate apprehension, anxiety, fear. He seemed to be remembering scenes of sexual interaction between his mother and himself. They were fragments of experiences contained in bursts of emotion and words. Some of these fragments were:

> "happened before I was two years old; bad smell . . . suffocate me; what could I have done; terror . . .; I see her cunt . . .; 'between my legs . . .' 'have a real pet'."

When Winston said he had finished with his experience, we began to talk about what had emerged. He reported he had been in an altered state, similar to the immersion tank and the intensive group experiences. His conclusion matched my observation. I read back to him the phrases cited above, also describing his affect and anxiety. Winston had associations that depicted a series of seduction scenes with his mother when he was a young child. Winston always was definitive in his recall and description of early childhood since he had eidetic imagery (near total recall), vivid dreams, fantasies, and recollections, and was able to freely associate in symbolic language usage and anagrams. This recall was different. Winston assembled all the data and believed that the following had taken place.

During early childhood, probably before three years old, his mother had several sexual experiences with him. Two such sexual seductions were reconstructed. While he was being washed by his mother she focused on his penis, washing it over and over again, playing with his penis and his testicles, including masturbating him. What is more, the mother became sexually stimulated by her sexual play with her son to such an extent that she moved from masturbating her son to holding him in her hands and using him as a penis, rubbing him up and down her vulva, using his entire body as a masturbating device. Winston recalled fragments of this scene as well as the look and smell of his mother's vagina.

In the sessions to follow, Winston increased his awareness about this early sexual trauma perpetrated by his mother to the point where he was convinced it had happened. This incest experience was consistent with other traumas he suffered in his relationship with his mother, characterized by her domination, control, intrusiveness, and narcissistic interaction with him. Continued exploration of the incest trauma occurred during the working through process. Winston's murderous rage toward his mother, the fantasies of dismembering her, his negative feelings toward women, and his sense of powerlessness were related to the incest trauma. This trauma also stimulated a profound sense of confusion and dissociation, so that when Winston began the analysis, he was severely emotionally and interpersonally disturbed, having no idea what had happened to him to cause his dysfunction. The employment of non-interpretative measures aided in helping Winston write the real narrative of his childhood traumas.

As has been mentioned, although Winston could be characterized as a cooperative, motivated analysand, he was very reluctant to volunteer any indications that he had made changes in his functioning. I accepted this reluctance as a psychodynamic related to Winston's negative relationship with his mother. His reluctance to acknowledge change was a defense against experiencing me as intrusive, controlling, and the seductive mother. There were times when I felt rejected by Winston's lack of recognition that change was taking place. By analyzing this countertransference reaction, I was able not to intrude his feelings of rejection into the clinical interaction.

A sense of clarity, focus, and relatedness replaced confusion and dissociation. Achievement replaced dysfunction. Aloneness was replaced by an ongoing interest in meeting a woman. He went to a holiday party his company gave and met a woman. They dated for about a year and married thereafter.

During his analysis, he significantly changed his work identity. He gained employment in a well-known financial firm. Returning to graduate school, he gained an MBA. Eventually, he became an executive vice-president. Although he did not enjoy his work, his superiors in the company were very happy with his intelligence, his presentations, and management skills. Work had always been problematic for two very important reasons. Winston felt imprisoned by work through having to perform at the behest of an authority to satisfy someone else's needs. He could never fully shake this negative mother transference to work. Equally difficult for Winston was the ever-present feeling that his mother was also the cause of the suppression of his creative impulses (a fuller discussion of the working through of this important issue will follow).

This is not to say that Winston became a gregarious, empathic, sweet individual. He still harbored intense prejudicial feelings towards others, became easily angered, and maintained social isolation. He had become psychologically sophisticated about the genetics of his emotional disturbance. In some instances, he did not have any motivation to explore changing his feelings or behavior. But, there was one area that was a source of constant frustration, resentment, and lack of fulfillment. Winston lamented his lack of creativity. It is to this important issue we now turn our attention.

The building block encounter: Suppression of creativity

We addressed a constant source of his frustration. He often voiced this verbalized lament:

> "I am always depressed. I go to work in a job I don't want to do. Since a child I wanted to express myself creatively. My mother wanted me to be the youngest Supreme Court Justice appointed to the bench. *I always had the desire to be an architect.*"

By then, I felt Winston had worked through some of his basic faults, such as his incest trauma, relationship to a woman, and career. He had partially fulfilled Freud's prescription for a meaningful life: to work, to love. But, he had not fulfilled a sense of inner satisfaction and fulfillment. Winston would never find happiness until he found a creative outlet for his energy. Balint had introduced the issue of creativity as a basic human need in his attempt to integrate Freud's oedipal theory with Ferenczi's confusion of tongues paradigm while extending these paradigms into an object relations perspective (Balint, 1968).

Our focus on Winston's suppressed creativity brought us back to his disturbed relationship with his mother during his early childhood. First, he went over, in detail, his life-time struggle with the intense dark feeling that he will never be creative in his lifetime. What is more, there were moments when he felt suicidal about this deficit. Our review of the suppression of his creative impulse was traced back to early childhood when he felt his mother had suppressed his creative impulse. It was the experience of her narcissistic intrusiveness and seductiveness that made him feel he had been robbed of a part of his true self. During this review process he was able to retrieve what seemed like a very early childhood memory. He closed his eyes and said the following:

> "I am sitting in a corner of my playpen, my back is to my mother. My mother is looking at me with her piercing gaze. Yes, it's like she's trying to control me with her look. It feels like she wants me to do something.
>
> "I am playing with large blocks, making a structure. As soon as I made the block structure she came over and knocked it down. I built the structure two more times. After she knocked down the structure for a third time, then, I crawled into a far corner and rolled up into a ball."

These retrieved memories became known as the building block trauma. Winston was confident that this recovered memory was a prototype of the suppression of his creative impulses. [The previous non-interpretative measures and the one to be described became the concept of reparative therapeutic experiences (RTE) (Rachman, 1998b).]

The building block encounter occurred as follows:

> All external stimuli were reduced. A symbolic play-pen was created by using large pillows from an office couch. Winston sat in a corner of the symbolic playpen with his back to me. He chose smaller pillows with which he would build a symbolic structure, as he did as a child. As he became engrossed in the activity, he had a smile on his face.
>
> When the structure was finished, I came from behind and knocked it down, as Winston had reported his mother had done. Winston made some unidentifiable sounds when the structure fell down. I remained silent. After a short period, Winston resumed building a similar structure. Once again, it was pushed down, and also for a third time. Then he became inactive, pulled his legs up to his eyes and remained in what seemed like a fetal position for a minute or two. When asked if he was all right, he answered he was. Then he indicated it was time to analyze the experience.

As in the other non-interpretative encounters, Winston indicated he felt he was sufficiently involved so that it became a meaningful emotional experience. Winston and I discussed his mother's pathological narcissism, which forced her to demand her son pay attention at all costs. She could never acknowledge any structure with which he was playing. He associated to this interpretation by remembering a childhood experience that was frightening and narcissistically intrusive. There were times, as a young child, he would awake in his crib to find his mother staring at him. Winston was frightened she was going to kill him. Our analysis suggested that his mother's ever-intrusive presence, aggressive demand for attention, actual sexual seduction, as well as emotional seductiveness, and relentless pursuit of his attention and love, made him feel vulnerable, penetrated, and assaulted. He added that he now understood from the recreation of the building block trauma encounter that his mother's physical and narcissistic behavior was an actual threat to his well-being. She physically aggressed against him by destroying the creation he enjoyed making. Now, he began to understand the meaning of the trauma that began the suppression of his natural creative impulse. His mother not only frightened him, demanded that he pay attention to her, did not affirm his creativity, but created a developmental crisis. She did not affirm his natural need to create. Her narcissism interfered with Winston's need to be affirmed as an individual in his own right. She contributed to his sense of powerlessness.

Changes in Winston's personality functioning: Beyond Freud's "to work and to love"

In discussions of what has constituted goals of mature human growth, both novelists and psychologists seem to agree. In a letter to Valeria Aresenyev on November 9, 1856, Tolstoy said: "One can live magnificently in this world if one knows how to work and how to love" (Troyat, 1967, p. 158). One could easily assume Freud was aware of Tolstoy's statement.

Erik Erikson wrote that Freud believed that sexual satisfaction (genital primacy) was not only the goal of a successful analysis:

> Freud was once asked what he thought a normal person should be able to do well. The questioner probably expected a complicated answer. But Freud, in the curt way of his old days, is reported to have said: "Lieben and arbeiten" (to love and to work). (Erikson, 1950, p. 229)

Using Freud's standard as a beginning, we will assess Winston's functioning as a result of his trauma analysis.

To love

Winston developed the capacity to have a meaningful marriage with a woman who loved him over a period of forty-five years. When his marriage is compared to those of other analysands who are as disturbed as him, or less so, or compared to those of individuals who are not in analysis or psychotherapy, his marriage seems successful and enduring. When he and his wife were seen for couple therapy, there were many signs of affection: They sat together each time; Winston held her hand as they talked; they never expressed harsh or mean-spirited words to each other; she clearly stated she was in love with him; he clearly demonstrated affection and dedication to her; there has never been a crisis of relationship where separation or divorce was considered.

Winston does not experience his wife as his mother. He worked through his rage at being overwhelmed, overpowered, betrayed, or treated like an object by a woman. Winston chose a woman different from his mother, someone who was passive, timid, and emotionally reserved. Winston was able to dominate her. There were times, however, when he was verbally abusive to her, an issue which needed attention during the couple analysis. He genuinely cared for his wife and he was able to respond positively to the couple counseling as well as able to curtail the verbal abuse. Winston's wife, in choosing him, found someone the opposite of her father, who was a raging alcoholic, physically abusive, emotionally and physically absent. In Winston, she enjoyed an emotionally and interpersonally responsive partner, who was genuinely committed to her. He never threatened her physically. As she developed medical difficulties, Winston was extremely invaluable to his wife, taking her to all her doctor's appointments, researching her problems, and being her medical advocate. She could not have dealt successfully with her medical problems without Winston. Although he had great difficulty verbalizing his love, there was no doubt Winston loved his wife and she knew it.

To work

Winston began analysis with a significant discrepancy between his intellectual capacities and his actual career achievements. Initially, he was working at the lowest level position for a college graduate from a prestigious university who was a member of an academic honor society. He had no work identity, having taken the least intellectually demanding job. One year after graduating from college, he was unemployed and adrift. At this point, Winston had no idea his intellect, work, and emotional interpersonal dysfunction were connected to his childhood traumas. As the incest and other traumas were being worked through, Winston's intellectual functioning was liberated. Through the years in analysis, he earned three post-graduate degrees: An MBA, a Master's Degree in photography, and a Law Degree. Winston had a career for more than thirty years as an executive assistant to a financial company's vice-president. This was a responsible position where he wrote position papers and gave speeches explaining the company's functioning. He was well rewarded for his efforts by formal recognition and financial remuneration. Winston felt frustration that he would never be able to employ his creativity in his work. Since he was a child he had dreamed of being an architect. When his company was downsizing, his boss left the company and Winston took the company's buy-out package and retired. He had invested his money wisely, so that he and wife could live in retirement without financial concern. Winston's retirement from formal work was salutary for him, as he gladly devoted his time to the kind of work he now enjoyed. This included photography, researching the Internet, and planning vacations.

To Freud's list of to love and work as indications of analytic success, we should also add to play, to create, to empathize, and to self-actualize.

To play

Ferenczi believed in play in both his personality functioning and his clinical interaction. He was described as the warmest and most responsive and playful of the analytic pioneers (Rachman, 1997a). When he came into a room, he would greet those present with a kiss on the cheek, including the dour Ernest Jones. As has been described, he and members of the Vienna Psychoanalytic Society visited a café where the American entertainer, Josephine Baker, was playing. She was drawn to him, going over to his table and playing with his bald head, creating an affectionate and warm interchange which everyone enjoyed. Ferenczi was not offended by this contact, enjoying the playful interaction (Rachman, 1997c).

In his paper, "Child analysis in the analysis of adults" (Ferenczi, 1980m), Ferenczi outlined his capacity to use play in the analytic encounter to communicate child-to-child with the adult analysand. He used his personal capacity to be comfortable with play to develop a non-verbal activity with a traumatized adult to help retrieve the childhood trauma:

> . . . a patient . . . resolved . . . to revive . . . incidents from his earliest childhood . . . I was aware that in the scene revived, by him, he was identifying me with his grandfather. Suddenly . . . he threw his arms around my neck and whispered in my ear: "I say, Grandpa, I am afraid I am going to have a baby?"
>
> Thereupon I had what seems to me a happy inspiration: I said nothing to him for the moment about transference, etc., but retorted, in a similar whisper: "Well, but what makes you think so?" (Ferenczi, 1980m, p. 129)

Among a host of relaxation, non-interpretative measures that have been described in this book, Ferenczi introduced analytic play, clinical interaction that employs heightened emotional and active experiences in the psychoanalytic situation, which allows the analysand to liberate their suppressed feelings. In so doing, the analytic encounter was expanded beyond interpretation towards a mutually active, dramatic, and emotional encounter. He valued and employed the language of children. Ferenczi appreciated the language of play, the language of children. Ferenczi realized he was using the play therapy of children with adults.

Winnicott also believed in the idea of play. For example, in his work with children, he developed the squiggle game to use in his consultations (Winnicott, 1958). He would draw a shape and invite the child to make something with it. He also used a spatula game, placing a spatula within a child's reach with which to play. Winnicott came to consider that

> Playing takes place in the potential space between the baby and the mother-figure . . . In other words, the initiation of playing is associated with the life experience of the baby who has come to trust the mother figure. (Winnicott, 1973, p. 146)

When analysis is going well, Winnicott believed "Creative play does not necessarily mean always playing alone . . ." (Casement, 1997, p. 162). Playing can also be seen in the use of a transitional object (Skynner & Cleese, 1993).

Play can be a vital aspect to help an individual cope with separation and independence. This is to be contrasted with incorporation of one person by another, which accounts for spurious maturity, the false self (Winnicott, 1973, pp. 201, 219). So, for Winnicott, "The task of the therapist was to enable the patient to become able to play, after which . . . it is in playing that the patient is being creative" (Winnicott, 1971, pp. 120, 163).

During Winston's participation in group psychotherapy, he became an advocate of employing active, non-interpretative measures. He not only enjoyed his participation, but helped create measures where he and group members enacted a series of encounters which helped liberate childhood traumas. He became an advocate of such measures believing that such analytic play is a valuable part of psychoanalysis. His belief and participation in play can be seen as a significant contribution to the success of his analysis (Rachman,

1979, 1981, 1988a, 1991a, 1994b, 1995c, 1998b, 2003a, 2004, 2007b; Rachman et al., 2005, 2009a,b).

Winston developed a rich capacity to play that has continued into his retirement. Every day he attempts to bring pleasure and play into his life. Each day, he and his wife use the afternoon meal to wine and dine. They go to a gourmet restaurant that Winston has researched, enjoying special meals, wine, and, for Winston, after-dinner brandy. He spends time working on his photography; taking pictures, organizing photographic books, and studying photography.

During the early phase of his analysis, Winston showed an obsessive–compulsive attitude toward the buying of clothes. He used this to soothe himself, giving to himself to replace the deprivation he felt. At one point, he had about 100 blue ties, each one with a slight difference in hue, texture, or design. Then one day, in a moment of anger, he threw them all in the trashbin. Now, he buys casual clothing to fit a less formal life style, where comfort is valued over formality. He still values good style and fit.

Travel is another important part of play. He and his wife travel to foreign countries, several times a year. He does a great deal of research prior to the trip, which adds to their enjoyment. They visit the significant places in the cities and plan to go to the great restaurants. Winston and his wife report great enjoyment from their trips.

Winston regularly reads books on history, biography, and photography. He is very interested in Sir Winston Churchill and English history. This reading for enjoyment has replaced the compulsive reading of Ancient Greek books in a psychological attempt to work on his oedipal issues (Rachman, 1981, 1988a).

A completely new form of play has developed for Winston and his wife. They regularly have movie night, where they both watch DVDs they have purchased from a catalog which has movies that express their interests. His wife is very positive about this experience, since she feels it brings them closer emotionally and interpersonally.

To create

As has been described, Balint described three distinct zones of personality development: The third relates to an individual capacity for the artistic, mathematical, philosophical, creation, and the acquisition of insight. The individual is "on his own and his main concern is to produce something out of himself and to understand others" (Balint, 1968, p. 24). For Balint, narcissism is seen as a protective expression against the bad or reluctant object. (Balint, 1965c).

Narcissism is only a detour to obtain for oneself what others did not give, and aggression is no more than a reaction to the missing primary love (Balint, 1965d). These conceptualizations by Balint were an attempt to integrate the confusion of tongues concept of trauma, expand upon it to include emotional trauma due to deficits in the primary object-love relationship with the mother, and to develop a conflict-free area of functioning where personal growth and creativity would be integrated (Rachman, 2003a).

Winston was extremely frustrated, angry, and resigned to a life without creativity. Much attention was paid to his intense fear that he had lost his capacity to be creative. The analysis revealed that his mother's narcissism had suppressed his creative impulse. When he was able to work through his rage towards his mother for suppressing his early attempts at creativity, he was able to explore creativity.

Winston's major creative activity became photography, which he had developed after the building block encounter. Since then, photography has been his major creative outlet. As mentioned, he earned a Masters of Arts degree in photography. His work has been shown in several photographic exhibitions, and has been reviewed in newspapers and magazines. He has also put selections of some of his photographs into books.

When he first discovered photography as an outlet for creativity, he developed a new technique to take pictures with the Diana camera. This specialized camera and his inventive technique allowed him to combine multiple images in one developed picture. He used his wife for the original series of these pictures (Rachman, 2003a). Winston has maintained his interest in photography over a twenty-year period.

His latest interests are photographs of abandoned industrial buildings. Winston says the photographs reflect his comfort with peopleless, stark, isolated, and dreary landscapes. He recently self-published a book of these striking and interesting photographs. These unusual sites are not generally examined or appreciated. Winston's work brings these industrial buildings and cityscapes into focus for study, examination, and appreciation. His most recent photographs are his innovative photographs of landscapes taken from a speeding train.

Retirement has allowed Winston to devote himself to other creative activities. In a surprising turn, he researched his German–Jewish family background. This seemed to be at odds with his admiration of Hitler and avowed anti-Semitism. In this apparent change of attitude, he read a definitive historical survey, entitled *Yiddish Civilization: The Rise and Fall of a Forgotten Nation*, by Paul Kriwaczek. When I expressed interest in the book, I was given a copy. What is more, he extended his previous interest in photographing cemeteries to taking a picture of the cemetery where his parents were buried. He printed the photograph on grainy canvas paper, with a greenish-gray color tint. It was a dramatic picture combining the drama of a cemetery embedded in a vivid image.

To empathize

Ever since Ferenczi introduced clinical empathy into psychoanalysis in his rule of empathy (Ferenczi, 1980r), this dimension of human interaction has become a significant part of any clinical interaction in psychotherapy and psychoanalysis. Clinical empathy became a turning point in clinical therapeutics and understanding human interaction (Rachman, 1989c, 1997a, 2003a). Ferenczi demonstrated that empathy was a necessary dimension to conduct a meaningful analysis with someone who has suffered from severe trauma (Ferenczi, 1988). In demonstrating the recognition for the need and the capacity to respond with empathy, Ferenczi's analysis of Severn helped establish empathy as a crucial way of being in a therapeutic relationship (Rachman, 2010a,b,c, 2012b,c,f, 2014a,b,c).

In the 1950s, humanistic psychotherapy, exemplified by the work of Carl Rogers, further developed the concept of clinical empathy and was developed as a necessary and sufficient condition for a therapeutic relationship (Rogers, 1959). Rogers believed in "accurate empathic understanding" (Truax et al., 1971), an empathic response should be an accurate understanding of the subjective experience of the individual (Truax et al., 1971). In this way, the therapeutic partners share intersecting subjectivities in the way Ferenczi attempted to do with Severn (Rachman, 2010c). Rogers' perspective, now referred to as person-centered psychotherapy, demonstrated that empathy was an essential dimension in a psychotherapeutic relationship.

In the development of the psychology of the self perspective, Kohut further elaborated the role of empathy as a method of observation as well as a method of response. Recreating Ferenczi's clinical work with difficult cases, Kohut demonstrated that empathy was a significant factor in the analysis of character, narcissistic, and borderline disorder (Kohut, 1984). Kohut believed that empathy was an emotional necessity for human existence, as water is a physical necessity for life (Kohut, 1977).

The advent of the relational perspective, originated by Stephen Mitchell (Mitchell, 1988), provides the most contemporary meaningful fit for Ferenczi and the Budapest School of Psychoanalysis's ideas and methods (Rachman, 2007a, 2010a). Ferenczi, Winnicott, and Kohut's formulations for empathy are a blueprint for considering personality growth and change. As all three clinicians–theorists work with difficult cases, empathy was essential in, at least, two basic ways. First, the analysand had developmental arrest in the necessary accurate empathic understanding from parental experience. They also lacked the capacity to recognize the need for, and to respond with, empathy with significant others. Their interpersonal relationships were marked by unempathic contact. These individuals were deficient in responding with empathy. A sign of personal growth during the course of an analysis would be a growing capacity to demonstrate accurate empathic understanding to others. This would mean the basic fault caused by defects in primary object-love was being repaired by the analytic contact. It would be anticipated that an individual such as Winston would show some indications of change in empathic responses.

Winston always had difficulty with empathy. Originally, we had explored the notion that his narcissistic and intrusive experience with his mother damaged his capacity for empathy. Then, there was a long period of time when Winston believed he was biologically blocked in expressing empathy. Although there were times when I shared my belief that his capacity to empathize was biologically blocked, very slowly, some changes appeared. Winston surprisingly, showed less rageful and angry feelings towards Blacks. Repeatedly, when I attempted to analyze his negative feelings toward African-Americans, he would say his feelings were based upon a generic, aesthetic, and biological standard which placed Negroes at the lowest level of the animal kingdom. For a period of time, I had not talked to him about the subject of Negroes because he was not open to analyzing it. Then, in an off-handed way, he mentioned that he no longer walked around in the street, murmuring to himself or cursing Negroes. I took this opportunity to rekindle the discussion about Blacks, or African-Americans. He asked me if I knew of any Negro whom I had admired? Then I told him that I went to Morris High School in the Bronx, where Colin Powell was a classmate. Mr. Powell had come from a similar family. Powell spoke Yiddish from having worked in the Jewish-owned furniture stores in the neighborhood. Through his own efforts, he became an international figure. I was flabbergasted when Winston responded positively, saying Colin Powell was different. Perhaps, this was some evidence of a change in attitude and perhaps some empathy toward a Black individual.

We also explored Winston developing greater empathy toward his wife. She would complain that he was not aware how hurtful he could be when he shouted her down in an argument, or, worse, told her to "shut up!" When we first discussed this issue, he offered his standard lament: He did not want his wife, or anyone for that matter, to stifle him in his emotional expression as his mother had done. Winston once again showed some indication of change in his capacity to empathize. He listened to my interaction with his wife as it was suggested to her that she develop a more assertive ability to respond to his bullying. In fact, he agreed with the recommendation and admitted to bullying his wife. She was expressing fear and anxiety, which was a re-enactment of her emotionally abusive interaction with her father. Winston's negative maternal transference was colliding with her negative paternal transference. They both accepted this interpretation. It was explained that in a permanent relationship, both members in a partnership deserve empathy. Reluctantly, he agreed; his wife was delighted. Winston stopped shouting her down. He promised his wife that he would "not shout her down" anymore. He was a man of his word. This, I believe, was an indication of further working through of his maternal rage. He was able to become more empathic with his wife in order to improve their relationship.

To relate with others

Ferenczi, Balint, and the Budapest School of Psychoanalysis laid the foundation for an interpersonal and relational approach to psychoanalysis (Rachman, 2003a, 2006, 2007a,b,g, 2010a). These contributions were the development of a two-person psychology, focused on the interaction between analyst and analysand, and the contribution of the analyst to the treatment process, which, among other factors, led to the origins of a relational perspective. Through the ideas of Balint (1965d, 1968) and Winnicott (1965b), the British object relations perspective further enunciated a human need for interpersonal experience to satisfy basic psychosocial experiences necessary for personality development.

Fromm (1959), Thompson (1964c), and Sullivan (1953), integrated the Budapest School and expanded upon it to develop the interpersonal perspective (Rachman, 2003a). Clara Thompson's analysis with Ferenczi was the conduit for this integration. When she approached Sullivan for a referral, since she was dissatisfied with her first analysis, Sullivan said there was only one person he would recommend, which was Ferenczi. Returning to America in the fall, after spending the summer months in analysis with Ferenczi in Budapest, she would share his ideas and experience with Sullivan, Fromm, and others (Rachman, 2003a). Fromm later became one of the American analysts who kept Ferenczi's ideas and importance alive in American psychotherapy and psychoanalysis. To these two we must also add Izette de Forest, a Ferenczi analysand and student whose book and articles helped introduce his work to an American audience (de Forest, 1942, 1954). De Forest described Ferenczi's approach as centering on the two-person experience of the analysis of countertransference.

To the emphasis on a two-person dialogue and the interpersonal situation in the psychoanalytic situation, we would add an analytic group experience as a meaningful part of developing the capacity to relate to others. Alexander Wolf pioneered the idea, which relates to an analysand's functioning in a group to widen one's capacity to relate to authority beyond the family and to one's peers (Wolf & Schwartz, 1962; Wolf & Kutash, 1991). In his analytic group method, he provided a Ferenczian therapeutic atmosphere. Wolf was a warm, tender-minded, and empathic person. He learned the value of empathy from his supervisor, Karen Horney (Wolf, 1989). Most importantly, his clinical training matched his natural personal capacity. To these personal and clinical qualities, we need to add his extensive knowledge of psychoanalysis. Wolf pioneered psychoanalysis in groups, from the perspective of the cultural interpersonal school. His unique contribution that is relevant to our discussion is the capacity to relate to others. Wolf pioneered a clinical methodology, "the alternate session" (Wolf & Schwartz, 1962). This adjunctive group method was a significant contribution to the idea of a peer's contribution to the interpersonal development of an individual's personality. He made an important distinction between relationship to authority (parents, analyst, teacher, etc.) and to peers (siblings, friends, age-cohort, peer group). This was compatible with Sullivan's ideas about the importance of age-cohorts in personality development. The alternate session met for an additional session during the week without the analyst leading the group. This combination of relating to authority (analyst-led group sessions) and to peers (alternate sessions) was Wolf's idea of the necessary combination for change in an psychodynamic therapeutic experience. Developing the capacity to relate to one's peers is then a necessary condition for personality development and an avenue for growth when psychological dysfunction is present.

As has been discussed, Winston regularly participated in analytic group and intensive group sessions. He was a very active and responsive individual in group. In fact, he became a peer-leader in these sessions. Not only did he encourage interaction, but he became the stimulant for exploring the unconscious. As has been discussed, his placement in group was made reluctantly, because of the concern that his lack of empathy and prejudicial feelings would create serious difficulties with particular individuals. Although he complained that he was never comfortable in group and he was forced to join, his interactions demonstrated an emotional vividness.

After the emotion of the intensive group experiences, where non-interpretative measures were employed, we returned to a focus on emotional issues. For the first time, Winston felt a connectedness between his experiences and emotions. He had never reported such a connectedness in individual sessions. Although he could not be considered an emotionally expressive individual, he became acutely aware of his own and others' feelings. Many group members turned to Winston for help when they were having difficulty. He was very responsive and helpful, for which the members were grateful.

Although Winston complained that he was not interested in relating to others, he responded to overtures by his co-workers to join them and their wives for dinner. Winston also had regular dinner meetings with his younger brother.

There were some changes in his interpersonal relations with me. As he became convinced that I was empathic and responsive, he also became aware of the difference between his emotionally distant and interpersonally unavailable father and me. Gradually, he began to express negative feelings. I was able to hold his criticisms with no withdrawal or retaliation, which strengthened the relationship. There were some difficult moments when he experienced me as being his intrusive and domineering mother. Then he would become angry and demand that I change my behavior towards him. I considered his demand, examined the interaction, and made meaningful changes. Winston was always grateful for the empathy and my change in function. Something began to change in his feelings toward me. On several occasions, he expressed positive feelings towards me, during his joint sessions with his wife. On one occasion, he said to her: "He is not like your abusive father. He is trying to help you. Yet, you always say he is picking on you!"

Winston's wife also had a severe trauma background marked by physical and emotional abuse by her father, which damaged her perceptions, feelings, and relationships to all male authority. In this instance, Winston was able to express positive feelings for me on behalf of his wife, which is something he could not do before. In addition, he had recommended to his wife, at an earlier time, that she consider joining a psychotherapy group. Winston said that his experience in group was helpful. He added that he believed that she would benefit from interacting with peers. Moreover, he thought she desperately needed to work on her relationships and social isolation. He was now advocating group psychotherapy, peer contact, and relationships.

To self-actualize

Abraham Maslow's concept of self-actualization (Maslow, 1954) can be viewed as a meaningful idea of a positive psychological measure to consider higher level of human functioning. It has a kinship to Balint's concept of the zone of creativity. Maslow's five-stage model of the hierarchy of needs was a pioneering attempt to go beyond the biological drive-theory of psychology. It provided a positive model of human behavior that is motivated to strive beyond fulfillment of basic needs. The five states are presented in descending order:

5. *Self-actualization*
   personal growth and fulfillment
4. *Esteem needs*
   achievement, status, responsibility, reputation
3. *Belongingness and love need*
   family, affection, relationship, work, groups
2. *Safety needs*
   protection, security, order, limits, stability
1. *Biological and physiological needs*
   air, food, drink, shelter, warmth, sex, sleep (Maslow, 1954, 1968; McLeod, 2007).

Maslow's framework integrates a spectrum of human functioning which provides a positive, humanistic goal to achieve one's full potential.

Winston's functioning over the course of the analysis did indicate some achievement in all five stages of Maslow's hierarchy of needs. For states 1 and 2, he has improved his biological and safety needs. When he began his analysis he was unemployed, and lived with his parents. During the first year of his analysis, he became employed. He progressed in his working career from an entry-level job as a social service investigator to becoming an officer of an important investment company. During this same period, he received Master's degrees in Business and Photography, as well as a Law degree. Changes were also made in Stage 3, *Belongingness and love need*. He married during the second year of his analysis, enjoying a more than forty-five year relationship with his wife. He also maintained an enjoyable friendship with his brother. There was some contact with former work colleagues. Winston never had expressed any desire for an ongoing connection with friends or a peer group.

In Stage 4, *Esteem needs*, Winston was able to establish himself as a responsible individual who was a high achiever in his firm. He became an executive associate to a vice-president, and was valued for his capacity to deliver presentations at meeting, Winston's capacity to self-actualize also indicated change. During a significant part of his analysis he was frustrated and angry that he could not fulfill his desire to be an architect. Analysis of this issue indicated his mother's successful attempt to suppress his creative impulse in order to fulfill her own narcissistic need for Winston's complete attention. With the help of non-interpretative measures in a series of adjunctive, intensive group experiences, Winston was able to emotionally confront and develop emotional insight into the suppression of creativity. Finally, he was able to translate these insights into action by creating a vocation in photography. Going into a twenty-five year period, Winston has also developed photography as an academic study. He experimented with new techniques. He pursued taking photographs in a variety of ways and unusual settings. During his retirement, he has devoted the largest portion of his days to walking around the streets of the city and the hills and byways of more rural areas looking for sites to take pictures.

CHAPTER NINE

Analysis of the incest trauma through the drawings of an outsider artist

Outsider art and psychotherapy

Outsider art, the art of visionaries, folk craftmen, reclusives, socially scorned, madmen/psychiatric patients, healers/spiritualists, or simply, peculiar/idiosyncratic individuals, has now received the recognition it deserves as the creative expression of extraordinary people. Their art, because they were not trained to paint, draw, sculpt, or build, reveals their inner selves in their raw creation (Maizels, 1996). The present discussion addresses the artistic productions of individuals who are regularly participants in psychotherapy or psychoanalysis, who are untrained in art, who either spontaneously, or through encouragement by the therapist, produce art which expresses their struggle towards self-understanding and self-actualization. Hans Prinzhorn was the pioneering psychotherapist who studied the art of the mentally ill to gain a better understanding of the process of artistic creation (Prinzhorn, 1972). Prinzhorn focused on the positive and growth potential of the art: "His basic objective was to demonstrate that insane artists are, so to speak, artists in a natural state, uncorrupted by society" (Ferrier, 1998, p. 9).

Prinzhorn paved the way to view the art of the mentally ill as not just curious productions of deranged minds, but art that arose from the deepest recesses of the human psyche. It was this special window into the soul that led Prinzhorn to believe that such art was visionary. This art was insightful, perhaps, containing ultimate truths, he believed. The question of what elevates the drawings or paintings of psychiatric patients, hospitalized psychotics, or analysands to the level of art is an important one. Outsider art, of which patient art is a subcategory, is presently enjoying some popularity. Spontaneously produced art by an analysand who is untrained in art, which occurs during the process of an analysis, and is the manifestation of an internally driven need to express the human condition, can be considered to be an example of outsider art. Of course, such productions will vary considerably, depending upon the individual's capacity to capture the essence of an inner struggle for self-definition and cohesion, as well as their talent to express themselves artistically and the visionary quality of their productions.

There is an existing tradition within psychoanalysis for the use of art as a means to help an analysand give expression to his/her psychopathology as well as aid the process of recovery. In the treatment of incest survivors, individuals have been encouraged to translate their trauma into artistic expression (Van der Kolk, 1988). In clinical work with incest survivors, art has been regularly employed to retrieve memories of trauma and to aid in healing the emotional splits that occurred due to the sexual trauma (Rachman, 2000).

Outsider artist as analysand: the case of W

When W. began his analysis in June 1993, he began to produce art on the advice of a female friend who was an artist and was in psychotherapy working on her own incest trauma. As John MacGregor has so poignantly observed, the artistic productions of an outside artist does not have the usual esthetics of traditional art: "The creations of a true outsider are invariably unsettling: raw, remote, even ugly" (MacGregor, 1989, p. 36).

W.'s drawings can stimulate in the observer archaic emotions usually repressed in the non-psychiatric patient, such as rage, fear, confusion, love, sexuality, perversion, dependency. The images that stimulate such emotions are not beautiful. They began as intense black and white lines, sometimes formed into an ambiguous shape.

Sometimes, the elements in the picture defy identification or analysis. Early in the analysis, W. had an idiosyncratic response to any persistent attempt to encourage associations or analyze the drawings. He became agitated and made it clear that he wished to continue his own associative process without interference. During the difficult analytic process with an incest survivor, empathy maintains attunement to the subjective experience of the analysand. Using the subjective experience of the analysand as the therapeutic compass also encourages and fulfills the necessary empathy for the productions of an outsider artist:

> Totally self-contained and self-motivated, the outsider artist is, nonetheless, vulnerable. Exposed to the un-accustomed attention and admiration of an audience, he is invariably confused by vague and ill-understood ideas and assumptions about his works coming from outside ... The well meaning art-lover, critic, or teacher unwittingly begins to bring about change; to manipulate and to mold the artist and his art in the direction of greater conformity with aesthetic conception and norms. (MacGregor, 1989, p. 36)

The basic issue in the particular artistic expression of outsider artists is that they are not exposed to external manipulation (no matter how well meaning), so that their art ceases to become a function of internal need. The history and evolution of W.'s artistic productions will indicate the extent to which I was able to maintain an non-intrusive role (Balint, 1968), so that the empathic milieu could be a holding environment (Winnicott, 1965b) for the expression of the anlaysand's deepest traumas (Ferenczi, 1988).

Childhood traumas

W. was overwhelmed by his childhood traumas, which helped form a barrier to direct communication with significant others. The mechanism of repression of feelings, avoidance of interpersonal contact, and development of a false self (a social mask) are characteristic of individuals who have suffered severe childhood traumas. W., through the course of his analysis, uncovered a catastrophic experience in his family interaction, which he characterized as living through an emotional holocaust. He was convinced, and the clinical data bears him out, that during his early childhood years, his father anally raped him and his mother fondled his penis and pressed him to her breasts and vagina. He was also a witness to his younger sister's incest experiences. Because these sexual traumatic experiences occurred at a very tender age, when his sense of self was being formed, and the traumas were intense and persistent, he was overwhelmed by betrayal, confusion, hurt, shame, guilt, and rage. Developmental arrest interfered with a sense of trust, belief in parental goodness and nurturance, safety in interpersonal relations, and protection from evil forces. In order to cope with the emotional shock of sexual abuse, he employed a variety of psychological mechanisms to reduce the shock and pain, to remove himself emotionally and interpersonally from the abusers, and to maintain a sense of self-cohesion (Ferenczi, 1980n, 1988; Rachman, 1994b, 1997c, 2000).

W.'s existence from childhood and adolescence into adulthood intensified this pattern of emotional inhibition, social isolation, symbiotic ties to his parents, and intense sexual repression. His relationships outside of the family were meager during his adulthood. W. lived in his parents' apartment until he was forty years old. He did hold a job during this time as a payroll clerk in a large corporation, but he did not have regular contact with a woman until an artist befriended him. W. was sixty-seven years old when he began a platonic relationship with this married woman. This relationship helped change his life and create a pathway toward interpersonal relationships.

W. was overwhelmed by his childhood traumas, describing the experience of violence and annihilation:

> "I remember images of my childhood. They are traumatic."
>
> "I am sixteen months old. I'm naked, lying at the foot of my parent's bed. My father is hitting my back with his clenched fist. One blow hit the center of my spine. The sound was so terrible, it took sixty years to go away. I thought he had broken my spine in two."
>
> "At Coney Island, I'm about fourteen months old. My father is holding me in the crook of his arm. He was wading into the water. Waves looked ominous. I began to scream in terror."

These memories of early childhood with his father are filled with physical and emotional pain. What emerged was a rageful father who placed his son in physical and emotional danger. His first memories are of abuse and neglect. These images of physical abuse and emotional terror at the hands of his father seemed to be the first level of childhood trauma:

1. "I lived in [my parent's] bedroom for the first year of my life" (Session 3.31.04).
2. "My sister admitted to me that she tried to kill me when I was nine years old . . ." (Session 3.31.04).
3. From a poem he composed, entitled "Oblivion", he had this vivid image:

   ". . . every Sunday morning on his knees with a razor across my throat and a knife across my thighs. [These lines are an image.] There were knives, a cat o'nine tails on the wall in the kitchen. I was raped. I have no memory, *but I know it was true*" (Session 5.5.04).
4. "I was told I was toilet trained by nine months. I don't remember, but as an adult, when I try to shit it's an adventure. There are so many layers of feelings connected to my rectum" (Session 5.5.04).
5. "When I [first] went to therapy, about 1965, when I became conscious of my homosexuality, I had the taste of a man's cock in my mouth. The taste lasted for a year—*this I swear by*. I don't remember, *ever* having a homosexual experience. If I did, I would kill myself [?] Because this was not the person I sensed I was. [Then he adds] I didn't know my father was the biggest faggot in my family" (Session 5.5.04).
6. "When I closed my eyes, an eye looked at me. I was being observed, watched, while I was awake. Lasted for thirteen years (?1969–1981).

   "I was forbidden to do things. The eye was watching . . ." Referring to his father, he said: "The horror of the domination of this man. I was a slave."
7. During the course of the analysis, W. uncovered incest memories and images. He talked about his mother and sexuality with anger.

   "My mother's various appetite for my body . . . my mother *fucked me*" (I asked him does he mean this in a literal sense). "Yes," he answered, enraged. "This is like being in Auschwitz" (Session 2.19.05). "My mother never gave me her breast. *I was her breast.* I needed to give to her completely."
8. Finally, he said of the sexual experience with his mother ,"My mother devasted me as a phallic woman. I had a fantasy of her breast as German lugers. Her breasts were weapons she used like a man, fucking me. *She was a monster!*" (Session 11.17.04).

9. W. described what he termed the rape scene, the prototypical sexual abuse scene, which came to him recently in a spontaneous moment of a recall of a childhood sexual trauma: "I was going down on my father; my mother was going down on me; my sister was sticking something in my ass" (Session 2.19.05).
10. W. felt he was a "sexual slave" to his family. He described a severe dissociative response to this sexual abuse, which he called "auto-immune reaction to sexuality." As an adult, his body was shut down to sexuality. He felt he didn't know where his genitals were located.

Autism, and Asperger disorder

As W. felt safer and more trusting, he became more willing to share his childhood experiences. He began to label himself as autistic, or having Asperger's disorder. He also read a *New York Times* article on Asperger's syndrome. He took exception with the article's idea that Asperger's is a neurological disorder. He quotes Winnicott's idea about autism and infantile schizophrenia and Frances Tustin's similar idea (Tustin, 1995; Winnicott, 1965a). W. described his symptoms of autism as:

1. "My mother told me a year before she died, that when she was outside with me with the carriage, I would rock the carriage *for hours* . . . [she did not realize] the autism in the rocking" (Session 3.31.04).
2. "I did not make eye contact."
3. "I couldn't make friends."
4. "I had no motivation."
5. "When I was fourteen years old, I realized I walked looking at the ground."

In 1965, when he entered his first psychotherapy, W. told his therapist of his first nightmare. Then he masturbated to fantasies about his fifteen-year-old niece:

> "I went to sleep, I saw the coastline of the United States and Florida, with a cock into the Atlantic Ocean. The letter 1500 was in the dream. At this

instant, a black cat originated on my left shoulder and dug his nails into me."

W.'s associations to the dream were as follows:

1. "The cat is my mother."
2. "My mother retaliated."
3. "The coast reminds me of a body; a cock into the body."
4. "Pain, her claws" (Session 6.9.04).

A second early dream, occurring in 1968, which he reported lasted all night, was as follows:

"Storks were sticking their beaks into my body. All night agony."

His associations were again to his mother:

1. "Her fingers had nails that stuck into my body when she changed me, washed me."
2. "I have no memory of my mother during my entire childhood." (Did he mean no positive memories of his mother? He did not respond.)

The clinical experience: being with W

The analysis of W. was a unique experience in several meaningful ways. There was W.'s spontaneous production of hundreds of drawings, and as well as a collection of paintings. The artistic expression of his inner self was one of the fulcrums of the analysis. Understanding W.'s traumas and responding empathically to them was another essential dimension of the analysis.

Unraveling the traumas was closely connected to the mutual analysis of the drawings and paintings. Analysis of countertransference was as essential to this therapeutic experience as were the two previous dimensions. Countertransference analysis maintained an empathic connection to W., especially during periods of rage. Finally, this analysis indicated that an individual can transcend severe sexual trauma and move toward sexuality during the latter part of his life.

The therapeutic interaction

The initial consultation session occurred in June 1993. W. came to the session referred by his best friend, Y. This friend, who was already in therapy, suggested it was time for him to focus his psychic energy on working through his childhood traumas. Y. was, at the time, having a successful experience working on her incest trauma. They enjoyed an emotionally close and interpersonally connected relationship. What is more, they influenced each other's lives in very important ways (a theme that was to become crucial for W.'s recovery). As has been discussed, W. suffered from intense and persistent sexual emotional and physical trauma. In his previous treatment, he had been in individual and group psychotherapy for about a six-year period. These experiences did help him move out of this parent's home, to work, and to have some interpersonal contact. However, he was resentful that his childhood traumas were not analyzed and worked through.

During our initial consultation session when he mentioned this failing in his previous therapy, I said to him that we would devote as much time and energy as was necessary to uncover and work through his childhood traumas. I agreed with him that he had not analyzed his traumas, and said it was time to do so. During his first year of his analysis, W. said that the idea that he had not integrated his traumas was a profound moment in our initial clinical interaction. When he learned in the consultation that I would intensely focus on his traumas, he decided he would return to therapy with me. He said he knew he had the right person with whom to work therapeutically: "When I came to you, I was ready. I spent thirty years getting ready for you."

The drawings

During the course of his analysis, W. spontaneously made hundreds of drawings and a small collection of paintings, which we have used to understand and analyze his traumas. In January 2005, he gained formal acceptance as an Outsider Artist. One of his pieces was part of a show. He was recommended to the gallery by his nephew, who is a photographer. The art show was curated by the Ricco/Maresca Gallery and entitled "Autism/Aspergers/Art". A poster for this show is found in Figure 1. The drawing is called "ABC", and is valued at $750 (Figure 2).

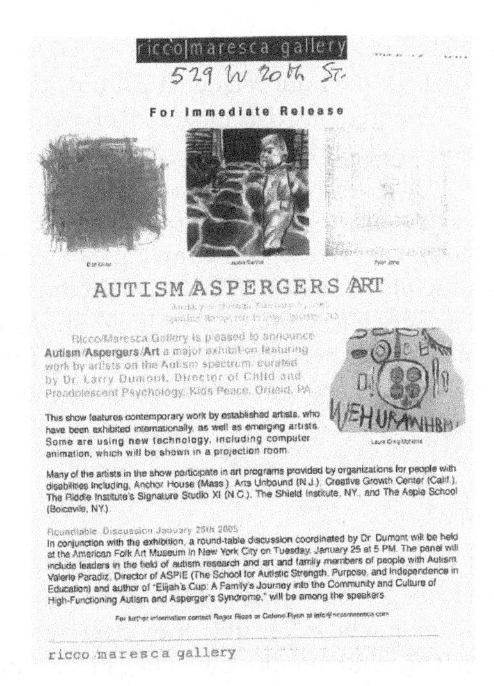

ricco|maresca gallery

529 W 20th St.

For Immediate Release

AUTISM/ASPERGERS/ART

Ricco/Maresca Gallery is pleased to announce **Autism/Aspergers/Art** a major exhibition featuring work by artists on the Autism spectrum, curated by Dr. Larry Dumont, Director of Child and Preadolescent Psychology, Kids Peace, Orfield, PA.

This show features contemporary work by established artists, who have been exhibited internationally, as well as emerging artists. Some are using new technology, including computer animation, which will be shown in a projection room.

Many of the artists in the show participate in art programs provided by organizations for people with disabilities including, Anchor House (Mass.), Arts Unbound (N.J.), Creative Growth Center (Calif.), The Riddle Institute's Signature Studio XI (N.C.), The Shield Institute, NY., and The Aspie School (Boicevile, NY.)

Roundtable Discussion January 25th 2005

In conjunction with the exhibition, a round-table discussion coordinated by Dr. Dumont will be held at the American Folk Art Museum in New York City on Tuesday, January 25 at 5 PM. The panel will include leaders in the field of autism research and art and family members of people with Autism. Valerie Paradiz, Director of ASPIE (The School for Autistic Strength, Purpose, and Independence in Education) and author of "Elijah's Cup: A Family's Journey into the Community and Culture of High-Functioning Autism and Asperger's Syndrome," will be among the speakers.

ricco/maresca gallery

Figure 1. The poster for the art show at which W.'s work was exhibited.

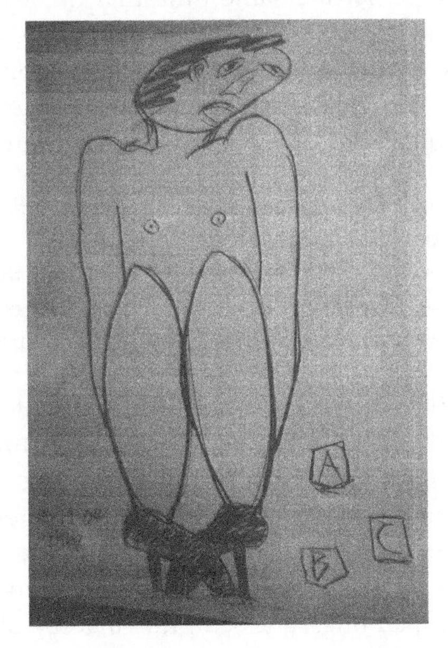

Figure 2. W.'s drawing "ABC".

W.'s drawings began as exclusively black pencil, crayon, or charcoal on white paper. Of the hundreds of such drawings, perhaps five or so had some crayon color. Also included in many of these early drawings are notations of either the subject's name or some hint of the emotional theme of the particular artistic production. In some ways, W.'s drawings have some resemblance to the outsider artist, Dwight Mackintosh (MacGregor, 1989). W.'s drawings are characterized by intense black and white strokes, the obsessive productions of a single subject matter, clear manifestations of an inner struggle, a personal vision of the human form, archaic material emerging from the unconscious, a self-motivated need for a creative outlet, and a talent for artistic expression.

Automatic drawings

W. reported that he began to do automatic drawings around September, 1989, before he began our analysis. The drawings were originally triggered by a dream in which "... [the drawings] showed me I didn't know about myself. Several months later, I began the automatic drawings." Apparently, the dream helped him realize he was becoming emotionally stronger. At the same time that he began feeling more adequate, he also realized his progress was slow. He said: "I was living on 5% of knowing myself. I was hopelessly out of touch."

Ferrier (1998), in discussing the French outsider artist, Raphael Lonne, made an interesting observation about his automatic drawings:

> Guided by the spirits, he began producing automatic drawings for which he was completely unable to account. He was unwittingly engaging in a form of psychic automatism similar to the experiments carried out by the surrealists. Unconscious his drawings were, since he was not even aware of the existence of the unconscious. (pp. 75–76)

Ferrier's description of the psychic function of automatic drawings accurately described the function of W.'s automatic drawings. He needed an outlet for his emotional struggles and, as is often the case, incest survivors naturally turn to some form of creative outlet like drawing, poetry, or sculpture. The world of outsider art is filled with individuals who have expressed their inner emotional struggles through drawings, paintings, and sculpture that reveal an unconscious world to the viewer (Ferrier, 1998). In fact, there are outsider artists who have created outdoor environments, which reflect their view of a world (Ferrier, 1998).

Copying art reproductions

A second development in W.'s artistic expression arose when his artist friend, Y., encouraged two important directions. She said to him: (1) "You should go to a therapist who is equipped to deal with your abusive background"; (2) "You should try to draw."

He trusted and valued her. As he said, "Because it was her, I tried." W., inspired by Y., moved from automatic drawing to copying art drawings from various art books. He enjoyed doing this because it moved him from the scribbling of the automatic drawings to attempting representational art (Figure 3).

Figure 3. An attempt at representational art by W.

Without my ever suggesting he draw, W. took the next step toward outsider art. In his own words, he revealed this psychological and artistic evolution: "My drawings began when I started therapy with you. I *never, never, never dealt with the trauma*. When I saw you for the first session, you told me I never integrated my childhood trauma. *This was a revelation*. Right then and there, I knew I would see you for therapy."

From the first session of our analysis onward, W. began to draw human figures, mostly women. At first, they were studies in the facial expressions. Gradually, the drawings included different versions of a torso. These drawings were the beginnings of the expression of unconscious feelings derived from childhood trauma represented by interaction within the family. W. reported this aspect of the process: "When I saw you I began to draw what was inside of me."

Drawings made during the analysis

The integration of W.'s spontaneously produced drawings was a key to our analysis. Our interaction in the clinical session consisted of free associating and then analyzing the drawings, much like a projective test is given by a psychologist. Each session, he would bring in an artist's sketchpad with about 10–20 drawings he had made between sessions. Each session began with W. showing me the drawings, free associations to the events of the day, telling of a dream, discussion of a poem he had written, or the uncovering of childhood memories. About half-way through the session, he presented the drawings he had produced. At first, he made it clear he did not want me to rush to interpret them. The drawings were reviewed one by one. I asked W. to say what would come to his mind, much as one would do if showing the Rorschach inkblots. At that point, the only other interaction initiated was to ask him for clarification on any aspect of the drawing that I did not understand. This interaction was similar to the inquiry phase of giving the Rorschach, where clarifying the data proceeded interpretation. After W. began to feel safer and more trusting, he would ask the analyst for thoughts about the drawings. This was a turning point. Before that point of openness on W.'s part, he was practicing a one-person psychology, where he was the sole authority in creating our clinical interaction. When he asked me for my associations, our analysis became a two-person experience. I began to cautiously introduce aspects of his trauma that were relevant to his drawing. He had a very enthusiastic response to these interpretations, as if he had been waiting all his life to have someone help him understand the catastrophe that had overtaken his childhood.

Drawings of Barbara

W. began to draw human figures, mostly of women early in the analysis. At first, they were studies in facial expressions. Gradually, the drawings included the different versions of a torso. His first series of drawings, which covered a four-year period, produced hundreds of pictures of a woman named Barbara. She was a young woman who waited on him in the neighborhood restaurant where he had his breakfast and lunch. W.'s experiences with women at this stage of his analysis was with family members, such as his sister and his niece, or through what he called business contacts, women whom he met through his interest in art, such as gallery owners. Also, he maintained a platonic relationship with his artist friend Y., who later will become the major sexual figure of his life. These kinds of limited contact with women helped W. to titrate his anxiety and reduce the sexuality of the interaction. It was necessary for him psychologically to negotiate his dissociated sexuality, intense feelings of inadequacy, castration feelings, and concern about a woman abusing him.

As W. saw Barbara every day for years, their customer–waitress relationship became friendly and warm. One day, Barbara confided to him that she was a lesbian. Her self-disclosure, although traumatic for W., was an empathic gesture by Barbara. She realized he was falling in love with her. He was able to recover from the trauma by drawing hundreds of pictures of Barbara, eventually adding sexual elements to her torso (Figure 4). In his own words, W. discussed the evolution of the Barbara's drawings:

> "The Barbara drawings were a prologue to the Susan drawings. I needed a face. I loved her from my heart, not my loins. She was a prologue to a real woman emerging. She was unobtainable. Barbara *opened up* my heart."

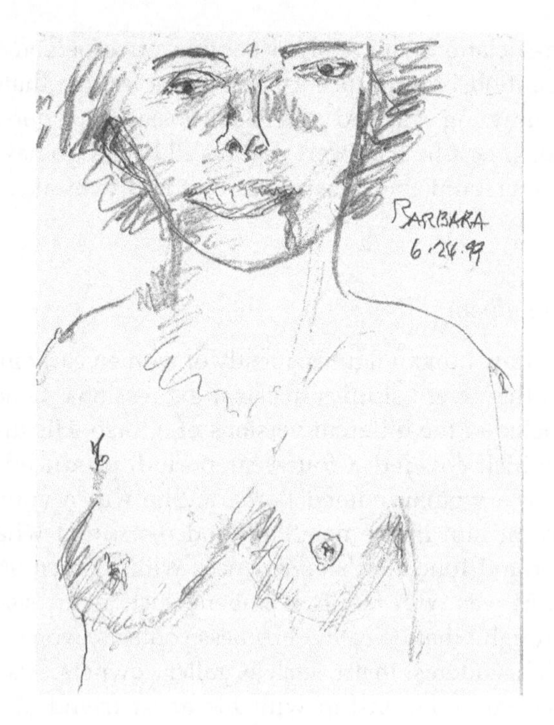

Figure 4. W.'s drawing of Barbara, 6.24.99.

Drawings of Susan

The next drawings began in 1999, inspired by his relationship with an art gallery owner, Susan. W. visited her gallery, as he had others, and usually made friends with a woman in the establishment. It would be someone with whom he felt an empathic, warm, and compassionate connection. He has the remarkable emotional sensitivity that is born of trauma. W. spent a lifetime searching for a mother who could control her sexuality so it would not contaminate her nurturance. This was embedded in the interaction with Susan, the gallery owner. W.'s description of Susan is as follows:

> "Met her when I started collecting prints at the gallery where she was the Associate Director. A lovely, kind woman who was married. I recall never believing in a million years that I would ever be interested in her as a woman. She subsequently opened her own gallery and we became friends and I would talk and she would listen (a great

listener!) She entered my dream life as a helper and a guide that has continued for ten years.

> "She is like a nun; extraordinary skin and mouth, I don't believe she has ever come on to me, but I must confess, in my fantasies, I lust for her to an exceptional degree. Combining my heart and loins has made her an extension of how I probably felt about my mother. They seem so much alike, repelled by sex, yet hopelessly wanting its license."

Between 3.28.99 and 5.19.99, W. produced twenty-one drawings of Susan (Figure 5). He described the Susan drawings as representing the most important work he had done up to this time: "The drawings are like breaking through the earth's crust . . . These drawings reach to the core of my mother, her breasts. This was impossible until now . . . The female has finally emerged through Susan."

In assessing the meaning of these drawings, I wondered whether W. was on the verge of change, moving toward a relationship with a

Figure 5. Susan in her gallery, 3.28.99.

woman where he can feel nurtured and express the fullness of his being. In the analytic sessions, he hinted at this development. He described increased body sensations, intrapsychic rearrangement of archaic material, the reduction of interpersonal anxiety and the rediscovery of what W. called "my genital area" (pointing downward from his midsection to his genitals). The analyst believed that W. was discovering and expressing his manhood, both literally and figuratively, in a new, positive way.

Drawings that indicated change

A series of drawings slowly began to emerge from the years of 2000 to 2005 that indicated intrapsychic and interpersonal changes. Six drawings depicted these changes.

A Young Woman is a painting W. produced on January 7th 2002 (Figure 6) when he began to move from black and white drawings to

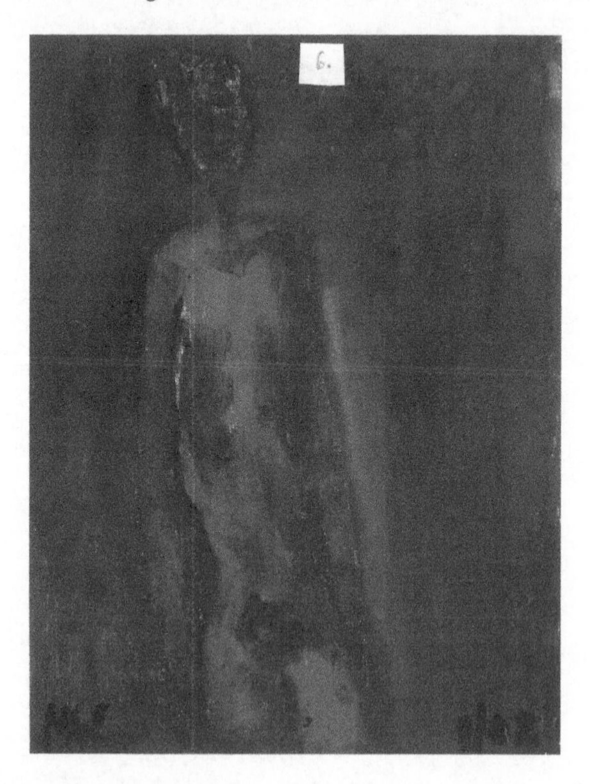

Figure 6. A Young Woman, 1.7.02.

producing drawings and paintings which contained color. He commented that the change reflected an emotional opening up where he felt more capable of expressing feelings other than anger or pain. The genital area seems to contain pubic hair, but it is not entirely clear. What is clear is that it is a painting of a full figure of a woman in vibrant red. "Is there a woman causing a fire to burn inside you?" was an interpretation offered tentatively. His response was noncommittal; but he didn't reject it, and neither did he verify it. However, he added: "[I] felt wonderful when I completed it" (Session 3.7.02).

In Figure 7, a drawing of 12.8.04, W. created a picture of a woman who, for the first time, is depicted in full figure, having recognizable breasts, a genital area that looks like a vagina, although one can also

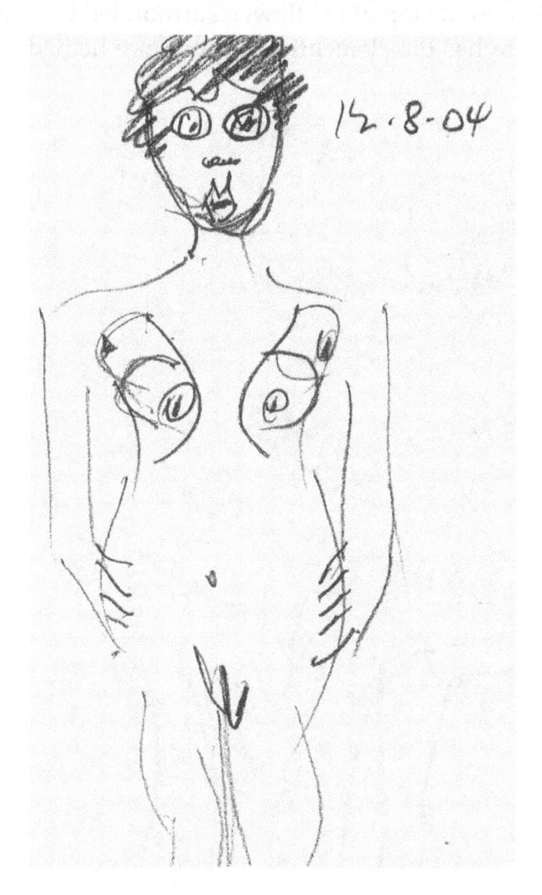

Figure 7. W's picture of his friend, Y, 12.8.04.

visualize a penis on the right side of the genital area. We both respond to this drawing as indicating that a significant change has taken place. The woman is relatively intact. It was clear to both of us that this was a woman who was not depicted as a phallic mother, or as a mad woman. These were the characteristics depicted in the previous drawings. Past depictions also contained women who have a penis. W. said this was a picture of his artist friend, Y.

On 5.1.05, W. produced *Viva,* the first drawing he had made of a flower (Figure 8). The flower takes up the majority of space in the drawing. It has a fullness and certain sense of sweetness, which W. acknowledged. *Viva,* the title of the drawing, indicated a celebration, aliveness, and life. The other elements of the drawing show a "phallic-type" object on the top of the flower, surrounded by two windows. The flower stem has the elements of disturbance he had identified in

Figure 8. Viva, 5.1.05.

many other drawings. On the two corners of the bottom of the drawing, there is a repetition of the windows in the upper portion of the drawing. W.'s response indicated that he was very pleased with the drawing. He felt it indicated a positive feeling was emerging. I offered that there was an emergence of a sense of well-being, a blossoming, and a sense of being able to look into something. W. accepted the interpretation gladly.

The drawing of 6.11.05 (Figure 9) indicated something new and something old. The old is the dark black markings at the bottom of the drawing, rising up to the middle of the page. In hundreds of other drawings these kind of lines and configurations indicated chaos, anger, disturbance, pain, or trauma. But, in this drawing, there is a decidedly new element. Two hands, seemingly free of angst, drawn in

Figure 9. An exchange of traumas.

a kind of sweet, tender way, are intertwined. The hands are drawn above the disturbance below, seemingly apart from the chaos. We agreed the inert intertwined hands are a sign of tenderness, a coming together of two people. W. again suggested the drawing is connected to his friend Y. When they first attempted intimacy, Y. said it was like,"an exchange of traumas."

A drawing that was made on 6.15. 05 (Figure 10), four days after the tender hands drawing, is even more remarkable. A one-eyed nude male with outstretched arms shows his penis. As soon as I saw this drawing, it seemed to me to be a picture of W. symbolizing a significant internal change. I waited patiently for W. to associate to the drawing. W. did not hesitate to say he had drawn himself as a full-fledged

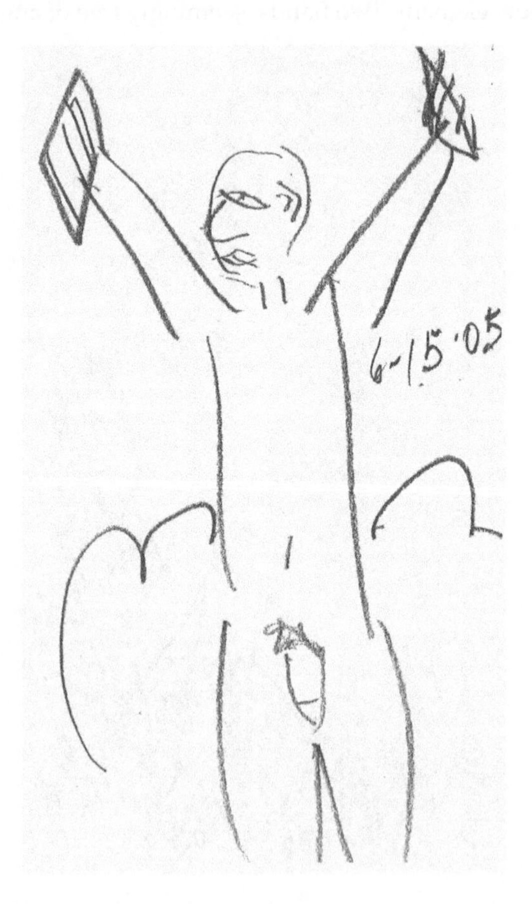

Figure 10. Discovering Who I Am as a Male.

male. This is the first drawing of himself as a male with clearly defined intact male genitalia. He had reported that he was now "feeling my body below the waist. I am discovering who I am as a male. I have some fiber in my being now" (Session 7.22.05). This drawing appears to depict this developing trend. What is more, it appears to be an aggressive statement of masculinity. This same one-eyed figure in Figure 11 appeared to have been transformed from a trauma victim to an assertive male.

"The Face of Death" drawing produced on 4.20.01 (Figure 12) became a therapeutic expression for W. of his traumatic childhood. "The Face of Death" reflected W.'s emerging feelings of the negative impact that recalling his intense childhood sexual abuse was having on his sense of self. In other words, recovering of childhood trauma is

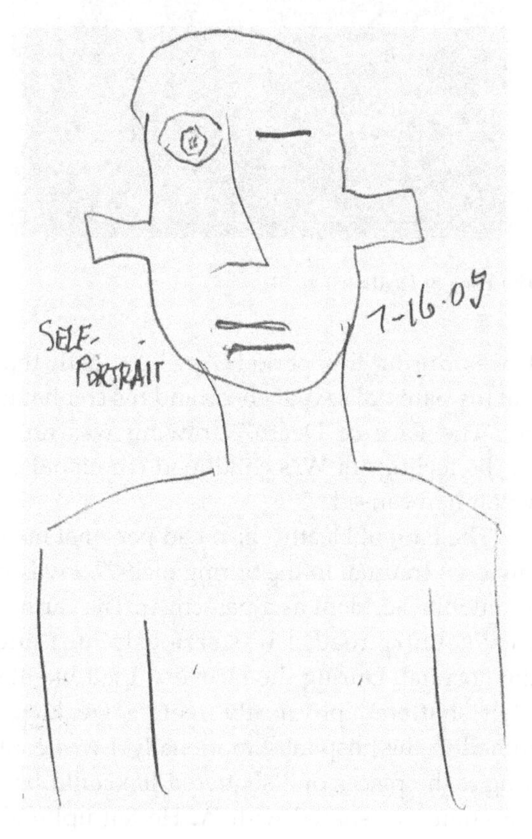

Figure 11. Self-Portrait, 7.16.05.

Figure 12. "The Face of Death", 4.20.01.

traumatic. It was during this period, April 20, 2001, that he became more aware of his parental sexual abuse and his combatant feelings of annihilation. "The Face of Death" drawing was an overt, active expression of the feelings of W.'s childhood emotional death that the sexual seduction had caused.

Figure 12, "The Face of Death", also had personal meaning for me; it depicted my own trauma. In the Spring of 1999, I was involved in a near-fatal automobile accident as a passenger. The car hit a tree, skidding on an icy country road. I was seriously hurt and spent two months in the hospital. During the recovery, I felt like the face in the drawing. I felt shattered physically, feeling weak, losing twenty pounds, confined to the hospital. Emotionally, I was confused, angry and wondering if the pieces of a shattered life could be put together again. This reaction was shared with W. He felt uplifted by the self-disclosure.

The therapeutic experience

Once the analysis formally began in the session after the consultation, the interaction changed. In the consultation session, I was firm, direct, and focused on collecting data in order to understand W.'s traumas. This focus and direct interaction seemed very helpful for W., because he felt I could understand and confront his traumatic childhood. Instead of continuing the direct focus on W's trauma, it became abundantly clear that W. was an intensely emotionally fragile individual who needed prolonged empathic understanding. He was also brimming with both anxiety and intense angry feelings. W. would have many moments of fitful rage. In our earliest interactions, I would inquire about an issue in a gentle, empathic manner. The issue might be something W. offered about his childhood, parents, interpersonal interaction, or one of the drawings he had produced. Without provocation, he would attack me, saying in an angry tone, "I don't know what that means! I don't know why I said that!"

At that point, it felt as if any questions, comments, or observations were experienced as traumatogenetic. It was clear that what W. needed was an extended empathic presence, who provided him with affirmation and acceptance. At this earlier period, he did not need to be pushed toward interpretation and insight. With someone so vulnerable and traumatized, I needed to focus on countertransference analysis. This was a moment where a two-person experience took precedence over my need to know.

The analysis was characterized by allowing the analysand to use the analyst as he needed, first as an empathic presence, then as a co-responder to the material brought into sessions, for example, dreams, poems, drawings, and observations, then as a co-creator of the process, when he was *invited* to give his ideas about the theory and technique about the treatment process (Rachman, 2006, 2007a,b).

The confusion of tongues theory of trauma indicated that the retraumatization is a natural development in the analysis of the incest trauma. As Ferenczi first suggested, then Kohut reaffirmed, the exact nature of the interaction in the psychoanalytic situation can determine whether the analysand will feel safe or retraumatized (Ferenczi, 1988; Kohut, 1984). It was clear, in this analysis, that W. would only feel safe if he could co-create the clinical interaction and could depend on the analyst's empathically attuning to his needs (Rachman, 1997a, 2000, 2003a; see also Chapter Eight).

W.'s rage

Dealing therapeutically with W.'s rage was a significant therapeutic challenge. As one can see from his earliest images and nightmares, he had developed his personality in response to physical and emotional abuse at the hands of both parents. His anger was never expressed directly towards them, but, transferentially, towards other people in enactments of his childhood traumatic experience. During the first three or four years of his analysis, W. would report disturbing incidents of anger in his daily life. He would, for example, be in a restaurant waiting to be served his meal and feel he was being mistreated by the waiter or someone in the restaurant. He would show his displeasure in an overt angry and hostile way, which led to a verbal altercation with one or more persons. The same kind of angry incident would occur on public transportation or when he was sitting on a park bench. W. would feel the person next to him was moving too close to him, invading his space. He would become enraged, often initiating an angry interchange. These hostilities were not confined to strangers. W. would also report feeling enraged at his sister, niece, his best friend, and me.

A good example of his rage and the analysis of the countertransference to it was contained in a clinical example that spontaneously occurred in one session during the winter months of the year 2000. I had just purchased an area rug for the consultation room. A plastic covering was placed over it on a snowy day so it did not get wet and dirty. During a prior session with a couple, no mention of the plastic cover was made. No sooner had W. entered the consultation room to begin the session than he erupted into a rage. The next fifteen minutes of the session were taken up by W.'s rants and raves toward me. He pointed his finger, shouting at the top of his lungs: "Who do you think you are! Boy, do you have problems! You are a sadist!" He then walked toward a picture displayed of Sandor Ferenczi. "You have betrayed your mentor, Ferenczi. Do you think he would do this to me" (Rachman, 2004, p. 230).

It was a very difficult moment in the analysis. W. clearly was in the throes of a retraumatizing experience that threw him into a borderline or psychotic rage. I was frightened and confused. From previous experiences with W., when he raged about his experiences with his family, friends, and strangers he met in a park or restaurant, he was unreachable until the rage subsided. While he continued his angry tirade, I thought silently: "I have no fucking idea what I've done to stimulate his rage. If I knew what it was I'd sure do what is necessary to calm him. I hope he will let me talk to him. In the meantime, it is scary to have him yelling at me like this. I wish he would stop. I hope he doesn't try anything physical."

W.'s reaction clearly created a confusion of tongues trauma between us. W. was acting as if I had deliberately recreated a terrible experience from his childhood. The analysis of this trauma began when W. finished his rage and became amenable to exploring the experience. When we both recovered, we began the exploration of the emotional experience. I was focused on understanding the anger: "It seems as if I have done something that is causing you much difficulty . . . I would like you to consider talking to me about the anger . . . so we can begin to understand it . . ." (Rachman, 2004, p. 231).

I also told him I would try to understand the crisis from his point of view. W. responded, beginning to reveal the meaning of his rage. His rage was a negative maternal transference reaction. For much of his life, he lived with a mother who covered all the family furniture in plastic. Since he suffered from sexual seduction and emotional deprivation from his mother, he interpreted his mother's covering the furniture as her protecting, valuing, and loving her furniture more than him. His mother never took such pains to protect him, "cover him from abuse." As soon as he walked into the consultation room, his eyes were drawn to the plastic cover on the floor rug and he was immediately, and emotionally returned to his family home and his mother's plastic furniture coverings. I had unwittingly (unconsciously) contributed to an enactment of a basic fault of W.'s personality. In an instant, I became his emotionally neglectful, abusive mother. The rage he had suppressed as a child emerged in a volcanic eruption. As we opened up this exploration of his rage and its meaning, W. became thoughtful, emotionally connected, and insightful, as he generally was. When I realized how traumatic my covering the rug was for W.'s psychology and psychic functioning, I decided to initiate a reparative therapeutic measure (Rachman, 1998b) by saying to W., "I am truly regretful that I contributed to your pain. Covering the rug with plastic is not as important as my being responsive to your needs."

The plastic covering for the rug was gathered up and thrown in the trash. I returned in a moment or two to find W. smiling and feeling grateful. It was now possible to analyze the empathic failure that had occurred between us as well as its connection to his childhood trauma. The trauma of the plastic cover became a symbol for the *abusive way he was treated in his family.*

Of course, abusive treatment is a crucial issue for an incest survivor. When W. saw the plastic rug cover, he experienced me as the plastic mother, someone who was unempathetic, narcissistic, and abusive. Since the analysis had helped reduce his dissociative process, his angry feelings connected to parental abuse were more available to him. Although it was emotionally uncomfortable for me to experience his rage, it was therapeutic for W. to openly react in an emotional way to perceived abuse. The more W. experienced me as abusive, the more it was necessary to be empathic and provide non-interpretative measures to create a reparative therapeutic experience for his childhood trauma (Rachman et al., 2009a,b). Additionally, when retraumatization occurs in the psychoanalytic situation, it is necessary for the analyst to practice judicious self-disclosure (Rachman, 2003d) to curtail clinical hypocrisy (Ferenczi, 1980n, 1988), to contribute a curative function to the confusion of tongues trauma. Judicious self-disclosure in this instance meant admitting that I had made a therapeutic error (Ferenczi, 1980b). The plastic rug cover was intended to do something positive, to protect a rug. But, it created a trauma, so it needed to be removed to reduce W.'s pain. The mandate was to repair the empathic rupture (Rachman, 1998a). W. was correct—his needs should take precedence.

W. was appreciative of my words and behavior, because he felt he was being helped with his childhood trauma. We were able to analyze, in this session, and in sessions to follow, his trauma and reach the following insights; his rage was caused by his maternal trauma; initially, he could not distinguish the analyst from his mother: the more developed was his insight into his abusive childhood experiences and his rage, the less angry he became. Several years later, he recalled the plastic cover trauma when he was analyzing his anger toward his mother. Turning toward me, he asked about the rage he had displayed in that disturbing session. I responded with, "When you became enraged about the plastic cover over the rug it was frightening and disturbing" (Session 2.19.05).

W. reflected that he now realized how angry he was at that moment; how angry he can become in an instant. This was the first time in years of analysis that he had examined his angry reactions. Furthermore, he reported that he was also less angry in interpersonal experiences in his daily life. After the plastic cover trauma, his angry outbursts diminished. W. indicated an internal process of change had occurred with this response: "I'm containing my rage. I've changed a lot. I'm getting along with people" (Session 2.19.05).

Sexuality transcends trauma

When W. began his analysis, his sexuality identity was not a major issue. Years after his analysis began, he reported his original reason for seeking therapeutic help was his anxiety over homosexual feelings. But, in the clinical interactions, he never reported homosexual anxiety of contact. W's family background included homosexual childhood experiences with his father, such as anal penetration. It is an important question to ask why W. did not focus on his homosexual feelings in either his report of his first therapy, or in his analysis.

W.'s childhood traumas were based upon multiple experiences. His sexual traumas with his father produced an experience of neglect, fear, and abuse. When his father was not sexually abusing him, he was emotionally neglectful and verbally and physically abusive. W. reported that his father showed no interest in him, and, on occasions, would "slam [me] against the wall." His mother, as he reported, was only interested in him as an object for sexual satisfaction. His younger sister was lured into his sexual abuse by his parents. With this emotional holocaust as his basic family experience, W. had lost the feeling of hope, trust, and safety in human relationships.

A relational concept, living in the transference (Rachman, 1997a, 1998b, 2003a), can be used to explain therapeutic change through the creation of a reparative therapeutic experience (Rachman, 1998b). In this experience, the nature of the empathic, responsive, flexible, and active relationship contributes to the repair of the childhood traumas. As Ferenczi (1988), Kohut (1984), Searles (1975), and Winnicott (1965a,b) have discussed, an analysis which stresses empathy, responsiveness, and tenderness over interpretation, silence, and clinical detachment is best suited for trauma analysis. The analysand needs and wants to be analyzed in an atmosphere of a non-abusing parental figure who demonstrates concern, compassion, and affection when attempting to understand and confront the analysand's traumas.

It is believed that such an experience creates a therapeutic alternative to the traumatogenic parental interaction of childhood, so that some emotional issues are lived through in the therapeutic relationship, rather than spoken through. Emotional insight, changes in the experience of the other, can occur in the subjective matrix of accurate empathic interaction. The ideas discussed above are all in the way of saying that W.'s homosexual anxiety was reduced in the therapeutic relationship. There might have been one or two dreams that had a homosexual theme, which were analysed, but it was never a significant issue to which W. devoted time and energy. There was no clinical data in the interaction, whether verbal or non-verbal, that indi-cated a necessity to analyze the issue. W.'s homosexual fears significantly dissipated. The issue of heterosexuality, however, was a significant issue for W. from the very beginning of his analysis, to which we now turn.

Sexual recovery and renewal

Drawings of Miss B

Both W. and I followed his retrieval, recovery, and renewal of his sexual feelings and functioning with great interest and delight. During his first therapy, as well as several years into the analytic experience, W. indicated that he had great doubts about being a senior citizen in his seventies who could begin to have an active sexual life. I hoped that all the intensive work toward uncovering his childhood sexual traumas, revealed in his drawings, and the analysis of the actual relationships with three key women in his adult life, would produce some breakthrough.

Over a period of several years, W. began to integrate the analytic work that had begun in June 1993. As discussed, he first cited his vicarious sexual relationship with Miss B., who was a waitress in the restaurant in his neighborhood he most frequented. He described the meaning of this relationship: "Remember Miss B., the lesbian! I had to go through experiences with this lesbian. I wanted to embrace her. It helped me feel more alive in my body [points to his thighs]" (Session 4.19.05).

W. yearned for a romantic relationship with Miss B. during a two-year period. He did approach her for a date, but she was not interested. The relationship remained a vicarious sexual relationship. It was a beginning attempt for W. to retrieve and recover a sexual sense of self. During the many discussions of his restaurant visits with Miss B., it was abundantly clear that W. was verbally expressing his sexual feelings for her. Miss B. did not share his sexual interests because she was attracted to women and saw W. as a father figure, not as a lover. He possessed a special quality of wanting to pursue the truth in analyzing his sexual trauma and to make whatever changes possible. What is more, he used his fantasy life, as well as Miss B.'s compassion, friendliness, and social interest in him, to encourage a positive paternal transference. If you will, he wanted to try on for size a sexual relationship with an adult woman. Although Miss B. was not his peer (she was probable thirty or more years his junior), W. needed a woman who would respond to him as a man. Moreover, he also needed a woman who would not act abusively to him as did his mother and sister. It was very important that the first woman he found the courage to turn to, after analyzing his sexual traumas, was receptive to him as a person. It was a credit to his developing sense of self that he chose a responsive, kind woman, not an exploitative or abusive one.

The drawing of Miss B. (Figure 4), produced on 6.24.99 during the time he was having contact with her, was one of the most significant productions. It was a drawing that illustrated a woman's face free of distortion, although one might interpret the mouth and nose as having masculine components. Even if one accepts this interpretation, the masculine mouth and nose might reflect his perception of her lesbian masculinity. The rest of the drawing of Barbara is feminine, showing a feminine torso, including clearly articulated female breasts. Such a drawing has emotional, feminine, and sexual appeal, no matter how crudely it depicts a woman.

Susan

The relationship with Susan, which became active after Barbara, was also a vicarious sexual relationship. But, the difference was that W. had an intense sexual response to Susan. He was ready for a more overt, sexual response to a heterosexual woman. W. was aware of his complicated sexual response to Susan. His physical relationship consisted of regular visits to her workplace, where they would have friendly conversations. The calm, friendly intellectual talks belied the intense sexual arousal and attraction that was churning in W. every time he saw Susan. He stated this intensity years after the relationship had faded: "Susan, helped me too. It was lust that was I running away from. If I had that lust, I was like my father" (Session 4.19.05).

Clearly, connecting his lust to his father's abusive sexual feelings towards him and his mother and sister made feeling sexual towards Susan intensely conflictual.

The drawing that W. made of Susan on 3.28.99 (Figure 5) clearly expressed the lust, conflict, confusion, and anxiety. The structure of the drawing indicated the bold, dark, black chaotic strokes that characterize his early drawings. Such drawings described the internal struggles W. had to negotiate to both uncover and work through his sexual conflicts. Also visible in the drawing is the figure's breasts, indicating W.'s capacity to express his sexual desire. The area of the figure's genitalia, at this point in W.'s analysis (1999), was expressed in conflictual terms. Emerging out of the vaginal area are two large objects, which have phallic-looking properties. These phallic-like objects seem connected to the figure's breasts. The female figure in the drawing has an unusual facial expression, perhaps some unhappiness. These characteristics of Figure 5 discussed above indicate an expression of sexuality and lust that caused as much difficulty as it did pleasure. With these difficulties evident, the drawing also indicated a full-figured sexual woman. Tucked away in the lower right corner of the drawing seems to be an apple, further suggesting the notion that W.'s discovery of his sexuality is a forbidden fruit. These ideas were originally suggested to W. when he brought the drawing into a session. At that time in his analysis, W. was not able to fully integrate the analysis of his sexual conflicts. My response to the drawing was empathic, stressing the positive qualities of his emerging willingness to express sexual feelings. W. integrated what he could of our clinical interaction during that therapeutic period.

The nature of this kind of empathic clinical interaction is based on the analyst's faith in the analysand's capacity to search for the truth and move toward self-actualization. The faith in W.'s capacities was verified when, in a session five years later, he reported that he had his first overt, positive, sexual dreams about a woman, using Susan as the projective device:

> "I am kissing Susan and I am holding one of her breasts" (Session 5.5.04).

A week later he had the second dream reported in the same session.

"I am kissing Susan and I am holding both of her breasts in my hand. There was nothing going on below the waist" (Session 5.5.04).

W.'s associations contained several significant statements. These were the first two dreams of W. having sexual contact with a woman. Although he had not seen Susan in a year or so, she remained a sexual figure for him. Susan still sent out "sexual vibes" to him, or, perhaps more accurately, he still felt sexual vibes for her. There was also a growing sense of greater sexual awareness. In the second dream, W. said: ". . . There was nothing going on below the waist," suggesting that he was still preoccupied with women's breasts, but afraid of their genitals. Yet, in his association to the dreams, he said: "There is something going on in the genital area" (Session 5.5.04). The contrast in these statements reflected W.'s growing sexual feelings in contrast to Susan's sexuality, which W. had described earlier in his analysis as: "She's like a nun: extraordinary skin and mouth. I don't believe she has ever come on to me, but, I must confess in my fantasies I lust for her to an exceptional degree. Combining my heart and my loins has made her an extension of how I probably feel about my mother. They seem so much alike: repelled by sex, yet . . . wanting its license" (Session 5.14.99).

In a drawing of 8.13.00 (Figure 13), W. depicted his mother in a nude pose with a disturbed look on her face, expressing his sexual preoccupation with her. Susan was a projective device for W. to work on and through those disturbing feelings, ". . . nothing [something] going on below the waist," depicted in the undefined genital area in the "Mother" drawing.

Y., his artist friend

W. met Y. at an art gallery in 1987. At that time, W. was a collector of fine art drawings and Y. was an artist. When they met, Y. was more interested in W. than he was in her. In his own words, he described these early feelings: "I paid no interest [to her] until 1991, when all of a sudden, she seemed to change . . . I walked Y. to her loft. *Big thing for me, I didn't know to be with a woman.* She didn't reject me. Y. was thrilled by my contacting her" (Session 9/20/04).

At first, W. did not know that Y. was married. He hesitated to contact her. Y. called him in April 1992, asking him out to lunch. It was

Figure 13. "Mother".

then he found out she was married. They got to know each other. W. found out her marriage was based upon sex, not love. She introduced W. to her husband, and W.'s reaction was: "She was his slave. He owned her lock, stock and barrel. I took the side of the victim" (Session 9/20/04).

In July of 1992, W. cut off contact with Y. because she was married and there was no opportunity for a romance. It was then Y. revealed her history to W.: "I found out that she was acting out with men. I was the 36th. When we met, she told me her amnesia about being abused by her father was breaking apart. It was good for her to talk about this" (Session 9/20/04).

Y. sensed in W. an empathic person with whom she could share her emotional problems. This quality of W. being a lay therapist was indicated in all his relationships, for example, Barbara, Susan, his sister, niece, nephew, and a male friend. The same dedication W. brought to the analysis of his traumas he conveyed to others. What is more, he vigorously encouraged these individuals to pursue psychotherapy and psychoanalysis to work through and recover from their traumas. W. used these special characteristics to help Y. Their relationship helped her to stop taking medication and she started psychotherapy, particularly to deal with the childhood sexual abuse by her father. As W. described it, they "blundered into sex, not genital sex." Their first sexual contact was oral sex at W.'s apartment. After this initial sexual contact, they continued the oral sexual contact for about a dozen times. W.'s reaction to this sexual contact was: "I felt warm as toast. I never felt like that before. She began to fall in love with me" (Session 9/20/04).

Y. described their sexual contact as an exchange of traumas (Session 10/25/04), knowing they both were wounded individuals attracted to each other to share and work on their traumas. The drawing, "An Exchange of Traumas" (Figure 9, 6/11/05), expressed this feeling. Two hands, a woman's on the right and a man's on the left gently come together. The woman's hand seems to be reaching out to the man's somewhat more agitated hand, paralleling the experience of contact which happened between W. and Y. when they met in real life. Below the gentle embrace of hands is the chaotic markings of W.'s drawing, which indicated intense anxiety, fear, and danger, indicative of trauma (compare Figure 9 to Figure 14, "Trauma", 9/21/99). But, they also shared a great affection and mutuality. When Y.'s psychotherapy for her sexual trauma became helpful to her, she encouraged W. to seek getting similar help. As previously discussed, W.'s first therapy experience did not uncover his childhood sexual trauma. Y.'s therapist recommended W. to the me. Another shared experience that became essential for W.'s recovery was Y.'s encouraging W. to draw, which allowed the unfolding of his childhood sexual traumas.

The new relationship with Y. was to develop over a three-year period. It was W.'s first romantic and genital sexual relationship. He realized that his view of Y. needed to change in order to move toward sexuality: "I think that I am trying to see Y. as a woman who was raped by her father. Maybe I can see her as a woman . . . I want to turn straw into gold, turn (our relationship) into love. I am forbidden to lust after her [is there something holding you back?], I have an autoimmune reaction to sexuality" (Session 10/25/04).

Figure 14 Trauma.

When he mentioned the auto-immune reaction to sexuality he was very emotional, for example, angry, upset, tearful. Slowly, carefully, not wanting to exacerbate his disturbance, I explored his feelings of intense sexual anxiety. W. said about the feeling: ". . . it can't be put into words. It is a feeling from the earliest time of life. You can't have sex—'I will cut it off'" (Session 10/25/04).

As we explored it more deeply, he not only indicated he suffered from crippling castration anxiety, but this anxiety was not only psychological, it was physiological. In essence, he felt that his very early and persistent sexual traumas resulted in the feeling that his body rejected sexuality. In many sessions when W. explored his sexuality he would point from his mid-section to his genital area. This gesture indicated that sexual functioning was severely restricted in his body and his sexual organs were unknown and taboo areas. Another serious issue in the sexual relationship with Y. was her husband. W. had intense negative feelings about him. He felt the husband was a "manipulator," living off Y.'s family inheritance, basically "homosexual" and not interested in Y. as a woman. Theirs "was not a marriage of love," W. concluded. More importantly, W. saw the husband as "evil." W. felt this sense of evil because the husband reminded him of his father's evilness. The husband became the contemporary embodiment of evil, an abuser, a sexual predator.

On 11/17/04, W. began a session expressing a change in his functioning: "The extent to which I could pay attention to my body, my sensations or lack of them, this was my bedrock. It was the equivalent of melting the *Antarctic Circle*" [W. became emotional] (Session 11/17/04). This session became a revelation for both analyst and analysand. After being in analysis for eleven years, W. was ready for a full analysis of his sexual fear, anxiety, and inhibition. In a way in which he was not available before, W. accepted every intervention, even the most penetrating interpretation. We were on the cusp of change. W. gave new meaning to Ferenczi's notion of the primary defense mechanisms associated with the confusion of tongues paradigm (see Chapter Six). Specifically, he showed the psycho/physical mechanisms that a survivor of a childhood sexual abuse suffers. He had lost the capacity to speak of the trauma. The trauma survivor becomes tongue-tied, using dissociation to protect himself from further harm and disturbed interpersonal relations. There is no better way to highlight this inner struggle toward change then to quote W. His words are beacons of light in the darkness of childhood sexual abuse: "I had to deal with the trauma in my throat, not daring to speak. Associated with that was the terror of breathing. I breathed so that one could not hear me. I was forbidden to breathe . . . The great defense is not to be seen or heard, even though I was there. I became a stone. Since I decided to stay alive, I evolved every defense I could. No one talked to me, played with me . . . I knew nothing about life, morality. I was staying alive, but I wasn't living. Everything is make-believe. You're hungry, but not too hungry. *You believe all the lies of your enemies.* I literally turned everything inside out" (Session 11/07/04).

W. began a session years ago, saying, "Something very important has happened." He said Y.'s husband died in June 2005. Y. called and invited him to visit her. He accepted the invitation in July 2005, unaware of what would happen. A year earlier, W. had said: "Y. represents someone I would live with and have sex with. She no longer has a penis. Not the 'phallic woman'" (Figure 7, Session 11/17/04).

During the July 2005 visit to Y., they had sex, on two nights, their first sexual experience. W. was seventy-nine and Y. was sixty-five years old at that time. W. said Y. was very open about being with him. He was characteristically frightened of her and sex, even though he had found the emotional courage to willingly enter into a sexual and romantic relationship with Y. He also found the fortitude to tell her to slow down. Whether he would have been able to enter into a sexual relationship with a woman if she was not assertive enough to initiate and maintain the relationship is an interesting thought.

Another aspect of that developing is that W. saw himself with Y. as a couple: "I'm in a new place. I never identified with couples, [but] now I do. I admire families now. We love each other and we're friends. To recover, it has been a monumental event. I now know what Buber said, 'The greatest entry into sexuality is the heart'" (Session 7/22/05).

The development of the coupling of W. and Y. was evident in a series of drawings produced prior to their sexual union (see Figures 15–17). W. had very few associations to these drawings, but, accepted my interpretations. Figure 15, *They Meet*, 3/4/00, was a rare drawing

Figure 15. They Meet.

that contained vibrant color. The couples are face-to-face, looking at each other, looking more concerned than joyous. The positive affect was contained in yellow, red, pink, and green colors of the drawing, which both facial figures share. The male figure's green color, and darker accents, are contrasted to the white, yellow, and pink coloring of the female face. The female of the couple seems more open, less conflicted than the male. Yet, *They Meet*, the drawing's title, suggested an event to be noted.

W. agreed with these interpretations. At this time, W. had no idea who the couple was he had drawn. Figure 16, "Untitled", 2/15/04, delineated a full-figured male and female with genitalia in a black and white drawing that shows the couple together. The woman's femininity is clear and unconflicted, but her face suggested anxiety. The male figure's genital area is defined, but the rest of him is literally drawn in the shadows. He is anonymous and full of anxiety. The drawing was produced a year before the July 2005 sexual union with Y. The drawing was W.'s unconscious talking to both of us. W., at this point, found

Figure 16. Untitled.

the drawing interesting, and positive. He hoped it meant a sexual awakening for him. But he also felt it was too late, that he was too old, his sexual repression was too deep, and the damage irreversible.

In a dream, W. also indicated how difficult it was for him to see himself in a heterosexual coupling:

> ". . . it is my father who has taken over my sister's soul . . . [My] father and sister were a couple . . . My father and sister were the role model of a couple for me. The only couple I could base my life on" (Session 7/22/05).

His associations show a new expression of anger toward his father for contributing so dramatically to his emotional, physical, and interpersonal damage. On the other hand, he is overwhelmed by his new sexuality. However, he is struggling to overcome the damage.

Two drawings, Figure 9, "An Exchange of Traumas," 6/11/05 and Figure 17, "Coupling," 8/27/05, depicted a breakthrough in sexuality.

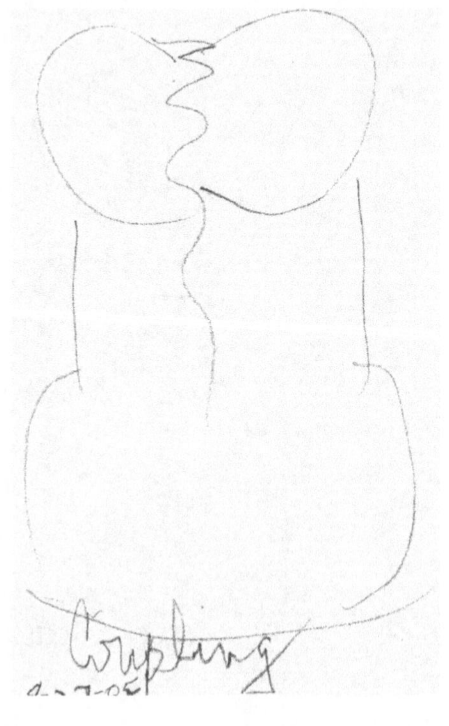

Figure 17. Coupling.

As has been discussed, "An Exchange of Traumas" illustrated W. and Y. coming together as a couple knowing they were two wounded people. They were two incest survivors who came together to help and give to one another. "An Exchange of Traumas" was created about one month before the sexual union between W. and Y., illustrated by a union between a man and a woman's hand. By this date, W. had been openly yearning for Y., clearly angry at her husband's abuse of her and wishing for her to leave her husband. Y. wished she could fulfill his wish, but indicated she was too dependent on her husband to leave him. When her husband died in June 2005, she was freed of her dependence. One month later, she contacted W. and their relationship began.

Figure 17, "Coupling," 8/27/05, was produced shortly after their union. Now, the couple as drawn appeared merged with no indications of traumas. Their relationship began in a very intense way. W. and Y. spoke day and night for two months, telling each other their dreams. W. reported this dream:

> "She stands naked in my bedroom ... She reaches for me, touches me from my shoulder to my knees. She felt very good. Like she is healing me. I'm not resisting her" (Session 9/7/05).

He had positive associations to the dream, which indicated he had opened to sexuality, even though he still struggled with intense anxiety. He continued to use the actual sexual experience to explore his unconscious. Y. did not allow W.'s anxiety to deter her. She was available for sex as often as W. would like. He was not as emotionally available as she was, but, she did not discourage his advances. Y. expressed her love for W. in a poem:

> I come at it slowly
> By way of Greece
> I protest too much
> It is my choice
> My thought and desire
>
> My passion, whim, and wish
> Trespass willfully and
> Stumble precisely at
> Your door step ... to share and
> Hear it all

Blow in my ear
Your tongue and mine
Need no introduction
Only proximity

Beethoven curls my heart
You melt it.
Pools of impatience
Block my walk to you

It is you to me this time
Have no fear my gentle man
I'll be here
I love you

(Reported in Session 9/7/05)

Living with Y. exacerbates a physical–sexual problem for W.: "One of the difficulties is defecating in the presence of the other. There is some special issue . . . Will I be able to relax enough? The place where I was ruthlessly raped by mother, father and sister. No doubt I'm getting better down there. I have to be at the end of my abuse therapy to be better" (Session 9/7/05).

We explored these issues in his difficulty defecating over a year or so and began to understand its meaning. The problem was connected to trauma. Both his mother and father penetrated his anus, he believed, from the first months of his life onward. W. then developed the insight: "resistance to shitting a defense against penetration. Always had problems with defecating going back to childhood. My parents never took me to a doctor. They were *barbarians*" (Session 8/23/07).

After a summer holiday break, I asked W., "How are you doing?" His answer reflected his new feelings and life: "Fundamentally, the best of my life. Y. loves me, needs me, depends upon me" (Session 9/12/07). I had told W. before the summer break in July 2005, when he described his new romance and sexual relationship with Y., "I am so happy for you. You deserve to have a relationship like you describe with Y" (Session 7/22/05). Then I offered my hand to congratulate him. He drew me close, hugged me, and said: "I couldn't have done it without you" (Session 7/22/05). From the onset we always had affection for one another. As early as the first six-month period in the analysis he brought in a picture (Figure 18a). As discussed, the draw-

Figure 18a. W.'s drawing of Arnold.

ings of this period were often chaotic, intense, black strokes completely covering the page, which we identified as indicating anxiety and confusion. This drawing, although it has some of these kinds of primitive markings, has a more benign look. W. described the drawing as an expression of how he experienced me after six months of analysis: "Someone caught in the moment, a human being. I like you very much. I never felt so supported, I've never had a man support me. You listen to me. You don't get into power struggles. You are a very decent, kind human being. You surprise me with your kindness and goodness. No one ever treated me this way" (Figure 18b, Session 2/21/93).

Ferenczi's (1980b, 1988), Kohut's (1984), and Rogers' (1959) wisdom was verified by my experience with W., which the above quote and the entire description of the case study seemed to bear out. In order to successfully treat a severe trauma survivor, one must allow

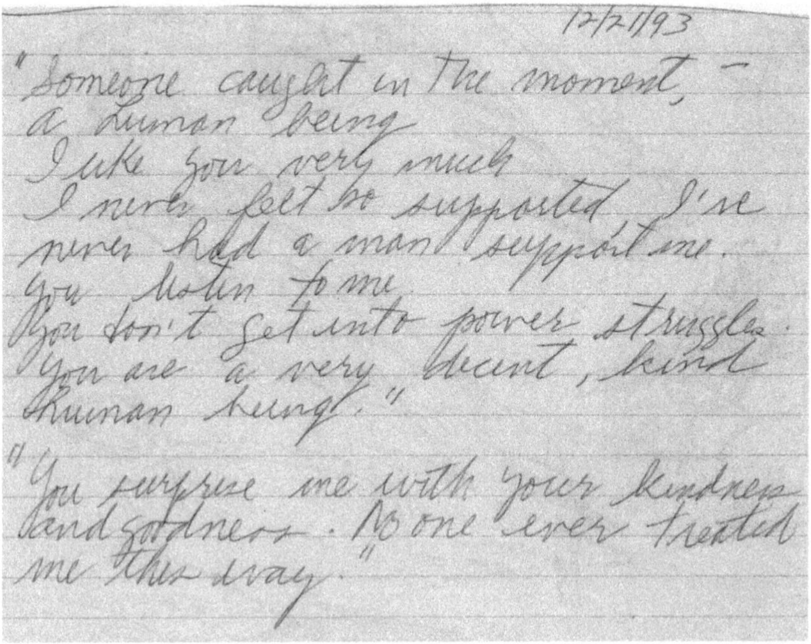

12/21/93

"Someone caught in the moment, —
a human being
I like you very much
I never felt so supported. I've
never had a man support me.
You listen to me
You don't get into power struggles.
You are a very decent, kind
human being."

"You surprise me with your kindness
and goodness. No one ever treated
me this way."

Figure 18b. Description of Arnold.

an emphatic relationship to unfold where the analyst not only contributes his/her intellectual clinical and interpersonal capacities, but also their humanity, affection, and love. With this kind of experiential, active, responsive human clinical interaction, the analyst and analysand help each other change and grow. Working with W. has helped me become a better analyst and person (Rachman, 2001b, 2003a, 2004, 2006).

CHAPTER TEN

View from the couch: an analysand's experience of trauma

In Chapter Nine, the analysis of sexual trauma in the case of W., an "outsider artist" was outlined. The description made reference to W.'s interest in psychoanalysis. W., like other incest survivors betrayed by his family, struggled to understand how his mother, father, and sister could have sexually assaulted him. As one incest survivor once said, "Your parents are God's agents here on earth. Their job is to protect you, to love you, *not to harm you*" (Rachman, 1997a). W. turned to the psychoanalytic literature in an attempt to understand why his parent did "evil things" to him.

A relational framework that is informed by the Budapest School of Psychoanalysis (Rachman, 1997a, 2000, 2003a, 2007a, 2014b) focused on a two-person clinical relationship. The analysand is a co-participant in the creation of the analytic dialogue, in the understanding of the clinical experience and co-creating clinical interactions. When W. volunteered that he regularly read the object relations literature, I incorporated his ideas into the clinical encounter. It had always been an interest to provide a forum for analysands to write about their analytic experience (Rachman, 1997c). W. welcomed my interest in his analytic reading and was flattered when he was asked to write about his ideas on their analytic encounter and therapeutic relationship.

I asked W. to write about his adventures in reading object relations theorists, especially D. W. Winnicott, who was his favorite. First, W. presented his reason for reading object relations theorists and then discussed how Winnicott's work had helped him. W. hand-wrote his comments on pages of yellow-lined 8 × 10 paper, in a scribbly hand that indicated a severe hand tremor. The handwriting was much like the black and white strokes of his early drawings discussed in Chapter Nine. It is all the more remarkable that W. is not impeded in his art or his writing by his hand tremors. This is truly a further example of his courage and determination to conquer his childhood traumas in the face of great obstacles.

The writing was much like the free association process we use in an analytic encounter. Some of the writing was omitted when it was not clear. Minor punctuation was added to help the reader. W's essay was produced during the first year of the analysis.

"How D. W. Winnicott helped me with my recovery"

You asked me a question, June 30th, why I read these books: in this instance Winnicott's *Discovery of Ideas* and Milner's *The Suppressed Madness of Sane Men* which was a good question.

It eases my loneliness, I am also trying to look at myself. . . . Is what they give only mere encouragement or might they be offering bits of a reflecting surface that I might see where once I could only hear? By seeing my ego, certain ideas might stick like fly paper . . . I cannot stop if by redoing a hundred hours work of the above I can metabolize one hour nay one minute it will be worth my while."

Notes on D. W. Winnicott

I had done lots of reading searching for myself; something recognizable and was not successful until I came across D.W. Winnicott in the spring of 1989. At first he did not make sense to me at all; little attention was paid to the first two years of my life; it was overlooked and taken for granted. When I came across the following quote of his, tears rolled down my cheeks: "In the presence of the schizoid I am in awe . . ." (I cannot lay my hands on the entire quotation). It said that the schizoid would die rather than betray his ideals. He knew me! I wasn't a freak! I had done what I had to do to stay alive hoping that one day there would be a light in the wilderness . . . For me Winnicott's ideas were and are revelatory and revolutionary. He says, and it is a paradox: "that the infant *believes* it has created the breast" (talk of omnipotence not knowing there is a "good-enough mother" adapting to his needs)! So at the very beginning life was essentially creative and the ruthlessness of the infant without anger and hatred; these would come later as *reactions* to an indifferent environment. (This kind of information relieved my guilt.)

Just prior to the time I began to read his work something unusual had taken place inside of me that had given me some respite from an overwhelming guilt and at the same time some vigor. I had no words to describe it until I read Winnicott, who described it for me: "that aggression must *fuse* with the erotic for the infant to evolve from absolute dependence". For him *these* are the two roots of instinct! For him the infant and the mother are a "nursing couple" and at the very beginning the mother has a "maternal preoccupation" almost like an illness to identify so completely with her infant and adapt accordingly.

For Winnicott, "being come first, then doing has meaning", quite unlike the satisfaction of instincts of Freud and his followers. (It is the female principle.) Winnicott learned most of what he conceptualized from his patients, and in his last volume, *Playing and Reality* completed just before he died in 1971, his dedication reads: "To my patients who have paid to teach me."

Shortly after my experience of the fusion of the aggressive and erotic I was dumbfounded to have a dream (content forgotten) and awaking from the dream to hear a voice of not known gender (probably a woman's) announcing this word: "integration". Frankly I had never known I hadn't! (Later on I would discover that my developmental line of experience was Winnicott's as well.)

In his theory, when the infant becomes aware that he is not omnipotent, that there is a *not-him* (my term rather than "not me"), the infant's first impulse is to "destroy the object". If the object survives the infant's destructiveness *without retaliation* the infant can conceive of an object outside his area of omnipotence and see that it is in his interest to *use* the object and relationship begins. Then the infant becomes concerned about harming the mother and does symbolic acts to repair the harm done. If these tokens of reparation and restitution (tokens of shit, first movement, smiles) are understood and accepted by the mother the unbearable guilt is transformed consciously and thus an

> authentic relationship begins based upon reciprocity characterized by play and creativity. If the mother rejects these acts of needing, forgiving, the guilt remains unconscious and Winnicott's conclusion is absolute: the infant will forever remain in limbo (my language). The hope is that later on in life the situation will be tackled anew and D.W.W says that development picks up at the precise place it had stopped.
>
> To help the infant bridge the gap between dependence and independence, Winnicott discovered what he called the "transitional object" and "transitional phenomena". A teddy bear, a doll, a piece of material. I had never had such an object and to my surprise and delight I *had* to buy a Paddington Bear in May of '92. Just at the same time I met Y., who has proven to be the most important person I have ever met in my life! (I hug the bear every day and two weeks ago Y. made a lovely scarf for him to wear this winter). In regard . . . the first mother: Winnicott says that the mother's face is a mirror which *reflect* the infant she is nursing. If he does not *see himself* in his mother's face (which is happening to him) but sees her preoccupations instead, ignoring his needs, *he is annihilated.* He cannot connect his instinctive and emotional charge, he is grounded in himself! Henceforth he will look at his mother's face not to validate himself but to acquiesce to her needs. Here the compliant "false self" emerges another Winnicott idea. Until I met Y. I was haunted by something missing in my life. Most of the time I was sure it was in history that I would be found: either in the story of a past or on the old and forgotten streets of a major city like New York. And so I walked the city streets in an attempt to recover myself and I always failed, whether inside of a building or outside of one looking in. Hopelessly lost (innately) until I met Y. Perhaps because I was ready, I would dare rejection which was the equivalent of death. But there she was accepting me as no one had ever done before, and the miracle happened! *I saw myself in her face as I felt myself to be at the moment* and almost immediately the city was no longer an abandoned playground. (Given to me as a hand-written copy in a Session 9/93).

A second series of self-reports was given to me by W. on October, 5, 1999, in response to a discussion we had in an analytic session, about my interest in collecting material about analysand's view of the analytic process. By then, I was planning a book about analysands' contributions to psychoanalysis (Rachman, 1999e). During that time I began asking analysands, colleagues, supervisees, friends, and acquaintances who were in counseling, psychotherapy, and psychoanalysis whether they were willing to share their reflections on their therapeutic experiences. W. had made it very clear he wanted to contribute to the project. W. believed that there was an arrogance in many psychotherapists and psychoanalysis. My idea to publish the analysand's point of view about how psychoanalysis is helpful had his complete approval. His contribution to this book follows.

"From the Couch"

Didn't know my fate and what to do about it; in relation to the world to be more exact: I didn't know what I lacked . . . .The value of an object like a book essentially meant that the book itself as a thing was more important than its content. Authority which I never questioned dominated my state of mind. Was I to please my therapist? Was I suppose to entertain him? Avoid being liked by him seemed to be much too important. If so, what was respect–self-respect? And how does that become the coin of the realm? My fear, for example, was a double-edged blade: fear of what is known and fear of what is not. Should I avoid both or do I choose only the fear I am least afraid of because it was relatively safe.

My homosexual fear was a constant source of anxiety. Being touched by a man and being seated next to a stranger in the subway or a movie were no little things. Standing inside a subway car to offset anxiety was weekly what I did. Watching a film I would try and sit apart. As I get stronger I would risk setting beside men and I progressed.

Touching a woman's private parts was next to impossible. If I took a maternal role, what I call caring, I could touch their hair, their arms and shoulders and maybe their hands. My omissions of not being able to relate to women intimately had to do with trauma. Its extent only known and becoming known through exploration. It cast a shadow; I might be taken from behind. My genital would be taken from me. It seems I gave my father absolute authority over my life. I looked backward and forward at the same time. This preoccupation with danger sapped my energy.

What I lacked took a long, long time for me to discover. From uncovering a two-dimensional image I had of myself that I kept in my unconscious was an autistic defense, plus confusion I had about body openings and their function. Obsessions like fear of raising my head above the window sill, crawling lighting the oven, asking for help, taking a shower and so many others of purely a functional nature. Sounds, not yet speech alarmed my abusers, it seemed . . .

Poetry betrayed my lack of connection. I could only write a line at a time, that might add up to a stanza or a paragraph if it were prose. I had no idea how to connect these individual lines. Conjunctions and prepositions were alien to my craft. There was no ongoing music. I believed I was stopped by unbidden threats from my super-ego. It took almost twenty-five years of effort to create a flow of words that might pause and take a breath but would continue to move without trauma.

The most obvious losses of my lifetime, completely eluded me till now. The acts of erection and penetration, copulation, of course, presupposes there be two acting in concert. There had to be a thou! and other for me. Who would have a value beyond anything I might have imagined; not knowing what it was that was going to get me to feel real, real in the most precious sense of the word meaning I would not have any doubts about my emerging self. Working at my drawings brought me many surprises: no hands; no wrists; missing breasts. A bewildering assortment of mouths upon the rightful one. No background (never even sensed), no floor, no ceiling. Becoming conscious of these omissions helped me considerably.

I did not exist grammatically. First person, second person, third person, were all jumbled up inside. I had answered more or less to a command I obeyed. Rather than answer to myself as an individual. I was summoned by command to present as an object to be dominated and determined. It was as a thing, as an object in the world was the way I saw myself. I was treated like a piece of furniture used, but never spoken too (see incident about the plastic covers and furniture). How then did I move from being a thing into becoming a first person singular?

It takes another person. The second person singular to move inertia. Year after year, I sat opposite my therapist and there was an air of respect in the room. I did my part. He did his. I trusted him. He more or less was the same person I saw over time and God knows I tried to be truthful. I brought my rages into that room and they were real for me, whether or not I was overacting was beside the point. I couldn't betray how I felt by being compliant, afraid of rocking the boat. And I was never discouraged from expressing what I really felt. A cynic might have said that rage was too easy for me, but it was all I had to offer at the time. There were too many areas unexplored and I needed the energy of outrage to do the exploring.

I came to reclaim myself out of bedrock; overwhelmingly dense and uninhabitable, not a please place to emerge from. Rock tends to be mute. A rock cannot claim to be human, though many do. I was one of them.

I arrived out of shame to claim my birthright which in its order of development allows every individual their right to obtain their right to be me. (So like a primate pounding his fists against his chest shouting "me! me! me!" as each fist hits, and so it appears to me.) And along the way comes the attribute of gender identification. I am me, knowing this that makes it so, and knowing this the world of form becomes my oyster. For the claims I shall be making on my behalf will be sentiment, not ruthless or ego-centric, could not be done unless I would allow the other half of the human race to make the same sort of claims on their own behalf. This is not like "The Bill of Rights," a document guaranteeing each citizen equal protection under the law. When these guarantees are not applied by a family towards each other, especially children, "The Bill of Rights" mean nothing, along with the "Ten Commandments." Mine is a personal assertion which I am making independent of authority; that I am one and one with the universe, that I am one and one with everyone else.

This is an achievement which was wrought and brought into being because of what happened between my therapist and myself. The I and thou of Buber! Change takes place in time and space when another is posited, not to be proven, but allowed for. There are many other givens beside faith and trust, a floor under my feet and walls that will not fall. A physical space must be guaranteed that ultimately becomes a psychic space in and of itself, which neutralizes chaos, reversing fore and aft, and a marriage of sorts takes place between two consenting adults, agreeing to respect each other's right to be.

This urgent space of reciprocity, is poetry: It is ethereal! It is magic! It is wondrous! When I say I am, I am already here referring to a thee! The space has become a contract, continuously being renewed by the parties involved. This is the space that Winnicott referred to as being that potential space of engagement which is presented to the infant for the first time, at four or five months of age, who begins to apprehend that there is someone there across from his surmise of omnipotence, who was always there, who always mattered and now he must deal

> with the space between them. This mother with the power to change our lives forever, does so by treating her infant with infinite respect, making the proverbial space between themselves immortal.
>
> In my therapy this nourishment for mutual respect came into being whenever I risked becoming more and more authentic—attacking him for mistakes I perceived he made and he did not retaliate. I was encouraged to be myself and a personal grammar evolved giving me the means to communicate what I do and what it meant. First and second persons are intimate channels of knowing what a relationship can mean in a mundane world of pure chance where image of commerce have become Dead Sea Scrolls of alienation and manipulation. (A hand-written copy given to the analyst in Session 10.5.99).

"You think you know what I've been through, but you can't really know, until I tell you" (W., June, 2007).

Analysts cannot be accurate in their descriptions of what has transpired between themselves and their co-participants in an analysis until they integrate the analysand's experience of what has transpired between them. We cannot continue to theorize about the course of an analysis from a one-person framework. The most accurate and meaningful idea of how an analysand has experienced the analytic relationship and has changed his/her functioning will only come from a mutually conceived two-person account of an analysis (Rachman, 1997c).

In a session in June 2007, W. was discussing my impending move from New York City. The conversation came around to my notion of W. writing about his analytic experience before I left. Suddenly, W. burst out with the statement, "You think you know what I've been through, but you can't really know, until I tell you!" When I first heard W.'s exclamation, there was a defensive reaction: "What do you mean, I've given a great deal of thought to our analytic experience and what is more, we've talked about it together on several occasions!" Although the above statements were accurate, I realized that W. was right. An analyst does not really know the experience of an analysand until he has the self-report of the analysand as part of the data for understanding the analytic encounter. To add to our understanding of the analysand's experience, W.'s self-report of what was his traumatic experience in his family as well as his experience of the therapeutic attempts to help him recover from the traumas was needed.

He began to bring in his hand-written notes as a response to my request for him to write about his experience of his analysis. There were six instalments, written between June and July 2007.

Installment No. 1—W. June 2007 Session: "You think you know what I've been through but you can't really know, until I tell you".

I recall an experience I had at the beginning of the first therapy, (Spring of '65). What precipitated my starting therapy was becoming aware of my homosexual impulses (which I had never consciously been aware of) and I began to fall apart; [experiencing] head off my shoulders, arms off my body, etc. If I saw a man on the sidewalk a block away, I would panic.

I was a truth teller (to the extent I knew the truth) and my therapist wondered at my seeming lack of resistance (little did he know). Somehow I believed (this after only four months) that I had exaggerated my symptoms and I would be back to normal by the end of the year. Back then I had no idea of words like integration and development and what would be the consequences of its not having occurred.

Early on I encountered unexpected things that would prove to be helpful in the long run, in dreams, for example, things would happen on my right side and other experiences on my left side, that I sensed was not random. Another example; in 1967 I picked up a book by an author I had never heard of, named Krishnamurte, and read the following: "To emphasize the negative is the most positive," and I knew it was true for me!

I moved out of my parents' home, two days before my fortieth birthday, too guilty to tell them about it beforehand. I left with 200 dollars, no job, no friends, hoping for the best. I rented a furnished room on the Upper West Side, lived there for ten years, and probably no more than a handful of visitors did I see in all that time. My social life consisted of a weekly therapy hour and a group I joined in 1967 run by my [first] therapist. By then I began working as a temp.

I was desperate not knowing what was wrong with me. I read a lot of books about clinical psychology, but could not find myself in them. One author interested me, Alexander Lowen, M.D. co-founder of

Bio-energenics, with its emphases on the body. I could not avail myself of that therapy because I could not allow anyone to touch me!

I did not realize how out of touch I was with my body and my feelings. I was being helped by happenstance. Looking at my face one morning in the bathroom mirror, I saw a psychic division between my head and my body (not right across!) No, the line was a diagonal; running from my upper left neck to my lower right neck. The awareness enabled me to call my condition schizoid—now that was something!

I backed into realizations of what was blocking my way; one, because I was motivated to find out the truth about myself; and two, trying to be creative; acting and writing plays, all these things frowned upon by my parents, brought about [by] an inner confrontation, which constellated into a symptom I would never have found out about otherwise. Whenever I closed my eyes I would see a pitiless eye looking at me. It was somewhat up on my right, as much to be looked at as well as to fixate me: this was a malevolent power to dominate. The symptom lasted thirteen years. I also became suicidal, not unexpected under the circumstances. The worst part lasted for two years, when I closed my eyes I saw myself leaping off of tall buildings. I would not stop trying to get well and would not take medication (which was an absolute!).

I began to meditate knowing nothing whatsoever about it. I sat stuck between illusions and magic (I was very naive). I can recall my first result, which was tangible. I felt a sensation in my lower right arm. It would take me three months more for me to experience a similar sensation in my lower left arm. At the time I was ignorant of physiology and anything to do with mind and body. I can illustrate the rigidity of my mind and my body by a fantasy I had way back then; should I jerk my head around abruptly, my neck would snap off and my head would roll on the floor like a billiard ball.

I entered therapy at the beginning knowing nothing about therapy and knowing nothing whatsoever about Sigmund Freud. My (first) therapist emigrated from Hungary after the '56 uprising. His father had run a school for delinquent children for 40 years and had once attended a lecture given by Freud in Vienna.

I entered therapy with him unaware of a tragic event was about to take place that would alter his life and my therapy. The suicide of his younger brother whom he disliked. He told me about it 18 months later wanting to know if I had noticed anything amiss in his demeanor and I said no (sincerely, I think). Only later did I suspect that his ambivalence towards his brother had been projected onto me. Knowing nothing about relationships I was [in] therapy to please, to entertain, never to be boring and God forbid never to confront.

I joined the group he ran and that became my social life for many years. I was an observer trying to help everyone else. At my best I was selfless and he labeled me "The Rabbi." It was there that I realized I was unable to talk to a *woman on a one to one basis*: I became mute I could easily be manipulated by those in the group who wanted to waste the group's time by asking me a question that was meaningless, and I went for the best hook, line and sinker that brought a smile to their coward faces (I was hopeless!).

One group (session) still stands out as significant: prior to going to the Group I bought a bouquet of flowers for one dollar! I had no idea why but I had to do it. The flowers were put in a vase that was placed on the low end table we sat around. I sensed that my therapist and some others sensed its importance. As the Group proceeded I began to feel terrible. Something in the middle of my chest—not my heart mind you, but my chest! I thought I was going to die. What was I going to do? Look at what I was doing to them. Dying in front of them! I had no other recourse I thought than to find a way to leave and crawl into a corner and die alone so as not to upset them!

The full length play I began to write in the Fall of '68 became the most important event of my life till then. Far more important than my passive involvement in WWII; a gunner aboard a B-29 flying over Japan. (Charles Bronson, the actor, was one of the crew.) Seven days a week, 18 hours a day I worked on that play. Previously I tried to be an actor and a director. Talent was beside the point: I could not risk being rejected, it was the equivalent of death. So I began to write one act plays and sent them out to various places throughout the country, receiving encouragement. One was Joseph Papp who wanted to read my next play, the play I was working on. The play was loosely modeled after my own family except that the family in the play was affluent and lived in the Suburbs while my family lived hand to mouth. My father was a nebbish, afraid to stand out. He wanted to be liked rather than confront life directly. His model took on the identity of Charlie Chaplin's Tramp. What a visage for a dirty old man!

The father in the play was a go-getter, needing to dominate, exulted in exercising power (except over his wife who manipulated him). She was somewhat more intelligent than my mother but just as stupid. In the opening monologue here's her take on keeping up with the Jones:

"The cream lives around here, as far as the eye can see, there's cream. A bungalow costs 35,000, we live in a bungalow but I'm not ashamed." Writing dialogue for the characters in the play especially the son, who was my alter ego, was like pulling teeth. But for the mother it flowed effortlessly. The night I finished the tank was dry. I had to literally push it over the finishing line. That night I had a momentous dream about my life that was devastating as well as hopeful, not aware of what I had to do, the particulars, to become a part of the Human Race. Prior to the dream, I had other dreams, that indicated a child of four had died.

The dream

It was early morning, overcast, no sky, gray light. I was up in the air, high above Brooklyn, near the juncture of the East River and the Greater New York Bay, looking down. There were no sounds, no bridges, no boats, no people, no cars, no lights, no planes, nothing. Suddenly the lower half of Manhattan, made up of skyscrapers, broke in two at their waists by an earthquake, the top parts falling down to the ground, everything happening in absolute silence. I looked up to see a huge barge with no superstructure moving several inches at a time, borne by the current of the East River, approaching where Fulton Street and the Manhattan side would be. I heard a man's voice coming from the vicinity of the barge addressing me:

"Where have you been? We have been waiting for you for thirty-eight years."

I woke up from the dream; I was forty-two and saw the connection between four and forty-two and wept for hours.

I had told the group about the play and how excited I was, and they didn't know what to make of it. When I was finished telling them I had mailed it to Papp and that I expected to receive a call from him in three weeks, they guffawed as if I were a stand-up comic. There was even derision coming from my therapist, which told me he was competing with me; cause for me to leave or to confront him; to my shame, doing neither, staying nine more years.

Just as I predicted his secretary [Joseph Papp] called me and I went downtown to meet with him. I remembered standing at the corner of St. Marks Place and Fourth Avenue, looking up to check the time as the clock on the North side of The Fisher Music Building, stepping off into oncoming traffic, pulling back just in time. He was late and I decided to wait for his arrival inside his spacious office, it was huge; with dozens of plaques lining the walls. When he entered he was taken aback: he had expected to meet a young man of twenty-one not a man of forty-two. He had a dynamic personality. My story took center stage over the next hour. He liked the play very much summing up his opinion when he said the following, word for word: "It's a classic of its kind that will be done generations from today!" Talk about praise! Wouldn't that grab you? It did me. He wanted to add music to it and already had a composer in mind. Recently I reread the play, liking it more today than I did then. It was fresh, it was alive. It was outrageously funny written out of the same rage I still feel today, though more coherently. I had anticipated Seinfeld by twenty-five years? When Papp walked me to the front door with his arm around my shoulder he said "this made your day didn't it?" And I knew he would never produce the play and he never told me why. In retrospect he closely resembled the father of my play.

By persistence and some luck I continued to send the play out into the world in the hope of a production. The luck was a letter I received from Papp after I had written him an angry letter accusing him of cowardice at not doing the play. My letter went out on a Monday. He received it on Tuesday. I got his reply on Wednesday. While defending himself at not doing the play—something about a committee not agreeing with him—he lauded my talent.

I photocopied his letter attaching it to a selective group of agents and theater producers who would not have read the play otherwise, he being the leading producer of theater at that time. Which led to a fateful afternoon I had in June, 1970, standing on the sidewalk at Fifth Avenue near Rockefeller Center. I received in the mail that day two letters that I was holding in my hands with some astonishment. One was a letter from the William Morris Agency who wanted to see me, having read the play. The other was from the University of Wisconsin who were administrating a program funded by the Rockefeller Foundation to obtain the production of new plays submitted by aspiring playwrights, and that my play had been chosen for that purpose. When without warning a black hole opened up underneath my feet. So quickly it took my breath away. A round abyss of no return. Nothing in my memory could compare to this! Sheer horror at the magnitude of the fall and the power it possessed over me. It was extinction. I took it as a warning and never wrote another play again.

I finally got a job in '73. Still a temp, I was lent to a small oil and gas company to cover their payroll desk until they hired someone. She came and went and they called me and I took the job. Giving me my fantasy life as an artist in waiting. It became a 14-year self-imposed incarceration. It was a nasty experience for me. The company was lethal. No one raised their voice. Top-heavy with executives, a place filled with intrigue and fear and even though I was treated conservatively: receiving the smallest pay raises, spied on—I prospered! It was the making of me (I learned to survive!) I began to grow up. When they pushed me out (on my 60th birthday no less) I took it in stride and worked out a deal. So I would never have to work again! Now I could devote my energy full time to work on a personal disaster I knew very little about.

It was during this time of my employment that I had significant things happen; I began to hear terrible wounds at the back of my brain. The base was imploded (the primitive part) where the corpus callosum was located between the two hemispheres was a crater which I likened to a World War I battlefield. It was open and the feelings about it tended to be awful: what was it? Where did it come from? It hurt to touch it. It removed toward agony. One afternoon in the early 1980s, on a lunch break, at 44th Street and 5th Avenue, going west, past the Seamans Savings Bank (now no more) I sensed that a psychic skin had covered the terrible wound (much to my surprise!) It was things like this that kept me going. On another lunch break I had an unexpected event that told me how behaviorosed I was to authority. Walking west again toward the corner of 43rd Street and 6th Avenue, a man who must've been 50 feet in back of me uttered "Hey" in a communicating voice and I froze in mid-stride. Of course it wasn't directed at me, but hearing it as I did indicated something was amiss.

To protect myself from others because I had porous boundaries and a limited ability to relate to strangers I was always aware who would be sitting next to me on a train or bus (since no one ever did unless it was jam packed) so if anyone tried to talk to me I knew they were up to no good. (I could not give them the benefit of doubt.) Still a wonderful thing happened to me one morning going to work [while] I was standing holding on to the white pole in the center of the subway car I was in when I noticed a pair of women shoes on the other side of the pole. A woman was actually standing there and I sensed was holding on to the same pole I was holding! I dared not breathe for fear of driving her away! (This had never happened to me before!) Nor did I dare to look up. Shortly afterward she disembarked (I never saw her face).

In the course of trying to find myself and having no idea of what to look for I remember an image I once had in a dream, of a blank piece of white paper and my insight that I was a two-dimensional creature at best!

I was confused for most of my life by what I was from and who I was. My biography was lost to me. To find myself and tell my story was contingent upon recovering my body with all its frozen parts and healing the shattered parts of my brain. I was an enigma to myself; adrift, no sail, no rudder, on an ocean of lies.

Through the use of the dream I began to realize the importance of geometric shapes in the unconscious. It took me twenty-five years to create a perpendicular (in the dream) and the attempt was agony. This once accomplished eventually led to the creation of the right triangle, a fundamental shape taken for granted by normal people.

It took me almost as long, to have a dream of a telephone ringing, picking it up, saying hello, and having a voice reply at the other end astonishing me when it happened.

Because of damage (I believe) to the occipital [lobe] I found it almost impossible to have images on behalf of my person, or to retain an image, as opposed to the images that impinged on me in my search for the truth. However, when I began to draw in my late sixties risking what I would see and what it might mean, my god-given right to perceive through a willed image became a possibility.

Prior to beginning therapy many years ago I filled out a questionnaire where I was asked what I was most afraid of and to my credit I put down the truth: the fear of death. Not only my own but in particular the death of my father. I prayed for the strength (which I didn't have at the time) to bury him with dignity, doing just that in 1985 when he died, taking care of all the details. Freud was right about the son coming into his own upon the death of the father. Something changed in me deep inside.

Nine months later two unusual events concerning women happened to me within a three-week period that were connected. The first experience was with my mother, the second with the wife of a friend I made at the company I worked for. I was in the kitchen of the apartment where my mother now lived alone, drinking a glass of water, when she walked up to me from behind and gently touched my left shoulder. It was the first time I ever remembered receiving such an act of tenderness from her. Three weeks later in the finished basement of my friend's house, where there was a gathering going on, I was sitting on an upholstered chair, hands clasping on the armrest, when the wife whom I liked avuncularly and no more, upon walking by gently touched my left wrist and I responded sexually! These two events presaged my first real attempt to deal with the death of the female inside my personality. Now I had the time to do so being retired.

I was reaching for something inside of me knowing nothing about it. I had a head trip about being aggressive, rather absurd when I think of it. I would not be like other men: combative (impossible)! Rather I would assert myself. How I had no idea.

I was suffering intensely having no clue about what was going on internally and what I could do about it. One night it came to a head. My ideas of passivity in the face of my aggression inside wanted to be recognized. Finally I relented to the agony that I was experiencing. I would allow my aggression to rear its ugly head. I had willed myself to keep it apart from what it needed to become connected to. Overnight half of the suffering disappeared. Shortly afterward I had a dream which surprised the hell out of me. I knew so little about myself and what had to be done. At the end of the dream came the voice of a figure outside of time and place, where Jung labeled the archetype, announcing at the foot of my bed (I didn't see her) "INTEGRATION." It was 1989, I was sixty-three. As the year came to the end I was provided information about my body that I cherish today. The wife mentioned above was a part-time talent agent: Opera singers, conductors, pianists. Her main source of income derived from teaching. I was invited to join her for a night at the opera. By now her marriage was on the rocks and I was too frightened to pursue her. When I met her, there was a well-dressed man joining us, something I had known nothing about, which had happened before. He was a conductor, leading a community orchestra in New Jersey. (We didn't like each other.) I sat in between them feeling I was privileged, cocky about what I thought I knew, as we sat watching a wonderful opera by Botto. I told him Faust was the myth of our time. He disagreed (we didn't get along) [and] I never saw him again. But he was much more aware than I had given him credit for and that I would soon find out. She called me a week or so later and during the conversation told me of an observation he had made about me both that I was not aware of, to wit: "He doesn't move anything below his waist." She had no idea why I received this devastating info so positively exercising the reverse I am sure. Thank God for enemies!

I came across Winnicott in 1990. At first his language was completely foreign to me—the first two years! I persisted and read *Playing and Reality* which blew me away! It was there that I came across an explanation of why my aggression was such an important experience for me to have when at last I surrendered to its inexorable power. It was axiomatic in his theory of the true self that the aggressive and the erotic components must fuse together early in the infant's life for the organic development of reality to occur. He told me something I had never known before and I was hooked.

I fell in love with Y. in 1992. She was married but acted as if she wasn't. For had I known (believing she was separated) I could never have asked her out for lunch. Such was the nature of my guilt. As it was the maître d' kept coming by reassuring me, patting me on the shoulder. She was married to a scoundrel and couldn't leave him. Hers was a tragic life: raped by her father, the death of an older and a younger brother because of parental neglect. Her amnesia of forty years was beginning to lift when we met. We actually were made for each other. Who but ourselves would be willing to take us on?

I was very passive. My head down looking at the sidewalk when I walked with her and when I was stimulated (sexual would connote an adult) I urinated in my pants. We liked each other. She was an artist and drew me, which I paid for. They were always short of money.

We eventually made love. But sex took second place for me. For me it was touching, holding, embracing, kissing, feeling her warmth and to my surprise caressing my warmth away afterward as if I were toast. She became my muse and I wrote half-a-dozen volumes of poetry, and in addition she was the one who recognized my doodling for what it might be: and I began to draw and it was she (we were no longer seeing each other) who suggested I needed to begin abuse therapy.

I liked Arnold immediately. He was the first man of authority, old enough to be a father figure, who supported me 100%! (And I flourished at the speed of light.) At our first meeting (I had no intention of starting) I told him everything I knew about myself, and at the end I asked him somewhat disingenuously "Why should I be in therapy?" And his answer, which I had never anticipated "You haven't integrated your trauma." He floored me and that was that.

I hid nothing from him as far as I know. My limitations were not as obvious then as they are today. Trauma only a word. My intentions (however admirable) mostly coming to protect me from my oblivion. Mostly in the dark about the consequences of my abuse I led with my heart and my soul that motivated a primary search for the truth. A stance I have never strayed too far from. To keep myself on the straight and narrow I have been skeptical at what I say I believe in. By and large I use my father as someone I would hate to be like. What afflicts me besides my fear is my guilt which appears to be a sentence of death pronounced against me in absentia. And it also appears it was a verdict I deserved based on no credible evidence. With this in mind I asked Rachman in session #29 about how I control my session (which I do) and his reply, which I did not expect, I felt so guilty, "Everyone is unique at how they do this. You use poems, drawings. You're into it. You could sing the whole session for all I care" moved me to say that no mature man has ever treated me this well.

The difficulty of trying to get well (whatever that might be) was a mystery to me. I could never predict what the next phase might be. Where am I today compared to yesterday? Why was the dream I thought to be "monumental" become just another step into damnation? For me the subtlety of the new was always a surprise. What is left, what is right? What is back and what is front? What is above and what is below? No maps to follow in a dark forest. I relied too much on redundancy: what passed for wisdom in a jaded world. Throwing my babies away with the bath.

September 25, 1995 marked a turning point in my therapy and in my life. I was sitting on a bench just inside Margaret Meade Park, at 81st Street and Columbus Avenue sketching a tree. Coming down the narrow path where I sat, heading for a dog run just beyond was a Doberman Pincher, not on a leash. The owner who brought up the rear, was throwing a tennis ball for the dog to snatch out of the air as it bounced. This time the ball after it flew over the dog's head hit a pebble lying in the path and went 90° left. The Doberman went for it, snatching the ball in its jaws right in front of the face of the homeless man who was fast asleep on the bench, who awakened with horrors as he jerked up his head at what he saw of the dog. (I had not noticed him until then.) The owner said "sorry" without stopping. And he and the dog went into the dog run. The homeless man calmed down and went back to sleep. Tranquility had returned and I stopped drawing the tree and began sketching the man. I showed the drawing to Rachman who was impressed not only with the drawing (it was good) but the content, of course! "The homeless man is you," he said (it never occurred to me). "Draw whatever you see in the drawing" he suggested. I could see, for example, a homeless child kneeling at his feet. This became the prototype of my drawings based on a previous drawing. (I've done thousands.) Eventually I called them "walking dreams" coined by Winnicott. Words such as incoherence, oblivion, annihilation arose, becoming commonplace.

True to the norm of dissociation I did not realize at the time that this experience with the homeless had happened on my father's birthday; his ninety-ninth birthday, were he still alive. And congruent to that coincidence was the fact I did not grasp until I began to write this; that the two digits of 99 was the square root of the street I was on—81!

One of the secrets I've kept from the world that I share with my therapist is the sexual obsession I have had for a married woman who runs an art gallery, a woman I still lust for to some extent. (It has gone nowhere sexually, why it continues) it runs like plumb line through my therapy. She mostly toys with me afraid of the consequences. I observe moth to the flames of incest. She lives in my loins while Y. lives in my heart which replicates the experience I had as an infant. Both married, both unattainable. I believe it was crucial that she not be a mother. She tantalizes me as if in fact she had a son and I was it. She wills herself into being and has no insight. She is beautiful (even today) and very shy. When I tried to take a photo of her ('96) she closed her eyes. In '99 I made 800 drawings of her and still do from time to time. She has a ravishing mouth and below her waist her thighs belie her modesty. Twenty years ago she listened to my story, as much of it as I knew of at the time, and I wasn't aware of any sexual connections between us. Her essence galvanized me (repression can do that) and the elements of slate arranged geometrically I once saw in her eyes was unforgettable. (I almost forgot to add myself to the mix: I am twenty years older, enough to be a father.) Like a sponge I took her into my unconscious and she became an archetype. In my dreams under her protection I have risen from the dead, brought to the frontiers of resurrection to enter the bedrock of desolation holding a sword in my grip, ready to die for my country.

Since I have begun to live with Y. she has changed and my dreams of both of them overlap: sisters, cousins, friends or women, just women? Of course, her husband (who recently appeared in a dream not as an enemy) was unhappy. (Believe me or not I never touched her inappropriately, and the few times I kissed her was against her wish). One day at an opening, he strode over to me with élan, and took both of my hands into his and said "Thank you! Thank you!" Years before in '97, she and I had lunch, one of two or three we ever had, and she told me the truth about how she felt, probably wished she'd never said it:

"When I'm with you, I feel alive." Looking back she did the right thing. I owe that lady a lot.

For me, lust arrives as a kiss of death, like salmon swimming up stream, to spawn and die in the heart of darkness: the autonomic and the anatomical disasters I uncounted at my mother's breasts.

Now I understand my guilt was not authentically acquired, but inflicted, imposed by terror. I was to be condemned in advance for my innate inheritance from God. Becoming victim enabled them to sin at my expense. I sacrificed my true self for their wellbeing. Which included rape, and other kinds of abuses. I was responsible for triggering their lust and their vengeance. To stay alive I disappeared and tried to stop breathing and for all I know I'm still holding my breath. Lust is linked with incest, is linked with violence, is linked with porn and perversions. My body was cremated, becoming a black hole.

At the very beginning I was fed sexually instead of lovingly and this abyss between the heart and the groin turned the real into the unreal. Everything based on heaven and hell can be traced back to touch and the absence of touch. The victim travels throughout his recovery unaware in the main of an unconscious reality for and against survival. A turn to the right and one to the left will do it, is wishful thinking like putting on a band-aid to heal a broken leg.

In my therapy I am aggressive. A person I could not be for most of my life. It's like I believe in the poetry of the event and I have been permitted to participate by a laid-back therapist who allows me to believe outrageously. He does not compete with me. He does not need to impress me, to show me how clever he is and how much he knows. He hardly says anything and when he does it suggests a crossroad that he seems to recognize before I do. I dive right in always feeling guilty of depriving him of equal time! How absurd, but it's true.

I believe I turned my body and mind inside out when the big bang occurred in the earliest days and weeks of my life. It was done at the speed of light: I reversed evolution in order to stay alive and the strange horror I believe I have been engaging in was reversing the original inversion.

Because I could think I thought I was real. I had no idea what fragmentation was about. I could not fathom I had no bottom drawers. Strangely, I was real because I was unreal. Function was not understood, let alone form. It would take time, lots of time for me to get a hand on integration and development. To stay alive I had turned the energy of life against my becoming real out of an unimagined catastrophe. I was in a birth state, and did not realize what it meant. That and the lack of development would come to a head in the summer of 2000. That summer I crossed the frontier between life and death. Death as the absence of form. Death as the absence of substance. Death as the absence of vitality. Death as the absence of light. Death as the absence of hope. Death as the absence of desire. It was and still is a grave disorder. Death begets death not life; becoming addictive. If I think I'm going to die I already have. If I think I'm going mad, I already have. Winnicott wrote about this.

I was faced with the monumental task of becoming real for the first time in my life, guided by an extraordinary intelligence that was feeding me incrementally, never knowing what the next feed would be. I began to see in the dark. I began to hear in the dark. I began to smell in the dark. I could hear the voice of the turtle. I could sense the fall of the sparrow. Everything was sacred and everything was true. Led by the work of God I had crossed the threshold of silence into the realized world of cause and effect, my body becoming the vehicle of my reincarnation.

Two weeks after I left the death state I had a dream which altered my perception of myself. Heretofore I never considered autism as anything to do with me. Just as I had never thought I was suffering from trauma. In the dream I am in the basement of a nightclub. It is Friday night, the beginning of the Sabbath (hardly Jewish). My body from my pelvis to my neck was encased by iron: thick, hard, impermeable. I was on the floor, my therapist was there to get the thing off of me. With all his strength, using both of his hands, he began to peel off the inhuman covering, petal by petal. The metal cover suggested the torso proper had no form *per se* that functioned. It was to keep the insides from spilling out! What suggested autism to me was the hardness of the protection I used to cover my body, something I had to do to go on living. It recalled what I had once read about hardness by Frances Tustin, an acknowledged expert on autism from England. Autistic children cannot bear separation from the mother. They delude themselves into believing that her body is continuous and everlasting with theirs by using autistic sensation objects and sensation shapes. In my case the sensation of hardness experienced within my body would sustain the delusion of net being separate.

In 1997, age 71, I experienced the reality of quality for the first time! It burst upon me and I began to write an epic poem about becoming real.

Witnessing an Heroic age;
The heroic arrival of quality!
An ice age having left,
A stone age having come
crashing through the cardiovascular windows
of desire . . . .

CHAPTER ELEVEN

Triumph of the human spirit: the emotional courage of a young woman who confronted her incest trauma

Several years ago, I was contacted by a young adult incest survivor who desperately needed an analyst to help her retrieve her childhood incest trauma. Soma (a pseudonym) intuitively knew that "Something happened in my childhood that is connected to physical problems that I have now, but I just don't know what happened." She had been to many different kinds of counselors and therapists who could be considered "new-age." Soma felt they were helpful to her, but she continued to have the gnawing feeling that something happened that she needed to confront. Finally, her last counselor became very concerned when Soma began having new serious physical symptoms and she came closer to confronting her trauma. Her last counselor, who was genuinely interested in Soma's welfare and knew he was in over his head, referred her.

Her parents were totally unaware of her childhood trauma and suffering. What is more, when she began to uncover her incest trauma, her mother was incredulous and was vehemently opposed to the idea that incest had occurred. In the light of her parents denial, this young woman's emotional courage in confronting her childhood incest trauma is an example of the triumph of the human spirit. I was profoundly moved by her courage and determination to get well. One of the most heart-warming examples of this phenomenon is the struggle of this young woman. She worked as diligently and courageously as anyone I have ever known.

Soma, was an attractive young woman who was in her early twenties when she began the exploration of her incest trauma. She was from a privileged family background. The family had wealth, status, and international political connections. Both parents were highly intelligent and achievement-oriented. In many ways, this family is much like the ones Freud originally described (Freud, 1954) and those Ferenczi described in the confusion of tongues theory (Ferenczi, 1980n). As originally reported by Freud and verified by Ferenczi, it was the fathers who were the sexual abusers of their daughters. Freud's (1954) and Ferenczi's clinical findings (Ferenczi, 1980n, 1988) uncovered an important fact about the incidence of childhood incest trauma. Previously, childhood seduction had been theorized to be the province of strangers who seduce children. Freud and Ferenczi's significant findings indicated, on the contrary, that the seducers of innocent children where their parents, not strangers (Rachman, 1997a). In modern times the same father–daughter dynamic regarding sexual abuse has been verified (Herman, 1981, 1992).

Privilege allows access to any necessary resources, whether it be objects or people. Soma's father had access to his beautiful wife, who was sensual and responsive. What is more, he had affairs outside the marriage with other beautiful women, both in the United States and overseas. His womanizing occurred all through Soma's childhood and adolescence. There were no limits to his sexual appetite, which were not satisfied by a loving, responsive wife, or a bevy of international beauties. Perversity is not easily satisfied. Women did not satisfy the father's appetite. Only a child would do. A child allows the adult male to be in total control, exercising complete power. As Ferenczi so clearly indicated, *sexuality with a child is not love, it is aggression* (Ferenczi, 1988). It does not provide nurturance, as does genuine affection and love. Rather, it harms and confuses the child and leads to developmental arrest (Rachman, 1994a).

Soma told the analyst that she was subjected to sexual abuse from the time she was four years old until her tenth or eleventh birthday. Her father, in essence, carried on an affair with his daughter. Apparently, the abuse was unknown to the mother. Sexual seduction, if it defines childhood, produces serious consequences for the survivor.

Such was the case for Soma. She was an innocent child who was asked to be a woman before her time. The demand to be sexually available for her father produced a nightmare of an existence. Her father would come to her bedroom in the middle of the night, from four years onward. We could not discern a rationale for this onset of abuse. Was it that at four, the father had some crisis with his wife or his women? Or was the father going through some emotional or physical crisis in his own psyche that propelled him towards his daughter?

While her mother slept in her marriage bed, her daughter was asked to be the marriage partner of her husband. The psychodynamics of sleeping when your daughter is being seduced by your husband is a fascinating issue. Do such mothers physiologically sleep so soundly that they do not hear their husbands leave the marital bed? Or, is such sleep a metaphor for semi-consciousness, denial, or dissociation. The mother does not want to be present for the traumas. Ferenczi talked of a robot-like presence as one of the consequences of the confusion of tongues trauma (Ferenczi, 1980n). My hypothesis that was offered to Soma was that her mother was probably sexually abused as a child, which she never acknowledged, confronted, or integrated. If I was correct, her mother was functioning in a state of dissociation, perhaps at the level of a dissociative disorder. What is more, her mother needed to continue this state of dissociation to protect herself from the emotional crisis of becoming aware of her own childhood seduction to protect herself from confronting it.

During the course of our analysis, Soma retrieved the memory of her father forcing her to perform fellatio and sexual intercourse, including anal penetration. What manner of man performs these evil acts on his own daughter? Clinical work with incest survivors makes one believe in evil, even though such an idea is the province of philosophers and clergymen, not usually psychoanalysts (Rachman, 1981, 1989a, 1991b, 1992b, 2000b, 2003a).

Why was there no way for Soma as a little child to protect herself from the midnight sexual intrusions of her father. There was no lock on her bedroom door, because her parents felt they should have access to their daughter in case of an emergency. What is usually a meaningful rationale for child safety, ironically, became a blueprint for terror. The emergency from which the parents were trying to protect her was actually in their midst. Locks, whether open or closed, cannot protect a child from a determined predator. Soma frantically tried to protect herself as a child. In the earlier years of molestation, she would lock herself in the bathroom adjacent to her bedroom by placing a chair under the door handle. There she would sleep on the cold, hard tile floor during the night. She had frequent nightmares that her parents attributed to a childish fear of animals. Soma's sense of terror was partially abated as she forged a plan to escape her tormentor. She became preoccupied with an elaborate and dangerous plan to escape her father's abuse. Soma soothed herself during her night terrors by an escape fantasy. She had a plan of going out of her bedroom window, sliding down the shingled slanted roof, and climbing down the tree that abutted the house. Imagine a little girl being preoccupied with a plan to escape from her father's sexual abuse. As Soma became older, sometime between eight and ten years old, she actually practiced her escape plan. No one in her family ever knew that she had actually practiced going out the window, down the tree, re-entering through a basement window, and going back to her bed.

When Soma became a preteen, she finally found the emotional strength to resist the sexual advances of her abuser. One day, as if she were reborn, Soma said "no". In the moment when she was nearly eleven years old, Soma found her lost voice. The sexual abuse was over, but the psychological effects of her tragic childhood were not. The most profound effect of the incest trauma was the development of a chronic disease that would cripple her functioning as an adult. The somatic connection began at her mouth and traveled through her gastro-intestinal system to her anus. The G.I. pathway was the pathway of abuse, from fellatio to anal penetration. She was trapped in her body, a body that now turned on her. Her childhood trauma infiltrated her adult life, retraumatizing her body, mind, and soul. One cannot exaggerate the negative effects childhood sexual abuse had on Soma's functioning. Because she was alone in coping with her trauma and its effects on her as a child, adolescent, and young adult, there was no acknowledgment that Soma needed medical help for gastro-intestinal symptoms or psychotherapy for her incest trauma. She was left to cope with intense physical and psychological issues by herself. She suffered in secret, and alone. Soma could not, therefore, develop the necessary coping mechanisms to deal with stress.

The obvious, observable symptoms were stomach pains, frequent bathroom trips, inability to metabolize certain foods, weight loss, and lack of appetite. Her mother and father zeroed in on the medical issue of their daughter's dysfunction. She was sent to the best physicians. Tests were taken. Her body was scanned, X-rayed, scoped, and fully examined. She was given an official diagnosis of peptic ulcer that both the physicians and her family accepted as the issue. Her parents even searched their family histories in order to find a precedent for her medical condition. Try as they may, there was no information in either family history that would indicate any disorder resembling their daughter's array of symptoms. After this exhaustive and thorough search, not one physician, and certainly not the parents, entertained the idea that Soma's medical condition could be of psychological origin. Actually, the medical disorder was a result of the incest trauma overwhelming the child's psyche, causing stress that could not be adaptively integrated. The stress found its way to Soma's most vulnerable organ, her gastro-intestinal system.

A child needs a parent or parent surrogate to protect her from further trauma. A child needs her mother, father, relative, or family friend to literally take the child into their arms and convey: "I'll stop this evil from hurting you anymore. I am so sorry you have suffered so much."

Soma never had this experience as a child, or as an adolescent. Consequently, not only was her sense of self damaged, but her interpersonal relation with adults was disturbed, especially with her mother and father. A false self developed, which showed to the world politeness and good manners; what was masked was her angry, withdrawn, emotionally distant, passive-aggressive, and dysfunctional self.

Soma's relationship with her mother was a perfect example of the false self–true self split. She never yelled at her mother, rarely showed any visible signs of anger. However, their relationship was a silent war. Soma manipulated her mother into catering to her every whim. The mother became a "servant" to her daughter. Soma rarely heard the word "no" from her mother or father. Another factor that led me to believe the mother was herself an incest survivor was that the psychodynamics of the mother's response was very similar to Soma's. The mother would never openly be angry, but seethe with anger. Her passive–aggressive maneuvers involved ignoring her daughter at times when a response was needed. The mother was not aware that she ignored and distanced herself from Soma during times when her daughter was in physical and emotional pain. Soma accepted this neglect as her mother's self-absorption and her silent anger. There was also the mother's emotional fatigue from servicing her daughter.

Soma's relationship with her father was characterized by emotional distance, intense manipulation, and suppressed rage. The father's career involved frequent international trips, sometimes with only an hour's notice to his family. The trips lasted from days to weeks. Upon return, the father would always bring his daughter and wife expensive presents. Besides these presents Soma would ask for, and receive, anything she wanted. Father and daughter both knew, but never overtly expressed, that these presents were born of the father's guilt for abusing his daughter. These were silent reparations for the emotional holocaust he inflected on her, as well as to buy her silence. What a nefarious bargain they forged in the aftermath of the incest. They both knew what they were doing, but neither could break this perverse bargain. Soma profoundly hated her father. During her recovery from the incest trauma, she was to express her rage and separate from him.

During her high school years, Soma's anger toward her parents began to surface. The inner struggle of adolescent turmoil broke through with negative feelings suppressed since early childhood. When she was first sent to a boarding school, she enjoyed some relief from her medical condition and the emotional trauma. There was reduced stress from not living with their parents, safely tucked away in a country locale, far from the urban scene of her sexual molestation. Boarding school provided a respite from the stress and disturbance of parental interaction. Soma was able to form responsive and empathic relationships with teachers and peers. She began to bloom, using her intellect, physical attractiveness, and desire to form healing bonds.

As the details of her childhood sexual abuse began to be analyzed, her anger toward her mother surfaced first. Soma became openly critical of her mother's friends, lifestyle, and, especially, her marriage. The mother was dumbfounded by her daughter's verbal attacks. She rationalized that these mean-spirited slings and arrows were the manifestation of her daughter's long suppressed adolescent rebellion. Soma's anger toward her father was much greater than towards the mother. She did not want to come home during vacation time, choosing to be with school friends. The tight fabric of an upper-class family forged from faulty mortar was beginning to show cracks. She threatened to never talk to her father again. When he called her at school she would not take or return his calls. When he switched to writing she would not answer his letters. It was clear to Soma's parents something was changing, but they hadn't a clue what was behind the change.

The mother expected Soma to maintain the same loving, attentive, and responsive relationship to the father as her mother had shown. What is more, the mother was completely puzzled by her daughter's noticeable indifference and hostility in Soma's relationship with her father. The mother never confronted her daughter about the emerging anger, rather, she pleaded with her daughter to respect and continue to love her father.

It was during her young adulthood that Soma's physical problems produced a threat to both her physical and emotional survival. A confluence of forces increased the intensity of the medical situation to produce emergency conditions. The demands of college academics at a first-tier school would not have been a difficulty to this highly intelligent and academically prepared adolescent, were it not for her deteriorating physical condition. Soma was not able to rise early in the morning to attend classes, had periods of prolonged absence from school, and had difficulty completing assignments on time. She was accused by some teachers and administrators as being unmotivated and having a behavioral problem. Soma did contribute to her own difficulties. She got caught up in drinking and drug taking. The alcohol and drug use was recreation and psychological. It was a way to soothe the emotional distress that her somatic misery was causing her, and an expression of anger to her parents.

On several occasions during her college years it was necessary for Soma to be hospitalized. She had difficulty eating, became weak lost weight, and had serious gastro-intestinal problems. These were emergency situations, which were devastating for her and her parents. Everyone, including medical personnel, maintained the idea that her symptoms were solely of a physical origin. Not one person, either parent, physicians, or school personnel, ever gave a thought to a psychological cause.

While in high school, Soma had her first therapy experience with a counselor at her boarding school. At this first experience, Soma did get help with her family issues, her physical ailments, and her negative sense of self. Since this was a counseling situation aimed at adaptation, not uncovering, Soma's dissociation remained intact. There was no exploration of the childhood sexual abuse during the high school counseling experience (which seemed appropriate at the time).

By the time she entered college, Soma was dedicated to therapy. She had developed an interest in New Age healing. Incest survivors have indicated a sense of comfort with non-traditional therapeutic relationships. They have lost faith in traditional authority and institutions because they did not protect them from abuse. Rather, they feel betrayed by their parents, school, and church. For Soma, therapeutic contact with a variety of New Age healing experiences was a mixed blessing. Soma did find the relationship therapeutic, which allowed her to have an empathic individual to whom she could express her inner feelings. This was in marked contrast to her relationship with her family, where she had to be the polite, *anger-free child*. Soma had lost her voice. She was tongue-tied (Ferenczi, 1980n). She could not speak of her trauma, because her dissociation mechanism was still in place. However, the therapeutic experiences did create a new beginning for Soma (Balint, 1965c).

Without recovering from, or analyzing, her childhood incest trauma, Soma began to have some emotional stirrings about her trauma. She began to regularly attend New Age healing workshops. These workshops were experientially oriented. They helped participants to focus on their inner feelings, to feel positive about themselves, the other participants, and the healing-oriented leaders. Soma also became a regular participant in physical healing massage. For the first time, Soma was emotionally developing differently from her family's emotional ethic of suppression. Any time she would bring up the kind of emotional encounters and responsiveness she experienced in the workshops, her mother and father began to question her mental health. They voiced the concern that she was becoming emotionally unstable and addicted to these New Age counselors and workshops. They did what they could to discourage her participation in such workshops. The emotional chasm between Soma and her family was to widen to such an extent that an emotional crisis was to develop which broke the family apart. Her family was very threatened by the idea that her medical condition might have psychological roots. But, there was a much more disturbing idea to emerge, that is, the family secret of incest.

A combination of the emotional stirrings of the childhood trauma and the continued use of powerful drugs to reduce Soma's physical discomfort brought about new difficulties. In order to reduce the ever-present debilitating physical symptoms brought on by drinking, smoking, and drug taking during her early college years, she was asked to take more powerful medications.

Her latest therapy combined New Age talk therapy with psychodrama and emotionally expressive methods. Soma had begun to open up to childhood trauma and now became emotionally connected to the uncovering process of the incest trauma. Her New Age therapist was professionally responsible and emotionally astute, realizing Soma needed a more exploratory and analytic therapy on a more frequent basis. When Soma finished college, she returned home and was referred to me, as an incest trauma specialist, by her New Age counselor. Soma was ready and willing to enter into an intense analytic relationship focused on uncovering her intense trauma. She began a regularly scheduled, three times a week sessions of analysis. During periods when retrieved memories caused intense emotional stress, we scheduled five times a week sessions.

As is often the case, the analysis of the incest trauma can produce retramatization. She again experienced night terrors, intense, sometimes crippling, anxiety, overpowering phobias, and debilitating gastro-intestinal problems. There were many indications of Soma's emotional courage during this disturbing period: She did not become addicted to alcohol or drugs. Soma would contact me between sessions when she felt overwhelmed by the experience. When necessary, Soma was asked to consult her physician when increased physical symptoms developed. Soma was dedicated to confronting the incest trauma and initiating the process of recovery. She expressed the need to have a therapist who was dedicated and clinically competent to explore the depths of the evil that befell her as a child. She said she needed: "Someone with compassion and empathy that would not flinch from confronting the depths of my trauma." This expressed need was born of her parents' denial of the trauma and their dedication to unconsciously preventing the family secret from being revealed.

Once she set a course for the confrontation with her childhood demons and with the evil of parental sexual abuse, however, she never wavered. Sometimes, she would awake in the middle of the night, afraid, confused, physically shaking, as if she were about to be molested as she had been as a child. She was encouraged to contact her boyfriend. If he wasn't available, she turned to a girlfriend. When no one was available, she learned to soothe herself through music, comforting baths, or television. There were nights when she would be walking in the street near her apartment, suddenly, overcome with fear, not knowing why this was happening to her. What was happening was the re-experiencing of her childhood sexual trauma that occurred during the dead of the night. I told her that she could call when she felt the anxiety was becoming overwhelming, but she wanted to develop the emotional strength to cope with the trauma.

Soma courageously confronted her childhood incest trauma. She never flinched from uncovering the details of her sexual abuse. She recovered many of the sexual experiences with her father in dreams, free associations, fantasies, as well as physical and emotional symptoms. The pieces began to fit together, had an internal consistency, explained many psychological issues, and began to hold the promise of recovery. She was able to have satisfactory sexual relations with her boyfriend, including performing fellatio. She had never been able to do this before, because it was part of her incest trauma. Now she was able to participate without any intensification of physical symptoms. Their relationship lasted for about one year. Soma was thrilled to be able to participate in a fuller relationship with a man.

The intense physical symptoms became less of an emergency situation. In the analytic sessions Soma was helped to make insightful connection between her medical condition and her childhood sexual trauma. She readily accepted this connection and was grateful for it. She was to sustain schoolwork in a way that had not been possible, when she was frequently ill. Soma was able to finish college. What is more, she began graduate school. Another significant change occurred in her social relations. Her self-image improved as she was able to reduce her identity as a medical patient. Her change in her self-image allowed her to feel less of an outcast. There was a very significant change in Soma's feelings of anxiety, dread, and depression. She felt there was an emotional liberation.

Her next challenge was to test all her emotional strength and courage Confrontation with her mother and father was going to take all the courage Soma could muster. She turned to me to help her with this very difficult task. Soma and I created an encounter with her mother and father in a step-by-step method. It was clear that to push her would create anxiety beyond her emotional capacity. Soma was also told she might have some retraumatization and recurrence of symptoms as she went through this part of the recovery process. Soma also needed to help to be aware of the intensity of her parent's defensiveness so we could create a confrontation they could tolerate. Soma was encouraged to find her voice and openly and directly express any feelings she was having about the confrontation process and my behavior during this difficult process. Above all, I urged Soma to create an attitude of empathy and patience in going through the process of sharing her feelings about the incest trauma with her mother and father. It was abundantly clear they would not welcome the idea of incest into their lives.

It was Soma's idea to talk to her mother first. She began what was to become a two-year process of unending difficulty, not knowing, at the time, her mother would be the more difficult of the two parents to confront. Any time Soma tried to talk to her mother about the origin of her negative feelings about her father, her mother would challenge the daughter's perception and feelings, iterating the father's goodness. The mother vehemently denied such a horrific act could have occurred. Her mother needed to defend her choice of a mate, and her long-standing marriage. The comfortable life she enjoyed, and, perhaps, most importantly, psychologically maintained the dissociation of her own childhood seduction. As often happens in conflictual parent–child relations with adolescents and young adults, tensions mount without any meaningful dialogue (Rachman, 1975a). The mother's capacity to have a therapeutic dialogue was hampered by her own rigid defensiveness. Apparently, it was psychologically more important to protect her own sense of self-cohesion than become vulnerable enough to respond to her daughter's need for empathy about being the victim of incest. This dilemma is faced by any parent, partner, or friend who feels so threatened by the other's need that self-protection is more essential than stretching oneself to empathize.

In her way, the mother did as much as she was psychologically capable of doing. To her credit, the mother did agree to support Soma, when she was a teenager, to see counselors to deal with her anxieties. At that time, the mother believed these anxieties emanated from her daughter's medical problems.

The counseling was seen as an avenue to maintain her health, deal with adjustment issues, bolster her confidence, and help her maintain a positive attitude. One could say there was an irony to the mother's behaviour, which eventually led her daughter to confront her incest trauma. The mother was a very anxious woman who needed counseling to deal with the daughter's difficult behavior, her husband's frequent sexual adventures, and her own repressed childhood sexual trauma. The mother was not at peace and would spend parts of each year going to religious retreats sponsored by synagogues. Her counselor was the Rabbi from the family's synagogue. The Rabbi was a student of Zen Buddhism, and the mother became a follower of Zen Buddhism.

The mother had, in some fundamental way, as all incest survivors have, lost faith in a traditional God. Her family's God and their traditions did not protect her from incest. Turning away from her tradition and towards Zen was the mother's attempt to heal her own trauma. The mother was using self-help therapy to find serenity and peace, without having to confront her incest trauma. Her false self was so well developed in her poised, responsive, and engaging façade no one could detect the horror of her early life. In her family tradition and social group, keeping emotions in check was demanded. Emotional messiness, which confrontation with trauma always brings, was highly undesirable and to be avoided at all costs. Soma's mother tried, as best as she could, to give her daughter a role model for dealing with trauma by turning to Zen spirituality. This model encouraged peace and serenity without confrontation with your demons. The mother knew she was an incest survivor, but never confronted this issue.

Soma's trepidation about confronting her sexual secret with her mother was palpable. As she chartered a course of confrontation with evil, she developed increasing emotional strength and courage from every experience that unearthed the truth. About a month after she recovered the full extent of her childhood incest, she wanted to tell her mother about it. She was angry about her discovery and felt her mother was complicit in it. I told Soma to find outlets for her anger by verbally expressing it in her sessions, and physical means of expression through vigorous exercise. She accepted this advice, and, for the first time, in her life, joined a gym. What I was trying to help Soma do was to reduce her anger so that she could create a therapeutic zone to talk to her mother. It was clear the topic would cause an emotional holocaust in the family. It was suggested that Soma think of the confrontation as a process to be done in stages, with emotional integration before each next stage. She needed to guard against overwhelming herself and her mother. When some of her anger subsided, she was encouraged to call her mother to schedule a meeting.

Soma began the process, even though in the days preceding her first meeting with her mother she had a re-occurrence of severe gastro-intestinal symptoms. They met for lunch at a place Soma knew her mother would like. Emphasizing her desire to conquer her emotional anxieties and fears as well as her physical problems, Soma talked to her mother about her belief that her father had regularly molested her. The mother was stone-cold silent. It would take all the courage and emotional strength Soma could muster to continue with the conversation. After what seemed like a lifetime, her mother held her daughter's hand, which Soma greatly appreciated. It was Soma who did all of the talking, and her mother who did all of the listening during this luncheon meeting that launched the exploration into the dark side of their family life. The mother said she would need time to digest this "bitter pill that she was asked to swallow." She asked Soma for a month before they could talk again. After two weeks, the mother asked if they could see a family counselor. The mother did not want to see me. I referred Soma to a colleague who worked with families. Soma felt that she could work with my colleague and arranged for her mother and her to begin counseling sessions.

For the next several months Soma's mother went into an emotional crisis disguised by her research project. There was not a book on the incest trauma that the mother did not read. She took copious notes on 8 × 10 yellow legal pads, as if she had been given a college honors thesis assignment. The mother had considerable intellectual talent. She graduated Phi Beta Kappa, Summa cum Laude, from one of the most prestigious colleges in the United States. The mother's intellect was a gift she had that she used to academically achieve, gain status and self-esteem, and even marry well. She was proud of her gift and had great confidence in her capacity "to figure things out for myself."

Soma shared with me the data of the family sessions, with her mother's approval. This material was integrated into her analysis. Unfortunately, the mother could not intellectually integrate her daughter's incest trauma. The fundamental confrontational statement the mother would offer, over and over again, clearly more angry than concerned, was: "Don't you think I would know if my husband had sex with my daughter?"

On the surface, her question has some superficial validity. It seems inconceivable that a mother would be totally unaware of a regular sexual experience between her husband and her daughter. Yet, all the research on father–daughter incest indicated, from Freud onward, that mothers were fundamentally unaware of the sexual crimes in their own homes (Alpert, 1995, Ferenczi 1980n, 1988; Freud, 1954; Messler-Davies & Frawley, 1994; Herman, 1981; Masson, 1984; Shengold, 1989; Van der Kolk, 1988). Soma's mother actually fitted the psychological description that clinical researchers have indicated about mothers of daughters who are incest victims. She was a bystander to sexual abuse. The families were psychologically affected by the sexual violation, the abuser, the victim, and the bystander. The incest trio share major psychological mechanisms, such as denial and dissociation, which are used to cope with the incest trauma (Ferenczi, 1980n, 1988; Herman, 1981; Masson, 1984). Soma's mother used dissociation to split the incest experience into separate fragments of thoughts, feelings, and experience. It is likely she used dissociation to an intense degree for two important reasons. First, the mother had a well-developed sense of dissociation because she had been a victim of incest herself as a child (my hypothesis, not clinical data). Consequently, the mother was never fully emotionally present in her own life. Second, the vehement denial of her daughter being the victim of incest that was indicated in her question: "Do you think I would do that to my own daughter?" Incest was an inconceivable thought that could not be entertained, even for a moment. Also, this is a remarkably defensive statement which further distances the mother from her own trauma and her daughter's experience of incest.

When her daughter told the mother about the father's sexual abuse, a cacophony of emotional chords ran through the mother's brain as if she were going through shock therapy against her will. There was only one way to reduce the emotional shocks. The mother had to take control of the crisis herself, using her considerate intellect as the major tool. First, she read all the self-help books on incest. Then she moved on to professional material. She was actually creating a tutorial course for herself on incest trauma. But this tutorial had a particular focus. Ferenczi has been credited as being the first analyst to empathically understand the child's emotional crisis of incest, accepting the child's report as psychologically valid (Masson, 1984), Soma's mother, on the other hand, focused on trying to prove that her daughter was a hysterical liar about incest. In her research, the mother found, and completely embraced, the false memory syndrome. What the mother did not research was the history of the founding of the False Memory Foundation (FMF), which developed the false memory syndrome. The FMF was founded by Pamela Freyd, PhD, as a response to her daughter, Jennifer Freyd, accusing her father of incest as a result of retrieving memories in her psychotherapy experience. In other words, rather than empathically explore her daughter's claim of paternal incest, Pamela Freyd and her husband Peter founded an organization to discredit their daughter's accusations. Soma's mother, in what she called "her extensive research," used the Freyds as a role model, rather than Alice Miller (1986, 1990), Judith Herman (1981, 1992), or Leonard Shengold (1989), all scholars on childhood sexual abuse and readily available to the public. Of course, the mother might have also run across the book, *Betrayal Trauma: The Logic of Forgetting Childhood Abuse* (1996), by Jennifer Freyd, who has become a scholarly contributor to the literature on childhood memory and sexual abuse.

After months of negotiating, Soma's mother agreed to a joint session with a family counselor. Soma did her best during the month hiatus to stay focused and positive. She had an individual session prior to the joint session with her mother. The family counselor reassured her she would help her talk honestly to her mother. Soma was prepared to understand her mother's intellectual approach to emotional trauma. She needed to accept her mother's method of coping with severe emotional issues. Neither the counselor nor Soma was prepared for the mother to enter the joint session with a lawyer's briefcase filled with hand-written notepads, typed papers, reprints of articles, and bound and paperback books. After a brief exchange of pleasantries, the mother used almost three-quarters of the session defending the false memory syndrome and the absurdity of her not being aware of her husband's molestation of her daughter. The counselor was empathic to the emotional crisis that her daughter's revelation had caused the mother and the family. In a non-defensive way, the counselor said that she believed the daughter was telling the truth. She had consulted with Soma's analyst (me) who presented meaningful psychological data of the origins of Soma's anxieties, fears, and symptoms. There was an internal consistency about her story and her personal functioning that, as a specialist in treating families of trauma survivors, she experienced for over twenty years. Soma's story could be found in the trauma literature to which she could refer the mother. The mother was speechless, but nodded yes, she would accept the references.

As the time approached for the end of this joint session, it was clear to everyone present that ending the session would be a blessing. Soma graciously thanked her mother for being willing to attend such a difficult meeting. Her mother had tears in her eyes as her daughter's kind words helped soothe her wounds. The counselor waited until the mother and daughter had had their moment and then asked the therapeutic duo if they wished to have another session. Soma deferred, and her mother softly said "yes."

I told Soma the joint session she described was a triumph of her capacity to empathize with her mother's emotional struggles at a time when her own were uppermost in her mind. She showed emotional courage and interpersonal maturity in the way she was relating to her mother. At that time, her mother was having a more difficult time with her incest trauma than was Soma. All these comments seem to help Soma.

Soma's mother asked her for permission to call me to discuss the incest issue. We scheduled a consultation session. The mother told me about being unaware of her daughter being subjected to incest by her husband, and her extensive research on the false memory syndrome. I empathized with her struggle and the difficulty in understanding and accepting this tragedy. Soma's mother found the courage to ask directly: "Do you think my daughter was incested?"

There was only one way to answer the question, so I offered her the following: "There is no way I can really know if Soma was incested. I tend to take her word for it because she has described the experience in the same way I have heard from the incest survivors with whom I have worked for over thirty years. I don't understand why your daughter would make this up. If you don't want to believe it is true, I can understand this too. Just see Soma's trauma as something that is real to her, whether it's real to you or not. Help her come to peace with it by being on her side. One final word. Don't lose your relationship with your daughter over this issue. *Please, this is the emotional test of your life*. You have all the emotional intellectual, social, and maternal instincts to pass this test."

She did not fight me about what was said to her. I was hopeful she would move from the darkness into the light. The mother needed a rest from the trauma that the daughter's awareness of incest had caused her.

No one would have predicted the experience Soma was about to have in finding the courage to confront her abuser, her father. Soma remembered her father expressing his guilt, confusion, and desperation, feeling completely baffled by her gastro-intestinal illness and its never-ending toll on his daughter's body and mind. To herself, she said: "Dad, I know what caused my physical problems, if I could only tell it to you." Once again, Soma's emotional courage came to the fore. She decided to attempt a first meeting with her father to share the insights she had struggled so hard to gain in her analysis. She had great trepidation, afraid he might deny the molestation even more vehemently than her mother had done. What is more, she was afraid he would blame her for the incest or blame me for planting the ideas in her head. Finally, she feared he would remove financial support for her treatment. Soma was determined to find a way to continue her analysis if her father removed his financial support. In essence, by the time she conceived of discussing her childhood sexual trauma with her parents, Soma was determined to finish her recovery process no matter what it took to do so. It was uplifting to experience her life-saving force.

Soma's father returned from Europe to see his daughter, not realizing the agenda was emotional, not physical, illness. She met her father at the airport where he landed from overseas, wanting to capture his attention without any other distractions. They had lunch for about one and half hours, which for Soma seemed like a lifetime. She had to use the toilet many times that afternoon, as the stress of telling her father about the sexual abuse mounted. In a manner that mimicked her childhood distress and terror and the psychological damage of molestation, she retreated to the bathroom. Soma simply said she had recovered the sexual experiences of her childhood with her father. As soon as she let the words slip from her mouth, she wanted to run into the bathroom and hide as she had done as a child to escape her father's abuse. She actually put her hands over her eyes and opened her fingers so she could peek through her hand. Her father completely surprised her. First, he gently took her hand from her face, held it in his hand and softly started his response. As tears welled up in his eyes, he said he had dreaded this day since Soma was a child, and, yet, he was glad it was finally here: "I am so very, very, sorry for what I did to you. It was wrong. I was wrong. It was a sick thing to do. In those days, I could not keep my sexuality under control. But, that's no excuse. *Please, please,* forgive me."

Was this a miracle? Was Soma dissociating? Was it a fantasy or a delusion? Just then her father took both her hands in his, iterating his lament of forgiveness. They both began to sob, not caring that they were in a public place. Only they knew what shameful secret they shared. What is more, some of the tears were for the joy of shared tears cleansing each other and feeling less stained by incest. Soma did not verbally forgive her father at that fateful meeting in the airport; it would take days, months, and years before she could even think of that impossible task.

When Soma evaluated the results of the two confrontations with her parents, she felt she had accomplished a great deal. She found her voice, lost since childhood, and was able to share her secret of incest with them. Now, the family of origin knew about the psychological derivation of their daughter's illness. Confusion, criticism, and improper treatment could give way to empathy, understanding, and recovery from trauma. And most of all, they could observe in their daughter's struggle to uncover her incest trauma, confront her demons, and tell her secret to them not a sickly, passive, rebellious dropout, but a vital, determined, courageous young woman.

When she told me about her courageous experiences with her mother and father, a trophy to celebrate her triumph was sent in the form of a letter that said:

> Dear Soma
>
> I congratulate you for confronting your childhood trauma. You have taken an enormous step towards health and recovery. You are an emotionally courageous, intellectually insightful and emphatically attuned human being.
>
> I am very proud of you.

CHAPTER TWELVE

Countertransference encounters: the analyst's experience of trauma analysis

As Balint (1968) so poignantly described, working in the zone of regression, which is characteristic of the treatment of individuals who have suffered the incest trauma, makes significant emotional demands on the analyst as well as the analysand. Regression, in this instance, refers to the process when the actual childhood seduction is first recovered, then re-experienced, and finally integrated into the contemporary adult personality. Each stage of the experience causes upheaval, even chaos. Balint cautioned that maintaining the regression to a therapeutic, rather than a malignant, level was a formidable task for the analyst to negotiate. He developed the concept of therapeutic regression based on his observations of his teacher, Ferenczi's, difficult clinical work with Elizabeth Severn (Rachman, 2010a,b, 2012b,c,e, 2014a,c, 2015). Balint was privy to the entire analysis of Severn, 1925–1933, as Ferenczi's most cherished student and analysand. Balint observed first hand the emotional issues that were evoked in what he called "the grand experiment" (Balint, 1992).

No one has struggled more than Ferenczi, either in pioneering or contemporary psychoanalysis, to maintain a therapeutic attitude and clinical interaction with a difficult analysand (see Chapter Five, for a fuller discussion of the emotional struggles that an analyst can face with an incest survivor). In fact, Ferenczi is a role model for an emotionally courageous clinician and professional who developed countertransference analysis for psychoanalysis. Ferenczi's countertransference analysis with Severn highlighted his special personal qualities as an analyst:

1. Great emotional courage in analyzing his own personal issues to what he termed rock bottom. He continued until he reached his emotional contribution to the difficulties in the therapeutic relationship.
2. A dedication to consistently creating a democratic and mutual analytic atmosphere in his clinical interaction, in spite of substantial emotional challenges. Once he accepted the challenge to co-create an analytic encounter, he did not resort to interpretations of resistance. Rather, he would intensify his empathic understanding and his self-examination.
3. He showed a remarkable capacity and willingness for empathic understanding as well as sharing his subjective experience. After all, he demonstrated this empathy for Severn under the most difficult of emotional and interpersonal circumstances (see Chapter Five). But, with Sigmund Freud, he also demonstrated great empathy by remaining within the boundaries of psychoanalysis and never founding his own school of psychoanalysis. Thompson (1964c) felt Ferenczi showed a personal failing by not challenging Freud, something she was able to do, as Ferenczi's student and analysand, by helping to found interpersonal psychoanalysis. Ferenczi, contrary, to Freud's anxiety, never intended to leave the fold. He wanted to help psychoanalysis integrate trauma study and treatment (Rachman, 2013).
4. His special willingness to self-disclose his personal contributions to the countertransference encounters. No one in the history of psychoanalysis has been his equal in self-disclosure. Sometimes, his self-disclosures have been questionable (Rachman, 1993d). Judicious self-disclosure is a contemporary concept that can modulate such questionable disclosures (Rachman, 1988d).
5. He had special personal qualities of flexibility, responsiveness, tenderness, and emotional enthusiasm in analyzing his own countertransference. These qualities allowed for a lively and

passionate interaction that motivated both parties in the therapeutic dyad.

The change encounter

The analysis in the case of Winston was a study in the analysis of countertransference (see Chapter Eight). As an example of this experience, three countertransference encounters are discussed. An initial countertransference encounter, which was labeled the change encounter, occurred in the first year of the analysis. As mentioned in Chapter Eight, one of the central dynamics of Winston's maternal trauma was the feeling of being controlled by the sexual seduction and emotional domination of his mother. So, it was not surprising that during one session we had an intense countertransference encounter over the issue of control. It might not have been surprising, but it was still a difficult moment. Winston often made it clear he needed to gather a sense of hope from me, since he had all but given up hope of ever overcoming his sense of powerlessness and fulfilling his creative desires. He came to a session during the latter part of the first year and began describing how much better he felt and ran off a series of what seemed like changes in his functioning.

At the time, I offered what was thought to be an empathic statement which could give him some hope: "It sounds like you are describing that you are changing."

No sooner had I finished the sentence than Winston became enraged. He said: "Changing? What are you talking about?" I was puzzled by his negative reaction and was going to try to understand it by creating an open dialogue with him. I said: "You seem irritated with me, what did I say, or how did I say it, that is causing you a problem?" With that, Winston got up from his seat and left the room. He did not respond to my attempt to persuade him to stay and discuss his upset. Since this was during my first year of training, I was upset about the failure to maintain Winston in the session. As a first-year analytic candidate, I brought this difficult case to a weekly training seminar, hoping for some emotional relief and intellectual insight. Unfortunately, neither emotional nor intellectual insight was received. In this traditional analytic institution, I was "blamed" for the analysand leaving the session because of my unresolved countertransference reaction. It was felt that neither the supervisor nor my fellow analytic candidates understood my empathic relationship with Winston. They jumped to the conclusion that, when an analysand leaves a session, the analyst is to be blamed. Yet, I did accept there was some difficulty in our relationship that needed to be analyzed.

I decided to rely on my previous training as a client-centered psychotherapist at the Counseling and Psychotherapy Research Center at the University of Chicago to focus on the issue of empathic failure during the session when Winston walked out. He did return for our next session, was on time, as usual, and was ready and willing to explore our difficulty. I learned a great deal from the session after the walk-out. I definitely learned more from this session than from the supervisory session with my peers and supervisor. Winston readily entered into a mutual dialogue. He said what angered him was that he experienced me as being "controlling, wanting to take credit for the fact I was changing." What is more, this experience evoked his negative feelings about his mother. He experienced me as his mother trying to control him, to get him to do what she wanted him to do and feed her narcissism in his accomplishments.

In those early days of my analytic training, it was difficult to accept Winston's judgment that I was being unempathic and retraumatizing him. This was a turning point for me. I needed to put aside my narcissism and reinvest in understanding Winston's subjective experience. The task was to understand Winston's experience of me as his controlling mother. We went over this controlling mother countertransference encounter in detail, with a specific focus on empathically understanding his subjective experience of my behavior as his controlling mother. "You are changing" was heard as me saying: "You are changing because of *my analysis of you*! I wanted you to change and *I am fulfilling my desire* for you to change." He left the session because of the anger that overwhelmed him because he believed I was trying to manipulate and control him. His leaving was not due to my inability to explore this issue or any feeling that I was being defensive or insistent on my point of view. Rather, Winston's feeling of being overwhelmed with rage dominated his thinking and feeling. Leaving was a protective device. He had to remove himself from the perceived toxic object so he could maintain his sense of self. Removing himself from the toxic situation also protected me from his rage. This relational analysis made more sense than blaming the analyst for poor technique.

I was relieved to hear about, and understand, Winston's subjective experience of my perceived controlling behavior. When I searched for my contribution to the countertransference encounter, I became aware that I was capable of being controlling. My assertive and enthusiastic tone could be experienced as demanding and/or intrusive. What is more, I was aware of this issue in my clinical/personal functioning (Rachman, 2003a). Winston was very responsive to the empathic attunement to his experience of the clinical difficulties. He was grateful that I was so willing to try to understand his aversive reaction to be being controlled. When I was willing to admit to the contribution to the countertransference encounter, Winston felt he *was not* experiencing his mother. According to his report, he never had an experience with someone trying to understand him so well or admit to having a responsibility in the difficulty. He never walked out of a session again. He became increasingly more aware of the transference implications that the analyst was controlling him.

The Hitler encounter

Winston and I did not stop having our countertransference encounters. Two additional such countertransference situations indicated change in both of our functioning. The Hitler encounter occurred after our analysis had been running for about ten years. There had been no relational crises for many years. Winston had been hard at work analyzing hundreds of dreams and fantasies, leading to an uncovering of early memories. He was able to develop insight into his traumas, primarily with his mother, and, secondarily, with his father. What continued to be troubling was his intense and puzzling negative feelings toward Jews. Winston had been railing against the Jews for several years, making anti-Semitic remarks, knowing I was Jewish. And, not incidentally, he came from an observant Jewish family where his father had been the president of the synagogue. We had explored the emotional connection between his anger toward the Jews and his mother and father. He acknowledged an emotional connection, and seemed to accept my interpretations that it was due to rage against his parents for their abuse and neglect. But, from time to time, he would have an outbreak of an anti-Semitic rant, in the same way as he would have an anti-Black rant.

Many years later, an analytic session began by Winston telling me he had seen a television program which focused on the holocaust. The analyst sensed that he was going to give a rant about the Jews, which he did, saying: "Hitler had the right idea killing all the Jews. They didn't appreciate how he was trying to cleanse Europe of undesirables who didn't share his vision of a pure race."

He went on a non-stop angry criticism of Jews who deserved to die because they were inferior. The analyst had heard the rant many times before. In the past, Winston would be allowed to go on until he stopped. But, this day for a reason I was not fully aware of, he was stopped in the following way: "Winston, you're not going to like what I'm going to say, but I have to say I don't appreciate your ranting and raving about how Hitler was right to kill the Jews. I would appreciate your stopping this."

He became very angry, saying: "I have a right to say whatever I please. You are my analyst, you have to listen to me no matter what I say."

I agreed with him, saying: "You are right! You have an inalienable right to say anything. And you're also right, as your analyst I should listen to it. I have listened to this same kind of rant before and didn't stop you. But, this time I find it difficult to hear."

Winston defended his position, continuing with the following: "I still don't like that you're trying to *stifle me*."

As soon as I heard the concept of "stifle", I changed my intervention: "I know you don't like to be stifled and I don't blame you. You're mother tried to stifle your functioning. I just feel I can't be therapeutic with you when you continually assault me with your admiration of Hitler and his hatred of Jews."

These comments began to soften his frustration and anger. The relationship crisis diminished as the session ended. The following session we fully analyzed our interaction. Winston admitted he was expressing a need he has to rant and rave from time to time, and this time he used Hitler and the Jews as the vehicle. What is more, he was able to understand that his reaction to the analyst was a transference reaction he felt for his mother's manipulation, control, and domination of him. Trying to stop him from talking about Hitler was akin to his basic childhood trauma when his mother stifled him.

What was so significant about this session was that the countertransference reaction allowed Winston and the analyst to co-create new meanings in the analytic narrative of his maternal transference experience. He became more insightful about his mother's narcissistic need for attention and how it stifled the expression of his creative impulse. Winston began, in this countertransference experience, to reduce his need to stimulate a negative transference. In the months to follow, he did not have the same need to express his rant about Blacks, Jews, or feel stifled by me. What is more, there was never again a countertransference encounter where he got so angry or felt so disturbed that he left a session prematurely. This experience was very helpful for me in contributing toward change. This countertransference encounter encouraged me to more fully examine the personal need to control and manipulate. I did have a need to control, which dates back to a childhood relationship with my mother. Some of this personal dynamic has been discussed. In an autobiography of a countertransference reaction, a similar maternal dynamic was analyzed so that a therapeutic relationship could be maintained with another difficult case (Rachman, 2003a,c). I became aware that my control dynamic could be very subtle, so that it had a psychological effect on Winston, even though I was not aware of its occurrence.

The Obama encounter

Changes in the countertransference encounters over the course of the analysis charted differences in functioning of both the analyst and analysand. This can be seen in a discussion of the Obama encounter. I had thought that Winston's negative feelings toward Blacks had diminished. He had only reported minor incidents where he expressed negative attitudes toward African-Americans. From time to time, he would make negative remarks about his boss: "I guess he got his job because he was a Negro; he was able to go to college because of the equal opportunity law." Other general comments at the time included, "It's a fact, Negroes are intellectually inferior to whites; I can't stand the fact that Negroes get an advantage over whites." But, in these ensuing years, he did not reveal the hateful, sadistic, and mean-spirited fantasies he had told me previously, "eliminating negro children", which occurred during the early years of our analysis (see Chapter Eight).

Did I think his anger and hatred toward blacks had been worked through? There was hope that some diminution in his negative feelings had happened, since he had almost completely stopped expressing the same kind of hateful feelings towards his mother that had preoccupied his thoughts during the early part of our analysis. There was some meaningful diminution of negative feelings toward his mother and Blacks. Dare I conclude that the analysis had been instrumental in this change? As we shall see, there is a complicated yes/no answer. The issue of Winston's negative feelings towards Blacks forced itself back into the analysis with the election of Barack Obama, the first African-American president of the United States of America. In anticipation of the election of Barack Obama, Winston began a campaign, both with his wife and me about his fear, anger, and disgust that America was, "actually electing a Negro to be head of the country." He warned both his wife and me that if "Hussein Obama, the Muslim," were elected he would be very emotionally upset and he would need some form of a palliative to survive the next four years of "the Negro's administration."

There was no rational or psychodynamic way to discuss Winston's anger toward and fear of "Hussein Obama", as he called him. It did not matter to him that Barack Obama and he were honor students at the same university, or that Barack Obama's mother was white. It was clear that Winston needed empathy, not interpretation, for his hatred or, should we say, fear. I needed to empathize with the fear that was emerging in him as Obama's election approached. He responded that it was fear that stimulated his anger. The fear was a loss of control. He felt a liberal Democrat would loosen governmental controls. He preferred the conservative Republican politicians because they keep the controls on human functioning. Their political policy suited him psychologically. He wanted to be left alone to take care of his own money, health care, living conditions, and way of life. When I attempted some interpretative interaction, linking his fear, anger, and anxiety about Obama to his life-long struggle with the ghost of his mother's domineering, controlling, and manipulative personality, he said: "Perhaps that's true, but, I believe it is more basic than that. I think it is more neurological. I can't stand losing control because it is an assault on my nervous system. Because of my neurological defects, my whole nervous system is threatened."

The neurological answer to understanding all of his behavior had become standard for Winston since a neuropsychologist told him that was the cause of his difficulties (see Chapter Eight). Rather than interpretation, I now offered empathy. I told him it must be intensely frustrating and frightening to feel the person in control of the country is trying to take something basic away from him. Such an empathetic response was not only helpful, but essential for Winston, even after decades of analysis. When he was threatened with loss of control, he would become very anxious and develop the obsessive need to rant and rave about his abuser, in this instance, "Hussein Obama." In the past, I would have tried harder to introduce some interpretative aspect to our interaction about Obama. But, my change in functioning towards greater empathic understanding when Winston becomes agitated, no matter how analytical he is capable of being, was important for both of us. I also helped his wife to accept his latest disturbing and peculiar campaign against Blacks. He would constantly make disparaging remarks about "The Mud People," especially when his wife and he were watching television and African-Americans appeared on the TV screen. He would yell at her, "Get those Negroes out of my house. I don't want to be exposed to them in my own home." She felt he was controlling her capacity to watch what interested her. I asked them to consider that some accommodation was necessary for a peaceful existence to be fashioned in the era of Barack Obama. After much discussion about control, manipulation, and intrusiveness, they both agreed to make some changes. Winston agreed to try to curtail his ranting and raving about Hussein Obama and the Negroes, especially when his wife was watching TV. She agreed to mute any commercials or programs that contained African-Americans while he was present. Since they had very different sleeping schedules, it also became possible to watch TV at times he was sleeping. They also began to watch movies together, where he could exercise control over whether there were African-Americans in the movies. Their watching movies together most weekend evenings pleased his wife very much.

The Obama encounter reinforced the idea that Winston's childhood had left him with enduring traumas that would never fully heal. An ongoing relationship with him meant revisiting these traumas on a regular basis. My notion of his capacity to analyze out his traumas had to be amended whenever his anxiety mounted to threaten his homeostasis.

The Obama encounter highlighted a change in my own thinking about Winston's personality structure and functioning. When he first began our therapeutic odyssey, I had reached the conclusion that he had developed a borderline personality organization. There were also periods of intense anxiety when psychotic-like features were evident. At times, I also thought the diagnosis of pseudo-neurotic schizophrenia was appropriate (a term popular in the 1960s when I was an analytic candidate). But, in this last decade of our analysis, Winston believed his fundamental issues were no longer a function of a psychological disorder, but a function of neurological deficits. As discussed in Chapter Eight, Winston had, on his own, arranged for several consultation sessions with a neuropsychologist in Cambridge, Massachusetts, whom he found on the Internet. The neuropsychologist diagnosed him with neurological–cognitive deficits based on her interviews and testing. She seriously influenced his thinking and they both concluded his issues were of a fundamental neurological basis. Although I did not accept the conclusion that all of Winston's issues were neurological, it did seem plausible that he had neurological problems both as a child and adult, which interfered with his capacity to self-actualize. What we began to discuss was the concept of Asperger's syndrome (Asperger, 1991; Szatman et al., 1989). Winston never felt satisfied that either my psychodynamic explanations or the biological explanations of the neuropsychologist were sufficient to fully understand his unusual and peculiar behavior. For example, after decades of analysis, with the use of non-interpretative measures such as neuropsychological consultations, extensive reading of psychological, biological, and genetic literature, and regular searching of the internet for medical information, Winston would routinely walk around his apartment, giving the Nazi salute, shouting "Heil Hitler." He would also log onto YouTube or My Face on the Internet and find Nazi or Hitler material. He did talk to me about it, but not as a sign we needed to analyze the issue. Rather, he was reporting a peculiar, obsessive interest in Hitler and the Nazis. This interest caused him no difficulty. It did cause his wife great difficulty, which provided some motivation to work on the interest as an issue. However, he sounded a familiar note: "I don't want to be stifled in my own house!" I agreed his home should be a sanctuary, but, I said, it also needed to be a "place of peace" where his partner would not be bombarded by sounds or images of Hitler, which she loathed. As he had done before, he was willing to examine this dilemma in the light of his wife's well-being. He agreed to stop walking around the apartment saluting Hitler and confine these activities to his study, in private. I was reminded of his willingness, many years ago, to accept my negative reaction to our Hitler encounter and not to re-evoke his need to praise Hitler for the destruction of the Jews. Winston, it should be added, never fully accepted the interpretation that his "anti-Semitism" had any link to a hatred of his destructive Jewish mother or his absent and unavailable Jewish father. However, several years ago, he began reporting that he was researching his ancestry and had established that his family origins were in Austria. He enjoyed doing the research. At this time he also began reading the book, *Yiddish Civilization: The Rise and Fall of a Forgotten Nation* (Kriwaczek, 2005), which he said was an excellent book. When I expressed interest in this book, I was given a copy as a gift. The two changes, his willingness to accept a limitation on his ranting and raving about Hitler and the seemingly positive response to his Jewish ancestry were not analyzed. I felt it was sufficient to accept it as it was manifested since Winston had not accepted the psychodynamic link of these issues to his relationship to his parents.

But there was something more that was driving a new view of his peculiar behavior. I had done some reading and talking to colleagues about the Asperger syndrome, wondering if a personal rigidity was being shown in insisting that Winston's childhood traumas were the only explanation for his disturbed behavior. There was one particular experience in researching Asperger syndrome that provided an insightful experience for me. In March, 2009, on the cable channel TBS (Turner Broadcasting System), a program was shown on Asperger syndrome featuring twin middle-age sisters who had an all-consuming obsession with the TV celebrity Dick Clark. First, the program presented a series of medical and psychological experts who examined the twins and agreed they had Asperger syndrome. The twin sisters were in middle age, living with their non-Asperger sisters and their families. They were very friendly, interactive, sweet, and innocent in a childish way. All interaction with others was focused on endless discussions about their obsession. In the room where the sisters lived, the walls were plastered with pictures of Dick Clark. A television set was the other prominent feature of the room. The sisters watch television daily, not only to see Dick Clark, but to fill in charts they both kept of the type, color, and style of the clothing he wore. When the clinicians investigated the twins' obsessive preoccupation with Dick Clark, they could not find any psychological or biological reason that would explain it. Their behavior was ego-syntonic. A moment of great joy occurred for the sisters when, through a local TV host, an appointment was made for them to visit Dick Clark in California. It was the greatest moment in their lives.

I found this documentary very helpful in furthering my understanding of Winston's peculiar behavior. I began to conceptualize his Negro obsession, Jewish obsession, and Hitler ranting and raving, which had continued for about forty years, as being very similar to the Asperger twins' Dick Clark obsession. Years of analysis of the psychodynamics of Winston's obsessions about Hitler, the Jews, and Blacks actually provided no meaningful insight. The inability to analyze the obsessions was unusual, because Winston was very open and cooperative in exploring all other aspects of his functioning. I could never reconcile this difference, finally reaching the conclusion, that, at present, there is no available psychodynamic explanation for Winston's obsessions. His ranting and raving about Hitler, Jews, and Negroes need to be accepted as an obsessive–compulsive symptom of Asperger syndrome. My change in thinking about Winston's obsessions helped me to discontinue trying to analyze the obsessions and work toward accepting it as a part of his personality. When this insight was shared with Winston and his wife in a couple's session, he was very pleased. He felt that I was able to understand his need to express himself in the privacy of his own home. This was a reversal of the feeling he had that I had stifled him on previous occasions. It was also an important opportunity to help his wife develop a new attitude toward her husband's peculiar behavior. She had always felt Winston's statements about Hitler, Jews, and Blacks were verbal attacks on her, since she had the opposite feelings about these people. She hated Hitler and had positive feelings about Jews and Blacks. She had a great deal of difficulty giving up the idea her husband was deliberately trying to cause her harm. She did not understand the Asperger syndrome. I asked her to look up the issue on line as well as send for a DVD copy of the Asperger's TV program. She reluctantly agreed to do so. What was pinpointed for both Winston and his wife was that an understanding of the Asperger's syndrome would be a help in working through some of the interpersonal difficulties they were having. Eventually, Winston did curtail his negative behavior with his wife.

Countertransference encounters with W

There were two countertransference encounters in the case of W. (see Chapter Nine), that were both disturbing, but aided self-actualization. They were (1) the plastic rug cover encounter (Rachman, 2003a) and (2) the "You think you know about me, you don't know anything" encounter. After about four years of trauma analysis with W., I experienced a very dramatic example of how the analyst's behavior can lead to retraumatization.

"Plastic rug cover" encounter

It is difficult to convey the surprise and shock that I experienced during the session when W. emotionally attacked me. At such moments of an intense countertransference encounter, it feels as if one does not know the analysand. It was as if all our clinical work and the establishment of what was experienced by me as a positive, significant working relationship was a fiction. Is it my need to view our relationship as positive and meaningful for me? Am I neglecting the darker aspects of the analysand's functioning? Have I forgotten that a transference relationship is ambivalent by its very nature?

One snowy day in January, I had decided to place a plastic cover over a new rug that I had placed in my consultation room. It was clear that the rug was going to get very dirty from the snow and slush that people would bring in from the outside. Covering the rug to protect it seemed like a reasonable idea at the time, and I never thought I would offend anyone by doing this. First, I saw a couple for therapy that day of the countertransference encounter. Our session was meaningful and uneventful. I noticed the couple saw the plastic covering the rug, smiled knowingly, as if to approve of the idea, and went through the session without incident. W.'s session followed the couple therapy session. *As soon as W. noticed the plastic covering on the rug, he became enraged.* He did not sit down as he usually did, but began pacing up and down the floor, remarkably agitated. He would not let me speak. Instead, he began to angrily attack me saying: [Pointing to a picture of

Sándor Ferenczi I had displayed on my office wall], "Dr. Rachman you are not being true to your mentor, Sándor Ferenczi. He would never do this to me! You sir, are not a true practitioner of empathy and analysis."

I wish to put my reaction in the vernacular, since that was my immediate internal emotional reaction: "What the fuck is going on? Why is this guy so angry? What the fuck did I do to him?"

I tried to develop a dialogue with W. about what I had done to him to cause him so much distress, but it was not possible. It was clear that I had done something (of which he was not consciously aware) that had triggered a traumatic experience. When W. refused to allow a dialogue about it, it became clear he needed to be given full expression to vent his emotional reaction to the trauma, without an analysis of it.

It is never easy to sit still while an individual attacks you verbally for a half hour. What is more, while remaining silent, one still needs to convey, non-verbally, some form of empathy. Although I was confused, feeling stupid, frustrated, and angry, I did feel empathy for W.'s distress, which was conveyed with facial and hand gestures. He seemed so emotionally out of control, needy, and lost. I hoped this would be a temporary empathic failure. I reminded myself that, even though W. was enraged, he did not leave the session. Finally, W. sat down on the couch and voluntarily started talking to me. He was much less angry and willing to understand what had transpired. At the end of this session and others to come, he was willing to analyze the retraumatization. Apparently, seeing the plastic cover over the rug instantly reminded W. of his hated mother, who put plastic covers on the furniture in the living room. He hated sticking to these uncomfortable chairs all his childhood and adulthood. The plastic covers symbolized his mother: "*choosing concern for her furniture over my needs.* What did she care about what I wanted, what made me comfortable?"

I, with the plastic rug cover, was like his mother, more concerned about my rug than him. When I realized how intrusive, disturbing, and traumatic the plastic rug cover was for W., I told him his comfort was more important than my new rug. I gathered up the plastic cover and put it in a bag and threw it away. W. was very grateful to view this marked change in my behavior as a result of empathizing with his pain. My self-analysis helped me realize that my narcissistic needs could be experienced as taking precedence over W.'s needs, given his traumatic background; I did not have the need to defend myself. In a way, it was irrelevant to W. that I did not intend to harm him. The fact of the matter was that my behavior had retraumatized him. I knew it was unintentional. Perhaps, one day, W. would come to realize this. Once again, the fact that he did walk out of the session when he felt so angry and traumatized indicates he also knew this. He needed to be emotionally held in a safe experience so he could therapeutically regress to the level of his basic fault.

"You think you know about me, you don't know anything!" encounter

Another clinical encounter with W. threatened my sense of intellectual and professional identity. What made this experience so disturbing was that it occurred after about eight years of analysis with W. Prior to this encounter, we had developed an inquiry into, and a basic understanding of, the psychodynamics of his childhood traumas. W. expressed gratitude for this. I was comfortable in being a partner in his self-discovery and self-definition.

All of a sudden, in a flash of a second, W. made me feel that rather than being his therapeutic partner, I was a stranger to him. One day, as we were discussing his childhood traumas he blurted out in an accusatory way, "You think you know about me, you don't know anything!"

This was a narcissistic blow. With confusion and concern, I asked him to help me understand what he meant by this statement, admitting to him I was surprised and disturbed about what seemed to be a fundamental criticism of my clinical work with him. During our extended discussion of this encounter, both of us learned a great deal. My original emotional reaction was disappointment, rejection, inadequacy, and hurt. I felt that my clinical work with W. was being questioned in the most fundamental way. I heard him saying that I was incapable of understanding and helping him. After eight years of analysis, which we created together, I did not understand him.

As I was able to do in the plastic rug cover encounter, he needed to arrive at some form of empathic understanding. W. had the emotional right to believe that I did not understand him, even if he believed I did. What was crucial was his experience of my not understanding him. As I began to focus on his experience rather than my own, W. could not explain why he was angry and critical towards me.

He just had the impulse to express his anger, disappointment, and rejection to me. I needed to contain his feelings, without always looking for explanations.

Analyzing my own need to feel intellectually and professionally competent, I realized that W.'s deep-seated trauma was at the root of his difficulties. There were times when he could not analyze his functioning because he was overwhelmed by anxiety and anger and felt speechless. As Ferenczi had said, childhood trauma produces a loss of one's voice (Ferenczi, 1980n). Yet, he also felt what I knew about him was "good enough" to understand and help him. What I needed to do was transform my countertransference reaction into an empathic understanding.

Countertransference and the sexual abuse of children

As analysts, one of our clinical mandates is to discover our enduring core countertransference reactions. These potential core countertransference reactions are usually identified in our training analysis. But, as one gains clinical experience, especially with difficult cases, re-enactments of the analyst's childhood traumas become more known. I identified one of my core countertransferences as a negative maternal transference to analysands who are very critical, hostile, and demeaning. This kind of interaction evoked a negative maternal transference (Rachman, 2003a).

Another one of my most enduring core countertransference reactions involve the intense feelings of anger, sometimes rage, as well as a desire to retaliate against and punish parents who sexually abuse children. During my clinical career, I have worked with children and adolescents with a wide array of problems in many different settings (Rachman, 1962, 1968, 1969, 1971, 1972, 1973, 1974, 1975a, 1976, 1977, 1987). As a consequence of these professional experiences, I developed a desire to protect children from harm. I wanted to be the good parent to help them recover from abuse. These countertransference vulnerabilities came into play in the consultation sessions with a young woman called Soma.

Countertransference encounter with Soma's parents

The case of Soma, which is described in Chapter Eleven, highlighted this kind of countertransference encounter. I had very intense feelings of anger towards both Soma's father, who regularly sexually abused her as a young child, and her mother, who was oblivious to the abuse. Her father, as in all instances of childhood sexual abuse, used his daughter to service his own perverse needs without any concern as to the effect his behavior would have on his developing child. Although, in analyzing incest survivors, I understand and accept that a father's abuse of his daughter is a function of his own childhood trauma, I still feel anger at the father for mistreating his child. Perhaps this is why I have never treated an abuser. My emphasis has always been the treatment of sexually abused children, adolescents, and adults. My countertransference reaction to the abuser does not allow me to treat them. My countertransference reaction also is germane to the mother of the abused daughter, what Dusty Miller (2005) called the bystander. I also have emotional difficulties with an empathic response to a mother who becomes a bystander to her daughter's sexual abuse by denying, dissociating, and rationalizing the abusive experience. Once again, I understand that the bystander can be the result of a mother's childhood trauma. In the case of Soma, I was able to maintain an empathic response. I did talk on occasion to the mother, since she contacted me for advice.

My focus with the mother, to whom Soma gave me permission to talk, was to help empathize with her daughter's need to have an ally in believing that she was a victim of sexual abuse. Soma's mother had enormous difficulty accepting the reality of her child's sexual abuse at the hands of her husband. First, she told Soma that there was no possible way her father abused her since she had no memory of such an experience. Besides, the mother emphasized her father would never do such "a horrible thing to you." Her daughter felt seriously rejected by her mother's inability to empathize with her childhood abuse. It was then that Soma asked me to help her with her mother. Her mother and I talked about Soma's "abuse accusations against her father." Both the mother and father were convinced that Soma's psychotherapist had "implanted these ideas in her head." The mother, in typical intellectual fashion, began an intensive study of the incest trauma. On the Internet, she found the false memory syndrome and the False Memory Syndrome Foundation. Soma's mother found emotional refuge in the false memory syndrome, reading all the articles and books she could find on the subject. She felt she had found support for her own conviction that children who report they have been sexually abused by a parent have had this idea implanted in their minds by psychotherapists.

When I first tried to engage Soma's mother in a psychological understanding of her daughter's claim of sexual abuse, she responded with a rigorous intellectual argument about the false memory syndrome. It was very difficult to find an empathetic response to this intellectual argument. I was actually angry at Soma's mother for closing her mind and heart to her daughter's need for empathic understanding. I knew I needed to search for an empathic connection with the mother in order to be able to help her daughter. What I found that was helpful was developing the interpretation that Soma's mother's vehement objection to the idea that her daughter was sexually abused by her father could be a result of the mother's own history of sexual abuse. I did not share the interpretation with Soma's mother. Rather, I used it to change my own feelings and attitude toward the mother so I could create an empathic dialogue with her. I empathized with her disturbance in her daughter's accusing her husband of being a sexual predator. She appreciated my response to her feelings. It was then that I attempted to help the mother empathize with her daughter's feelings. I asked her to consider that there was no meaningful reason for her daughter to fabricate a sexual abuse scenario. Forty-odd years' experience in treating the incest trauma seemed to verify her daughter's claim. She did not budge in her insistence that there was no validity to her daughter's claims. Then I suggested that her daughter needed her empathy, even if the daughter had some psychological reason to falsify the abuse charge. If it were false, Soma needed her understanding even more. Falsifying sexual abuse meant her daughter was suffering from some serious psychological issues. The mother did accept this idea and reduced her judgmental and negative attitude toward her daughter. The mother's change in feeling and attitude did allow her to have a more empathic dialogue with her daughter about the sexual abuse claim. Without ever changing her basic notion that her husband did not sexually abuse her daughter, she agreed to join her daughter in a series of short-term counseling sessions. The mother and daughter were able to reduce their animosity, have a form of reconciliation, and resume their relationship. Whether or not they will fully enjoy an emotionally close relationship is open to question. Incest survivors find it difficult to feel safe and affirmed with a parent who has not understood or empathized with their trauma. They feel the trauma destroyed their childhood and belief in parents as protectors of children.

CHAPTER THIRTEEN

Understanding an erotic transference as an enactment of a childhood incest trauma

An early learning experience about erotic transference

Analytic training rarely provides education and supervision about the difficult phenomenon of an erotic transference. One of the authors of this book, Arnold Rachman, remembers only two instances that dealt with this issue. The first instance occurred in a classroom discussion about transference. A senior analyst who taught the course said, in essence, that candidates should all try to prevent an erotic transference from developing because, once it occurs, it is almost impossible to analyze. The training analyst also added that the development of an erotic transference was causally linked to an erotic countertransference reaction by the analyst. The analytic candidates were so shocked and fearful to hear these warnings that none of us ever discussed the topic among ourselves. This class was given in our second year of analytic training. From then on, there was almost a complete silence on the topic of an erotic transference. It was given the silent treatment (*Totschweigen*) (Rachman, 1999a).

During the final year of training in individual analysis, all the candidates received a special notice that the founder and director of the Institute, the late Larry Wolberg, MD, was going to give a clinical demonstration. This was a very special event. As candidates, our contact with the director of the institute was minimal. We missed having contact with him since he was a recognized authority on integrating various techniques and methods into psychoanalytic practice (Wolberg, 1977). Not all of the candidates were enamored of his approach, which was then called eclectic. Now, it is referred to as an integrative approach. I was very interested in the director's approach because I had come to analytic training with a background in Carl Rogers' humanistic psychotherapy, phenomenology, and humanistic psychology (Rachman, 2006, 2007b, 2009b). I anticipated the director's clinical presentation as an opportunity to aid a theoretical and clinical integration, which was very much needed (Rachman, 2014b).

One day in the fourth year of analytic training, the candidates, the supervisors, and a group of senior analysts gathered in the one-way mirror demonstration classrooms to see a demonstration of supervision of an erotic transference crisis. The director and a senior analyst met in a one-way mirror room. The rest of us met in the two observation rooms on either side of the one-way mirror room. There was great expectation as we settled in for this unique supervision session. The analyst being supervised, to our surprise, had asked the director for a consultation because he was involved in an intractable case of erotic transference. He attempted to analyze the transference crisis, consulted colleagues and experts, but the problem persisted. With no other place to turn, he contacted the founder and director of his former training institute for a consultation. The director agreed to the consultation with the stipulation that the consultation could be used as a teaching session for the Institute's analytic community. The analyst agreed to have the consultation session in the Institute's one-way mirror teaching classroom.

Everyone was excited to see the director deal with the issue of an erotic transference, which was, as discussed, treated with silence. The candidates admired both the senior analyst and the director for their courage, daring, and willingness to expose their clinical functioning to the scrutiny of a community of analysts who had a reputation of being very critical of each other. The director's supervision of the analyst's erotic transference crisis was the only time during my four-year period in analytic training that the issue of an erotic transference became a part of my education or a focus in our analytic community.

A remarkable event emerged out of this consultation, which demonstrated a daring and innovative recommendation for solving the erotic transference crisis. The analyst first presented the erotic transference dilemma. For several years, he had been seeing a young woman who had developed an obsession, an intense desire to have a baby with him. The analyst, over a period of several years, had attempted every method he had been taught to analyze this erotic transference. His interventions included interpretation, empathic understanding, and confrontation. He was in great distress, feeling helpless and hopeless. The director first respectfully listened to the analyst's presentation of his clinical crisis. When the analyst made it clear he had finished with his presentation, the director did not hesitate to offer his perspective.

As has been mentioned, the director was a leader in psychodynamic eclecticism, so the audience expected innovation. But we did not expect what some analysts thought of as a shocking recommendation. First, the director empathized with the clinical crisis and the analyst's clinical work, saying that he had done an admirable job attempting to resolve the erotic transference by traditional analytic means. In his manner and words, the director did not blame the analyst for the intractable erotic transference. Rather, the focus of the supervision was three-fold: empathic attunement to the analyst's struggles with a difficult case, meaning anyone would have difficulty with this analysand; acceptance of the situation as intractable (he made it clear no amount of interpretation, empathy, or confrontation would change the situation); the analysand needed an active intervention where a real experience should be introduced. None of the analysts gathered in the one-way mirror classroom that day expected the recommendation of the director. He recommended that the analyst needed to: "live in the transference, with the analysand, for a limited time." The analyst was told to give the female analysand a symbolic baby, either a cat or dog (whichever animal the analysand preferred) as a present. The pet would constitute the baby the analysand wished to have with her analyst. The gift of a symbolic baby was also thought to be within ethical and professional standards. Finally, the director made it very clear that no seductive or actual sexual behavior by the analyst was to be part of the attempt to resolve the erotic transference.

It is fair to say, that the general reaction by the majority of the analytic community of the Institute was negative and critical. Senior analysts and many of the candidates thought the director had crossed the border of analytic activity with the giving of a symbolic baby recommendation. The analytic community of the Institute was more conservative than the director. I was excited by the recommendations. Through the Institute's grapevine, it was suggested that the analyst had carried out the director's recommendation. The erotic transference stalemate was apparently resolved, and the analysis was resumed. When the difficult analysis was brought to termination, the analyst, in the months to follow, moved to the West coast.

I believed the director's recommendation of a symbolic baby was in the tradition of Ferenczi's non-interpretative measures that he developed for his most difficult cases, as in the analysis with Elizabeth Severn (see Chapter Five). In fact, there was a connection between the director's recommendation and his analytic lineage and education. Larry Wolberg, MD, the director, was analytically educated at the William Alanson White Institute, which was founded by analysts such as Eric Fromm and Clara Thompson, who were influenced by Ferenczi. Thompson was Wolberg's analyst. Thompson helped introduce Ferenczi's ideas into American psychoanalysis (Thompson, 1942, 1944, 1950, 1964a,b,c), as well as using them as one of the underpinnings of interpersonal psychoanalysis (Thompson, 1964c).

The clinical interaction of providing a symbolic baby for the analysand can be viewed from a relational perspective.

With very difficult analysands, active/empathic intervention based upon an understanding of childhood trauma and the resultant developmental arrest, non-interpretative measures target the unfulfilled needs (Ferenczi, 1988; Rachman, 2003a). Although Wolberg's clinical acumen addressed the technical issue in resolving an erotic transference, no theoretical discussion occurred. This chapter, in part, addresses the gap in theoretical understanding of the meaning of an erotic transference and the use of non-interpretative measures to deal with it clinically. We wished to change the *Totschweigen* experience, where silence about an erotic transference prevails (Rachman, 1999a). There is a theoretical clinical perspective influenced by Ferenczi to confront this issue.

In retrospect, the above-mentioned teaching experience had a profound effect on me. Wolberg became a role model for clinical daring and integrative analytic functioning. A combination of researching the history of psychoanalytic pioneers, discovering the empathic and active innovations of Ferenczi, while integrating the previous training in phenomenology and humanistic psychology and psychotherapy became a bridge to relational psychoanalysis (Rachman, 1997a; 2006, 2007b, 2009b, 2010a, 2011b, 2012a, 2014b).

The issue of an erotic transference continues to be a neglected topic in psychoanalysis (Rachman et al., 2009a). Ferenczi's *Clinical Diary* became an important avenue to understanding the role of trauma in difficult cases (Ferenczi, 1988). Ferenczi described eleven clinical cases which had at their origins childhood sexual trauma. In Chapter One of this book, an insight-provoking case helped further an understanding of childhood sexual trauma. In the early 1980s, another insight-provoking case appeared, which became the conduit for being able to integrate the supervision learning experience with Larry Wolberg, the research on Ferenczi, the acquaintanceship with humanistic psychotherapy, and clinical experiences with trauma cases.

An insight-provoking case of erotic transference: the case of Miss M

Miss M. came to analysis in a state of intense confusion, anxiety, and dysfunction. She exhibited severe symptoms of uncontrollable crying, emotional outbursts of anger, intense depression, and the feeling she did not know where she was going in her life. She described herself as being at loose ends. Her emotional, interpersonal, and work life were in shambles.

Miss M. had a fundamentalist Christian religious background, which had a significant impact on her emotional development. When she was a child, this religious background provided a conservative, strict ordered life. A spirited daughter was born to a controlled mother. The mother was described as a strictly religious woman who found her spirited daughter difficult to understand and control. When the mother saw Miss M. masturbating as a young child, she chided her to stop, but never explored the obsessive motivation of her child. She did not realize that it was a symptom of abuse. The father was a quiet, strong, emotionally reserved individual. But the trauma of parental unresponsiveness was overshadowed by an even more intense and damaging childhood trauma. The strict religious extended family background did not prevent Miss M. from having a early childhood incest trauma. When she was two years old, she was molested by a cousin who was about seventeen years old. She described him as mentally or socially retarded. As a very young child, she also remembered masturbating with the rubber end of a pencil, which she inserted into her vagina. The sexual abuse by her cousin continued during her childhood. She also remembered instances of her cousin locking her in the bathroom of his parent's home, and sexually abusing her. The sexual abuse usually involved the cousin fondling the young Miss M.'s vagina with his fingers. A second form of molestation involved the cousin teaching her to perform fellatio. The emotional and physical deprivation from her parents made her hungry for physical and emotional attention. The cousin, in the usual confusion of tongues experience, promised his two-year-old cousin affection and love. But it was passion and exploitation. Again, as is characteristic of a seduction, Miss M. lost her voice; she became tongue-tied. She could never speak of the trauma. The extended family and the community in this rural setting took a protective attitude toward the cousin. He was taken care of by the family, never seen by a physician or sent to a clinic for an evaluation of his retardation. Both the community and Miss M.'s silence about the abuse supported denial and dissociation. The split-off confusion of tongues trauma found its way into Miss M.'s adolescent and adult behavior.

The development of an erotic transference

Miss M. quickly developed an erotic transference as she began her analysis. First, her seductiveness was expressed through endless verbal *double entendres*. She was a very attractive woman in her twenties. It was necessary to perform an ongoing countertransference analysis of her seductiveness in order to maintain a therapeutic relationship. There are two examples of the way Miss M. accentuated her seductiveness in the analysis. On one occasion she sent me a greeting card. On the outside cover of the card a saxophone was depicted. Inside the card, the greeting said: "Do you want to have sax with me?"

When we discussed the card, she clearly expressed a desire to have a sexual relationship. It was clear I needed to clarify the therapeutic boundary: "I appreciate that you find me attractive. Our relationship is for the purpose of helping you understand the difficulties you're having in your life. Our relationship does not include any romantic or sexual contact."

Miss M. was angry at my words. But, after further discussion, she reluctantly accepted the therapeutic boundary. Our discussions in the sessions to follow, however, became the key to the analysis. The hypothesis was introduced that her intense erotic feelings and her desire to act them out with her analyst were an indication of a psychological issue she needed to understand. By understanding and confronting the issue, she could begin to work out her relationship with men. She clearly reported her relationship with men as unsatisfying and preventing her from reaching her goal of being married and having children.

Miss M.'s overtures to have sexual and romantic contact were also voiced in her interaction in group analysis. She would present to the group endless sexual adventures that she had since her high school years. These reports provided an important avenue for exploring the erotic transference. One such example of a sexual adventure illustrated her hyper-sexuality. At a friend's wedding, she spotted an attractive young male during the ceremony and became sexually aroused. After the ceremony, which took place outdoors at a country club, she approached the sexually desirable man and seduced him. They had sex behind a group of bushes in the country club's grounds. She presented this sexual adventure as an example of her attractiveness to men and men's sexual response to her. Then she would go into her lament that she could find all the sexual partners she wanted, but she couldn't find a suitable man to marry and have a child. The group therapy members echoed the analysis that I had begun in our individual sessions. During this group session, when she finished her sexual adventure story and began her lament of the lack of having a suitable man to marry, she then exclaimed: "What I want is Arnold! He's the kind of man I want."

One of the members of the group, who was a peer-leader (see Chapter Eight, the case of Winston), commented on this lament. It initiated an interaction with Miss M. focused on helping her work through the erotic transference issue inherent in her above cited exclamation. He said in an assertive/emphatic way: "If you want someone like Arnold, then use the understanding you gather in group and individual and find someone, in your real life, like him. Part of your problem is that you keep wanting your romance to be with Arnold. Don't you get it? Your job, all of our jobs, is to take what we learn here and apply it in our lives."

It was very clear from Miss M.'s emotional and interpersonal responses to the member's emotional insightful intervention that she was beginning to develop an introspective attitude toward her sexual acting out. She did listen and respond to the group's and my mandate that she needed to analyze her need to have a romance with her analyst. In individual analysis, the opportunity was taken to further Miss M.'s understanding of her erotic transference by introducing the psychological connection between her childhood incest trauma and her sexual acting out as an adult. There were four basic phases to the exploration of the erotic transference: (1) exploration of the recall and re-experiencing of the sexual molestation by her cousin; (2) the manifestation of her erotic transference in the analysis as an enactment of her childhood sexual trauma; (3) the sexual acting out of the childhood sexual trauma in her relationships with men; (4) integrating the data from the analysis (individual and group) into an emotional insight which could help her change her behavior to fulfill her stated goal of getting married and having a child.

Revisiting the childhood sexual trauma was a very difficult emotional experience for Miss M. She was able to elaborate on her cousin's abuse of her. One such incident she described happened sometime before her third birthday. In this exploration of the trauma, she now remembered her cousin penetrating her, while she screamed in horror. The analysis also included the parental denial and dissociation as well as the community's protective attitude toward her abuser. We worked on her confusion of tongues experience, which included her suppressed anger, and a loosening of the dissociation process.

With the focus on her childhood seduction firmly established, we turned our attention to the enactment in the analytic relationship. Miss M. very reluctantly entered into this phase of our analysis. Slowly, but persistently, we maintained a focus on establishing an emotional/interpersonal connection between Miss M.'s childhood incest trauma and her adult sexuality with men and her analyst. Analyzing our relationship, although difficult for her, became an important vehicle for change. She was encouraged to fully express her erotic feelings. We analyzed the manifestation of these erotic feelings having its origin in her cousin's seduction and the subsequent effect it had on her personality development. Miss M. tempered her disappointment in giving up her romantic attachment to me with the realization that she was making therapeutic advances. There was a marked reduction in her anxiety. She became less preoccupied, more open and self-exploratory. Her hysterical outbursts became significantly less frequent. Miss M. was also able to use her considerable talent in her field of media to become a valued member of staff of a newspaper. Most significantly, she became determined to work through her incest trauma.

Resolution of the erotic transference

Our shared subjectivities contributed to the development of an erotic transference experience. It was exciting, stimulating, flattering, and disturbing to be in the sessions with this very attractive sexual woman who was trying to seduce me. As Ferenczi pioneered, the analysis of the analyst was crucial in maintaining a therapeutic relationship, especially when analyzing an erotic transference (Ferenczi, 1988). On an ongoing basis, my countertransference analysis focused on working through the allure of her seduction. I needed to remind Miss M. and myself that she used sex as a way to gain attention and affection to repair a childhood maternal deficit and actual sexual molestation.

During the second year of our analysis, the erotic transference seemed to have vanished. It was no longer an issue as Miss M. now focused on her childhood trauma and her relationship with men. One year later, Miss M. began dating men where sexuality was not the primary issue. She met a man with whom she began a serious relationship. Eventually, they developed plans for marriage and having a child. Miss M. terminated her analysis after she solidified plans for marriage. After another year had passed, she sent me a letter telling about the joys of being married even though her husband had alcohol issues. She proudly announced that she had given birth to a daughter. I sent her a gift for the baby.

Supervision and the erotic transference

When I first tried to apply my ideas about an erotic transference to supervisory cases, I found confirmation of the causal link to childhood incest trauma (Rachman et al., 2005; 2009a,b). An analytic candidate, who was in the third year of a four-year training program, had a very dramatic experience with an erotic transference. He was seeing a highly educated woman in her mid-twenties who was bright, verbal, and in the middle of a divorce when she entered analysis. In a few weeks, after beginning the analytic experience, she developed an intense erotic transference that seriously frightened the analyst (perhaps, once again, a version of the case of Elizabeth Severn—see Chapter Five). She was aggressive and demanding in her expressions of love for her analyst. One day, she suggested, then begged, to leave the consultation room in order to rent a hotel room so that they could make love. When the analyst did not respond to her request she became angry, throwing a book at him. The candidate's silence in the face of this woman's acting out was the best he could offer in response to her assaults on him, which frightened him. He felt it would be better not to intensify her acting out by responding verbally: "I felt it was better to shut up rather than open my mouth and say the wrong thing that would send her into orbit. Besides, what do you say to an analysand who is physically trying to sleep with you?"

The woman's determination and aggressiveness was to reach a crescendo during this first year of the analysis. At the beginning of a supervision session during that first year, and at the height of the manifestation of the erotic transference, the candidate unloaded to me his shocked, intensely anxious and fearful reaction to the analysand's latest acting out. As he shook with anger and fear, he then told me the following: "I am completely in shock and I don't know what to do. You got to help me!" ["I will help you with this difficult person. Tell me what she's done this time."] "You won't believe this one. She came into our session carrying a blanket and suggested we both lie down on the couch and make love."

It was clear the candidate needed both theory and technique, a sense of empathy and a frame of reference to understand erotic transference. In actuality, giving him an understanding of this difficult situation can also be considered an empathic response (Rachman & Mattick, 2012). He was told that such sexual seduction was probably a function of the analysand's childhood sexual trauma. I asked the candidate if he explored any aspect of an incest trauma with his analysand. He said he had not. What is more he was never educated to do so. From then on, I said, our supervision would focus on helping him uncover the analysand's childhood incest trauma. This incest trauma exploration would reduce the acting out of the erotic transference, and help him conduct a therapeutic exploration of the issue. As we began this focus, the candidate did reveal that the analysand had previously spoken of her father molesting her as a child. She did not express any negative feelings towards him. As a function of her confusion of tongues trauma, she believed her father was trying to show her affection in the only way he knew how. Besides, the father had told his daughter that her mother had rejected him emotionally and physically. He needed affection. The candidate had unwittingly joined his analysand in the denial of the incest trauma. Prior to our supervision, he had been taught in his training institute by a well-known and respected analyst that "Sexual abuse for a child is not always traumatic. If the therapist does not make an issue of it, then perhaps, it would not be a significant issue for the child."

The candidate was very much influenced by this teacher. Both the teacher's denial of the incest trauma and the candidate's unconscious need to join the denial provided an enactment of the erotic transference. We have discussed throughout the present volume Freud's endorsement of the oedipal theory and neglect of the seduction theory. We have argued this has fostered not only a neglect of the incest trauma, but a negative, anti-therapeutic attitude toward understanding and analyzing the incest trauma (Rachman, 2012d,e). All the research and clinical evidence that has been collected since Ferenczi pioneered the confusion of tongues paradigm and relaxation therapy has demonstrated that trauma disorders are more prevalent than psychoanalysis is willing to admit (Alpert, 1995, 2001; Bass & Davis, 1994; Carlson, 1997; Messler-Davies & Frawley, 1994; Herman, 1981, 1992; Howell, 1997; Justice & Justice, 1979; Miller, 1986, 1990, 2005; Shengold, 1989; van der Kolk et al., 1996). The recognition of trauma disorders needs more attention from well-trained mental health professionals, especially from psychoanalysts, because they can provide meaningful psychodynamics (Rachman, 2012d,e,f).

The supervisory focus on the incest trauma produced a significant change in the candidate's clinical functioning with the difficult analysand who aggressively attempted to seduce him. When the candidate began to integrate the supervision and introduced the idea that the analysand's erotic behavior with him was an expression of her father's sexual seduction of her as a child, he was surprised that the analysand readily accepted this idea. In fact, she exhibited no resistance to this interpretation. With both the candidate's and the analysand's acceptance of the incest sexual trauma focus, the therapeutic dyad was able to explore both the childhood seduction and the erotic transference. She revealed that as a child she had developed an obsession with seeing her father's penis. Her original interpretation of the obsession was a function of her hyper-sexuality. In essence, she seduced the father. With the new focus, the analysand became aware that the father was her seducer. Her obsessive need to see her father's penis had at its origin his ongoing need to have her perform fellatio. The exploration of her seduction lessened her confusion of tongues trauma. She became able to speak of the trauma, liberated her anger toward her father and men, and became aware of her developmental sexual arrest.

The candidate became able to interpret the erotic transference as a function of her father's molestation. This was now linked to the analysand's hyper-sexuality and violating of the therapeutic boundaries. Her sexual seduction was emotionally connected to her father's seduction of her. What is more, the father's seductions were manifested in the analytic situation. She acted out the violence, rage, intrusiveness, and sexual seduction by her father with the analyst. We also examined the candidate's countertransference reaction to the clinical crisis. The candidate became aware that his fear, sense of victimization, and powerlessness had its origin in his own childhood experience with his father. The candidate was able to process his countertransference reaction to the analysand as seducer and abuser. She developed her love for her abuser that she preserved through identification with the father/abuser. He also helped the analysand understand the terror she felt when she was abused by her father.

Towards the end of their clinical experience, the analysand divorced her husband and began a new life. Eventually, she earned a doctorate at a prestigious university. She contacted the analyst, from time to time, with a card, phone call, or gift. At such times, he reported, she would call him by a nickname she used while she was in the throes of the erotic transference, and then they would both laugh.

Theoretical understanding of an erotic transference

The emergence in an erotic transference in the psychoanalytic situation can be understood as a function of the enactment of a childhood incest trauma. The confusion of tongues theory of trauma is the theoretical underpinning for this assumption (see Chapter Four). Childhood sexual seduction leads to the dissociation and the splitting off of the trauma. A detailed sexual history of the analysand's childhood and the extent of any abuse should be gathered as it would alert the analyst to the possible emergence of an erotic transference. The emergence of an erotic transference, when it occurs, is an essential condition to the unfolding of the analysis and should be welcomed as a positive development. We need to erase the silence and fear in the psychoanalytic community. In our experience, the analysis of an erotic transference is often essential to the analysis of the incest trauma. *The emergence of an erotic transference can be seen as a pre-condition to the unfolding and working through of the incest trauma.* What is more, a childhood incest trauma, when conceptualized as a confusion of tongues trauma, can help to create an empathic holding environment in which the split-off, dissociated aspects of the experience can emerge in the psychoanalytic situation. The relational experience in the therapeutic dyad becomes the enactment stage in which the sexual trauma becomes known and understood. As Ferenczi, then Balint, suggested, empathic non-intrusive therapeutic activity is a meaningful dimension which aids the unfolding of a trauma disorder (Balint, 1968; Ferenczi & Rank, 1925). At all times, the integrity of the analytic encounter is maintained. In a relational perspective, informed by the Budapest School of Psychoanalysis, clinical activity is employed to understand and respond to the analysand's developmental arrests. In addition, the analyst must continue his/her countertransference analysis to guard against seductive and erotic behavior. In this perspective, seduction in the psychoanalytic situation is retraumatizing and recreating of the childhood incest trauma. Countertransference analysis (See Chapter Twelve) is an ongoing essential dimension of the analysis of the incest trauma (Rachman, 2003a, 2014a).

Initially, the analyst can develop intense anxiety when he/she experiences the boundary in the clinical encounter has been breached through the emergence of an erotic transference. Feelings of intrusiveness, erotic stimulation, self-blame, and intense anxiety and panic can predominate. If an analyst has had traditional analytic training, superego feelings of guilt and shame can develop because of the feeling that the erotic transference is the fault of the analyst. On the other hand, an analyst has to guard against not allowing the emergence of an erotic transference. Preventing the emergence of an erotic transference involves an emotional dampening of any sexual feelings existing in the relationship. Creating a sexually neuter atmosphere is an antitherapeutic experience. When the analyst is uncomfortable, suppressive, denying, or critical of emerging sexual feelings by the analysand, the development of an erotic transference is suppressed. If an erotic transference does not emerge in a case of childhood incest, the analysis of the incest trauma may be prevented.

An empathic compass, the analyst's capacity to attune and respond to the subjective experience of the analysand, allows maximum emergence of an erotic transference. Equally hovering attention must be paid to all sexually laden material. In this way the erotic transference will emerge without judgment, criticism, or any other negative countertransference reaction. The analyst invites the sexuality of the analysand to be contained in the safety of an empathic, nonerotic, but compassionate therapeutic relationship. In the supervisory example discussed, the analyst was eventually able to treat the erotic transferences by creating a holding environment for the sexuality without responding punitively to the analysand. Empathic understanding of the analysand's intensity of feelings and authenticity of longings was a necessary first step in the direction of diminishing focus on sexual enactments. The analyst's presence fulfills the function of an anchor, with clear and containing boundaries, that creates the sanctuary of safety in the therapeutic alliance.

It is necessary for the analyst to establish countertransference as an essential dimension of the analysis of the incest trauma (de Forest 1954, Ferenczi, 1988). In this way, the dramatic shifts in the transference relationship will not be used to express defensive reactions. The analysis of the countertransference maintains the therapeutic relationship as a container for the incest trauma. A psychological space is provided to explore the sexual material with the analysand. Rather than believe the analysis is faltering, the emergence of an erotic transference can be an indication that the conditions of safety, trust, and empathy have been established. Instead of feeling shame, the analyst could understand his/her positive contribution to the unfolding of the analysis and the welfare of the analysand.

The concept of enactment, as developed by McLaughlin (1981, 1987, 1988, 1991), is a valuable concept in the understanding of the psychodynamics of an erotic transference and the role of early childhood trauma in personality development.

In the discussion of the clinical supervisory examples, we have tried to demonstrate the value of enactments that is contained in the unconscious communication that the erotic transference represents. It is only when one understands the analysand's erotic behavior toward the analyst as a mode of communicating their incest trauma that the emotional–interpersonal experience can be viewed as an opportunity for a therapeutic encounter. As has been discussed, the incest survivor, in order to maintain self-cohesion turns toward denial, dissociation, and splitting. Ferenczi's original description of the psychodynamics of the incest trauma and the effects on developmental arrest (Ferenczi, 1980n, 1988), remains a helpful perspective for establishing a clinical encounter in the psychoanalytic situation. Somatic memory becomes the avenue for the safe keeping of the seduction experiences. It is through the dimension of non-intrusive empathic activity in the psychoanalytic situation that the analysand, in an emotional climate of safety, trust, and empathetic understanding, dares to communicate her incest secret stored in her body as somatic memory. In the analysis of the incest trauma, enactments can constitute the essence of the treatment (Messler-Davies & Frawley, 1994; Rachman, 2000, 2007a). If the analyst develops his/her empathic compass so that he/she becomes finely attuned to the unconscious/conscious, verbal/nonverbal communication of the analyst's childhood trauma in the psychoanalytic situation, the analysis of the incest trauma can begin.

Enactments not only illuminate the subjective experience of the analysand, but, importantly, of the analyst. An essential dimension of the relational perspective is the two-person psychology of the analytic encounter (Rachman, 2003d, 2010a,c, 2011b, 2012a), and elaborated in a contemporary clinical method of mutuality (Aron, 1991, 1996; Messler-Davies & Frawley, 1994; Rachman, 1997a, 2003a). From a relational perspective, the analyst's subjective experience is crucial to understanding and treating the incest trauma. As has been discussed, an enactment can be the first clue that the erotic transference is being manifested. It is through the erotic elements in the transference that the analysand engages the analyst in the enactment of the original childhood trauma. The immersion in the emotional details of the incest trauma, which is in dissociation, is an unconscious attempt to engage and involve the analyst in lifting the veil of denial which has protected the incest survivor from the psychological effects of the abuser (Rachman, 2004). The enactment signals the analysand's desire to communicate the trauma to her/his analyst, who is the fantasized reparative therapeutic parental figure:

> Enactments disguised by the unconsciously determined affective and behavioral involvement of the analyst, result from the patient's attempts to create an interactional representation of a wished-for object relationship. (Chused, 1991, p. 628).

Daring to trust the ideal parent, the analysand wishes to penetrate the subjective experience of the analyst (Ellman, 1998). The analyst must allow penetration and develop an integration of subjectivities so that analyst and analysand can mutually engage in the struggle to uncover the incest trauma embedded in the erotic transference.

The insight-provoking case of Miss M. helps us to understand an important issue about the issue of an erotic transference. Following Balint's assessment that therapeutic regression is a positive phenomenon in an analytic encounter with difficult cases (Balint, 1968), an erotic transference can also be a positive phenomenon in the analysis of the incest trauma. It can be seen as a necessary and sufficient condition to analyzing the incest trauma. Moreover, the development of an erotic transference should no longer be considered a taboo subject in psychoanalysis. Our field needs to openly discuss this issue on a regular basis in our institutes, conferences, papers, and books, from both a theoretical and clinical perspective. Analysts need to be more self-disclosing in discussing their own experiences in an erotic transference. We need to remove the stigma that revealing one's sexual feelings, reactions, and clinical behavior is pathology. An erotic transference is not a clinical phenomenon of which to be afraid or to avoid. We need to develop meaningful theoretical frameworks for understanding and analyzing an erotic transference. A clinical framework that integrates an empathic, flexible, and responsive attitude is most helpful in responding to an erotic transference. As Balint suggested, interpretation gives way to understanding and responding to the analysand's fundamental empathic needs (Balint, 1968). Such responsiveness allows the therapeutic exploration of an erotic transference.

The discussion of the treatment and supervision of the erotic transference issue can be summarized in the following way.

1. The analysis of the incest trauma helps inform the analyst of the importance of childhood sexual molestation as a factor in personality development.
2. Such an understanding allows the analyst to apply understanding to the supervision of an analytic candidate and the very difficult clinical experiences with an erotic transference.
3. Ferenczi's development of the confusion of tongues paradigm and the issue of relaxation measures to treat trauma survivors is a meaningful framework for understanding and treating an erotic transference.
4. When an erotic transference emerges in an analytic situation, it is not an indication of a negative transference effect or of an intense countertransference reaction. Rather, it may be an indication of a positive development where the analysand feels safe and trusting enough to unconsciously communicate their childhood incest trauma. Once emerged, the erotic transference, if allowed to develop in a natural way (without premature interpretation, intense anxiety in the analyst, or a fear of a regressive transference experience), can become the vehicle for the analysis of the childhood incest trauma.
5. To push the theorizing about the incest trauma and the development of an erotic transference to the fullest, one would speculate that to analyze the incest trauma, it would be necessary for an erotic transference to develop so the trauma can fully be experienced and worked through. This would be a meaningful consideration in circumstances where there is a history of childhood incest.

CHAPTER FOURTEEN

Education, training, and supervision for analyzing the incest trauma

Education

Psychoanalysis has lost its voice about the incest trauma. There is no major theoretical orientation in psychoanalysis that has a focus on the incest trauma and its relationship to the development of psychopathology (Rachman, 1997a,b). In fact, the only theoretical orientation that does integrate childhood sexual seduction as a significant psychodynamic is Ferenczi's confusion of tongues paradigm (see Chapter Four). Yet, Ferenczi's theory was originally condemned (Rachman, 1997a,b) and then ignored (Rachman, 2006, 2007b). It is essential that psychoanalysis acquaint itself with this missing legacy so that it can make a contemporary contribution to the study and treatment of the incest trauma, pedophilia, and child abduction (Rachman, 2012d,e). Such a return to these neglected areas of study would not only advance our field, but contribute to the public welfare.

Over the past thirty-five years, I (Rachman) have been writing about the Budapest School of Psychoanalysis and its unique contribution to theory and technique, the present volume being the third book devoted to this topic (Rachman, 1997a, 2003a). Taken together, these three books, as well as many presentations and papers, have outlined the unique contribution that Ferenczi and the Budapest School (Rachman, 2014e) have made to the study and treatment of trauma.

As has been mentioned elsewhere, one of us (Rachman) had no analytic educational or supervisory experiences that constituted preparation for treating the incest trauma (Rachman, 1997a, 2003a). I was trained to be a psychoanalyst in the late 1960s, when there were discussions of "difficult cases" as ambulatory psychotic, pseudoneurotic, schizophrenic, or borderline psychotic. These were individuals who were designated as suffering from severe emotional issues, *beyond* the oedipal complex. Gradually, non-traditional perspectives, such as object relations, interpersonal psychoanalysis, self psychology, and relational analysis contributed to a discussion of narcissistic, borderline, and psychotic disorders. In the discussions of these alternative perspectives, however, there was almost no mention of the incest trauma or its influence on personality development or psychological disorder. The neglect of the incest trauma occurred in interpersonal analysis, which was founded by Henry Stack Sullivan, Clara Thompson, and Eric Fromm, who appreciated Ferenczi and the Budapest School of Psychoanalysis. But, like others who appreciated Ferenczi's work, they did not emphasize the importance of childhood trauma. Roazen believed that Ferenczi's non-interpretative methods led to a split with Freud and the analytic community (Roazen, 1975). This is a meaningful assessment (Rachman, 1997a). Now, another dimension can be added to this issue. Ferenczi's clinical findings and theoretical ideas about the significance of trauma, and the incest trauma in particular (Ferenczi, 1980n, 1988), was the issue that separated him from Freud in his final years. Freud could not accept that Ferenczi was returning to an abandoned theory (seduction hypothesis), and was regressing in his clinical interaction with analysands, in order to treat the incest trauma (Rachman, 1997a,b, 2013, 2014b,c). Ferenczi was undaunted in his belief that he had discovered something that was meaningful and important. Ferenczi's discovery of the importance of the incest trauma is still not appreciated by contemporary psychoanalysts and psychotherapists (Rachman, 2012d). The education of analytic candidates about the incest trauma is mandatory.

The Budapest School of Psychoanalysis's contributions to the study of the incest trauma

There are several unique contributions that the Budapest School made to the incest trauma. Ferenczi's ideas and clinical work, as has been mentioned in these pages, helped describe the incest trauma as an emotional disorder based upon childhood sexual seduction by a parent or parental surrogate. He described this experience as an actual event in family interaction, causing a trauma to which the child reacted with a series of ego defenses which he identified as a confusion of tongues. What is more, he felt the psychodynamics of the incest trauma, its effect on personality development, and developmental arrest, needed to be understood in a new framework which he developed (Ferenczi, 1980n, 1988). Originally, this paradigm was an explanatory device for the incest trauma. Ferenczi's student, Balint, expanded this paradigm into a theory of emotional and interpersonal trauma. The basic fault paradigm (Balint, 1968) expanded Ferenczi's idea of trauma to emotional trauma experiences between mother (the caretaker) and the child. In Chapter Four, "A confusion of tongues theory of trauma", we presented a framework that integrates the Ferenczi and Balint paradigms into a general theory of trauma from the contemporary perspective of relational theory.

The Budapest School has also made a significant contribution to the methodology of treating the incest trauma. Ferenczi initiated clinical experimentation with the introduction of clinical activity in psychoanalysis. Activity morphed into his trauma analysis and non-interpretative measures for the analysis of the incest trauma (Rachman, 1997a, 1998b, 2003a). Balint's concepts, such as the child's need for object love, the non-intrusive analyst, and benign and malignant regression were important contributions to the treatment of trauma, which helped develop the object relations perspective (Rachman, 2003a, 2007a). Both Ferenczi's and Balint's clinical ideas and new methodology introduced the Budapest School's alternative to traditional analytic functioning. Freud was originally a champion of the evolution of psychoanalysis in the direction toward Ferenczi's activity (Freud, 1955b), and empathy (Ferenczi, 1980k). What is more, Freud, even after the breach that was created in their relationship because of the Ferenczi–Severn analysis (Rachman, 2010b,c), said of Ferenczi: "he has made all analysts into his pupils" (Freud, 1933c, p. 228). In other words, although he differed significantly from his student toward the latter part of his clinical career, Freud realized his favorite son and cherished student had made a significant contribution to the evolution of psychoanalysis (Freud, 1933c).

Ferenczi's "Confusion of tongues" paper (Ferenczi, 1980n) and his *Clinical Diary* (Ferenczi, 1988) provided a comprehensive theory and treatment of the incest trauma. The confusion of tongues paradigm was a comprehensive and meaningful extension of Freud's seduction hypothesis (Masson, 1984). It did provide a theory for studying and treating the incest trauma (Rachman, 2000), a theory of emotional trauma (Balint, 1968), a relational perspective of the psychoanalytic encounter (Rachman, 2003d, 2007a, 2010a), and the first alternate or dissent theory of psychoanalysis (Gedo, 1986).

The confusion of tongues theory helped establish childhood seduction as a factor in the development of psychopathology, psychological disorder, and developmental arrest. It changed the focus from only a study of unconscious forces as a determinant of human behaviors to a focus on conscious factors and the actual interaction of family members. Ferenczi's work demonstrated that it was no longer the stranger luring a child into a back alley to molest them, but the parent in the child's family who was the abuser, breaking a myth of seduction. The confusion of tongues theory placed emphasis, for the first time, on the role of traumatic disorder as a distinct psychological factor. Such an idea provides psychoanalysis with a step in its evolution (Fromm, 1959; Rachman, 2007a). Freud and his orthodox followers, however, did not appreciate the value of dissidence in the evolution of psychoanalysis as a science (Rachman, 1999a).

Complementing the understanding of the incest trauma was Ferenczi's creative clinical experiments in treating trauma. In fact, one can say that his career was dedicated to developing ways to respond to the needs of analysands in an ever-empathic therapeutic way. His therapeutic responsiveness was of a different sort than Freud's. Rather than find intellectual ways to convey an understanding, he struggled with understanding the subjective experience of the individual (Rachman, 2010c). Even more importantly, Ferenczi was open to the analysand's contributing to his/her own treatment. Such a philosophy of therapy allowed for co-construction of the analytic encounter and the introduction of non-interpretative measures (Ferenczi, 1988; Rachman, 2007a, 2014a,b). These non-interpretative measures proved helpful in treating the incest trauma (Rachman, 2000, 2003a; Rachman et al., 2005, 2009a,b).

We need to study the confusion of tongues theory, realizing its significance for understanding the incest trauma as well as for emotional, physical, and interpersonal traumas. Educating analytic trainees and colleagues about the efficacy of employing non-interpretative measures in treating trauma is also necessary. In the past twenty-five years or so, our field has accumulated a body of literature on the theory and technique of working with incest survivors. We need to begin to develop study sequences in the incest trauma.

A special mention should be made of the value of Ferenczi's *Clinical Diary* (Ferenczi, 1988) as a device for education. The *Clinical Diary* provides a blueprint for studying and analyzing the incest trauma that continues to have relevance for contemporary clinical thinking and practice.

Supervision

There are three instances in a supervisory teaching experience that indicated the need for a study of the incest trauma. A distinguished late member of the analytic community who had received her analytic training at the Vienna Psychoanalytic Institute in the early 1930s, before the Freuds left Vienna for London, told me there was no interest in the incest trauma. Although this classically trained analyst had evolved into a self-psychologist, when the issue of the incest trauma was discussed she became quiet and made few responses. She showed no enthusiasm for what the supervisee considered an interesting case. Finally, when the lack of responsiveness was noted, the supervisor, in essence, conveyed that the incest trauma was not an area of interest and she could not offer anything to help the supervisee.

In another example, a supervisee was having great difficulty with an erotic transference in his clinical experience at an analytically oriented training institute. He was very anxious about this particular experience, seeking out senior members of the institute for advice and help. One such training analyst was considered a non-traditionalist who emphasized contemporary ideas and methods. When the supervisee raised the issue of childhood sexual abuse and its potential connection to adult psychopathology and disorder, the senior analyst said to him: "In my experience, if you don't overemphasize childhood sexual seduction and exaggerate its importance, I find the negative effects are minimal in the adult."

To this day, these seem like shocking words. Was this a statement about the analyst's personal struggle to cope with her childhood incest? Clearly, the supervisee needed help to understand both theoretically and clinically the incest trauma. Only then could he respond meaningfully and explore the analysand's childhood incest trauma. It seems shocking that the incest trauma was summarily dismissed as an analytic issue.

Finally, an analytic candidate submitted a case study for examination as the requirement for graduation at an analytic institute. The chairman of the examining committee and a second committee member were surprised to see that data presented in the case history on childhood sexual abuse of the analysand were never examined by the analytic candidate. When she was asked about the omission, she responded that her classically oriented supervisor never encouraged her to explore the incest trauma. The committee recommended that she must, at the very least, indicate she was aware that an incest experience had occurred. The committed told her to indicate that the issue was not explored, based on the advice of her senior supervisor. The supervisee reluctantly agreed. When she contacted the supervisor again, it was decided that oedipal conflict was the correct focus. The candidate was given a pass on her case study despite the objection of the committee. Her senior supervisor insisted her student receive a passing grade because she had done a meaningful job in analyzing the individual's oedipal complex. The supervisor's seniority overruled the committee's decision. It was reminiscent of Masson's experience when he reported trying to understand psychoanalysis's insistence on the oedipal complex as the only explanation for behavior (Masson, 1984, 1988, 1990).

An analytic candidate uncovers her own incest trauma

One of the most dramatic examples of how a theoretical and clinical understanding of the incest trauma can lead to insight and improved functioning occurred in a supervisory experience with an analytic candidate from a contemporary institute. The candidate was a highly intelligent dedicated student of psychoanalysis, who was emotionally open and honest in supervision. She voluntarily presented her countertransference reactions. The supervisee also displayed the same emotional courage in her clinical work with analysands. One of her more difficult analysands was an incest survivor whom she would regularly present in supervision. The case generated a great deal of emotional reaction for the supervisee. Then, during one session, in an obviously agitated state, she voiced her belief that her present anxiety might have been stimulated by a recent session with her incest survivor analysand. She was encouraged to discuss the nature of her interaction with the analysand that could have triggered her anxiety. What became clear was that her analysand was struggling with early memories of having had a favorite doll that had become a self-object which helped her survive the darkest moments of her incest trauma. As we began to explore this material, the supervisee began to cry. Without intruding upon her emotional state, she was asked whether she wanted me to explore the issue of the analysand's doll and its emotional effects upon her. I continued to be cautious in the interaction with her, but she was fearless in her exploration of the meaning of the clinical interaction.

She used this opportunity to uncover a childhood memory of her own sexual abuse. When she was a child, she had a stuffed animal as her favorite toy; it was her transitional object as a young child and then became her self-object. A relative, who lived with her family, was her abuser. During the supervisory session, she uncovered a childhood memory of running away from the grandfather as he attempted to sexually abuse her. She hid under a kitchen cabinet clutching her stuffed animal, screaming and crying. She was successful in preventing abuse that day. The stuffed animal helped her maintain self-cohesion and provided the necessary self-soothing to maintain her contact with reality.

I had no intention of turning the supervisory session into an analytic session. The uncovering of the supervisee's childhood memory was a confluence of the supervisee's openness and the empathic atmosphere of the supervisory session. These factors allowed the uncovering of the childhood sexual trauma. The supervisee was able to use her new understanding of her own trauma to help better treat her analysand. What was also significant was that the uncovering of her own sexual trauma enhanced her own analysis. Her analysis did not focus on the issue of childhood sexual abuse. She worked through her own incest trauma in supervision, not in her own analysis.

Uncovering the incest trauma in a spinal cord injured patient

A unique event occurred in a series of supervisory sessions with an analytic candidate who was working clinically with a spinal cord injured patient (Rachman, 1995a). The supervisee began a session saying she had two emergency sessions with a spinal cord injured patient she was seeing in a hospital setting. The patient was brought in several days before the supervisory session in a state of physical deterioration and emotional regression. Spinal cord injured patients need to maintain good body hygiene so that their skin does not deteriorate. This patient's skin was seriously deteriorated with severe sores. Emotionally, he was diagnosed as having a psychotic episode.

When the supervisee interviewed her patient, he was so uncommunicative that she could not gain any understanding of what had happened to produce such pathology. Although the case seemed puzzling, the supervisor believed that the patient had suffered an emotional trauma. With that thought in mind, I suggested to the supervisee that she focus her next session on uncovering any possible recent trauma. The supervisee was noticeably relieved that there might be a way to understand and help this deteriorated individual.

In two sessions, where she focused on the issue of trauma, the supervisee discovered that there was a traumatic event that had recently occurred. At first, the patient could not talk about it. The supervisee was encouraged to offer a hypothesis that some difficult and disturbing event had occurred in the patient's family interaction which could help understand the present crisis. Then the patient revealed that his mother had recently revealed to him that the person whom he thought was his uncle was really his father. Furthermore, he remembered that this uncle had sexually abused him when he was ten years old when they were on a camping trip. The supervisee was encouraged to focus on the incest trauma. When the patient was told by his mother that his uncle was his father, and he remembered him as a sexual abuser, he went into a deep depression. He became mute, refused to talk to his mother, with whom he lived and who was his caretaker. She was not allowed into his room to cleanse his wounds, and turn him over regularly, so that sores would not develop. He rarely ate. In essence, the patient went into a passive suicide mode, by not eating and allowing the physical deterioration. Additionally, he was symbolically expressing his anger toward his mother for not protecting him from the abuse and then shattering his illusions about his father and his family.

With the introduction of a comprehensive supervision about theory and treatment of the incest trauma, the supervisee was able to help the patient confront his emotional reaction to becoming aware of his incest trauma. He welcomed the analysis that allowed him to develop insight into the childhood trauma he had split off from consciousness. The patient, with the help of the active empathic relationship with the supervisee, made very significant progress. Within three weeks his psychotic reaction was significantly reduced, aided by psychotropic drugs. His physical hygiene was restored. He began eating regularly, and, very importantly, he developed an interest in exploring his childhood incest trauma. The supervisee, who had never had any training in dealing with the incest trauma, became adept at helping this seriously disturbed patient. They entered into a more intensive analytic relationship that continued on an outpatient basis when the patient was released from the hospital.

A contemporary analytic curriculum that provides study in a variety of theoretical orientations friendly to the issue of a trauma studies and the use of non-interpretative measures is necessary for the analysis of the incest trauma. We need to integrate the lessons learned from a study of the history of psychoanalysis. In particular, we need to integrate the damage that political intrigues have cost our field (Rachman, 2012d). We need to appreciate creative dissidence, being open to new ideas, clinical experimentation, and maintaining the capacity for surprise (Rachman, 2004). In our clinical interactions, we need to emphasize being emotionally open, judiciously self-disclosing, creating an atmosphere of trust, empathy, and democracy (Rachman, 2003a). Finally, we need to develop respect for the history of psychoanalysis and the contribution of its dissident pioneers (Masson, 1984; Roazen, 1975).

REFERENCES

Albach, F., & Everaerd, W. (1992). Posttraumatic stress symptoms in victims of childhood incest. *Psychotherapy and Psychosomatics, 57*(4): 143–151.

Alpert, J. L. (1995). *Sexual Abuse Recalled: Treating Trauma in the Era of The Recovered Memory Debate*. Hillsdale: NJ: Analytic Press.

Alpert, J. L. (2001). No escape when the past is endless. *Psychoanalytic Psychology, 18*(4): 729–736.

Anderson, L. (1981). Notes on the linkage between the sexually abused child and the suicidal adolescent. *Journal of Adolescence*, 4: 157–162.

Anzieu, D. (1975). *L'auto-analyse de Freud et la decouverte de la psychanalyse* (Vol. I) (pp. 311–315). Paris: Presses Universitaires de France.

Aron, L. (1992). From Ferenczi to Searles and contemporary relational approaches. *Psychoanalytic Dialogues*, 2: 181–190.

Aron, L. (1996). *A Meeting of Minds: Interpretation As Expression of The Analyst's Subjectivity* (pp. 95–121). Hillsdale, NJ: Analytic Press.

Aron, L., & Harris, A. (Eds.) (1993). *The Legacy of Sandor Ferenczi*. Hillsdale, NJ: Analytic Press.

Asperger, H. (1991). Austistic psychopathology in childhood. In: U. Frith (Ed. & Trans.). *Autism and Asperger Syndrome* (pp. 37–92). Cambridge: Cambridge University Press.

Bacal, H. A. (1988). Reflections 'Optimum frustration.' In: A. Goldberg (Ed.), *Progress in Self Psychology* (Vol. 4) (pp. 127–131). New York: Guilford Press.

Balint, A., & Balint, M. (1939). On transference and countertransference. *International Journal of Psychoanalysis, 20*: 223–230.

Balint, M. (Ed.) (1949). Sandor Ferenczi number. *International Journal of Psychoanalysis, 30*: Whole No. 4.

Balint, M. (1958). Letter to the editor: Sandor Ferenczi's last years. *International Journal of Psychoanalysis, 39*: 68.

Balint, M. (1965a). Early developmental stages of the ego: primary object love. In: *Primary Love and Psychoanalytic Techniques* (pp. 77–90). London: Tavistock.

Balint, M. (1965b). New beginning and the paranoid and the depressive syndromes. In: *Primary Love and Psychoanalytic Technique* (pp. 223–230). London: Tavistock.

Balint, M. (1965c). Character analysis and new beginning. In: *Primary Love and Psychoanalytic Technique* (pp. 159–173). London: Tavistock.

Balint, M. (1965d). *Primary Love and Psychoanalytic Technique.* London: Tavistock.

Balint, M. (1968). *The Basic Fault: Therapeutic Aspects of Regression.* London: Tavistock. [Reprinted Evanston, IL: North Western University Press, 1992].

Balint, M. (1992). The area of the basic fault. In: *The Basic Fault: Therapeutic Aspects of Regression* (pp. 12–23). Evanston, IL: Northwestern University Press.

Bass, E., & Davis, L. (1994). *The Courage to Heal.* New York: HarperCollins.

Berendzen, R., & Palmer, L. (1993). *Come Here: A Man Overcomes the Tragic Aftermath of Childhood Sexual Abuse.* New York: Villard Books.

Bettelheim, B. (1950). *Love is Not Enough.* New York: Avon Books.

Bettelheim, B. (1959). Feral children and autistic children. *American Journal of Sociology, 64*(5): 455–467.

Bettelheim, B. (1990). *Freud's Vienna and Other Essays.* New York: Knopf.

Bollas, C. A. (1987). *The Shadow of the Object*: New York: Columbia University Press.

Bonomi, C. (1999). Flight into sanity: Jones's allegations of Ferenczi's mental deterioration. *International Journal of Psychoanalysis, 80*: 507–542.

Bowlby, J. (1969). *Attachment and Loss* (Vol. 1). New York: Basic Books.

Brandchaft, B., Doctors, S., & Sorter, D. (2010). *Toward an Emancipatory Psychoanalysis.* New York: Routledge.

Bryer, J. B., Nelson, B. A., Miller, J. B., & Krol, P. A. (1987). Childhood sexual and physical abuse as factors in adult psychiatric illness. *American Journal of Psychiatry, 144*: 1426–1430.

Carlson, E. B. (1997). *Trauma Assessments: A Clinician's Guide.* New York: Guilford Press.

Carroll, J., Schaffer, C., & Abramowitz, S. (1980). Family experiences of self mulitating patients. *American Journal of Psychiatry, 137*: 852–853.

Casement, P. (1997). *Further Learning From the Patient.* London: Routledge.

Chodoff, P. (1990). Post-traumatic stress disorder and the holocaust. *Academy Forum, 34*: 3–4. *Cahiers Confrontation, 12*: 63–78.

Chused, J. F. (1991). The evocative power of transference. *Journal of the American Psychoanalytic Association, 39*: 615–639.

Covello, A. (1984). Lettres de Freud du scenario de Jones du diagnostic sur Ferenczi. *Confrontations, 12*: 63–78.

Cozolino, L. (2002a). The interpersonal sculpting of the social brain. In: *The Neuroscience of Psychotherapy: Building and Rebuilding the Human Brain* (pp. 172–214). New York: W. W. Norton.

Cozolino, L. (2002b). The anxious and fearful brain. In: *The Neuroscience of Psychotherapy: Building and Rebuilding the Human Brain* (pp. 239–261). New York: W. W. Norton.

Cozolino, L. (2002c). The impact of trauma on the brain. In: *The Neuroscience of Psychotherapy: Building and Rebuilding the Human Brain* (pp. 257–285). New York: W. W. Norton.

Cremerius, J. (1983). Die Sprache der Zärtlichkeit und der Leidenschaft: Reflexionen zu Sandor Ferenczis Wiesbadener Vortrag von 1932. Sandor Ferenczis bedeutung für theorie und therapie der psychoanalyse. [The language of tenderness and passion: reflections on Sandor Ferenczi's presentation at the Wiesbaden conference of 1932. The meaning of Sandor Ferenczi's work for the theory and therapy of psychoanalysis]. *Psyche, 37*(11): 988–1015.

De Forest, I. (1942). The therapeutic technique of Sandor Ferenczi. *International Journal of Psychoanalysis, 22*(1): 121–139.

De Forest, I. (1954). *The Leaven of Love: A Development of The Psychoanalytic Theory and Technique of Sandor Ferenczi.* New York: Harper and Row.

Dupont, J. (1982). The source of inventions. In: *The Sandor Ferenczi–Georg Groddeck Correspondence (1992–1933).* Translation, notes and comments by the Groupe de traductionzi: Groddeck. *Cahiers Confrontation, 12*: 33–42.

Dupont, J. (Ed.) (1988a). Introduction. In: *The Clinical Diary of Sandor Ferenczi* (pp. xi–xxvii). Cambridge, MA: Harvard University Press.

Dupont, J. (Ed.) (1988b). *The Clinical Diary of Sandor Ferenczi*. Cambridge, MA: Harvard University Press.

Eissler, K. R. (1965). *Medical Orthodoxy and the Future of Psychoanalysis*. New York: International Universities Press.

Ellman, S. (1998). *Enactment, Transference and Analytic Trust*. In: S. Ellman & M. Moskowitz (Eds.), *Enactment Toward A New Approach to the Therapeutic Relationship* (pp. 183–203). Northvale, NJ: Jason Aronson.

Erikson, E. H. (1950). *Childhood and Society*. New York: W. W. Norton.

Fairbairn, R. D. (1954). Observations of the nature of hysterical states. *British Journal of Medical Psychology, 27*: 105–125.

Falzeder, E., Brabant, E., & Giampieri-Deutsch, P. (Eds.) (2000). *The Correspondence of Sigmund Freud and Sandor Ferenczi 1920–1933* (Vol. 3). Cambridge, MA: Belknap Press of Harvard University Press.

Farber, S. K. (2000). *When the Body Is the Target: Self-Harm, Pain and Traumatic Attachments* Northvale, NJ: Jason Aronson.

Ferenczi, S. (1933). Sprachverwirrung zwischen den Erwachsenen und dem Kind (Die Sprache der Zärtlichkeit und der Leidenschaft) [Confusion of tongues between the adults and the child: (the language of tenderness and passion)]. *Internationale Zeitschrift für Psychoanalyse, XIX* (1–2): 5–15. Original title: Die Leidenschaften der Erwachsenen und deren Einfluß auf Sexual- und Charakterentwicklung der Kinder [The passions of adults and their influence on the sexual and character development of children]. Reprinted in 1936 in *Bausteine zur Psychoanalyse* (Vol. III). Berne.

Ferenczi, S. (1949). Confusion of the tongues between the adults and the child—(the language of tenderness and of passion). *International Journal of Psychoanalysis, 30*: 225–230.

Ferenczi, S. (1980a). *First Contributions to Psycho-analysis*, Ernest Jones (Trans.). New York: Brunner/Mazel.

Ferenczi, S. (1980b). *Further Contributions to the Theory and Technique of Psychoanalysis*, J. Rickman (Ed.), J. I. Suthe and others (Trans.). New York: Brunner/Mazel

Ferenczi, S. (1980c). On forced phantasies: activity in the association technique. In: J. Rickman (Ed.), *Further Contributions to the Theory and Technique of Psychoanalysis* (Vol. 2), (pp. 68–77). New York: Brunner/Mazel.

Ferenczi, S. (1980d). On the technique of psychoanalysis. In: J. Rickman (Ed.), *Further Contributions to the Theory and Technique of Psychoanalysis* (pp. 177–189). New York: Brunner/Mazel.

Ferenczi, S. (1980e). Technical difficulties in the analysis of a case of hysteria: including observations on larval forms of onanism and onanistic equivalents. In: J. Rickman (Ed.), *Further Contributions to the Theory and Technique of Psychoanalysis* (pp. 189–197). New York: Brunner/Mazel.

Ferenczi, S. (1980f). The further development of the active therapy in psychoanalysis. In: J. Rickman (Ed.), *Further Contributions to the Theory and Technique of Psychoanalysis* (pp. 198–217). New York: Brunner/Mazel.

Ferenczi, S. (1980g). Contradictions to the "active" psychoanalytic technique. In: J. Rickman (Ed.), *Further Contributions to the Theory and Technique of Psychoanalysis* (pp. 217–230). New York: Brunner/Mazel.

Ferenczi, S. (1980h). On influencing of the patient in psychoanalysis. In. J. Rickman (Ed.), *Further Contributions to the Theory and Technique of Psychoanalysis* (pp. 235–237). New York: Brunner/Mazel.

Ferenczi, S. (1980i). Psychoanalysis of sexual habits. In: J. Rickman (Ed.) *Further Contributions to the Theory and Technique of Psychoanalysis* (pp. 257–297). New York: Brunner/Mazel.

Ferenczi, S. (1980j). The problem of the termination of the analysis. In: M. Balint (Ed.), *Final Contributions to the Problems and Methods of Psychoanalysis* (pp. 77–86). New York: Brunner/Mazel.

Ferenczi, S. (1980k). The elasticity of psychoanalytic technique. In: M. Balint (Ed.), *Final Contributions to the Problems and Methods of Psychoanalysis* (pp. 87–102). New York: Brunner/Mazel.

Ferenczi, S. (1980l). The principle of relaxation and neocatharsis. In: M. Balint (Ed.), *Final Contributions to the Problems and Methods of Psychoanalysis* (pp. 108–125). New York: Brunner/Mazel.

Ferenczi, S. (1980m). Child analysis in the analysis of adults. In: M. Balint (Ed.), *Final Contributions to the Problems and Methods of Psychoanalysis* (pp. 126–142). New York: Brunner/Mazel.

Ferenczi, S. (1980n). Confusion of tongues between adults and the child: the language of tenderness and of passion. In: M. Balint (Ed.), *Final Contributions to the Problems and Methods of Psychoanalysis* (pp. 156–167). New York: Brunner/Mazel.

Ferenczi, S. (1980o). Notes and fragments. In: M. Balint (Ed.), *Final Contributions to the Problems and Methods of Psychoanalysis* (pp. 216–231). New York: Brunner/Mazel.

Ferenczi, S. (1985). *Journal Clinique: Janvier–Octobre 1932*, Le Groupe du Coq-Heron (Eds.). Paris: Payot.

Ferenczi, S. (1988). *The Clinical Diary of Sandor Ferenczi*, J. Dupont (Ed.), M. Balint & N. Z. Jackson (Trans.). Cambridge, MA: Harvard University Press.

Ferenczi, S., & Rank, O. (1925). *The Development of Psychoanalysis*. New York: Nervous and Mental Disease Publishing.
Ferrier, J. L. (1998). *Outsider Art*. Paris: Pierre Terrail Editions.
Finklehor, D. (1984). *Child Sexual Abuse*. New York: Free Press.
Forward, S., & Buck, C. (1979). *Betrayal of Innocence*. Harmondsworth, Middlesex: Penguin.
Freud, A. (1933). Report of the Twelfth International Psychoanalytical Congress. *International Journal of Psychoanalysis, 14*: 138.
Freud, A. (1936). *The Ego and the Mechanisms of Defense*. New York: International Universities Press.
Freud, A. (1967). *The Writings of Anna Freud, Vol. II*. New York: International Universities Press.
Freud, S. (with Breuer, J.) (1895d). *Studies on Hysteria. S. E., 2*. London: Hogarth.
Freud, S. (1896). The aetiology of hysteria. *S. E., 3*: 189–221. London: Hogarth.
Freud, S. (1915a). Observations on transference-love. *S. E., 12*: 157–171. London: Hogarth.
Freud, S. (1918b). *From the History of an Infantile Neurosis. S. E., 17*: 3–104. London: Hogarth.
Freud, S. (1919a). Lines of advance in psychoanalytic therapy. *S. E., 17*: 157–168. London: Hogarth.
Freud, S. (1919e). 'A child is being beaten'. *S. E., 17*: 177–201. London: Hogarth.
Freud, S. (1925j). Some psychical consequences of the anatomical distinction between the sexes. *S. E., 19*: 243–258. London: Hogarth.
Freud, S. (1933c). Sandor Ferenczi: Obituary. *S. E., 21*: 227–232. London: Hogarth.
Freud, S. (1954). *The Origins of Psychoanalysis: Sigmund Freud's Letters—Letters, Drafts and Notes to Wilheim Fliess 1887–1902*, M. Bonaparte, A. Freud, & E. Kris (Eds.), E. Mosbacker & J. Strachey (Trans.). New York: Basic Books.
Freyd, J. (1996). *Betrayal Trauma: The Logic of Forgetting Childhood Abuse*. Cambridge, MA: Harvard University Press.
Fromm, E. (1955). *The Sane Society*. New York: Henry Holt.
Fromm, E. (1959). *Sigmund Freud's Mission*. New York: Harper and Row.
Gabbard, G. O. (1996). Glenn O. Gabbard replies. *Journal of the American Psychoanalytic Association, 45*: 2, 571.
Gay, P. (1988). *Freud: A Life For Our Time*. New York: W. W. Norton.
Gedo, J. E. (1986). Ferenczi: psychoanalysis' first dissident. In: *Conceptual Issues in Psychoanalysis: Essays in History and Method* (pp. 36–50). Hillsdale, NJ: Analytic Press.

Gedo, J. E. (1987). Personal communication. Letter to Arnold Wm. Rachman.

Goldberger, L. (1966). Experimental isolation: an overview. *American Journal of Psychiatry, 122*: 774–782.

Goldwert, M. (1986). Childhood seduction and the spiritualization of psychology: the case of Jung and Rank. *Child Abuse and Neglect, 10*: 555–557.

Greenspan, G., & Samuel, S. (1989). Self cutting after rape. *American Journal of Psychiatry, 146*(6): 789–790.

Grosskurth, P. (1986). *Melanie Klein. Her World and Her Work.* Cambridge, MA: Harvard University Press.

Grosskurth, P. (1991). *The Secret Ring: Freud's Inner Circle and The Politics of Psychoanalysis.* New York: Addison-Wesley.

Grossman, C. M., & Grossman, S. (1965). *The Wild Analyst.* New York: George Braziller.

Grossman, F. K. (1997). The destructive debate over recovered memories. *Bostonia: The Alumni Quarterly Boston University, Spring*: 73–75.

Grünberger, B. (1980). From the "active technique" to the "confusion of tongues:" on Ferenczi's deviation. In: S. Lebovici & D. Widlocher (Eds.), *Psychoanalysis in France* (pp. 127–152). New York: International Universities Press.

Harrison, K. (1993). *The Kiss.* New York: Random House.

Hartley, H. (1997). *Henry Fool.* Motion Picture. Sony Picture Classics.

Haynal, A. (1989). *Controversies in Psychoanalytic Method: From Freud and Ferenczi to Michael Balint.* New York: New York University Press.

Haynal, A. (1993). Elma Palos' "sexual behavior" with Ferenczi. Personal communication.

Herman, J. L. (1981). *Father–Daughter Incest.* Cambridge, MA: Harvard University Press.

Herman, J. L. (1986). Histories of violence in an outpatient population. *American Journal of Orthopsychiatry, 56*: 137–141.

Herman, J. L. (1992). *Trauma and Recovery.* New York: Basic Books

Hidas, G. (1993). History of Hungarian psychoanalysis. The talking therapy: Ferenczi and the psychoanalytic vocation. Presented to the Fourth International Conference of the Sándor Ferenczi Society, Budapest, Hungary, July 21st.

Howell, E. F. (1997). Masochism: a bridge to the other side of abuse. *Dissociation, 10*(4): 240–245.

Jacobson, E. A. (1964). *The Self and The Object World.* New York: International Universities Press.

Jones, E. (1953). *The Life and Work of Sigmund Freud Vol. I: The Formative Years and The Great Discoveries*. New York: Basic Books.

Jones, E. (1955). *The Life and Work of Sigmund Freud. Vol. II: Years of Maturity, 1901–1919*. New York: Basic Books.

Jones, E. (1957). *The Life and Work of Sigmund Freud. Vol. III: The Last Phase: 1919–1939*. New York: Basic Books.

Jones, E. (1959). *Free Associations: Memories of A Psychoanalyst*. New York: Basic Books.

Jung, C. (1961). The theory of psychoanalysis, *C. W., 4*. New York: Pantheon Books.

Justice, B., & Justice, R. (1979). *The Broken Taboo*. New York: Human Sciences Press.

Kafka, F. (1948). The metamorphosis. In: *The Penal Colony and Other Stories*. New York: Shocken Books.

Karpe, R. (1956). Freud's reaction to his father's death. *Bulletin of the Philadelphia Association for Psychoanalysis, 6*: 25–29.

Kempe, R. S., & Kempe, C. H. (1984). *The Common Secret*. New York: Freeman.

Klein, M. (1935). A contribution to the psychogenesis of manic–depressive states. *International Journal of Psychoanalysis, 16*: 145–174.

Klein, M. I. (1981). Freud's seduction theory: its implications for fantasy and memory in psychoanalytic theory. *Bulletin of the Menninger Clinic, 45*: 185–208.

Klein, M. I., & Tribich, D. (1982). Blame the child: Freud's blindness to the damaging influence of parents' personalities. *New York Academy of Sciences, 2*(8): 14–20.

Klett, S. (2014). Sandor Ferenczi's legacy: his influence on my work with difficult patients. *Psychoanalytic Inquiry, 34*: 175–176.

Kohut, H. (1971). *The Analysis of the Self*. New York: International Universities Press.

Kohut, H. (1977). *The Restoration of the Self*. New York: International Universities Press.

Kohut, H. (1984). The role of empathy in psychoanalytic cure. In: *How Does Analysis Cure?* (pp. 172–191). Chicago, IL: University of Chicago Press.

Krüll, M. (1986). *Freud and His Father*. New York: W. W. Norton.

Kriwaczek, P. (2005). *Yiddish Civilization: The Rise and Fall of a Forgotten Nation*. London: Phoenix.

Landecker, H. (1992). The role of childhood sexual trauma in the etiology of borderline personality disorder: considerations for diagnosis and treatment. *Psychotherapy, 29*(2): 234–242.

Levine, H. B. (Ed.) (1990). Introduction. In: *Adult Analysis and Childhood Sexual Abuse* (pp. 3–20). Hillsdale, NJ: Analytic Press.

Lewis, H. B. (1984). Book Review. *The Assault on Truth: Freud's Suppression of the Seduction Theory* by Jeffrey Moussaieff Masson. *Psychoanalytic Psychology, 2*(33): 353–378.

Lifton, R. J. (1986). *Nazi Doctors: Medical Killing and the Psychology of Genocide*. New York: Basic Books.

Loftus, E. F. (1979). *Eyewitness Testimony*. Cambridge, MA: Harvard University Press.

Loftus, E. F. (1991). The glitter of everyday memory . . . and the gold. *American Psychologist, 46*(1): 16–18.

Loftus, E. F., & Ketcham, K. (1991). *Witness for the Defense: The Accused, the Eyewitness and the Expert Who Puts Memory on Trial*. New York: St. Martin's Press.

Loftus, E. F., & Ketcham, K. (1994). *The Myth of Repressed Memory*. New York: St. Martin's Press.

MacGregor, J. M. (1989). *The Discovery of the Art of the Insane*. Princeton, NJ: Princeton University Press.

Mahler, M. S. (1963). Thoughts about development and individuation. *Psychoanalytic Study of the Child, 18*: 307–324.

Mahler, M. S., Pine, F., & Bergman, A. (1973). *The Psychological Birth of The Human Infant: Symbiosis and Individuation*. New York: Basic Books.

Maizels, J. (1996). *Raw Creation: Outsider Art and Beyond*. London: Phaidon Press.

Malcolm, J. (1984). *In The Freud Archives*. New York: Alfred A. Knopf.

Maslin, J. (1998). *Henry Fool* (1997). Film review: Faustian wonders and a mythic queen. *New York Times*, June 19.

Maslow, A. H. (1954). *Motivation and Personality*. New York: Harper.

Maslow, A. H. (1968). *Toward a Psychology of Being*. New York: D. Van Nostrand.

Mason, L. E. (1997). Divided she stands. *New Yorker Magazine, 30*(29): 44–49.

Masson, J. M. (1984). *The Assault on Truth: Freud's Suppression of the Seduction Theory*. New York: Farrar, Strauss & Giroux.

Masson, J. M. (Ed.) (1985). *The Complete Letters of Sigmund Freud toWilhelm Fliess 1887-1904*. Cambridge, MA: Belknap Press of Harvard University Press.

Masson, J. M. (1988). *Against Therapy: Emotional Tyranny and The Myth of Psychological Healing*. New York: Atheneum.

Masson, J. M. (1990). *Final Analysis: The Making and Unmaking of a Psychoanalyst*. Reading, MA: Addison Wesley.

Mattick, P. (1984). Confusion of tongues translation. Personal communication.

McGrath, W. J. (1986). The collapse of the seduction theory. In: *Freud's Discovery of Psychoanalysis: The Politics of Hysteria* (pp. 197–229). Ithaca, NY: Cornell University Press.

McGuire, W. (Ed.) (1974). *The Freud/Jung Letters: The Correspondence between Sigmund Freud and C. G. Jung*, R. Manheim & R. F. C. Hull (Trans.). Princeton, NJ: Princeton University Press.

McLaughlin, J. T. (1981). Transference, psychic reality and countertransference. *Psychoanalytic Quarterly, 50*: 639–664.

McLaughlin, J. T. (1987). The play of transference: some reflections on enactment in the psychoanalytic situation. *Journal of the American Psychoanalytic Association, 35*: 557–582.

McLaughlin, J. T. (1988). The analyst's insights. *Psychoanalytic Quarterly, 47*: 370–389.

McLaughlin, J. T. (1991). Clinical and theoretical aspects of enactment. *Journal of the American Psychoanalytic Association, 39*: 595–614.

McLeod, S. A. (2007). Maslow's Hierarchy of Needs. Available at: www.simplypsychology.org/maslow.html.

Menaker, E. (1982). *Otto Rank: A Rediscovered Legacy*. New York: Columbia University Press.

Menaker, E. (1986). Announcement of Ferenczi's death. Personal communication, April.

Messler-Davies, J., & Frawley, M. G. (1994). *Treating the Adult Survivor of Childhood Seuxal Abuse: A Psychoanalytic Perspective*. New York: Basic Books.

Miller, A. (1986). *Thou Shalt Not Be Aware: Society's Betrayal of the Child*. New York: New American Library.

Miller, A. (1990). *Banished Knowledge*. New York: Doubleday.

Miller, D. (2005). *Women Who Hurt Themselves: A Book of Understanding and Hope*. New York: Basic Books.

Mitchell, S. A. (1988). *Relational Concepts in Psychoanalysis: An Integration*. Cambridge, MA: Harvard University Press.

Modell, A. W. (1990). *Other Times, Other Realities: Toward A Theory of Psychoanalytic Treatment*. Cambridge, MA: Harvard University Press.

Molnar, M. (1992). *The Diary of Sigmund Freud: 1929–1939. A Record of the Final Decade*. New York: Charles Scribner's Sons.

Nemes, L. (1988). Freud and Ferenczi: a possible interpretation of their relationship. *Contemporary Psychoanalysis, 24*(2): 240–249.

Nusbaum, G. A. (2000). A case illustration of combined treatment using a psychodynamic group for women sexual abuse survivors to address and modify self-punitive trends. *Group, 24*(4): 289–301.

Ogden, T. H. (1979). On projective identification. *International Journal of Psychoanalysis, 60*: 357–373.

Paskauskas, R. A. (Ed.) (1993). *The Complete Correspondence of Sigmund Freud and Ernsest Jones 1908–1939*. Cambridge, MA: Harvard University Press.

Perry, B. D., Pollard, R. A., Blakely, T. L., Baker, W. L., & Vigilante, E. (1995). Childhood trauma, the neurobiology of adaptation, and "use-dependent" development of the brain: how "states" become "traits". *Infant Mental Health Journal, 16*(4): 271–291.

Prinzhorn, H. (1972). *Artistry of the Mentally Ill*. New York: Springer.

Putnam, F. (1989). *Diagnosis and Treatment of Multiple Personality Disorders*. New York: Guilford Press.

Rachman, A. W. (1962). *Counseling Mentally Retarded Teenagers in a Sheltered Workshop. Report*. Chicago, IL: Jewish Vocational Service.

Rachman, A. W. (1968). A new technique for group psychotherapy with delinquents. *Newsletter: Eastern Group Psychotherapy Society, 11*: 3–4.

Rachman, A. W. (1969). Talking it out rather than fighting it out: prevention of a delinquent gang war by group therapy intervention. *International Journal of Group Psychotherapy, 19*(4): 518–521.

Rachman, A. W. (1971). Encounter techniques in analytic group psychotherapy with adolescents. *International Journal of Group Psychotherapy, 21*: 319–329.

Rachman, A. W. (1972). Group psychotherapy in treating the adolescent identity crisis. *International Journal of Child Psychotherapy, 1*(1): 97–119.

Rachman, A. W. (1973). Adolescent group psychotherapy. *Pediatric Annals, 2*(3): 17–31.

Rachman, A. W. (1974). Identity group psychotherapy. In: S. Gordon & G. Williams (Eds.), *Clinical Child Psychology: Current Practices and Future Perspectives* (Chapter 30). New York: Behavioral Publications.

Rachman, A. W. (1975). *Identity Group Psychotherapy with Adolescents*. Springfield, IL: Charles C. Thomas.

Rachman, A. W. (1976). The role of fathering with adolescent delinquent males. *Journal of Social and Correction Psychiatry, 20*(4): 11–22. Reprinted in: C. V. Martin (Ed.), *Basic Readings in Juvenile Delinquency*. Olathe, KS: Martin Psychiatric Research Foundation.

Rachman, A. W. (1977). Encounter techniques in analytic group psychotherapy with adolescents. *International Journal Group Psychotherapy,*

21(3): 319–329, 1971 (reprinted in J. F. McDermott & S. Harrison (Eds.), *Psychiatric Treatment of the Child*. New York: Jason Aronson, 1977).

Rachman, A. W. (1978a). The first encounter session: Ferenczi's case of the female Croatian musician. Presentation to the American Group Psychotherapy Association Convention, New Orleans, February.

Rachman, A. W. (1978b). Combined therapy from a humanistic perspective. Presentation to Three Day Annual Workshop in Analytic Group Therapy. Postgraduate Center for Mental Health, New York.

Rachman, A. W. (1978c). Intensive psychotherapy from a humanistic perspective. Presentation to Schalvata Psychiatric Center, Ramat Hasharon, Israel.

Rachman, A. W. (1979). Active psychoanalysis and the group encounter. In: L. R. Wolberg & M. Aronson (Eds.), *Group Therapy 1979: An Overview*. New York: Intercontinental Medical.

Rachman, A. W. (1980). The role of activity in psychodynamic psychotherapy. Presentation in Invited Lecture Series, Pine Crest Christian Hospital, Grand Rapids, MI.

Rachman, A. W. (1981). Humanistic analysis. *Groups. Psychotherapy: Theory, Research and Practice, 18*(4): 457–477.

Rachman, A. W. (1987). Identity group psychotherapy with adolescents: a reformulation. In: F. J. C. Cramer-Azima & L. H. Richmond (Eds.), *The Group Therapies for Adolescents* (pp. 21–41). New York: International Universities Press.

Rachman, A. W. (1988a). Liberating the creative self through active combined psychotherapy. In: N. Slavinska-Holy (Ed.), *Borderline and Narcissistic Patients in Therapy* (pp. 309–340). New York: International Universities Press.

Rachman, A. W. (1988b). Sandor Ferenczi's influence in modern psychoanalysis. Presentation to the History of Psychoanalysis Course, Institute for Modern Psychoanalysis, New York, February 25th.

Rachman, A. W. (1988c). Introduction. Symposium: Child Abuse, Sexual Trauma and the Group Context. Presented to the American Group Psychotherapy Association Conference, New York.

Rachman, A. W. (1989a). Confusion of tongues: the Ferenczian metaphor for childhood seduction and emotional trauma. *Journal of the American Academy of Psychoanalysis, 17*: 181–205.

Rachman, A. W. (1989b). The analysis of the incest trauma. Presented to Grand Rounds, Brookdale Hospital, Brooklyn, NY, October.

Rachman, A. W. (1989c). Sandor Ferenczi: psychoanalysis' fallen angel (unpublished).

Rachman, A. W. (1990). The retrieval of the incest trauma through the use of drawings. Presented to the Psychology Department, Bellevue Hospital, November.

Rachman, A. W. (1991a). An oedipally conflicted patient. In: A. Wolf & L. Kutash (Eds.), *Psychopathology of the Submerged Personality* (pp. 215–238). Northvale, NJ: Jason Aronson.

Rachman, A. W. (1991b). Dreams of incest: the literal interpretation. The Royal Road to the Unconscious: A Conference on Dreams, C. G. Jung Foundation of New York.

Rachman, A. W. (1992a). The confusion of tongues between Hedda Nussbaum and Joel Steinberg: dynamics of an abusive relationship. Presented to the International Conference of The Psycho-Historical Society, John Jay College, New York City, June.

Rachman, A. W. (1992b). The seduction of the child. Lecture to the Jungian Foundation, New York.

Rachman, A. W. (1992c). Ferenczi's discovery of the confusion of tongues theory. Presentation to the Division of Psychoanalysis, American Psychological Association, Philadelphia, PA, April.

Rachman, A. W. (1992d). The analysis of the incest trauma in group analysis. Lecture to the American Group Psychotherapy Association Conference, New York, February.

Rachman, A. W. (1992e). Reviving and retrieving incest memories. Lecture to the Psychology Department, New York University, Bellevue Hospital Medical Center, New York, November.

Rachman, A. W. (1993a). Ferenczi and sexuality. In: L. Aron & A. Harris (Eds.), *The Theoretical and Clinical Contributions of Sandor Ferenczi* (pp. 81–100). Hillsdale, NJ: Analytic Press.

Rachman, A. W. (1993b). The evil of childhood seduction. Presentation to the American Academy of Psychoanalysis, New York, December.

Rachman, A. W. (1993c). The abusive parental transference in group analysis of the incest trauma. Presented to the American Group Psychotherapy Association Conference, San Diego, California, February 19.

Rachman, A. W. (1993d). Judicious self-disclosure by the psychoanalyst. Presented to the Fourth International Ferenczi Conference, Budapest, Hungary, July 19th.

Rachman, A. W. (1994a). The confusion of tongues theory: Ferenczi's legacy to psychoanalysis. In: A. Haynal & E. Falzeder (Eds.), *100 Years of Psychoanalysis* (pp. 235–255). London: Karnac.

Rachman, A. W. (1994b). Oedipus from Brooklyn: a Ferenczian analysis. Presentation to the Circulo Brasiliano de Psicanalise, Belo Horizonte, Brazil.

Rachman, A. W. (1994c). The examination and analysis of the psychotherapist's emotional reactions to a "difficult analysand." Presented to the Seminar, Sandor Ferenczi Institute, Michigan Group, Grand Rapids, Saturday, January 29th.

Rachman, A. W. (1995a). Sandor Ferenczi's pioneering contributions to the analysis of the incest trauma. Plenary Presentation to the First Ferenczi Congress of Latin America, Sao Paulo, Brazil.

Rachman, A. W. (1995b). Theoretical issues in the treatment of childhood sexual trauma. *SCI Psychological Process, 8*(1): 20–25.

Rachman, A. W. (1995c). Ferenczi's reformulation of the seduction theory. Presentation to the Psychoanalytic Society of Campinas, Campinas, Brazil.

Rachman, A. W. (1996a). Art of the abused. Guest lecture to the Psychology and Art Course, New School for Social Research, New York.

Rachman, A. W. (1996b). The confusion of tongues between Sigmund and Anna Freud: Issues of seduction. Presentation to the Eighth Biennial Conference, Psychoanalytic Society, New York University Postdoctoral Program, New York.

Rachman, A. W. (1997a). *Sandor Ferenczi: The Psychotherapist of Tenderness and Passion*. Northvale, NJ: Jason Aronson.

Rachman, A. W. (1997b). The suppression and censorship of Ferenczi's confusion of tongues paper. *Psychoanalytic Inquiry, 17*(4): 459–485.

Rachman, A. W. (1997c). The view from the couch: listening to an analysand's ideas about theory and technique (unpublished).

Rachman, A. W. (1998a). Judicious self disclosure by the psychoanalyst. *International Forum of Psychoanalysis, 7*: 263–269.

Rachman, A. W. (1998b). Ferenczi's "relaxation-principle" and the contemporary clinical practice of psychoanalysis. *American Journal of Psychoanalysis, 58*(1): 63–81.

Rachman, A. W. (1999a). Death by silence (Totschweigen): the traditional method of dealing with dissidents in psychoanalysis. In: R. M. Prince (Ed.), *The Death of Psychoanalysis: Murder? Suicide? or Rumor Greatly Exaggerated* (pp. 154–164). Northvale, NJ: Jason Aronson.

Rachman, A. W. (2000). Ferenczi's confusion of tongues theory and the analysis of the incest trauma. *Psychoanalytic Social Work, 7*(1): 27–53.

Rachman, A. W. (2001a). The analyst's trauma. Presentation to the Postgraduate Center for Mental Health, Spring.

Rachman, A. W. (2001b). Boychielich: the boys of Leggett Avenue (unpublished).

Rachman, A. W. (2003a). *Psychotherapy of Difficult Cases: Flexibility and Responsiveness in Contemporary Practice*. Madison, CT: Psychosocial Press.

Rachman, A. W. (2003b). Freud's analysis of his daughter Anna: a confusion of tongues. In: A. Roland, B. Ulanov, & C. Babre (Eds.), *Creative Dissent: Psychoanalysis in Evolution* (pp. 59–71). Westport, CT: Praeger.

Rachman, A. W. (2003c). Oedipus from Brooklyn (OFB): a Ferenczian analysis. In: *Psychotherapy of Difficult Cases: Flexibility and Responsiveness in Contemporary Practice* (pp. 45–113). Madison, CT: Psychosocial Press.

Rachman, A. W. (2003d). Die relationale Dimension in der Psychoanalyse [Sandor Ferenczi's contributions to the evolution of a relational perspective in psychoanalysis]. *Integrative Therapie, 3–4*: 356–367.

Rachman, A. W. (2004). Beyond neutrality: the curative function of analyst self-disclosure. In: J. Reppen, M. A. Schulman, & J. Tucker (Eds.), *Way Beyond Freud: Postmodern Psychoanalysis Evaluated* (pp. 127–142). London: Open Gate Press.

Rachman, A. W. (2006). Finding Ferenczi: a personal odyssey. Invited address to the Postgraduate Psychoanalytic Society, Oak Room, Baruch College, September, New York City.

Rachman, A. W. (2007a). Sándor Ferenczi's contributions to the evolution of psychoanalysis. *Psychoanalytic Psychology, 24*(1): 74–96.

Rachman, A. W. (2007b). The road to creative dissidence. Sándor Ferenczi's clinical journey and the evolution of psychoanalysis. Invited Address, Postgraduate Psychoanalytic Society, Friday Evening Series, "Learning From Our Past," New York.

Rachman, A. W. (2009a). The papers of Elizabeth Severn (letters, papers, books, photographs, announcements, personal items): a lost legacy of psychoanalysis. (Unpublished).

Rachman, A. W. (2009b). From phenomenology to client centered psychotherapy to relational analysis. Faculty Recognition Address: The Institute of the Postgraduate Psychoanalytic Society, New York, December 6th.

Rachman, A. W. (2010a). The origins of a relational perspective in the ideas of Sandor Ferenczi and The Budapest School of Psychoanalysis. *Psychoanalytic Perspectives, 7*(1): 43–60.

Rachman, A. W. (2010b). Sandor Ferenczi's analysis of Elizabeth Severn: "wild analysis" or pioneering attempt to analyze the incest trauma. Presentation to Division of Psychoanalysis (39), American Psychological Association Spring Meeting, Chicago, March.

Rachman, A. W. (2010c). An "in vitro" study of intersubjectivity: Sandor Ferenczi's analysis of Mrs. Elizabeth Severn. Presentation to the XVI International Forum for Psychoanalysis, October 20–23, Athens, Greece.

Rachman, A. W. (2011a). The discovery of Elizabeth Severn's papers. Distinguished Faculty Award: Postgraduate Psychoanalytic Society, New York, September 23rd.

Rachman, A. W. (2011b). From client centered psychotherapy to the Budapest School of Psychoanalysis to relational analysis: collected papers, personal recollection, and interpersonal experiences (unpublished).

Rachman, A. W. (2011c). Confusion of tongues: understanding trauma and human behavior. Unpublished.

Rachman, A. W. (2012a). The relational dimension in psychoanalysis: from Ferenczi to Mitchell. Presentation to The Psychoanalytic Society, Prague, Czech Republic, May 26th.

Rachman, A. W. (2012b). The confusion of tongues between Sandor Ferenczi and Elizabeth Severn. Plenary Presentation, The International Sandor Ferenczi Conference, "Faces of Trauma". Budapest, Hungary, Saturday, June 3rd.

Rachman, A. W. (2012c). The Elizabeth Severn papers, No. 2. The International Sandor Ferenczi Conference, "Faces of Trauma" Panel Discussion. The Ferenczi House: Residents and Patients. Budapest, Hungary, Sunday, June 3rd.

Rachman, A. W. (2012d). Psychoanalysis' neglect of the incest trauma. Presentation to The Psychohistorical Association, The Kimmel Center, New York University, New York, Friday, June 8th.

Rachman, A. W. (2012e). The psychodynamics of abduction: confusion of tongues theory of trauma. Presentation to the XVII International Forum of Psychoanalysis, "Working with Conflict and Alienation: 50 years of IFPS", Mexico City, Mexico, October 10–12.

Rachman, A. W. (2012f). The analysis of the incest trauma: from the seduction hypothesis to the confusion of tongues theory of trauma. Presented at the Symposium of the Institute of the Postgraduate Psychoanalytic Society, The Hungarian House, New York. Saturday, November 17th.

Rachman, A. W. (2013). A semi-trance session: Elizabeth Severn's clinical idea of "therapeutic regression" (unpublished).

Rachman, A. W. (2014a). Sandor Ferenczi's analysis with Elizabeth Severn: "wild analysis" or pioneering treatment of the incest trauma. *Psychoanalytic Inquiry*, *34*(2): 145–168.

Rachman, A. W. (2014b). Sandor Ferenzci as "the bridge:" my journey from phenomenology and humanistic psychotherapy to relational analysis. *Psychoanalytic Inquiry, 34*(2): 182–186.

Rachman, A. W. (2014c). The "evil genius" of psychoanalysis: Mrs. Elizabeth Severn, Dr. Sandor Ferenczi's partner in the study and treatment of trauma. Presentation: Freud's Archives, The Library of Congress, Washington, DC, June 20th.

Rachman, A. W. (2014d). The Budapest School of psychoanalysis. *Psychoanalytic Inquiry* (in preparation).

Rachman, A. W. (2015). Elizabeth Severn: Sandor Ferenczi's analysand, colleague and collaborator in the study and treatment of trauma. In: A. Harris & S. Kuchuck (Eds.), *The Legacy of Sandor Ferenczi: From Ghost to Ancestor*. London: Routledge (in press).

Rachman, A. W., & Mattick, P. (2009). Freud's confusion of tongues with Dora: the need for empathy not interpretation (unpublished manuscript).

Rachman, A. W., & Mattick, P. (2012). The confusion of tongues in the psychoanalytic relationship. *Psychoanalytic Social Work, 19*(1–2): 167–190.

Rachman, A. W., Kennedy, R., & Yard, M. (2005). Erotic transference and the relationship to childhood sexual seduction: perversion in the psychoanalytic situation. *International Forum of Psychoanalysis, 14*(3/4): 183–187.

Rachman, A. W., Kennedy, R. E., & Yard, M. A. (2009a). Erotic transference and its relationship to childhood seduction. *Psychoanalytic Social Work, 16*: 12–30.

Rachman, A. W., Yard, M. A., & Kennedy, R. E. (2009b). Noninterpretative measures in the analysis of trauma. *Psychoanalytic Psychology, 26*(3): 259–273.

Rachman, R. B. (1978). The feral child. Junior Essay, Friend's Seminary, New York.

Roazen, P. (1969). *Brother Animal: The Story of Freud and Tausk*. New York: New York University Press.

Roazen, P. (1975). *Freud and His Followers*. New York: Alfred A. Knopf.

Roazen, P. (1989). Lecture. Jung Institute, New York City.

Rogers, C. R. (1942). *Counseling*. Cambridge, MA: Houghton Mifflin.

Rogers, C. R. (1951). *Client Centered Therapy: Its Current Practice Implications and Theory*. London: Constable.

Rogers, C. R. (1959). A theory of therapy, personality and interpersonal relationships as developed in the client centered framework. In: S. Koch (Ed.), *Psychology: A Study of Science* (Vol. III) (pp. 184–256). New York: McGraw Hill.

Rudnytsky, P. L. (1991). *The Psychoanalytic Vocation: Rank, Winnicott, and The Legacy of Freud*. New Haven, CT: Yale University Press.

Sabourin, P. (1985). *Ferenczi, Paladin et Grand Vizier Secret*. Paris: Editions Universitaires.

Schore, A. (2001). The effect of early relational trauma on right brain development, affect regulation, and infant mental health. *Infant Mental Health Journal*, 22: 201–269.

Schore, A. (2003). *Affect Regulation and the Repair of the Self*. New York: W. W. Norton

Schur, M. (1972). *Freud: Living and Dying*. New York: International Universities Press.

Searles, H. F. (1979). The patient as therapist to his analyst. In: *Countertransference and Related Subjects*. New York: International Universities Press.

Shapiro, S., & Dominiak, G. M. (1992). *Sexual Trauma and Psychopathology: Clinical Intervention with Adult Survivors*. New York: Lexington Books.

Shengold, L. (1989). *Soul Murder: The Effects of Childhood Abuse and Deprivation*. New York: Ballantine Books.

Skynner, R., & Cleese, J. (1993). *Families and How to Survive Them*. London: Cedar Books.

Solomon, P., Kubzansky, P. E., Leiderman, P. H., Mendelson, J. H., Trumbull, R., & Wexler, D. (Eds.) (1966). *Sensory Deprivation: A Symposium Held at Harvard Medical School*. Cambridge, MA: Harvard University Press.

Stepansky, P. E. (1983). *In Freud's Shadow: Adler in Context*. Hillsdale, NJ: Analytic Press.

Sterba, R. F. (1982). *Reminiscences of a Viennese Psychoanalyst*. Detroit: Wayne State University.

Sullivan, H. S. (1953). *The Interpersonal Theory of Psychiatry*. New York: Norton.

Sulloway, F. (1979). *Freud: Biologist of the Mind*. New York: Basic Books.

Sylwan, B. (1984). An untoward event: ou la guerre du trauma de Breuer à Freud, de Jones à Ferenczi. *Cahiers Confrontation*, 2: 101–115.

Szatman, P., Bremmer, R., & Nagy, J. (1989). Asperger's syndrome: a review of clinical features. *Canadian Journal of Psychiatry*, *34*(6): 554–560.

Thompson, C. (1942). The therapeutic technique of Sandor Ferenczi: A comment. *International Journal of Psychoanalysis*, *16*: 64–66.

Thompson, C. (1944). Ferenczi's contribution to psychoanalysis. *Psychiatry*, *7*: 245–252.

Thompson, C. (1950). *Psychoanaysis: Evolution and Development. A Review of Theory and Therapy*. New York: Hermitage House.

Thompson, C. (1964a). Ferenczi's relaxation method. In: M. R. Green (Ed.), *Interpersonal Psychoanalysis: Papers of Clara M. Thompson* (pp. 67–82). New York: Basic Books.

Thompson, C. M. (1964b). Sandor Ferenczi, 1973–1933. In: M. R. Green (Ed.), *Interpersonal Psychoanalysis: Papers of Clara M. Thompson* (pp. 65–66). New York: Basic Books.

Thompson, C. M. (1964c). Ferenczi's contribution to psychoanalysis. In: M. R. Green (Ed.), *Interpersonal Psychoanalysis: The Papers of Clara Thompson* (pp. 72–82). New York: Basic Books.

Troyat, H. (1967). *Tolstoy*. New York: Doubleday

Truax, C. B., Wittmer, J., & Uargo, D. G. (1971). Effect of the therapeutic conditions of accurate empathy, nonpossessive warmth and genuineness of hospitalized mental patients during therapy groups. *Journal of Clinical Psychology, 27*: 137–142.

Tustin, F. (1995). *Autism and Childhood Psychosis*. London: Karnac.

Van der Kolk, B. A. (1988). The trauma spectrum: the interaction of biological and social events in the genesis of the trauma response. *Journal of Trauma and Stress, 1*: 273–290.

Van der Kolk, B. A., McFarlane, A. C., & Weisaeth, L. (Eds). (1996). *Traumatic Stress: The Effects of Overwhelming Experience on Mind, Body, and Society*. New York: Guilford Press.

Wakefield, R., & Underwager, R. (1992). Recovered memories of alleged sexual abuse: lawsuits a gain to parents. *Behavioral Sciences, 10*: 483–507.

Weniger, G., Lange, C., Sachsse, U., & Irle, E. (2009). *Journal of Psychiatry and Neuroscience, 34*(5): 383–288.

Winnicott, D. W. (1949). Hate in the countertransference. *International Journal of Psychoanalysis, 30*: 69–74.

Winnicott, D. W. (1958). *Through Pediatrics to Psychoanalysis. Collected Papers*. London: Tavistock.

Winnicott, D. W. (1965a). Ego distortions in terms of true and false self. In: *The Maturational Processes and the Facilitating Environment: Studies in the Theory of Emotional Development* (pp. 141–152). New York: International Universities Press.

Winnicott, D. W. (1965b). *The Maturational Processes and the Facilitating Environment*. New York: International Universities Press.

Winnicott, D. W. (1967). Postscript: D. W. W. on D. W. W. In: C. Winnicott, R. Shepherd, & M. Davis (Eds.), *Psychoanalytic Explorations* (pp. 569–582). Cambridge, MA: Harvard University Press.

Winnicott, D. W. (1969). The use of an object. *International Journal of Psychoanalysis, 50*: 711–716.

Winnicott, D. W. (1971). *Playing and Reality*. New York: Penguin.
Winnicott, D. W. (1973). *The Child, the Family, and the Outside World*. London: Penguin.
Wolberg, L. R. (1977). *The Technique of Psychotherapy* (Vols. I & II). New York: Grune & Stratton.
Wolf, A. (1989). Personal communication.
Wolf, A., & Kutash, L. (Eds.) (1991). *Psychopathology of the Submerged Personality*. Northvale, NJ: Jason Aronson.
Wolf, A., & Schwartz, E. K. (1962). *Psychoanalysis in Groups*. New York: Grune & Stratton.
Wolstein, B. (1989). Ferenczi, Freud, and the origins of American interpersonal relations. *Contemporary Psychoanalysis*, 25(4): 672–685.
Young-Bruehl, E. (1988). *Anna Freud: A Biography*. New York: Summit Books.
Zubek, J. (Ed.) (1969). *Sensory Deprivation: Fifteen Years of Research*. New York: Appleton Century Crafts.

INDEX